FICINO

COMMENTARY ON PLOTINUS

VOLUME 5 • *ENNEAD III, PART 2,*
AND *ENNEAD IV*

ITRL 82

MARSILIO FICINO

◆ ◆ ◆

COMMENTARY ON PLOTINUS

VOLUME 5 · *ENNEAD III, PART 2,*
AND *ENNEAD IV*

EDITED AND TRANSLATED
WITH AN ANALYTICAL STUDY BY

STEPHEN GERSH

THE I TATTI RENAISSANCE LIBRARY
HARVARD UNIVERSITY PRESS
CAMBRIDGE, MASSACHUSETTS
LONDON, ENGLAND
2018

Series design by Dean Bornstein

Library of Congress Cataloging-in-Publication Data

Names: Ficino, Marsilio, 1433–1499, author. | Gersh, Stephen, editor, translator.
Title: Commentary on Plotinus / Marsilio Ficino ; edited and translated with
an analytical study by Stephen Gersh.
Other titles: I Tatti Renaissance library ; 80.
Description: Cambridge, Massachusetts : Harvard University Press, 2017– |
Series: I Tatti Renaissance library ; 80 | Volume 4 published in 2017. |
"This is a facing-page volume: Latin on the versos; English translation on the
rectos"—Provided by publisher concerning volume 4. | Projected publication
from publisher: Volume 1: Ennead I—volume 2: Ennead II, part 1—volume 3:
Ennead II, part 2—volume 4: Ennead III, part 1 (Books I–IV)—volume 5:
Ennead III, part 2 (Books V–IX) and Ennead IV—volume 6: Enneads V and
VI. | Includes bibliographical references and index. Contents: Volume 4,
Ennead III, Part 1 (Books I–IV).
Identifiers: LCCN 2016049215 | ISBN 9780674974982 (alk. paper) (Volume 4)
ISBN 9780674974999 (alk. paper) (Volume 5)
Subjects: LCSH: Plotinus. | Plotinus. Enneads. | Neoplatonism.
Classification: LCC B693.Z7 F5313 2017 | DDC 186/.4—dc23 LC record available
at https://lccn.loc.gov/2016049215

Contents

ॐ ? ॐ

· CONTENTS ·

Abbreviations

☙❧

Basel 1580   *Plotini Platonicorum facile coryphaei operum philosophico-rum omnium libri LIV [. . .] cum latina Marsilii Ficini interpretatione et commentatione* (Basel, 1580); facsimile edition with an introduction by Stéphane Toussaint (Lucca: Société Marsile Ficin, 2010). Cited for Ficino's translation of Plotinus and for his commentary on *Enneads* I–II and V–VI.

Lettere   *Lettere*, ed. Sebastiano Gentile, 2 vols. to date (Books I–II). (Florence: Leo S. Olschki, 1990–2010).

Letters   *The Letters of Marsilio Ficino*, trans. Members of the Language Department of the School of Economic Science, London, 10 vols. to date (Books I–XI) (London, 1975–2015). Volumes 5 to 10 contain a photoreprint of the 1495 Venice edition, corrected against some of the early manuscripts.

Opera   *Marsilii Ficini Florentini [. . .] opera et quae hactenus extitere et quae in lucem nunc primum prodiere omnia*, 2 vols. (Basel, 1576); photographic reprint (Torino: Bottega d'Erasmo, 1959, 1962, 1983; and Lucca: Société Marsile Ficin, 2010).

Platonic Theology   Marsilio Ficino, *Platonic Theology*, ed. and trans. Michael J. B. Allen and James Hankins, 6 vols. (Cambridge, MA: Harvard University Press, 2001–2006). References are to the book, chapter, and paragraph of this edition.

Saffrey 1959   Henri-Dominique Saffrey, "Notes platoniciennes de Marsile Ficin dans un manuscrit de Proclus (Cod. Riccardianus 70)," *Bibliothèque d'humanisme et de Renaissance* 21 (1959): 161–84.

SF   Paul Oskar Kristeller, ed., *Supplementum Ficinianum: Marsilii Ficini . . . opuscula inedita et dispersa,* 2 vols. (Florence: Leo S. Olschki, 1937).

COMMENTARY ON PLOTINUS

[ENNEADIS TERTIAE] CAPITULA

[LIBER V]
ARGUMENTUM IN LIBRUM DE AMORE

CHAPTER HEADINGS OF
ENNEAD III [part 2]

[BOOK V]
ANALYSIS OF THE BOOK ON LOVE

3

[LIBER VI]
ARGUMENTUM IN LIBRUM QUOD INCORPOREA NON PATIUNTUR

Summa libri.

Anima neque patitur neque formas qualitatesque suscipit; item de duplici imaginatione.

Quod in vera essentia contineantur vita et intellectus; item de uno quod est super essentiam et de uno quod est infra eam.

Quod naturalia non sint entia vera; et quod materia dicatur non ens, et instar speculi videatur habere formas quas non habet veras.

Quantum anima materiam supereminaet; et quomodo certa quantitas materiae sequatur modum cuiuslibet speciei in materiam venientis.

[LIBER VII]
ARGUMENTUM IN LIBRUM PLOTINI DE AETERNITATE ET TEMPORE

Quid aeternitas et ubi sit; quid sempiternitas; quid perpetuitas. Quomodo se habeat aeternitas ad tempus.

De conformatione intellectus ad aeternitatem; item quid non sit tempus: scilicet quod non sit duratio in corporali motu vel mensura similis aut numerus aut consecutio comesque corporei motus.

Aeternitas est in mente divina, tempus in anima mundi, quo agitur mensuraturque mundi motus.

[BOOK VI]
ANALYSIS OF THE BOOK "THAT INCORPOREAL THINGS ARE IMPASSIVE"

Summary of the book.

The soul is neither passive nor the recipient of forms and qualities; also regarding the twofold imagination.

That life and intellect are contained in true being; also concerning the one that is above being and the one that is below it.

That natural things are not true beings; that matter is said to be nonbeing and seems to have forms which it does not truly have, in the manner of a mirror.

How much the soul is elevated above matter; and how a certain quantity of matter follows the measure of each and every form coming into matter.

[BOOK VII]
ANALYSIS OF PLOTINUS' BOOK "ON ETERNITY AND TIME"

What eternity is and where it is; what everlastingness is; what perpetuity is; how eternity relates to time.

On the conforming of intellect to eternity; also, what time is not: namely, that it is not duration in corporeal motion, or a similar measure, or number, or the succession and accompaniment of corporeal motion.

Eternity is in the divine mind; time is in the world soul, and is that by which the motion of the world is activated and measured.

[LIBER VIII]
ARGUMENTUM IN LIBRUM DE NATURA ET CONTEMPLATIONE ET UNO

Naturalia fiunt a vita quadam agente per rationes quasi contemplativas sibi infusas ab intellectu divino.

De fine intellectualis naturae; et quod in cognitione vera idem est cognoscens et cognitum; et de gradibus vitae et intelligentiae; et quod intellectus primus est omnia et perfecte totum.

Intellectus etiam primus est necessario multiplex et est omnia; igitur ante ipsum est principium omnium quod non est omnia sed super omnia.

Ipsum bonum est super essentiam, vitam, intellectum; neque intellect potest attingi.

Ipsum bonum est pater cuius filius est intellectus semper a patre plenus. Huius autem intellectus est imago mundus.

[LIBER IX]
ARGUMENTUM IN LIBRUM DE OCTO CONSIDERATIONIBUS

Propositio prima: quod mundi auctor sit intellectus primus ipsius boni filius.

Propositio secunda: quomodo anima potest colligere se in proprium intellectum et per hunc intellectu formari divino. Sunt et in

[BOOK VIII]
ANALYSIS OF THE BOOK "ON NATURE, CONTEMPLATION AND THE ONE"

Natural things come to be from a certain life acting through reason-principles that are quasi-contemplative, these being infused into them from the divine intellect.

On the end of the intellectual nature; that in true knowledge, the knower and the thing known are the same; regarding the levels of life and intelligence; and that the first intellect is all things and is perfectly the whole.

Even the first intellect is necessarily multiple, and is all things; therefore the causal principle of all things is prior to it, this principle being not all things but above all things.

The Good itself is beyond being, life, intellect; and it cannot be attained through intellect.

The Good itself is a father whose son is intellect, always filled by his father; the world is the image of this intellect.

[BOOK IX]
ANALYSIS OF THE BOOK "ON EIGHT CONSIDERATIONS"

First proposition: that the founder of the world is the first intellect, the son of the Good itself.

Second proposition: how the soul is able to gather itself into its own intellect and through this be formed by the divine intellect.

hoc capitulo tres aliae propositiones: duae de anima et una de Deo.

De intellectu etiam nostro: quomodo est semper in actu.

Quomodo Deus est super motum et statum et cognitionem; item de eo quod in actu est et quod in potentia.

There are also three other propositions in this chapter: two regarding the soul and one regarding God.

Concerning our intellect also; and how it is always in act.

How God is above motion and rest and knowledge; also regarding that which is in act and that which is in potency.

LIBRI PLOTINI PHILOSOPHI
EXCELLENTISSIMI
INTERPRETE MARSILIO FICINO
PLATONICO
TERTIA ENNEAS

THIRD ENNEAD OF THE BOOK
BY PLOTINUS
A MOST EXCELLENT
PHILOSOPHER
TRANSLATED BY THE
PLATONIST MARSILIO FICINO

[LIBER V]

ARGUMENTUM IN LIBRUM DE AMORE

: I :

Omnis potentia tum cognoscendi tum generandi respuit turpe;
nititur ad pulchrum, quoniam omnis ex prima pulchritudine
proficiscitur atque movetur.

1 Arbitror equidem, Magnanime Laurenti, te non longam de amore disputationem a Marsilio tuo nunc exacturum, tum quia multa de hoc in *Symposio* disputavimus, tum maxime quoniam tu plurima de amore divinitus invenisti elegantibusque carminibus cecinisti. Ergo summa sequar fastigia rerum. Omnis potestas animae sive rationalis sive naturalis ideo amore perpetuo nititur ad pulchrum attingendum atque generandum, quoniam potestas eiusmodi ab ipsa pulchritudine proficiscitur, ideoque in seipsa retinet formam pulchritudinis insitam perpetuumque ad ipsam velut ad finem amoris instinctum. Hanc utique causam quisquis ignorat non potest amorum naturas et amantium passiones exprimere. Profecto divinus intellectus est forma prima puraque prorsus et omniformis. Intellectus animalis est forma quidem secunda sed similiter omniformis. Natura est forma tertia pariter omniformis suisque ducta principiis eo spectat assidue ut informitatem materiae operiat mirabiliter et exornet. Siquid ergo deforme sub natura contingit, sic accidit praeter intentionem ipsam Dei primam atque naturae, sicut

[BOOK V]

ANALYSIS OF THE BOOK "ON LOVE"

: I :

*Every power both of knowing and generating rejects the ugly
and strives toward the beautiful, since every power proceeds
and moves from the first beauty.*

I believe, O magnanimous Lorenzo, that you will not now de- 1
mand from your Marsilio a long discussion concerning love, both
because we have discussed this matter extensively in the *Symposium*, and especially because you have discovered many things
about love by divine inspiration and have sung of it in elegant
verses.[1] I will therefore attend to the main points concerning these
matters. Every power of the soul, whether rational or natural,
strives with perpetual love toward the attainment and generation
of the beautiful because a power of this kind proceeds from beauty
itself. For the same reason, this power retains an innate form of
beauty in itself and an everlasting impulse toward that form itself,
as though the end of love. In any case, whoever is ignorant of this
cause cannot give expression to the nature of loves and the passions of lovers. Certainly, the divine intellect is the primal Form,
absolutely pure and omniform. The intellect of soul is the secondary form, but is similarly omniform. Nature is the tertiary form,
and is likewise omniform. Under the guidance of its own principles, nature continually applies itself to the covering and adornment of matter in a wonderful manner. If anything lacking form
occurs below nature, this arises outside the primal intention as
such of God and nature, just as that which happens to lack form

quod deforme contingit in artificio accidit praeter omnem artis intentionem. Sicut ergo naturalis, sic et rationalis ubique potestas a prima pulchritudine ducens originem turpe quidem respuit velut dissonum, pulchrum vero pro viribus asciscit velut consonum, pulchram formam generare conatur suamque in ipsa natura perpetuo conservare. Sed potentia rationalis parturit in animo pulchritudinem, naturalis autem pulchritudinem in materia parit, et utraque pulchrum pro viribus in quo generet subiectum naturaliter optat, ita demum aptius pulchritudinem creatura.

∴ II ∴

Duplex mundi anima, duae Veneres, amores duo qui non passiones sed existentiae quaedam sunt.

2 Cum videamus eatenus in nobis intelligentiam perfici quatenus et actus intelligendi et intelligenda res a materia condicionibusque materiae segregatur, coniectare licet primum ipsum simpliciter intellectum esse alienissimum a materia; praeterea et intellectualem animam inde proxime genitam ideoque summopere intellectualem non posse coire cum materia in communem unius compositi formam. Est enim haec et intellectus quidam et simpliciter anima; vita vero ex hac subinde nata velut anima quaedam et natura simpliciter—potest iam in unum cum materia congredi. Intellectualem itaque animam illam in mundo primam Venerem appellamus; vitam vero mundo illinc prorsus infusam Venerem appellato

in craftsmanship arises outside the entire intention of the art. Therefore, inasmuch as it is natural, so does rational power everywhere take its origin from the first beauty. It rejects the ugly as though dissonant but appropriates to the maximal degree the beautiful as though consonant, striving to generate a beautiful form and to preserve its own form in that nature for perpetuity. But the rational power gives birth to beauty in the mind, whereas the natural power brings to birth in matter. Each of these powers as much as possible naturally desires a substratum in which it might generate the beautiful, and will thereby at length create beauty more fittingly.

: II :

The twofold world-soul; the two Venuses; the two loves which are not passions but beings of a certain kind.

Since we see that intelligence is perfected in us to the extent that both the act of understanding and the thing understood are separated from matter and the conditions of matter, it is legitimate to surmise that that which is the first intellect *simpliciter* is the most alien to matter, and moreover that the intellectual soul which is most immediately generated from the first intellect and is therefore primarily intellectual is not able to come, together with matter, into the communal form of a single composite. For this soul is both an intellect of a certain kind and soul *simpliciter*, while the life that is immediately born from it is as though a soul of a certain kind and nature *simpliciter*, this latter being now able to come into union with matter. Therefore, that intellectual soul that is in the world we call the first Venus. Let the second life that is immediately infused into the world from that source be called the second

2

secundam. In utraque perpetuus viget amor, circa divinae mentis pulchritudinem incitatus, tum in prima ad pulchritudinem similem in se generandam, tum in secunda ad pulchritudinem in materia pro viribus exprimendam. Putat vero Plotinus, ex mente Platonis, intellectualem mundi animam, dum intrinsecus agit circa Deum intelligendo illum atque volendo, concipere in seipsa non imaginarium quiddam sed naturale aliquid et subsistens, (ut arbitror) Christianae trinitatis in hoc mysterium imitatus. Existimat autem, sicut lucere atque calere duo quaedam sunt in igne sed unum denique sunt in sole, sic cognoscere atque amare in potentia rationali quidem esse diversa, sed in substantia intellectuali actum unum existere. Cum vero actus eiusmodi in anima mundi sit intimus et circa intimum efficacissimusque, hinc effici penes seipsam prolem huic actui congruam quae, quoniam ex intelligentia nascitur, sit intelligibile quiddam, quoniam ex amore procedit, sit aliquid amatorium, immo sit amor ipse subsistens ex actu quodam amandi productus. Nam cum illic idem sit existere prorsus et agere, nimirum sic intus agendo existentia quaedam producitur intus, in qua quidem producta sit eadem quae est et producentis essentia, hoc ipso differens quod in illo quidem propagans est, in hoc autem inde est propagata. Differt insuper relatione quadam, siquidem existentia haec amatoria hoc ipsum quod est et amantis est et amati. Differt praeterea quod in existentia propagante ponitur potius ipsa visio pulchri, in existentia propagata voluptas ipsa potius circa pulchrum.

Venus. In both of these, a perpetual love flourishes and is stirred to excitement around the beauty of the divine mind toward generating in itself a similar beauty in the case of the first Venus and toward expressing to the extent of its powers this beauty in matter in the case of the second Venus. Indeed, Plotinus thinks — in line with Plato — that the intellectual world-soul, as long as it exercises an internal activity around God by understanding him and willing, conceives in itself something not imaginary but natural and subsistent. In this teaching he imitates (as I believe) the mystery of the Christian Trinity.[2] He also maintains that, just as shining and heating are two things in fire but are ultimately one in the sun, so knowing and loving are different things in the rational power but exist as one activity in the intellectual substance. Since such an activity in the world-soul is most internal, around that which is most internal,[3] and also most powerful, an offspring in harmony with this activity is produced from this activity within the world-soul itself. And since this offspring arises from intelligence, it is a certain intelligible, but since it proceeds from love, it is something lovable — or rather, it is love itself subsisting as something produced from a certain activity of loving. For since in that realm it is absolutely the same to exist and to act, a certain being is assuredly produced within in this manner by internal activity. And in this production, the substance of the produced and the substance of the producer are one and the same, differing in that the substance is generative in the latter case but generated thence in the former. There is difference also in a certain relation, seeing that that loving substance is the essential being of both the lover and the beloved. Moreover, there is difference where that which is situated in the generative being is rather the vision itself of Beauty, and that which is situated in the generated being rather the pleasure itself around that Beauty.

: III :

Confirmatio superiorum.

3 Si gravida mulier saepe ob miram imaginationis affectusque vehe-
mentiam naturali quadam foetum afficit qualitate ob hoc ipsum
quia sit matri connexus, si rursum motio similis animi in proprio
corpore subitas exprimit qualitates, quid mirum ex vehementia simili substantiale aliquid in ipsamet anima nasci, praesertim in ipsa
intellectuali anima, ubi actio vehementiaque et affectio non adven-
titia est, non mobilis, sed naturalis penitus atque firma. Et ipse qui
videt gaudetque et appetit efficacissimus est et obiectum eius est
potentissimum influitque potenter. Confirmantur haec ex eo quod
si ubique accidentalia rediguntur ad quaedam substantialia proportione quadam congruentia sibi, necesse est et amores qui passiones quaedam adventitiae sunt ad substantiales amores rite in-
ferri. Post haec, notabis iterum duas mundum habere animas
oportere: alteram quodammodo separatam quae corpori praesit
velut artifex, alteram vero coniunctam quae illinc insit corpori velut forma. Separatam quidem oportet adesse, tum quia talis quaedam ex intellectu puro proxime micat, tum quia mixtus artifex non
absolute imperat artificio. Oportet insuper animam mundo inesse
coniunctam, tum quoniam anima prima fecunda est ad hanc ex se
generandam, tum quoniam oportet mundum esse compositum
perfectissimum. Itaque necesse est habere formam suae materiae
perfectissimam: id est, viventem atque sensualem. Non fit autem
unum in mundo ex intellectuali anima proprie atque materia (ut

: III :

Confirmation of the above.

If a pregnant woman, on account of an amazing force of imagina- 3
tion and feeling affects her fetus with a certain natural quality because of the fetus' connection with the mother, and if again a
similar motion of the soul immediately expresses qualities in the
body proper to it, how is it surprising that something substantial
could be born in the soul itself through a similar force. This is
especially the case with the intellectual soul itself where activity,
force, and affection are not adventitious and changeable but absolutely natural and firm. And one who sees and rejoices and desires
is the most effective, his object is the most important and emanates powerfully. This is confirmed by the fact that, if everywhere
accidents are referred back to certain substances that are congruent
with them by a certain proportion, it is necessary that loves that
are certain adventitious passions are rightly traced back to substantial loves. After this, you will further observe that the world must
have two souls: one that is somehow separate and presiding over
the body as an artificer, the other however being joined and present in the body and as though a form. It is necessary for the separate soul to be present both because a certain thing of this kind
immediately springs forth from the pure intellect, and because an
artificer of a mixed nature does not totally command his handi-
work. In addition, it is necessary for soul to be in the world as
conjoined to it both because the primal soul is fertile in generating
this soul from itself and because it is necessary for the world to be
a most perfect composite. Therefore, it is necessary for the world
to have the most perfect form of its matter: that is, a living and
sensitive form. Unity does not come about in the world from the
intellectual soul properly speaking and matter, as Plotinus main-

vult Plotinus), quoniam intelligentia per actionem affectumque in oppositum materiae tendit; sicut neque fieri unum putat in nobis, siquidem nec in nobis intellectualis anima communicat cum corpore in passionibus corpori propriis neque corpus cum anima tali in actionibus ad eiusmodi animam proprie pertinentibus. Licet tamen dicere intellectualem animam tum in mundo esse mundanam, tum in nobis humanam, atque ex ea simul et animali unum ideo confici quoniam ex illius influxu simul atque materia fit unum animal sensuale cui et illa semper inspirat vitam absque continuo illius spiritu perituram. Has utique geminas in mundo animas iterum geminas Veneres esse memento quas gemini similes comitentur amores. Memento quin etiam amorem in secunda hac mundi anima non tantum per vim genitalem generare totam in mundi materia pulchritudinem, sed etiam per efficacem imaginandi potentiam tum divinam suspicere formam tum ad eandem et mundum et quae sunt in mundo pro viribus provocare.

: IV :

Duo amores cuilibet animae naturaliter insiti quasi duo sunt daemones.

4 Amores qui tamquam novi quidem animorum motus a rebus quae extrinsecus offeruntur cottidie incitantur in nobis tamquam notos leviter attigit. Diligentius vero prosequitur substantiales amores: id est, essentiales perpetuosque instinctus ad pulchrum animae

tains, since intelligence tends toward the opposite of matter through action and disposition. It is in the same way that he believes unity not to come about in us, since neither does the intellectual soul in us share together with the body in the body's own passions, nor does the body share with such a soul in the actions properly pertaining to a soul of this kind. However, one can say that the intellectual soul is both worldly in the world and human in us, and that a unity is produced from that intellectual soul and the animate being, given that simultaneously through the emanation of the intellectual soul and through matter, one sensitive animate being arises into which the intellective soul always breathes a life which will perish without its continual breathing. Assuredly, you must remember that these twin souls in the world are also twin Venuses that similar twin loves accompany. Indeed, you should also remember that the love in this second world-soul not only generates the entire beauty in the matter of the world through its reproductive power but also through its active power of imagining both looks up to the divine Form and calls forth toward that same Form, to the extent of its powers, the world and the things in the world.

: IV :

The two loves naturally implanted in any soul
are like two daemons.

Plotinus has lightly touched upon — as though a topic known to us — the loves which as though certain fresh motions of souls are incited by the things every day presented to us externally. He more energetically pursues the topic of the substantial loves: that is, the essential and perpetual impulses toward beauty naturally inborn in

4

naturaliter insitos et assidue, quamvis nec eligas nec advertas, trahentes ad ipsum, quorum alter in ipsa cognoscendi alter in generandi potentia naturaliter est insertus. Et quoniam velut praefectus ducit animam et more providentiae regit, appellatus est daemon, quamvis praestantior amor appellatur et deus. Dicitur autem hos anima generare non quidem cottidie sed ab initio, quando pro natura sua partim ab aevo sibi tradita partim pro electione vitae, quandoque contracta instinctus eiusmodi concipit ad saeculum regnaturos. Quorum occulto quodam nutu cottidie plures in nobis suscitantur affectus atque conceptus quos sane nec externa dumtaxat spectacula nec praesens affectio corporis nec nova consultatio porrigit.[1] Et profecto perpetuus quidam vitae tenor plurimum directus ad unum, praesertim quantum spectat ad vitae speciem scientiasque et artes naturalesque facultates unicuique proprias, ab eiusmodi daemone regitur, recto interim ab externo quodam sibi congrue daemone. Congruunt et rationales animae omnes per eiusmodi suos amores cum mundanae amoribus animae quatenus et ipsae sunt animae mundanae sorores. Quae simul amoresque sui ita dependent ab anima mundi et illius amore, non quia inde sortiantur essentiam sed quoniam ad motionis illius exordia quasi concinendo motiones proprias ordiuntur perque proprios fines ad finem denique moventur illius.

the soul and drawing it continually toward that object, although you neither choose it nor pay attention to it. Of these loves, one is naturally inserted in the power of knowing, and the other in the power of generating. And because it leads the soul as though placed before it and controls it providentially, love is called a daemon, although the more excellent love is also called a god. The soul is said to generate these, not on a daily basis but from its beginning, when on the basis of its nature which is partly transmitted to it from eternity and is partly in accordance with its choice of life, it is contracted at some point and conceives the impulses of this kind that will dominate during its temporal existence. At a certain hidden prompting from these impulses, many affections and concepts are daily aroused in us which neither purely external observations, nor a present affection of the body, nor a fresh deliberation puts forth. Indeed, a certain perpetual course of life mostly directed toward unity, especially to the extent that it looks toward the form of life, the sciences and arts, and the natural faculties proper to each individual, is controlled by a daemon of this kind, the latter having been ruled in the meantime by a certain external daemon in harmony with it. Through their loves of this kind, all the rational souls are harmonious with the loves of the world-soul, to the extent that they themselves are the sisters of the world-soul. These souls and their loves are dependent on the world-soul and on its love, not in the sense that they derive their being from it, but because they order their own motions as though in concordance with the beginnings of its motion, and are finally moved through their own ends to its end.

: V :

De daemonibus.

5 Oportere vero daemones esse medios inter stellas et homines in *Theologia* satis ostendimus, ut sphaera quaelibet supra nos hac nostra praestantior longeque amplior rationales habitatores habebat suae sphaerae conformes sicut habet et nostra. Nam et ignea quaedam animalia esse comprobat Apuleius hoc Aristotelis testimonio: in fornacibus ardentibus quaedam animalia propria visa sunt volitare pennulis apta quae totum aevum suum diversantur in igne—cum eo exoriuntur cum eo pariter extinguuntur. Profecto quod primum ab ipsa vivifica substantia, id est anima, vitam accipit solus est ignis. Est enim ignis inter corpora proximus animae quoniam excellentissimus, efficacissimus, mobilissimus: hinc efficitur ut fovente calore singula vivant, non fovente non vivant. Secundo per ignem aer igni proximus vitam sortiri videtur et pabulum esse caloris; per haec duo subinde subtilis aqua vicinior aere, per hanc similiter terra subtilis, per haec quattuor invicem congregata corpus ex quattuor non iam vaporibus sed materiis crassioribus compositum atque solidum—licet autem ubique quod prius est atque simplicius a sequente compositoque resolvere.

6   Sunt igitur animalium rationalium quinque genera. Prima sunt quorum corpora solus est ignis, ac si visibilis ignis, stellae sunt quos antiqui deos nominant, si invisibilis, daemones Orpheus

: V :

On daemons.

We have demonstrated sufficiently in the *Theology* that the dae- 5
mons must be mediate between the stars and men, on the consideration that any sphere that is more excellent and much more extensive than this sphere of ours had rational inhabitants in
conformity with its sphere just as does our own.[4] Apuleius confirmed that there are certain fiery animate beings on the basis of a
testimony of Aristotle to the effect that in burning furnaces certain
special animals equipped with little wings are seen to flit about
and live out their entire lifespan in the fire, rising up with it and
likewise being extinguished with it.[5] Indeed, it is fire alone that
first receives life from the life-giving substance itself: that is, the
soul. Among bodies, fire is that which is closest to soul, seeing
that it is most excellent, most powerful, and most mobile. Hence,
it comes about that individual things live when heat fosters them
and do not live when it does not. Secondly, the air that is closest
to fire seems to obtain its life from fire and also to provide the
nourishment for its heat. Thereupon, through these two the rarefied type of water that is closer to air obtains its life, and similarly
through this water the rarefied type of earth. And through these
four assembled with one another, the body that is compounded
and solidified now not from vaporized but from denser modes of
matter obtains its life, it being everywhere lawful however to release that which is prior and simpler from that which is subsequent and composite.

There are five kinds of rational animate beings. The first kind 6
comprises those whose bodies are fire alone. If this fire is visible,
these are the stars which the ancients call gods; if it is invisible, Orpheus calls these animate beings the fiery or celestial

igneos vel caelestes appellat qui in planetarum circulis stellarum
vicem teneant sub planeta duce—non enim decet ab innumeris
animalibus quae sunt in firmamento mox ad unicum infra descendere. Secunda quorum corpora sunt ignis et aer optime mixtus: hos daemones idem aetherios vel aerios nominat. Sunt et
animalia tertia in quibus ignis et aer cum subtili quadam aquae
componitur, quos daemones iam nominat aquaeos qui quandoque
paulo densiores facti aspici possint. Neque desunt quarta quae
tribus iam dictis subtilem adhibeant terram quasi quendam terrae
vaporem. Hi ab Orpheo terreni daemones appellantur qui et aliquando paulo ulterius condensati etiam valeant attrectari: hos
etiam nuncupat subterraneos quotiens videlicet subeunt terrae ca-
vernas. Quinta sunt hominum quasi infimorum daemonum corpora in quibus, praeter daemonicam illam ex quattuor subtilibus
mixturam qua daemones sumus quae in nobis spiritus est primoque vivit et sentit, mixtura solidorum est adiuncta. Spiritum
vero primo vivere atque sentire patet ex eo quod, retracto a membris spiritu, mox sensus et motus membra deserit ideoque et vita.
Cum vero quod prius cognatiusque accipitur firmius teneatur,
probabile videtur animas eiusmodi posteriora gradatim dimittere
corpora, prioribus interim diutius reservatis, ut quae fuerunt in
corpore solido diutius postea sint in tenui in quo pariter erant et
in quo potissimum sentiebant—quod et propter cognationem facile cedit animae conectenti. Quo vero sublimius simpliciusque
corpus est, eo tardius videtur ab anima deserendum, caeleste vero

daemons.[6] These daemons, in the manner of stars, have their station in the circles of the planets. They are under the guidance of a planet, for it is not fitting to go down—starting from the innumerable animate beings that are in the firmament—immediately to the unitary. The second kind of animate being consists of those whose bodies are fire and air mixed in the best way—the same authority calls these the aetherial or aerial daemons. There is also a third kind of animate being in which fire and air are compounded with a subtle type of water. This authority now calls these the watery daemons. These daemons are visible from time to time when they become a little denser. And a fourth kind of daemon is not lacking. These daemons add a subtle type of earth, as though some vapor of earth, to the three substances already mentioned. These are called the earthly daemons by Orpheus.[7] These daemons can even be touched at certain times when they are further condensed to a slight degree. He also calls this kind of daemon subterranean to the extent that they go down into the caverns of the earth. In fifth position are the bodies of man, as though the bodies of lowest daemons. In this case, in addition to that daemonic mixture of the four subtle bodies whereby we are "daemons"—this being in our case spirit and living and sensing for the first time—a mixture of solid bodies is annexed. That spirit is the first thing that lives and senses is clear from the fact that, when spirit is removed from the limbs, sense and motion immediately leave them, and therefore life does also. Moreover, since that which is received as more primal and more akin is retained more firmly, it seems probable that souls of this kind will gradually release their lower bodies, their higher bodies being meanwhile retained for longer. Thus, those souls that were in a solid body will remain longer subsequently in the rarefied one in which they were equally present, in which they sensed most powerfully, and which yields most readily, on account of its kinship, to the soul that binds it. To the extent that a body is more elevated and simple, the more slowly

numquam—in omni siquidem genere quod primo sit particeps, semper est particeps. Et merito vita sempiterna, ubi semel sempiternum corpus ipso suo esse naturaliter animavit, numquam desinit animare. Solis igitur hominum animabus inferiorumque daemonum datum est corpora caduca mutare, quia composita sunt ex dissonis et ideo solubilia, tum quoniam propter corpus eiusmodi et locum et ministerium a beatitudine distrahuntur. Nefas autem est animas rationales ad contemplationem absolutam naturaliter institutas diutius illa carere. Quando igitur ad finem perveniunt, in aetherio et caelesti corpore multa saecula vivunt: quod enim est ex intentione specierum earumque principii potissimum, id quamplurimum est et maxime diuturnum.

7   Caelestes quidem daemones et aetherios verisimile est et sempiternos esse et perturbationis expertes propter naturae simplicitatem puritatemque loci, aquaeos autem terrenosque esse quidem longaevos non autem indissolubiles habere et perturbationes animi ferme tales quales et nos habemus—vicinitas enim regionis atque naturae morum affert similitudinem. E duobus primis nihil effluit umquam: quare nec opus est nutrimento sed dumtaxat cantibus et figuris luminibusque delectantur colunturque et ita nobis conciliantur, illis praecipue temporibus quibus ea sidera regnant quae et illi sequuntur. E duobus sequentibus cum effluat aliquid, instaurare necessarium est. Sed in quibus nihil est terreum, satis odor facit conciliatque aromatum atque florum exhalatioque liquorum. Postremi daemones odoribus et vaporibus indigent crassioribus qui ex sanguine carnibusque mittuntur maxime coctis et a nobis

does it seem to be deserted by its soul, the celestial body indeed being never deserted, seeing that in every genus, that which participates first is always participant. And rightly, when everlasting life through its own being has once naturally animated an everlasting body, this life never ceases to animate. Therefore only to the souls of men and lower daemons is it given to change perishable bodies, since these are composed of dissonant things and are thereby capable of dissolution, especially since they are drawn aside from blessedness on account of such a body, a location, and a function. It is unlawful for rational souls which have been naturally instituted for unfettered contemplation to be without that contemplation for very long. Therefore, when they arrive at their final goal, they live for many ages in an aetherial and celestial body. Because it results from the intentionality of the Forms and especially of the Forms' causal principle, this body is the greatest and most long lasting.

It is probable that the celestial and aetherial daemons alone are 7 everlasting and free of perturbation on account of the simplicity of their nature and the purity of their location, that the watery and earthly daemons are indeed long-lived but not indissoluble and have perturbations of soul somewhat like the disturbances that we have, given that the proximity of the region and of nature yield similarity of dispositions. From the first two kinds of daemon nothing ever flows out. Therefore, they have no need for nutriment, but are at least pleased by songs, figures, and lights, are worshipped, and are therefore conciliated by us, especially at those times when the stars that they also follow are in the ascendant. When something flows out from the two following kinds of daemon, restoration must be made. But the smell of perfumes and flowers and the exhalation of liquids is sufficient to accomplish this restoration and to conciliate in the case of daemons containing nothing of the earthly. The last kind of daemon has need of the denser smells and vapors that are sent forth from blood and flesh, especially when cooked and consumed by us. For this reason, if

assumptis. Quare, si Porphyrio credis, dices hos induxisse nos ad animalia devoranda, ut ipsi penes nos atque e visceribus nostris haurirent sugerentque saepe concoctum sibique competens ab animalibus alimentum—est autem eis insita quaedam attrahendi sugendique facultas qualis membris inest animalium radicibusque plantarum. Nos autem eos tali quidam nidore ad nos allicimus unde, ut ait Porphyrius, homines ventri dediti vasa fiunt daemonum immundorum. Quamvis enim daemones si quo indigent nutrimento, ut ait Iamblichus, id absque nostra opera sibi passim suppeditare possint, tamen probabile est posse quasdam illecebras ab homine illis offerri et incontinentes daemones incontinentibus hominibus commisceri. Superbi vero superbioribus daemonibus agitantur, nam primum esse in eis superbiam Porphyrius ait adeo ut nihil vehementius optent quam supremos a nobis deos existimari et pro illis maxime coli—atque princeps eorum potissimum id contendat ut deus primus omnium habeatur—; incitare nos ad corporis huius oblectamenta quibus ipsi in nobis ferme similiter oblectentur; irritare ad contentiones et proelia quibus et ipsi inter se aliquando conflictantur et aerem conflictu conturbant, et assiduo gaudere mendacio; nos autem illis non posse resistere, nisi quatenus superiorum daemonum inspirationi mentem diligenter exponimus, sobrii castique vivimus ac deo nos suppliciter commendamus—sola enim puritate sanctimonia pietate genus humanum a potenti malorum daemonum incursu defendi. Hinc et Democritus orabat ut bonos daemones obvios haberet utpote qui, ut Plutarchus ait, existimaret multos daemones esse malos. Omnes vero appellavit idola in aere grandia inter se emittentia voces et

you believe Porphyry, you will say that these daemons have led us
to eat animals, in order that they may often in us and through our
intestines drink and suck in digested animal food suitable to themselves. There is implanted in them a certain power of drawing in
and sucking of the kind that resides in the members of animals
and the roots of plants. We entice those daemons toward us by a
certain sleekness of ours: for which reason, as Porphyry says, men
given over to their stomachs become the vessels of impure daemons.[8] Although the daemons, if they have need of some nutriment, are everywhere able to supply this to themselves without
our efforts — as Iamblichus says[9] —, it is probable that certain enticements could be offered to them by man and that intemperate
daemons could have commerce with intemperate men. Proud men
are urged on by prouder daemons, for Porphyry says that pride
exists in a primal manner in them, to such a degree that they want
nothing more than to be considered by us as the highest gods and
to be worshipped to the greatest degree in the place of those
gods,[10] the chief of those daemons striving most of all that he
should be held to be the first God of all. Porphyry says that these
daemons incite us toward those of our bodily pleasures through
which they in a more or less similar way enjoy themselves in us,
and that they arouse us to the disputes and battles in which they
sometimes contend among themselves and disturb the air with
conflict. He says that they also continually rejoice with falsehood,
and that we are unable to resist them unless, to the extent that we
diligently open our mind to the inspiration of superior daemons,
we live in a sober and chaste manner and commend ourselves to
God in a prayerful way, for it is only by purity, holiness, and piety
that the human race can be defended against the powerful assaults
of wicked daemons. Hence, even Democritus prayed that he might
have good daemons in his path: a man who, as Plutarch says,
thought that many daemons were bad.[11] He called all the daemons
idols swollen with air and emitting sounds among themselves, of

longaeva difficileque solubilia. Daemones vero multos esse malos qui et homines sub praetextu bonorum fallant Iamblichus asserit, sed eos bonorum numinum praesentiam subito fugere atque ita legitimum religiosum non posse decipere. Haec ab Aegyptiis et Chaldaeis. Proinde Plotinus ait daemonicas animas idcirco ad corpora procliviores exsistere, quoniam in eis materia quaedam regnet intelligibilis. Haec autem non solum est ipsa natura formabilis — haec enim et superioribus inest — sed intima quaedam essentiae dispositio in qua nec identitas alteritatem superat neque status motum neque natura communis particularem neque agendi facultas potentiam patiendi. Per quam sane dispositionem essentia talis tum corpori etiam caduto tum animi perturbationi videtur accommodari. Ob hanc rationem, quod et Iamblichus asserit, daemones providentiam non ut dii² communem habent sed singuli ad actiones proprias atque provincias.

: VI :

De origine daemonum.

8 Quid vero Plotinus in capite sexto dicit, daemones ex ipsa totius anima generatos, atque Porphyrius in libro *De Abstinentia* dicit, daemones ex tota anima pullulasse, ne intelligas substantias ipsas animarum quae sunt in daemonibus ex anima mundi creatas. Immo vero animam hic totam accipe illam pateram sive deam ideamque communem ex qua Timaeus, praeter mundi animam,

great age, and difficult to wipe out. It is asserted by Iamblichus that many daemons are bad and also deceive men in the false appearance of good daemons, but that they suddenly flee the presence of good divinities and therefore cannot deceive the lawfully religious person, this teaching being derived from the Egyptians and Chaldaeans.[12] Similarly, Plotinus says that daemonic souls exist with a proclivity toward body because a certain intelligible matter is dominant in them.[13] This matter is not only susceptible to form by its very nature, since it is also present among the higher things, but is a certain inner disposition of being, in which neither does sameness overwhelm otherness, nor rest motion, nor the universal nature the particular, nor the power of activity the potentiality of passivity. Through this disposition, such a being seems to become conformable even to the perishable body and also to the perturbation of the mind. For this reason, as Iamblichus also asserts, the daemons do not have the universal providence that the gods have, but rather relate individually to their own actions and provinces.[14]

: VI :

On the origin of daemons.

Regarding the question why Plotinus says in his sixth chapter that   8
the daemons are generated from the soul of the totality itself,[15] and Porphyry in his book *On Abstinence* that the daemons have sprung forth from the total soul,[16] you should not understand that the very substances of the souls which are in the daemons have been created from the world-soul. On the contrary, you should observe that "total soul" here means that bowl, or goddess and universal Idea from which Timaeus asserts that, in addition to the

seorsum sphaerarum animas iterumque animas daemonum homi-
numve asserit esse productas—nam et Proculus ait in *Alcibiade*
daemones a dea vivifica generatos a qua generantur et animae. Vult
quoque Plotinus et ab ipsa mundi et a qualibet anima rationali
suam quandam irrationalem animam emanare quam nominat daemonem. Eiusmodi vero daemones, etsi suas sequuntur animas,
tamen sub communi quodam influxu animae mundanae gignuntur
ab eis, nam in illius providentia est praecipue ut ipsius naturae
subserviant tot talesque naturae ad dispositionem universi complendam. Omnino vero, qualescumque sint daemones, ideo pendere dicuntur ab anima mundi quoniam eorum animas ipsa mundi
anima per vitales vires infusas materiae velut escas corporibus alli-
gat. Inter haec, intelligibiles deos ponit, id est, ideas et intellectuales caelestium animas, item sensibiles deos scilicet stellas, post
eas daemones qui sunt invisibiles sive in caelo sunt sive sub caelo,
quamvis ipsam daemonis appellationem ad eos qui sub luna sunt
proprie transferant.

9   Corpora daemonum in superioribus quidem descripsimus ratione quadam liberiore per quam a plerisque Platonicorum haud
longe discederemus. Possumus autem ratione forsitan magis physica dicere corpora daemonum sublunarium plurimum esse composita. Nam et elementa in globum unum undique commiscentur.
Erit igitur necessario ignis in eis—per hunc enim vita motusque
viget. Erit et aer ignis pabulum—nec solus cum solo ne subito
dissolvantur. Esto insuper aqua tenuis nec sine terra subtili,

world-soul, the souls of the spheres and also the souls of daemons and men were separately produced[17] — and indeed, Proclus says in his *Alcibiades* that the daemons were generated by the life-giving goddess by whom the souls also were generated.[18] Plotinus holds that both from the world-soul itself and from each and every rational soul there also emanates a certain irrational soul of their own, which he names a "daemon."[19] The daemons of this kind, even if they follow their own souls, are generated by the latter in subordination to a certain universal outflow from the world-soul, for it is primarily within the providence of the world-soul that so many and such natures should be subject to its nature in order to complete the ordering of the universe. In any case, the daemons, of whatever kind they are, are said to depend wholly on the world-soul because the world-soul itself binds their souls through vital powers infused into matter as food is infused into bodies. Among these powers, Plotinus posits intelligible gods: that is, the Ideas, and the intellectual souls of the heavenly bodies, and likewise sensible gods: namely, the stars. After these he posits the daemons which are invisible, whether in the heaven or below the heaven although, strictly speaking, people apply the name "daemon" itself in a metaphorical sense to the spirits that are properly speaking below the moon.

We have described the bodies of the daemons in the previous 9 passage, exercising a certain greater freedom of thought in which we did not depart very far from the majority view of the Platonists. However, we may perhaps say on the basis of a more physical argument that the bodies of the sublunary daemons are composite for the most part. The elements are mixed together on all sides into a unitary mass. Therefore, there will necessarily be fire in the daemons' bodies, for life and motion grow strong through it. There will also be air as the nourishment of fire, with neither element in splendid isolation, so that sudden dissolution is avoided. Let there also be subtle water not without subtle air, for

alioquin minimam habebit sub igne stabilitatem. Oportet sane spiritalia daemonum corpora, sicut et spiritus noster, esse admodum temperata ut sint illius vitae nobilis susceptacula. Oportet igitur in eis tyrannicam ignis voracitatem ita domari ut et trium numero et horum quidem quantitate maiore unius tyranni rapacitas refrenatur. Non potest autem terra illic esse multa,[3] nec etiam aqua plurima. Sit ergo quamplurimus aer, secundo loco humor aquaeus tenuissimus, tertio ignis sed admodum rarus ne forte sit edax; quartum teneat subtilissima terra locum. Et quamvis daemones omnes sint propemodum temperati, aliqui tamen temperatissimi sunt, in ceteris autem elementum hoc aut illud paulo magis excellit. Erunt igitur complexiones eorum quinque ferme sicut et nostrae, temperatae[4] videlicet, et quattuor non adeo temperatae, stellis quidem subditae consimilibus et praesidentes instinctu quopiam naturali hominibus complexionis eiusdem.[5]

: VII :

De amore subsistente, et de intelligentia
in nobis aeterna.[6]

10   In capite septimo ubi dicit 'ratio igitur,' et cetera, intellige pro ratione vim seminariam ab intellectu animali fluentem in animam velut patrem in matrem in qua gignit amorem tum ex copia sua tum ex quadam animae indigentia mixtum. Item amorem ponit

otherwise the daemonic body will have little stability underneath the fire. Indeed, the spiritual bodies of the daemons, as is the case with our spirit, must be tempered to a high degree so that they may be the receptacles of that noble life. It is therefore necessary that in them the overbearing greediness of fire should be sufficiently tamed that the rapacity of a single tyrant is curbed by both the number and the greater quantity of a threefold. However, there cannot be a great amount of earth in the daemons' bodies, and also not a large quantity of water. Let there be air in the greatest amount, a most subtle watery moistness in second place, and in third place fire of a very rarefied kind lest perchance it should become greedy. Let the most subtle earth hold the fourth position. Although all the daemons are tempered to some degree, some are most fully tempered, while in others one element or another is slightly more prominent. Therefore, there will be five combinations of elements among the daemons more or less as there are among us — that is, tempered combinations — and four combinations not tempered as much. These combinations are placed under stars of a similar nature and preside over men of the same complexion with a natural impulse of some kind.

: VII :

*On the subsistent love and on the intelligence
in us that is eternal.*

In the seventh chapter, where Plotinus says: "therefore, a reason-principle" and so on,[20] you should understand by "reason-principle" the seminal power flowing into soul from soul's intellect, as a father's semen flows into the mother in whom he begets his love blended from his own abundance and a certain want on the part of

perpetuum tum in intellectu animali ad pulchrum intelligibile contemplandum tum in natura ad generabile pulchrum. Et utrumque amorem esse aliquid arbitratur essentiale atque subsistens, quoniam ab anima per ipsam essentiam eius existant. Amores autem qui nuper excitari solent, cum non ab ipsa anima simpliciter sint velut agente, sed contingant in eam quasi patiente ab externis et corpore, non subsistentes daemonesve appellant sed passiones.

11   Post haec animadvertes intellectum ipsum omnium communem atque intellectum uniuscuisque proprium inter se longe differre, rursum potentiam cognoscendi quae non habet in essentia sua ipsum quod cognoscendum est secundum illius essentiam sed quandam eius imaginem esse fallacem, certam vero esse quae ipsum in se habet obiectum. Quod si non tamquam imaginarium habet potentia eiusmodi, ipsummet exsistit obiectum. Cognitio igitur perfectissima qualis est intellectus est res ipsae quae dicuntur obiecta, imperfectissima vero sicut sensus nec est quae sentienda sunt nec habet sed ad illa se vertit. Cogitatio vero. etsi non est illa quae cogitat, habet tamen, id est, notiones eorum, sive ex se ipsa proprie sive ab intellectu suo hauriat pro arbitrio. Si mundum contempleris intelligibilem, illic non solum universus intellectus est universum intelligibile, sed etiam in quavis idea intellectus certus est intelligibile certum. Praeterea intellectus uniuscuisque animae proprius est suum ipsum intelligibile, differt tamen et in hoc ab ipso simpliciter communique intellectu, siquidem non est ipse universum simpliciter intelligibile, est enim ipsum suo quodam pacto. Habet igitur intellectus noster universalium rerum intelligentiam, similiumque amorem, quoniam ipsum universum intelligibile et habet pariter et exsistit. At quoniam hic exsistit hoc

the soul.[21] He also posits a perpetual Love, both in soul's intellect toward contemplating the intelligible beauty, and in nature toward the beauty that can be generated. Plotinus also holds that each love is something essential and subsistent, since their existence derives from soul through the latter's being in itself. He calls the loves wont to be recently aroused not subsisting daemons but passions, since these are not derived from soul itself *simpliciter* and functioning as an agent but happen upon it as though it were passive to external things and the body.

After this, you should observe that that universal intellect of all things and the intellect proper to each individual thing are quite different from one another, and further that that power of knowing which does not have in its being that which is knowable according to the latter's being but a certain image is deceptive, whereas that power of knowing which has its object in itself enjoys certainty, for if a power of this kind does not have something image-like, then it exists as its own object. Therefore, that most perfect knowing that intellect constitutes *is* the things themselves that are said to be its objects, whereas the most imperfect knowing in the manner of sense *is not* the things that are sensed and does not possess them but turns itself toward them. Thinking, even if it *is not* the things that are thought, does possess them: that is, the concepts of them, whether it draws the latter properly from itself or from its intellect in the process of judging.[22] If you contemplate the intelligible world, there not only is the universal intellect the universal intelligible but also a particular intellect is a particular intelligible in each and every Idea. Moreover, the intellect proper to each soul is its own intelligible, although it also differs from the intellect itself that is universal *simpliciter* in that it is not itself the universal intelligible *simpliciter* but is that intelligible according to a certain specificity of its own. Our intellect therefore has an understanding of universal things, and a love of similar things, since it both has and is that universal intelligible itself. But since it is here

ipsum non tam simpliciter quam suo quodam pacto, id est, non prorsus efficacissimo modo, ideo in speciali qualibet notitione non omnino distincte comprehendit singula quae mens divina comprehendit—oportet enim intellectum ⟨nostrum⟩ ad rationem se imaginationemque convertere ut particularia distincte cognoscat. Quod autem praeter intellectum communem sint et alii non solum discursione sed statu perpetuo cognoscentes a primo distincti, ita confirmari videtur: Intellectus primus cum sit multitudo prima, merito est in plures intellectus naturaliter propagabilis. Est in eo diversitatis idea, est etiam identitatis idea longeque potentior. Quoniam igitur sub diversitate in plures intellectus distribuitur discurrentes, merito et in plures sub identitate derivatur stabiliter cognoscentes. Sed in iis inde naturaliter propagatis ita ratio discurrens subnectitur intelligentiae stabili, sicut in prima mente ipsa diversitas vel alteritas identitate subnectitur. Progredi vero in multitudinem infinitam intelligendo: id est, intelligere singula, datur intelligentiae nostrae rationis adiunctae imaginationisque ministerio. Cetera quae de amore diisque disputantur in libro *De Amore* satis confirmavisse videmur.

that very thing not so much *simpliciter* as according to a specificity of its own: that is, not in absolutely the most powerful way, it does not distinctly comprehend with any special mode of understanding all the individual things that the divine mind comprehends. This is because it is necessary for our intellect to turn itself toward reason and imagination in order to know particular things distinctly. That there are besides the universal intellect other intellects that know not only discursively but in perpetual stability and are distinct from the first one is confirmed in the following way: — Since the first intellect is the first multiplicity, it is rightly the natural progenitor of a multiplicity of intellects, for there is within it an Idea of difference and also an Idea of sameness, the latter being much more powerful. Therefore, since the first intellect is distributed in dependence on difference into a plurality of intellects that know discursively, it is rightly also distributed in dependence on sameness into a plurality of intellects that know in a stable way. But to these intellects produced naturally from the first intellect, a discursive reason is subjoined to the stable intellection, just as in the first mind itself difference or otherness is subjoined to sameness. It is given to our intellect to proceed into an infinite multiplicity in the process of understanding—that is to say, to understand individual things—, doing this with the assistance of the reason joined to it and the imagination. We seem to have dealt sufficiently with the other questions to be raised concerning love and the gods in our book *On Love*.

[LIBER VI]

ARGUMENTUM IN LIBRUM QUOD INCORPOREA NON PATIUNTUR

Summa libri.

1 Summa libri huius est asserere rem incorpoream pati non posse. Rem quidem incorpoream appellat quae vel nullam in sua ratione quantitatem includit, quamvis eam extrinsecus accipere valeat — haec autem materia est — vel quantitatem prorsus excludit — haec autem est mens et anima. Praeterea passionem esse vult mutationem quae substantiam perdere valeat sive divisione contingat qualis accidit quantitati rebusque necessariam habentibus quantitatem sive contingat alteratione qualis accidit contrariis inter se qualitatibus atque insuper formis quas necessario qualitates eiusmodi comitantur. Igitur tam materia prima quam anima res est incorporea neque quantitatem neque qualitatem eiusmodi propriam sibi vindicans — ideoque a passione seiungitur, ac multo magis anima quam materia. Anima enim non solum formas non admittit perniciosas verum etiam nec novas aliquando qualescumque sint formas videtur accipere. Multa igitur in sequentibus de immutabili animae rationalis essentia deque partibus eius, nonnulla insuper de essentia prima, plurima de illius opposito: id est, de prima materia disputantur, quatenus id denique confirmetur rem incorpoream esse passionis expertem.

[BOOK VI]

ANALYSIS OF THE BOOK "THAT INCORPOREAL THINGS ARE IMPASSIVE"

Summary of the book.

The main point of this book is to assert that an incorporeal thing 1
cannot be passive. Plotinus calls "incorporeal" either a thing that
includes no quantity in its reason-principle although it is able to
receive the former from the outside, matter being such a thing; or
else a thing that excludes quantity altogether, mind and soul being
things of this kind. Moreover, he understands passivity as equivalent to a change that is able to destroy substance whether this
arises through division of the kind that accrues to quantity and
things that necessarily imply quantity, or else through alteration of
the kind that occurs with qualities that are contrary to one another and additionally with the forms that necessarily accompany
qualities of this kind. Therefore, both primary matter and soul are
incorporeal things that claim neither such a quantity nor such a
quality as proper to themselves. For that reason, they are separated
from passivity, soul being much more in this manner than is matter. Indeed, soul not only does not admit destructive forms but
also seems not at any time to admit new forms of whatever kind
they may be. In what follows, therefore, many arguments are made
regarding the immutable being of the rational soul and its parts,
and also some regarding the first being, and very many regarding
its opposite: that is, prime matter. All this is in order to confirm
ultimately that an incorporeal thing is free of passivity.

Anima neque patitur neque formas qualitatesque
suscipit; item de duplici imaginatione.

2   In prima igitur libri parte quae capita quinque continet, ostendit
animam non esse passioni subiectam; in secunda deinceps ostendet
simile aliquid de materia. Quantum vero ad primam spectat, animadvertes nullam incidere a corporibus impulsionem vel qualitatem in potentia animae cognoscentem, sive enim modo quodam
naturali et, ut ita dicam, inciderit materiali — confundetur cognitio
et discretio protinus et iudicium — ; sive imaginali quadam condicione saltem id eveniat ut corpora forment animam: quod dictu
nefas, nam ad animam tamquam superiorem spectat formare corpora non inde formari. Omnino vero omnis cognitio et affectus
animae etiam ad corporalia vergens est actio quaedam animae circa
talia neque interim patitur inde. Neque enim convenit cum corporibus in materia, qualis communio solet aliquam passionis vicissi-
tudinem in agente committere. Quid igitur est sentire? Est quidem in anima hoc ipsum: scilicet adhibere seipsam et expedire vim
suam circa illa ad quae habet essentiam consentaneam et naturaliter aptam; recordari quoque similiter est expeditissime hoc ipsum
efficere. Nulla igitur potentia cognoscendi per novas formatur
imagines, sed intellectus quidem actu semper est illa ipsa quae
cognoscit; ratio vero et phantasia ex eo statu in quo sunt secundum potentiam illa quae ab ipsis excogitanda sunt actu quandoque
fiunt illa quae secundum actum in intellectu sunt semper. Sensus

The soul is neither passive nor the recipient of forms and qualities; also regarding the twofold imagination.

Therefore, in the first part of this book which contains five chapters, Plotinus shows that the soul is not subject to passion. Afterward in the second part he will show something similar with respect to matter.[1] As far as the former is concerned, you should observe that there comes upon it from bodies no impulse or cognitive quality in the power of the soul, whether this comes upon it in a certain natural and, so to speak, material manner — here, cognition and discernment and also judgment will be destroyed straight away —, or else comes about at least through a certain imaginative condition so that bodies might form the soul — a shameful suggestion given that it pertains to soul as superior to form bodies and not to be formed by them. To be sure, every cognitive act and every disposition of soul even inclining toward corporeal things represents a certain activity of soul around those things, and is not in the meantime passive with respect to the latter. Indeed, this action does not come together with bodies in matter, for such a communion is wont to introduce a certain changeability into the agent. Therefore, what opinion should we hold? That it is in the soul itself that this action takes place: in other words, that the soul applies itself and exercises its power around those things with which it has an essential being that is compatible and naturally suitable, recollection being similarly the accomplishment of this in the most effective manner. Therefore, no power of knowing is formed through new images. Rather, a certain intellect in act is those very things that it knows. Reason and imagination, according to the status that they have, are potentially those things that are to be thought by them, and sometimes become in actuality those things that are always actual in the intellect. The external sense perceives

2

exterior percipit sentienda, non accipit. Vegetativa nutrit movetque, neque nutritur interea vel movetur.

3   Haec omnia confirmat Porphyrius ostendens, quando anima dicitur pati, hanc ipsam passionem non esse alterationem ullam in natura vel aliqua qualitate sed accommodationem quandam et affectionem animae ad rem hanc aut illam, esseque id aliquam actionem animae circa externa sed angustam: quando scilicet suae potentiae affectusque amplitudinem ipsamet contrahit ad angustum. Concluditque Porphyrius omnes animae qui dicuntur motus non esse proprie motus in anima sed in corpore et in anima quidem esse actiones, in corpore vero eosdem fieri passiones. Addit actus vegetationis et sensus atque memoriae non imaginales esse sed ita quodammodo naturales ut calefacere calere illuminare lucere — eadem Plotinus existimat.

4   Notabis interea virtutem communiter in anima duplicem: alteram quidem velut privatam: scilicet alicui partium animae proprium — haec autem est ut quaelibet rite suum officium peragat —, alteram vero quasi publicam: scilicet ut cunctae partes invicem rite concinant; a mente regatur ratio, huic irrationales subinde vires obtemperent inter quas concupiscentia subsit audaciae. Neutra virtus est velut qualitas animae impressa sicut subiecto — similiter neque vitium — sed est potius velut motus et actus horumque vacatio. Si qua vero in nobis est qualitas, vel aliunde impressa per modum naturae imaginisve vel actionibus acquisita: eiusmodi quidem non est in anima sed in corpore potius sic proprie aut sic affecto, in quo et formationes passionesque fiunt dum anima vegetat sentit afficitur atque iudicat. Nulla denique in anima mutatio fit

the things to be sensed but does not receive them. The vegetative soul nourishes and moves, but is not in the meantime nourished and moved.

Porphyry confirms all this. He shows that, when the soul is said to be passive, this passion itself is not any alteration in its nature or in some quality but a certain accommodation and disposition of the soul toward one thing or another, and that this so-called passion is a certain action of the soul with respect to external things, but a narrowed one: namely, when the soul itself contracts the amplitude of its power and disposition toward narrowness.[2] Moreover, Porphyry concludes that all those things that are said to be motions of the soul are not proper motions in the soul but are actions in the body *and* the soul, although they become passions in the body.[3] He adds that the activities of imparting life, of sensing, and of memory are not imaginative in character but are somehow as natural as are warming, heating, lighting, and shining.[4] Indeed, Plotinus holds the same opinion.

You will note in the meantime that there is, in a general way, a twofold power in the soul. One power is as though private: that is, proper to one of the parts of the soul. It is this in order rightly to perform any of its tasks as its own function. The other power is as though public: that is, in order that all the parts might rightly harmonize with one another, the reason being ruled by the mind, the irrational powers subsequently obeying the reason, and among the latter concupiscence being subordinated to audacity. Neither power is like a quality impressed in the soul as though in a subject—the same applying to their deficiency—; rather, each power is as though a motion and an activity and likewise the absence of the latter. If quality is in any way in us, it is either impressed from somewhere else in the manner of nature or an image, or else it is acquired through actions. A quality of this kind is indeed not in the soul but rather in the body, the latter being qualified thus either properly or as affected. In the body, formations and passions

nisi progressio a potentia quaedam in actum—atque haec quidem non ab alio motore sed ab ipsamet anima—neque rursus[1] in actum qui adveniat quasi qualitas sed qui prodeat velut actio. Si qua vero pars animae passiva dicitur, non subiectum aliquod passionibus corporalibus intelligitur sed principium passionum.

5 Animadvertes iterum duplicem in nobis imaginationem: primam quidem in anima rationali discursionis et iudicii compotem, similem quodammodo rationi, secundam vero ab hac impressam in anima seu vita in nobis ratione carente, quae sane imaginatio non tam discursione utitur quam fertur instinctu—quamvis intimo sed circa corporis passiones—, quae ⟨et⟩ tamquam communis sensus principium est sensuum reliquorum. Ponit quandoque Plotinus per translationem quandam imaginationem in parte etiam vegetali, quae neque fit discursio per formas, sicut prima, neque intuitus formae, ut secunda, sed formae intus vigentis expressio in seipsa perque hanc impressio in materiam ubi naturalis actio est tamquam imaginatio quaedam substantialis agens nequaquam imaginando. Hic quoque notabis a facultate animae vegetali facultatem concupiscendi irascendique pullulare, quemadmodum ab intellectu naturaliter ratio profluit et subinde imaginatio prima a qua profluit et secunda.

arise when the soul imparts life, senses, is affected, and judges. In fine, no change occurs in the soul except a certain progression from potency to actuality, and this progression results not from another mover but from the soul itself. Again, this progression is not toward an actuality that arises like a quality but to an act that comes forth as an action. If a part of the soul is in any way said to be passive, it is understood not as something subject to corporeal passions but as a causal principle with respect to passions.

Further, you should observe that there is a twofold imagination 5 in us: the first being in the rational soul, sharing in discursiveness and judgment, and being in a certain manner similar to the reason; the second being impressed by the former in our soul or in our irrational life. This latter imagination does not so much employ discursive reason as it is driven by an impulse that is, although internal, in relation to the body's passions. Moreover, this imagination is the causal principle with respect to the other senses, as though being a common sense. Sometimes, Plotinus with a certain metaphorical usage places imagination also in the life-giving part of the soul.[5] This becomes neither discursiveness through forms, as in the case of the first kind of imagination, nor intuition of form, as in the case of the second kind. Rather, it is the expression in itself of the form living within, and through this form an impression in matter, where natural action is like a certain imagination acting substantially and in no wise by imagining. Here also you will note that from the life-giving power of the soul the power of concupiscence and irascibility springs forth, just as reason naturally flows forth from intellect, and afterward from the reason the first imagination, and from the first imagination the second.

Quod in vera essentia continentur vita et intellectus;
item de uno quod est super essentiam et de
uno quod est infra eam.

6   In capite sexto notabis ens verum esse illud quod omnino est: id
est, cui non deest aliquid ad perfectionem essentiae necessarium;
essentia vero perfecta actum intimum et perennem sui ipsius includit: id est, vitam, atque hunc quidem exigit maxime intimum. Talis autem est si intelligentia fuerit: haec enim est vitae reflexio in
essentiam. Ex prima ergo essentia velut ex radice pullulat in seipsam vita simul et intellectus, sed germen eiusmodi eatenus ex ea
nascitur quatenus fecunditatem habet ex ipso bono, communem
dico, ceu vitis ex sole. Ut autem fecunditas haec ad vitam proprie
intellectumque distinguatur, ex ipsamet essentia provenit, ceu ex
vite factum est ut virtus solis determinetur ad uvam. Munera igitur vivendi intelligendique et similia ex ipso quidem bono velut
principio communissimo atque fine. Ex ipsa vero essentia prima
profluunt velut ex radice propria et quadam potestate formali. Proinde verum ens veramque essentiam Plotinus hic non solum accipit ens ipsum omnium caput entium, sed etiam omnem formam
habentem esse suum atque exsistere in essentia propria ideoque a
materia separabilem, in qua propterea nulla est potentia et procli-
vitas ad non esse, nulla miscetur aliena natura, nihil deest ad suam
exsistentiam necessarium. Potentia speciei redacta est semper in
actu, in qua rursum una cum essentia pariter vita et intellectus

That life and intellect are contained in true being;
also concerning the one that is above being and
the one that is below it.

In chapter six you will note that the true being is that which 6
wholly *is:* namely, that to which nothing necessary for the perfection of its being is lacking. Perfect being includes an inward and
everlasting activity internal to itself: that is, life, and it performs
this action as its most intimate one. But it is being *of such a kind* if
it has become intelligence, for this is the turning back of life toward being. Therefore, from the first being there springs forth into
itself as though from a root the simultaneity of life and intellect.
But a shoot of this kind is born from the root to the extent that it
has fertility — a universal fertility, indeed — from the Good itself,
just as the vine has fertility from the sun. In order that this fertility might be demarcated in a proper sense from life and intellect, it
comes forth from being itself, just as it comes about from the vine
that the power of the sun is delimited in relation to the grape.
Therefore, the functions of living, understanding, and the like
arise from the Good itself, as though from a most universal beginning and end. They flow forth from the primal being itself as
though from their own root and a certain formative power. Accordingly, Plotinus here understands as the true being and the true
essential being not only being itself, the summit of all beings, but
also all Form that has its own being and existence in its own essence, the totality of Form being therefore separate from matter.
Moreover, in this Form there is no potency or tendency toward
nonbeing. No alien nature is blended there. Nothing necessary to
its existence is lacking there. The potency of form is always converted into actuality. Again, life and intellect are equally included
there in union with being. Of the same nature are all the intellects

includitur. Eiusmodi sunt intellectus omnes et intellectuales animae in genere veri entis connumerata, nam formae sensibiles inseparabiles a materia entia non vera dicuntur ob contrarias earum quas hic diximus rationes. Cum vero materia longius admodum a prima rerum forma distet quam formae sensibiles, atque hae non vere entia nuncupentur, nimirum ipsa vere non ens appellari a Plotino et Porphyrio consuevit, quoniam formale in seipsa nihil includit sed prorsus excludit. Esse vero formae munus est, siquidem essentia prima idem est quod et prima forma naturaliter omniformis.

7   Huc adducenda sunt quae de ipso uno in *Parmenide* tum negantur tum iterum affirmantur, et quae in *Sophiste* de ente simiiter atque non ente. Unum ergo tribus praecipue modis accipies: aut quod cum ente videtur aequari, aut quod ente superius est, aut quod est inferius. De uno quidem quod enti aequale est, praecipue de ipso ente primo, omnes rerum species proprietatesque pariter affirmantur: est enim fons entium omnium et exemplar. De hoc ergo dici solet: est idem et alterum, stabile, mobile, aequale, inaequale, magnum, parvum, atque similia : sunt enim hic ideales omnium rationes. De uno autem supremo haec similiter negantur omnia: est enim illic non horum forma sed causa. De uno tandem infimo: id est materia, omnia haec aeque negantur: nihil enim habet in se ipsa formale.

and all the intellectual souls that are enumerated within the genus of pure being, for the sensible forms that are inseparable from matter are, because of the reason-principles contrary to them that we speak of here, not said to be true beings. It is certainly because matter stands at a much greater distance from the first Form of things than do sensible forms, and because the latter are not truly called beings, that matter itself is accustomed to be called "nonbeing" by Plotinus and Porphyry given that it includes nothing formal within itself but totally excludes it.[6] The being of form is a gift, given that the first being is the same thing as the first Form that is naturally "omniform."

Here one should introduce the things that are at one point denied and at another affirmed of the One in the *Parmenides*,[7] and similarly the things that are said of being and nonbeing in the *Sophist*.[8] You will therefore understand "one" in three senses primarily: either that one which seems to be equal to being, or that one which is superior to being, or that one which is inferior to being.[9] Of the one that is equal to being, and especially of the first being itself, all forms and properties of things can be affirmed in like manner. It is the fount of all beings and the Exemplar. Therefore of this one it is customary to say that it is same, other, stable, mobile, equal, unequal, great, small and so forth, for the ideal reason-principles of all things are *here*.[10] Of the one that is highest, all these things are similarly denied, for it is not the Form of things but the cause that is *there*. Finally, of the one that is lowest: that is, matter, these things are equally denied, for it has nothing in itself that is formal.

7

*Quod naturalia non sint entia vera; et quod materia dicatur
non ens, et instar speculi videatur
habere formas quas non habet veras.*

8   Inter haec, ubi ait naturalia non tam esse re vera quam esse videri,
introducit Epicuream quandam obiectionem, qua contenditur res
quae corpulenter sunt solas veram essentiam possidere, idque e
duobus patere praecipue: tum quia soliditate sua dividenti resis-
tunt, tum quia vehementer obiecta percutiunt. Respondetur ad
primum corpora eiusmodi dura, dum videntur resistere, diutius
percutienti sunt exposita ictumque exspectant propterea quod in-
eptissima sint ad fugam, ac propter eandem ad motum ineptitudi-
nem inefficacemque naturam, postquam divisa sunt in partes, in
priorem formam redire non possunt; corpora vero subtiliora, ubi
cedere percutienti videntur, propter mirabilem efficaciam subterfugiunt[2] celerrime passionem, atque ob eandem similiter efficaciam
subito redeunt in se ipsa. Denique cum motus in rebus sit actio
quaedam vitaeque plurimum interioris indicium et ubique sit vitae
vestigium, et quae minime corpulenta sunt promptissima sint ad
motum, consequens est, quatenus ad incorpoream naturam res
accedunt, eatenus ad vitam motionis et efficaciae compotem ideoque ad essentiam accedere veram, corpulenta vero ab essentia
cadere. Qua in parte respondetur similiter ad secundum: scilicet
corpulenta, quando in aliquid incidunt, laedere gravius, non
quia firmiora sint sed quoniam sint prorsus infirma, adeo ut se

*That natural things are not true beings; that matter is said to
be nonbeing and seems to have forms which it
does not truly have, in the manner of a mirror.*

When Plotinus says, in the midst of this discussion, that natural 8
things are in reality not so much things that are as things that
seem to be, he introduces a certain Epicurean objection.[11] According
to this it is argued that things that are bodily alone possess
true being, this becoming clear through two considerations primarily:
that they resist division through their solidity, and that
they strike objects forcefully. The reply to the first objection is that
hard bodies of this kind, when they seem to resist, are exposed for
a long time to something that strikes them and await that impact
because they are totally unsuitable to flight. Moreover, because of
that same unsuitability to motion and the powerlessness of their
nature, after they have been divided into parts, they are not able to
return to their proper form. However, when more subtle bodies
seem to yield to the thing that strikes them, they very quickly
evade passivity to the striking on account of their marvelous powerfulness,
and likewise because of that same powerfulness immediately
return to themselves. Finally, since motion among things is a
certain action and very much an indication of inner life and everywhere
a trace of life, and since even those things that are least
bodily are very liable to move, it follows that, to the extent that
things come near to the incorporeal nature, to the same extent do
they approach a life that possesses motion and power and therefore
approximate to true being, whereas bodily things fall away
from being. Here, we respond in part similarly to the second objection:
namely, by saying that bodily things, when they fall upon
something, damage it more seriously, not because they are more
robust but because they are absolutely feeble: to such an extent

sustinere non valeant ideoque ipsa sui ruina casuque proxima quaeque laedant. Nam et qui ad equitatum ineptissimi sunt, hi equos premunt potissimum atque defatigant, et languentia corpora gestantibus onerosissima esse solent.

9   Post haec, memento materiam quidem esse inanem essentiae primae umbram, formas vero materiales esse varias imagines idearum quae in prima continentur essentia nullam habentes cum illis similitudinem in natura, quamvis in effectu representandi similitudinem aliquam videantur habere. Atque ideo materiam instar speculi, dum vel solas imagines accipit vel forte nec istas quidem accipit sed videtur accipere, re vera nihil pati, praesertim quoniam materia in aliud, cum ipsa sit ultimum, resolvi non potest, ideoque nec pati. Huic sane nulla formarum contraria est, cum omnibus aeque naturaliter sit exposita. A nulla igitur pati potest, quandoquidem nec quae in materia fiunt quaelibet a quibuslibet sed a contrariis patiuntur. Item materia ex praesentia formae nullam sibi propriam qualitatem contrahit vel virtutem et idcirco non patitur, alioquin iamdiu facta esset familiariter multiformis, ideoque non foret amplius subiectum communissimum ab omnibus aeque formabile. Iam vero, si in qualibet alteratione ipsam subiecti substantiam permanere oportet, qualitatibus interim permutatis, multo magis in transmutatione mundana necesse est materiam permanere. Denique cum substantiale aliquid in nihilum resolvi ipsa naturae bonitas minime patiatur, substantiae vero simplices nequeant in aliud quandoque resolvi, merito neque formae simplices in se subsistentes neque materia simplex perire aliquando pative

that they are not able to sustain themselves and therefore also damage everything closest to them through their own ruin and collapse. Those people who are most incompetent in horsemanship are the very ones who drive the horses most and wear them out, and inactive bodies are wont to become the most burdensome to those who carry them around.

After this, you should bear in mind that matter is the empty 9 shadow of the first being, and that material forms are the various images of the Ideas that are contained in the first being. The former have no similarity of nature with the latter, although they seem to have some similarity in the accomplishment of representation. Matter therefore is like a mirror. While it receives only images or perhaps does not even receive these but only seems to receive them, it is therefore not in reality passive. This is especially the case since matter, being itself the last term, cannot be dissolved into something else and therefore cannot be passive. To be sure, there is no form contrary to matter, given that it is naturally exposed to all forms. It therefore cannot be passive to any form, seeing that each and every thing that comes to be in matter is passive not to any other thing but only to its contrary. Likewise, matter does not derive any quality or power proper to itself from the presence of form, and for that reason is not passive. If that were not so, it would have been long since subjected to many interrelated forms, and so would no more be the most general substratum which is equally formable by all things. Moreover, if it is necessary that the substance itself of the subject endures within any qualitative change, the qualities in the meantime changing, much more so is it necessary that matter should endure within the transmutation of the world as a whole. Finally, since the goodness of nature does not allow anything substantial to be dissolved into nothingness, and simple substances are unable to be dissolved at any time into something else; then rightly, neither simple forms subsisting in themselves nor simple matter can ultimately perish or

possunt. Materia utique cum sit malum, id est, maxime distans ab ipso bono, non sic appetit bonum ut naturale aliquid inde sibi vindicat, sed ut quandam imaginariam inde vestem induat atque fallat, et quo magis in sua informitate permanet eo magis est mala sive malum. Neque calefit materia sed compositum: ipsa vero calorem sustinet mox depositura calorem quasi vestem minime permutata natura. Rursum quando dividitur aliquid, quantitas et quod hanc sequitur dividitur, non materia quae quantitatem natura praecedit. Atqui quemadmodum in processione colorum postremum, id est, nigredo nihil habet primi, id est, albedinis, sic materia ultimum in ipso entium descensu nihil vel intra se possidet simile primo vel in facie suscipit aliquid de natura primi, sed imitamina quaedam dumtaxat inania. Atque propter extremam ad primum diversitatem, nullum ex imaginum illius praesentia saporem entis sibi familiariter vindicat vel odorem, ut ad quaslibet formas in posterum adventuras, quantumcumque repugnet prioribus, ipsa sit ad capiendum aeque parata.

10   Maxime vero inter haec id observabis quod ait naturalia, si cum divinis comparentur, non maiorem habere substantiam quam imagines corporum in speculis apparentes, nec aliter haec a divinis perpetuo dependere quam imagines ab obiectis. Huc Salomonis illud tendit: Omnia vanitas. Huc illud Pauli: Videmus nunc per speculum in aenigmate. Sed quoniam nunc et corpora videmus et speculum a quibus in quo imagines omnino dependent, ideo ipsam in se imaginum deprehendimus vanitatem, alioquin nisi videremus illa, hanc redarguere non possumus, sed quae imagines sunt esse res veras arbitraremur, sicut et nunc quae naturalia nominantur

be passive. Undoubtedly, since matter is Evil: that is, standing at the greatest distance from the Good, it does not seek the Good in the way that some natural thing would lay claim to the latter, but does so in order to clothe itself with an imaginary garment derived thence and to deceive. And the more matter persists in its formlessness, the worse it is or the more it is evil. It is not matter that becomes hot but the composite: it indeed sustains heat but will soon put aside the heat like a garment with no change of nature. Again, when something is divided, it is the quantity and that which follows it that is divided, not matter which precedes the quantity in its nature. However, just as in the gradation of colors, the last term: that is, blackness has nothing of the first term: that is, whiteness, thus matter as the last term in the descent of beings neither possesses anything similar to the First within itself nor takes over anything on the surface from the nature of the First other than certain resemblances that are merely empty. And because of its extreme difference from the First, it lays no claim through affinity to any savor or redolence of being from the presence of images of the First: this in order that it itself may become equally prepared to receive whatever forms will arise in the future, however much they may conflict with previous forms.

Among these points, you will observe above all how Plotinus 10 says that, if natural things are compared with divine things, they have no more substance than do the images of bodies appearing in mirrors, nor do they everlastingly depend on the divine in any other way than do images upon objects.[12] This is the meaning of Solomon's statement "Everything is vanity"[13] and Paul's "We see now through a mirror in an enigma."[14] But since we now see both the bodies and the mirror on which and in which respectively the images have total dependence, we discover the vanity itself of the images. Otherwise, if we were not to see them, we would not be able to convict them of vanity but would think that the things that are images are true things. By the same token, we would believe

veras esse substantia opinamur, quoniam neque divina neque materiam aspicere possumus a quibus in quam ceu simulacra ab obiectis in speculum prosiliunt atque resiliunt. Profecto, vel sicut putant physici imagines rerum ipsae sunt in speculis, vel sicut perspectivi tradunt nullae in speculis sunt imagines sed radii rerum in speculum incidunt atque inde, si eidem reflectantur ad oculum—quod accidit ubi ad pares angulos reflectuntur, tunc res ipsae per eiusmodi suos radios oculis ita redduntur ut tamen sensus ibi fallatur, putans alibi se res videre quam videat—quomodocumque vero res se habeat, qualis est comparatio speculi ad res visibiles atque visum, talem esse Plotinus vult atque Porphyrius materiae ad res divinas et sensum, quam sane materiam, velut ipsi enti prorsus oppositam, existimant radios actusque primi entis et mentis non quidem intus admittere sed ceu densum quoddam et propter diversitatem entibus invium repercutere protinus actus eorum, atque hac ipsa quasi reverberatione apparere sensibus quasi sensibilia, quae in seipsis intelligibilia sunt adeo ut putemus in materia nos inspicere quae in primo ente intellectuque sunt atque inde movent animum ut cognoscat. Denique quoniam ipsa entia vel ideae, dum in materia agunt, neque de natura sua quicquam amittunt neque de statu moventur neque in proportione vel affectu conveniunt cum materia; ideo quid dari videtur inde velut inane debilissimumque materiali semper hac indiget sede. Atque interim materia haec, quia nec verum aliquid accipit umquam neque quale-

that things that are called natural things are the true substances, given that we cannot look upon either the divine things or the matter by means of which and into which the natural things, being as though phantasms from objects reflected in a mirror, leap forth and leap back. Indeed, whether, as the physicists think, the images of things themselves are in mirrors, or, as the Perspectivists[15] teach, there are not images in mirrors but only rays from things falling into the mirror and coming out of it if these rays are reflected back toward the eye—here, it comes about that, when the rays are reflected at angles equal to one another, then the things themselves through their own rays of this kind are returned to the eyes in such a manner that the sense is deceived there, thinking that it sees the things in a place other than that in which it really sees them—; either way, just as the mirror is compared to visible things and vision, so do Plotinus and Porphyry maintain that matter is in comparison with divine things and sensation. Indeed, they think that this matter, as though totally opposed to being itself, does not receive within itself the rays and activities of the first being and mind but immediately throws them back as though it were something dense and because of its otherness that is impervious to beings, and that these rays appear to the senses and as sensible things in that very reverberation,[16] so to speak. Moreover, these rays are in themselves intelligible, to such an extent that we think that we see in matter the things that are in the first being and intellect and from that source move the mind to know them. Finally, since the beings themselves or the Ideas, while they are active in respect to matter, do not lose anything of their own nature, are not moved from their rest, and do not come together with matter in any proportion or disposition: for this reason, that which seems to derive from them, as though empty and most feeble, always needs this foundation in matter. And in the meantime, given that it never receives anything true, never seems to receive any quality

cumque videtur accipere, ob naturalem falsitatem vere accipit, ideo impletur numquam sed semper affectans transmutationi perpetuae praebet occasionem.

Quantum anima materiam superemineat; et quomodo certa quantitas materiae sequatur modum cuiuslibet speciei in materiam venientis.

11 Quando lignum hoc esse dicitur extra lignum illud, seiuncta sunt duo haec inter se non multum, quoniam per terminos externos tantum, specie vero coniuncta sunt invicem. Magis ergo ignis est extra aquam: non solum enim exterioribus terminis sed qualitatibus contrariis seiunguntur, quoniam vero et genere conveniunt et materia possunt quandoque misceri. At anima toto genere a materia separatur ideoque, quamvis materiam penetret, longius tamen est extra materiam. Ideoque formas quas anima mundi ab intellectu divino nacta nititur per seminariam virtutem in materiam ubique traducere, materia secum conciliare non potest neque miscere sibi, quamvis illae invicem misceantur.

12 Tum vero materia sicut suapte natura formarum est omnium expers, ita etiam quantitatis: haec enim est forma quaedam. Et quoniam quantitas est postrema formarum, idcirco certa quaedam quantitas et figura rebus secundum speciei formaeque praecipue modum a mente et anima destinatur. In formalibus igitur rationibus specierum in mente et anima existentibus inclusa est atque definita certa quantitas et figura quae unamquamque speciem

whatsoever, and truly receives on account of its natural falsity, this matter is never filled but, in continuous aspiration, provides the occasion for perpetual transmutation.

How much the soul is elevated above matter; and how a certain quantity of matter follows the measure of each and every form coming into matter.

When this block of wood is said to be outside that block of wood, these two are not much separated from one another, since they are separated only through their external boundaries but are conjoined with one another according to form. Therefore, fire is outside water to a greater extent, these being separated not only in their external boundaries but also in their contrary qualities, being at times capable of blending, since they agree with one another in genus and matter. But the soul is separate from matter in its entire genus and therefore, although it penetrates matter, it is far outside the latter. Therefore, as to the forms which the World-Soul, having obtained from the divine intellect, everywhere strives to transfer into matter by means of the seminal power, matter can neither unite these with itself nor blend them with itself, although they blend with one another.

Indeed, just as matter in its own nature is devoid of all the forms, in like manner is it also free of quantity, for the latter is a certain form. Moreover, since quantity is the last of the forms, for that reason a certain specific quantity and shape especially according to the measure of species and form is appointed for things by mind and soul. Among the formal reason-principles of species existing in mind and soul, a certain quantity and shape that accompanies each and every species is included and delimited. In the

comitatur. In ratione quidem hominis formali vel equi decreta est hominis quantitas aut equi. Expeditur autem quantitas haec in effectum ob efficaciam rationis ubique formalis motumque eius quendam in actione atque propter processionem formae naturalis emanantis ab ea. Hac igitur efficacia motione processione super materiae faciem producitur in molem ipsa materia: tantam videlicet quantam exigit ipsa forma tum mundana mundo tum humana homini tum leonina leoni. Et sicut una cum qualibet specie propria venit quantitas in materiam, sic et abit una cum specie, et ad novae deinceps speciei adventum nova fit quantitas, sicut et qualitas propria speciei. Producitur autem quantitas in materia secundum distantiam ex quantitate virtutis agentis motuque formali. Materia quidem ob suam debilitatem nequit eiusmodi devitare motum vel absque tali quadam distractione suscipere formas. Anima vero quoniam et ipsa forma quaedam est speciesque subsistens, ideo cunctas rerum species in eodem quasi centro complectitur. Formas enim illas forma haec accipit modo formae: formarum vero modus est ut tum unaquaeque velut simplex in quolibet sui collecta sit tota tum cunctae in qualibet facillime concludantur. Hinc rursus efficitur ut ratio nostra possit formas tum absque multitudine numerali in ipsa speciei unitate comprehendere tum a quantitatis dimensione secernere. At materia cum extensione quadam semper accipit formas, quoniam ad motum formae super eam divinitus procedentis ubique protrahitur,[3] natura eius interim libenter protractioni[4] cedente, paratque cuilibet ubique moli, quoniam propriam sibi nullam possidet molem. Ac

formal reason-principle of a man or a horse, a certain quantity of the man or the horse is decreed.[17] This quantity is everywhere released into effectivity on account of the power of its formal reason-principle, on account of a certain motion of its reason-principle in activity, and also because of the procession of the natural form emanating from that activity. Through this power, motion, and procession over the surface of matter, matter itself is stretched out into bulk: namely, with whatever quantity the form itself demands, the form itself being at one time a worldly form for the world, at another a human form for a man, and at another a leonine form for a lion. And just as quantity comes into matter together with each and every proper form, thus it also departs together with the form. At the subsequent advent of a new species, a new quantity arises, just as does a quality proper to the species. The quantity is stretched out in matter according to its distance from the quantity of the active power and from the formal motion. Because of its weakness, matter is unable to avoid a motion of this kind or take on forms without a certain pulling asunder of this kind. But soul, since it is itself a certain form and a subsistent species, enfolds all the species of things in the same center so to speak. This form receives those forms in a formal manner, and the mode of existence of forms is such that each form as though simple is collected as a whole in a given object, while at the same time all forms are very easily embraced in each and every form. From this again, it comes about that our reason is able to comprehend forms in the unity itself of a species without numerical multiplicity, and also to separate them from the dimension of quantity. But matter always receives forms together with a certain extension, because it is everywhere drawn out with respect to the motion of the form above it proceeding from the divine sphere—its nature in the meantime freely yielding to the drawing-out—; and because it everywhere makes preparations for each and every bulk, given that it has no bulk proper to itself. While it is being extended

dum in dimensionem per totum extenditur mundi spatium, non dividitur in materias plures, sed unica restat atque continua, tum quia non est obnoxia passioni, tum quia non in vita, sed libens potestatem sequitur extendentem et ab una extenditur ratione ad unam universi formam.

13   Haec utique quasi mundi mater est ac minus etiam est quam mater. Pater autem est Mercurius ille antiquus quem esse volunt tum seminariam mundi rationem in ipsa animae mundanae natura, tum etiam rationem omnium idealem in mente divina. Et re vera idealis ipsa ratio pater est universi, seminalis autem ratio mater, quatenus commercium habet aliquod cum materia desuperque repletur. Materia vero matrix et locus est potius generationis atque susceptaculum. Tu vero memento in planeta Mercurio esse tum donum contemplationis a mente divina tum actionis a natura mundi, atque hinc ab eo dari ingenium vel contemplationibus vel actionibus et artibus aptum vel quandoque strenuum ad utrumque. Si Saturnum trino sextilive aspexerit vel eius domicilium occupaverit, favet contemplationi potissimum, si Martem aspexerit aspirat potius actioni, si Iovem utrique feliciter afflat officio, si Venerem intuetur suavitatem ingenii eloquiique simul ornatumque designat.

dimensionally through the entire space of the world, it is not divided into a plurality of matters, but remains unified and continuous both because it is not subject to passion and because it is not alive. It freely follows the potentiality of stretching out, and is stretched out by a unitary reason-principle to the unitary form of the universe.

This matter indeed is the mother of the world, so to speak, and is also less than a mother. The father of the world is that ancient Mercury who is understood to be both the seminal reason-principle of the world in the nature of the world-soul itself and also the ideal reason-principle of all things in the divine mind. And in truth, that ideal reason-principle itself is the father of the universe, whereas the seminal reason-principle is the mother to the extent that it has some traffic with matter and is filled from on high. Matter is rather the womb and place of generation and the receptacle. You should remember that in the planet Mercury there is both the gift from the divine mind of contemplation and that of action from the nature of the world, and also that there is given from that source a natural disposition that is suitable for contemplations or for actions and arts, being sometimes energetic toward both types of pursuit. If it has looked toward Saturn in trine or sextile aspect or occupied the latter's house, it favors contemplation the most. If it has looked toward to Mars, it aspires more toward action. If it has looked toward Jupiter, it is favorable and propitious to both endeavors. If it is looks upon Venus, it marks out sweetness of intelligence and eloquence and at the same time decorum. 13

[LIBER VII]

ARGUMENTUM IN LIBRUM PLOTINI DE AETERNITATE ET TEMPORE

Quid aeternitas et ubi sit; quid sempiternitas;
quid perpetuitas. Quomodo se habeat aeternitas ad tempus.

1 Aeternitatem Platonici primum ponunt in prima mente, deinde in mentibus aliis, tertio in corporibus quatenus in eis stabile aliquid reservatur. Similiter tempus primum in anima prima, deinde in ceteris animabus, tertio in corporibus quatenus in his reperitur et motus. Quaeritur quidnam in mente prima primoque ente sit aeternitas. Certe ibi sunt quinque entis genera vel elementa: scilicet essentia, motus, status, identitas, et diversitas. Sunt et rerum species quae nominantur ideae: humanitas atque similia. Genera quidem entis de se invicem minime praedicantur: ipse namque status neque motus est neque est mobilis. Identitas neque diversitas est neque diversa: haec enim opposita sunt. Essentia quoque ipsa in primo sui signo nullum habere videtur oppositorum. Ideae quin etiam de se invicem non praedicantur, nam idea leonis nec est idea hominis nec humana. Aeternitas autem ita de omnibus quae ibi sunt praedicantur ut quodlibet eorum sit aeternum. Aeternitas itaque neque aliquod genus entis est ibi nec idea quaedam: est enim cunctis commune donum. Cetera vero illic inter se distinguuntur vel secundum proprietates incommunicabiles, atque (ut ita dixerim) singulares sicut inter se ideae, vel oppositione quadam, ut

[BOOK VII]

ANALYSIS OF PLOTINUS' BOOK "ON ETERNITY AND TIME"

What eternity is and where it is; what everlastingness is; what perpetuity is; how eternity relates to time.

The Platonists situate eternity first in the primal mind, secondly in the other minds, and thirdly in bodies to the extent that something stable is retained in them. Similarly, they place time first in the primal soul, secondly in the other souls, and thirdly in bodies to the extent that motion also is found in them. But one might ask why eternity should be in the primal mind and the primal being. There are assuredly five Genera or elements of being there: namely, being, motion, rest, sameness, and otherness. There are also the Forms of things that are called "Ideas:" humanity and the like. The Genera of being are in no way predicated of one another, for rest itself is not motion and is not moved. Sameness is not otherness and is not other, since these terms are opposites. Also, being itself in its primal signification seems to embody no opposition. Indeed, the Ideas are not predicated reciprocally of one another. The Idea of a lion is not the Idea of a man and is not human. However, eternity is so predicated of all things that are there that any one of them becomes eternal. Therefore, eternity is not any Genus of being there, and is not some Idea, for it is the universal gift to all things. Other things there are distinguished among themselves either according to incommunicable properties, being individual in the way that Ideas are individual among themselves (if I may put it thus), or else according to a certain opposition, as motion is

motus et status, identitas et diversitas. Aeternitas sane etsi cunctis est commune donum adeo ut etiam ipsi motui et ipsi diversitati et multitudini illic existentibus competat—haec enim omnia sunt aeterna—, tamen secundum ipsum statum, ipsam identitatem, ipsam unitatem praecipue designatur a quibus illic et cetera possidentur.

2   Neque putandum est aeternitatem esse proprie ipsum statum. In formali enim ratione aeternitatis tria praecipue continentur: status scilicet et sempiternitas—quasi dicas ipsum semper—et identitas sive unitas sive (ut ita dixerim) indistantia. Ipse vero status non necessario haec in sua ratione comprehendit: non comprehendit ipsum semper. Possumus enim cogitare stare quidem aliquid sed non semper. Non complectitur necessario unitatem sive unum: potest enim in multitudine permanere. Item motus opponitur statui, non autem opponitur sempiternitati: quid enim prohibet quod movetur moveri semper? Atqui sempiternitas ipsa, etsi non sola sit tota aeternitatis ratio, est tamen in illius ratione potissimum. Cum itaque motus statui potissimum opponatur, non tamen adversetur sempiternitati quae est in aeternitate potissimum, nimirum non est idem penitus aeternitas atque status qui a ceteris illic quodammodo discretus est. Aeternitas vero cunctis est aeque communis: est enim aeternitas vigor quidam ipsius essentialis intellectualisque vitae, semper quidem ipse vigens, aeque simulque sua omnia possidens, nec amittens sui aliquid nec novum aliquando munus acquirens. Vigorem eiusmodi quaecunque ibi sunt aeque sibi vindicare videntur.

3   Interea meminisse debes sempiternitatem simpliciter esse quasi genus aliquod perseverantiam seu vitam significans principio fineque carentem. Sub qua duae sunt species, quarum prima est

opposed to rest, and sameness to otherness. But even if eternity is the universal gift to all things to such an extent that it pertains to the motion itself, otherness itself, and multiplicity that exist there — all these things being eternal —, eternity is nonetheless designated primarily according to rest itself, sameness itself, and the unity itself by which the other things there are possessed.

You should also not think that eternity is rest itself in the proper sense. Within the formal reason-principle of eternity three things primarily are embraced: namely, rest, everlastingness — as though one might say the "forever" itself — and sameness or unity or "nondiversity" (to coin a phrase). Rest itself does not necessarily contain these things within its reason-principle, since it does not embrace the "forever" itself: we are able to think of something as at rest yet not as *always* at rest. Moreover, rest does not necessarily embrace unity or the one, since it can persist in multiplicity. Again, motion is opposed to rest but is not opposed to everlastingness, for what prevents that which is moved from being moved forever? But everlastingness itself, even if it does not solely represent the entire reason-principle of eternity, is the most important component in that reason-principle. Given that motion is most opposed to rest but does not stand against everlastingness which is most powerful in eternity, then assuredly eternity is by no means the same as rest, the latter being somehow distinct from the other things there. Indeed, eternity is shared by all things alike, for it is a certain power of the essential and intellectual life, itself flourishing forever, possessing all its resources equally and simultaneously, neither losing anything of its own nor ever acquiring any new function.[1] All the things that are there seem to appropriate a power of this kind in equal measure.

In the meantime, you must recall that everlastingness *simpliciter* is as though a certain genus that signifies a persistence or life lacking beginning and end. Under this genus are two species, of which

aevum: scilicet aeternitas quae est vita vel perseverantia infinita permanens simul tota, secunda perpetuitas sive ipsum tempus: scilicet perseverantia infinita per partes successione progrediens. Unde ut ait Proculus utrumque mensura quaedam est: tempus temporalium atque mobilium, aeternitas aeternorum. Sed tempus crebra repetitione et quasi numerando metitur, aeternitas autem semel adhibita et coaptata mensurat. Propria aeternitatis ratio appellatioque non tam essentia vel intelligentia est quam vita. Est ergo vita, sed quanta? Infinita profecto, ut a parte qualibet temporis differat. Rursum qualis? Certe tota simul, ut a toto tempore differat. Est igitur aevum vita infinita tota simul et, ut brevius complectamur, vita iam infinita; tempus autem vita procedens per infinitum. Ipsum quidem aeternitatis esse praesens omnino fixum est velut centrum, ideoque sufficit unum. Cum enim numquam praetereat, non est opus aliquo succedente. Quod vero praesens in tempore dicitur, cum subito transeat, praesente alio indiget successore, ne tota temporis natura perdatur quae ex infinitis sibi invicem succedentibus momentis paulatim coacervatur. Ideoque si qua eius essentia est, ea ex esse miscetur atque non esse, dum praesens inter praeteritum futurumque quae non sunt intervenit et, utcumque potest, aemulatur ipsum aevi praesens per aliquod iugiter sui praesens, adhibens seipsum ad stabilem aevi praesentiam. Neque tamen stabilitur ideoque, quam non potest consequi permanendo, saltem succedendo consequitur, ut per plura momenta infinite procedens se pro viribus ad infinitatem aevi fixam simplicemque adaequet, dum unum permanens (ut ita dicam) aevi momentum

the first is the "always": that is, eternity[2] — infinite life or persistence enduring in totality and simultaneity —, while the second is perpetuity or time itself: that is, an infinite persistence proceeding through parts in succession.[3] For this reason, as Proclus says, each of these is a measure of some kind — time of temporal and mobile things and eternity of eternal things.[4] But time is measured by frequent repetition and as though by numbering, whereas eternity measures in being applied and fitted to something at once. When properly thought and named, eternity is not so much being or intelligence as it is life. It is therefore life. But what is its quantity? It is infinite, certainly, and therefore differing from any part of time. What is its quality? Assuredly, it is simultaneous totality, and therefore differing from the whole of time. Therefore, the always is infinite life in simultaneous totality[5] and — to express it more briefly — life that is already infinite, whereas time is life proceeding to infinity. The being itself of eternity is a present altogether fixed as though a center, and therefore holds the position of a unity. Since it has never been in the past, it has no need of something to succeed it.[6] However, that which is said to be present in time, when it suddenly passes away, needs something else to succeed it in the present, lest the whole nature of time, which is gradually accumulated through an infinity of moments succeeding one another, should be destroyed.[7] Therefore, if time has a being in some respect, the latter is blended from being and nonbeing, since the present intervenes between the past and the future which are nonbeings, and imitates as much as possible the present of the always through a certain presence-in-continuity of its own, applying itself to the stable presence of the always. Time is not stable, and therefore the presence that it is unable to achieve by enduring, it can at least reach by succession. It does the latter in order to make itself equal — as much as is within its power — to the fixed and simple infinity of the always, proceeding as it does infinitely through many moments, while the one enduring (if I may put it thus)

velut centrum innumerabilia momenta temporis velut puncta
quaedam in circumferentia perpetuo percurrentia e conspectu
pariter sibi praesentia contuetur atque complectitur: distant quidem inter se extra centrum lineae atque puncta in centro colliguntur in unum. Similiter et momenta temporis et temporalium
rerum progressiones inter se quidem distant sed in aeternitate
temporis temporaliumque principio ita rediguntur in unum ut una
sit praesentia omnium et vita eadem unusque conspectus.

4   Inter haec, ubi Plotinus de toto perfecto loquitur, memento
omne totumve quod in arte reperitur atque natura esse communem quandam formam post partes singulas ibi sequentem et ex
partibus resultantem. Non est igitur eiusmodi totum per se totum
sed per partes et per illud quod partes invicem congregavit: nec
igitur est primo totum. Primo itaque totum est quod est forma et
substantia quaedam simplex in se ipsa generans, si quas habitura
sit partes; et quia generat eas, ideo quodammodo praecedit eas et,
quo signo antecedit partes, est penitus individua. Iam vero, quoniam individua est ideo, dum partibus se inserit singulis, inserit
ubique se tota; atque hoc ipsum est absolute totum quod reservatur in quolibet sui totum. Talis utique divina mens est ad ideas,
talis universa natura vitalis ad semina rerum, talis aeternitas men-
tisque primae vita ad omnem sui praesentiam, manens semper in
uno atque ad unum. In uno quidem sui ipsius esse actuque praesenti, ad unum item quod super essentiam est bonum amando et
agendo se conferens. Manens inquam quoniam, quicquid expedit
habere, iam habet; manens item per infinitum — neque tamen ipsa

moment of the always, as though a center, surveys and encompasses the innumerable moments of time that are like certain points that move perpetually along the circumference and are equally present to its view, the lines and points being different from one another outside the center but collected into unity at the center. Similarly, the moments of time and the progressions of temporal things are indeed different among themselves, but are so reduced to unity in eternity, the principle of time and of temporal things, that there is one presence of all things, and a self-identical life, and a single view.

In the course of this discussion you should remember that, 4 when Plotinus speaks of the perfect whole, the "all" or the "whole" that can be found in art and nature represents a certain universal form following there upon the individual parts and resulting from those parts.[8] Therefore, a whole of this kind is not a whole through itself but through its parts and through the fact that it has brought together the parts among themselves. Therefore, it is not primarily a whole. That which is primarily a whole is a certain Form and substance that is simple and self-generating, even if it will acquire parts. Since it generates those parts, it is in some manner prior to those parts and, in the sense that it precedes those parts, is completely undivided. Moreover, since it is indivisible, when it inserts itself into individual parts, it inserts itself everywhere as a whole. And this is the absolute whole: that which is reserved as a whole in any aspect of itself.[9] Such is the relation of the divine mind to the Ideas, and such is the relation of the universal life-giving nature to the seeds of things, and such is the relation of the eternity and the life of the first mind to its self-presence as a whole, always remaining in one and toward one. This eternity remains "in" the one[10] of its own being and in the activity of presence, and also remains "toward" the one because above being is the Good that cleaves to itself in loving and acting. It "remains," indeed, because it already has whatever it is advantageous to have. It also remains

illic infinitudo est quantitas aliqua praeter vitam. Cum enim ipsa entis primi vita quae primus intimusque est actus illius quantitatem quamlibet antecedat, si qua ponatur in ea durationis et perseverantiae quantitas, nihil propterea intelligas additum individuae illius vitae praesentis simplicitati.

De conformatione intellectus ad aeternitatem; item quid non sit tempus: scilicet quod non sit duratio in corporali motu vel mensura similis aut numerus aut consecutio comesque corporei motus.

5 Ubi Plotinus post disputationem de aeternitate profundam descendit ad tempus, considerabis qua ratione probet mentis aeternitatem propterea quod aeterna tangat intelligendo, siquidem intelligere est quodammodo tangere. Cum enim sensus omnes tactu quodam rem percipiant sentiendam, multo magis supremae vires animae: ratio intelligentiaque cognoscendo tangunt, praesertim quia res penetrant earum intima discernendo, quod non efficit sensus. Atqui et obiecta earum efficacius veniunt ad tangendum — immo nec venire necesse est quae nusquam absunt. Cognatio igitur intellectus ad propria et aeterna eius obiecta maior est quam cognatio sensus ad sentienda. Cognatio inquam intelligentiae mutua: quatenus enim tangit, tangitur atque vicissim. Sicut igitur sensus est agitque in tempore, sic intellectus in aevo. Ratio vero

through infinity — not that the infinity there is some quantity in addition to the life.[11] Given that this life itself of the primal being, which is the primary and innermost activity of that being, precedes all manner of quantity; if any quantity of duration or continuity is posited with respect to it, you must understand that nothing is thereby added to the indivisible simplicity of that life of presence.

On the conforming of intellect to eternity; also, what time is not: namely, that it is not duration in corporeal motion, or a similar measure, or number, or the succession and accompaniment of corporeal motion.

When Plotinus after the profound discussion of eternity turns to time,[12] you will consider by what means he proves the eternity of the mind: namely, on the grounds that it touches eternal things by understanding, given that indeed understanding is touching in a certain sense. For since all the senses perceive the thing to be sensed with a kind of touch, it is much more likely that the highest powers of the soul: reason and intelligence, touch in the process of knowing, especially since they enter into things in grasping their innermost distinctions — something that sense does not do. In any case, the objects of reason and intelligence come to this touching in a more efficient way — or rather, it is not necessary for them to come since they are nowhere absent. Therefore, the connection between intellect and its proper and eternal objects is greater than that between sense and the things sensed. What is more, the connection on the part of intelligence is reciprocal to the extent that it involves touching and being touched in turn. Therefore, just as sense exists and acts in time, so does intellect in the always. Reason has a mediate status, so to speak, between these

tamquam media est in utroque, nam et aeterna tangit et temporalia. Medium quidem eiusmodi esse potest, nam et caelum est in utroque: per substantiam in aevo, per motum actionemque in tempore. Debet quin etiam universo eiusmodi medium non deesse, ut inter res supernas quae tam actione quam essentia sunt aeternae atque inferiores quae utrimque sunt temporales sint rationales animae per essentiam quidem in aevo per actionem vero motumque in tempore. Proinde notabis id admodum placere Platonicis animam rationalem eatenus seipsam accommodare foris tum his tum illis gradibus universi tum aeternis tum temporalibus tum etiam mediis, quatenus in eosdem intus seipsam expedit gradus sibi quodammodo naturaliter insitos, quemadmodum et corpus nostrum variis seipsum modis loco cuilibet aptat, prout variis seipsum figuris modisque componit.

6   Tempus est aut ipse motus aut aliquid proprium motionis: scilicet vel intimum motionis spatium vel mensura eius vel comes. Tempus non esse motum patet ex eo quod motus omnis peragitur tempore, quasi aliud quiddam sit tempus in quo motus agitur, aliud ipse motus. Praeterea, si corpus quod nunc movetur paulo post moveri desinat, deinde moveatur iterum, interceptus quidem erit motus, tempus vero non intermissum. Sicut enim cogitamus quamdiu motum fuerit, sic et quamdiu quieverit; atque eadem perpetuitate temporis tum vices motionum tum media quies agi mensurarique poterunt. Ac si desinat moveri corpus ab alio mobile, adhuc superfore tempus saltem in motore per se mobili possumus cogitare, quasi naturam temporis supra motum corporis quaerere debeamus. Item in motu velocissimo plurimum est de motu ipsiusque natura sed de tempore minimum; in motu

two, for it touches both the eternal and the temporal. It can have such a mediate status, because the heaven also mediates the pair of terms, being in the always through its substance and in time through its movement and action.[13] Indeed a mediator of such a kind must not be lacking in the universe, so that between the higher things that are eternal both in their action and in their being and the lower things that are temporal from these two viewpoints, rational souls exist through their being in the always and through their action and motion in time. Likewise, you will note that it is very much the opinion of the Platonists that the rational soul conforms itself to external things: now to these levels of the universe and now to these, now to eternal things and now to temporal things and now also to mediate things. It does this to the extent that it arranges itself internally into those same levels that are somehow naturally implanted within it, just as our body also adapts itself in various ways to a given location in accordance with the various shapes and rhythms in which it configures itself.

Time is either motion itself or some property of motion: that is, either its inner space, or its measure, or its accompaniment.[14] That time is not motion is apparent from the fact that all motion is carried through in time, as though the time in which the motion is executed is one thing and the motion itself another. Besides, if the body that now moves ceases to move shortly afterward and then moves again, the motion will be broken off whereas the time is not interrupted. For just as we think as long as there has been motion, so also do we think as long as there has been rest: indeed, both the phases of motion and those of intervening rest will be measurable by the same perpetuity of time. And if the body that is movable by something else ceases to move, we are able to think of time as continuing beyond that motion at least in the mover that is movable by itself, as though we ought to seek the nature of time above the motion of a body. Also, it is the maximum with respect to motion and its nature, but the minimum with respect to time,

tardissimo fit vicissim, quippe cum aliud sit tempus atque motus. Denique propria quidem temporis sunt brevitas atque longitudo, propria vero motus intensio atque remissio quae declarantur celeritate quadam et tarditate proventus. Quorum vero propria inter se differunt discrepant ipsa similiter. Probabilius est igitur tempus esse aliquid ad motum proprie pertinens quam ipsum proprie motum.

7   Dices forsan esse spatium non quidem loci quod est extra motum sed durationis atque perseverantiae quae est intima motui quasi proprium intervallum et ductus tractusque et progressio motus. Ad haec obiici duo possunt: primum quidem totidem esse eiusmodi intervalla motibus intima quot sunt et motus. — tempus autem unum esse debere mensuram quasi communem cuius usu quodam motus omnes quantumcumque inter se diversos metiri aliter aliterque possimus — ; secundum vero durationem eiusmodi non aliud videri quam motum: ipsam scilicet motionis continuitatem qua sublata non erit motus si factus subito fuerit. Et profecto haec est summa proprietas vel natura motus — sicut dimensio extensa per locum — aut est ipsum corpus aut corpori maxime propria. Atqui ipsa duratio motibus intima non est ubique sed in hoc motu servatur atque illo; tempus autem esse cogitamus ubique atque durationem et perseverantiam quamlibet motionis tempore metiri solemus. Unde videtur tempus esse intervallum aliquod mensurale et praeter intervallum proprium motionis, nec tamen ad locale pertinens intervallum. Proinde quaeremus de externo eiusmodi intervallo sive ductu, quidnam sit naturaliter in seipso ante hunc mensurationis effectum. Prius enim in se hoc ipsum quod

that resides in the fastest motion. The reverse situation obtains with the slowest motion, since time and motion are two different things. Finally, the properties of time are brevity and length, whereas those of motion are tightening and slackening, which are indicated by a certain quickness and slowness in which they arise. Things whose properties differ from one another are themselves different in a similar manner. Therefore, it is more likely that time is something that properly pertains to motion than that it is itself motion in the proper sense.

You will say perhaps that time is the space, not indeed of the location that is external to the motion, but of the duration and continuity that is internal to motion, this space being as though the proper interval, the connection and protraction, and the progression of the motion. Two objections can be made against this. First, there are as many intervals of this kind in motions as there are motions. But one time must be a sort of common measure, somehow using which we may measure in one way or another all motions, however much they differ from one another. Second, duration of this kind does not seem to be different from motion: that is, the continuity of motion whereby, when it has been removed, there will not be motion if the action of removal has occurred suddenly. And indeed the property or nature of motion in the fullest sense is that—just as in the case of the dimension extended in place—it is either body itself or a special property of body. In any case, the duration itself that is internal to motions is not everywhere but is kept in one motion or another, whereas we think that time is everywhere, and we are accustomed to measure any duration and constancy of motion with time. For this reason, it seems that time is a certain mensural interval and is in addition to the interval proper to the motion and is also not pertaining to the spatial interval. Therefore, we will inquire concerning this kind of external interval or connection as to what is naturally within it prior to this operation of measurement. For this measuring thing

est debet exsistere quam aliquid metiatur. Quaremus item numquid metiatur quietem et quo pacto: eatenus enim quiescit aliquid
quatenus movetur et aliud.

8   Tria quaedam proposita sunt de tempore ab his qui dicunt tempus esse aliquid motionis: primum quidem esse spatium durati-
onemque motus — de quo satis est dictum — ; secundum vero esse
mensuram quandam durationus eiusmodi; tertium esse aliquid
comitans sive consequens. Sed redeamus nunc ad mensuram ad
quam paulatim modo descendimus compulimusque respondere
quidnam sit in se antequam metiatur, et utrum externa mensura
sit vel intima, et — quaecunque sit — quomodo metiatur motum
similiter et quietem. Addimus insuper quomodo mensura numeralis esse dicatur quasi sit ex unitatibus congregata. Probabilius autem est tempus ob ipsam eius continuitatem simpliciter mensuram
quandam appellare quam numerum. Atqui si mensura quadam
est, ergo est quantitas quaedam, qualiscumque sit, sive quantum
quiddam motum dimetiens quatenus cum motu concurrit. Hic
ergo quaeretur: qua conditione cum motu concurrat et cur potius
metiatur motum quam mensuretur a motu Solemus enim tantum
tempus ex tanta motione metiri atque deprehendere tempus ex
actione non minus quam e converso. Summatim iterum dubitatur
an tempus sit motus ipse quadam magnitudine mensuratus an
potius magnitudo quaedam motum metiens an[1] tertium quiddam.
Quod magnitudine utatur ad motum dimetiendum et omnino de
hac ipsa magnitudine mensurali poterit dubitari: tanta enim est in
se sicut et motus est tantus. Numquid igitur sicut motus per eam

that exists must exist in itself before it measures something. We will inquire also as to whether it measures rest and how it measures it, for something is at rest to the extent that also something else is being moved.

There are three particular assumptions concerning time on the part of those who say that time is some aspect of motion. First, that it is a space and duration of motion [A] — on this point, enough has been said — ; second, that it is a certain measure of such duration [B]; and third, that it is something that accompanies or follows [C]. Let us now return to measure [B], a topic to which we turned a little just now and where we compelled its proponents to reply as to what the measuring thing is in itself before it measures, whether the measuring thing is an external or internal measure, and how — whatever the measuring thing is — it measures both motion and rest in similar fashion. We additionally ask how the measure may be said to be numerical, as though collected together from unities. On account of its very continuity itself, it is more credible to call time simply a certain measure rather than a number. But if it is a certain measure, it is therefore a certain quantity — in whatever form it comes about — or a certain *quantum* measuring motion to the extent that it is concurrent with the motion. Therefore the question here will be: on what condition is it concurrent with the motion, and why is it that it measures the motion rather than is measured by the motion? For we are accustomed to measure so much time by so much motion, and to grasp time on the basis of action not less than to grasp action on the basis of time. In sum, it is again a matter of doubt whether time is motion itself measured by a certain magnitude, or whether it is rather a certain magnitude measuring the motion or some third term. It will also be possible to have doubts as to whether one can use magnitude for measuring motion, and in general concerning the measuring magnitude itself, since it will be as great in itself as the motion is great. Therefore, just as the motion is

8

censetur tantus, ita et ipsa per superius aliquid existit tanta? Denique quidnam sit prius quam metiatur (ut diximus) investigare licebit. Similes quaedam dubitationes exoriuntur si tertia de motu opinio admittatur, dicens tempus esse aliquid quod comitatur motum. Cogimur autem ponere tempus ipsum esse aliquid, etiam si nullus animus electione utens metiatur tempore motum: generat enim anima mundi tempus naturali quodam suo intimoque motu, nulla ad hoc utens electione.

Aeternitas est in mente divina, tempus in anima mundi,
quo agitur mensuraturque
mundi motus.

9   In mente quidem divina non est tempus proprie sed idea quaedam temporis velut exemplar conceptum illic ad quandam aevi similitudinem imitantem quidem aevum sed interim diversitate degenerantem; tempus autem proprie est in anima mundi, in ipsa eius vegetali natura et imaginatione rursum quodammodo naturali assidue comitante naturam. In hac inquam gemina facultate animae actio ad generanda et imaginanda mundana ob debilitatem non simul tota peragitur, sed gradatim modo alia oritur modo alia ordinata quidem sed dissimilis, atque nunc ad haec vertitur nunc ad illa, secundum prius posteriusve procedens. Processio quidem deinceps secundum gradus eiusmodi motus est; continuitas et longitudo processionis est tempus. Iam vero, si qua ratione longitudo

judged to be so great through the magnitude, will not the magnitude itself exist as so great through something superior? Finally, it will be legitimate to investigate what the magnitude is before it measures (as we have said). Certain similar doubts arise if the third opinion regarding motion is entertained: that which states that time is something that accompanies motion [C]. We are forced to posit that time itself is something, even if no soul through its exercise of choice measures motion with time, for the world-soul generates time with a certain natural and inner motion of its own, exercising no choice to this end.

Eternity is in the divine mind; time is in the world soul, and is that by which the motion of the world is activated and measured.

In the divine mind there is not time in the proper sense but a 9 certain Idea of time in the manner of a paradigm that is conceived there according to a certain similitude of the always, imitating the always but having meanwhile a certain declension through difference.[15] However, time is in the world-soul in the proper sense, in its vegetal nature, and again in the imagination that is natural in a certain sense and closely accompanies nature. In this twofold power of the soul indeed, the action of generating and imagining earthly things is, on account of its weakness, not performed all at once, but in a stepwise manner. It now arises in one form or another, ordered indeed yet dissimilar. Now it turns to these things, and now to those, proceeding according to the before or the after. Indeed such a procession in sequence according to steps is motion; the continuity and the length of the procession is time. Moreover, if the length of a body differs from the body according to some

corporis ab ipso corpore differt, eadem differt et tempus a motu. Longitudo inquam motionis a motione, atqui et haec ipsa longitudo ita se ad aeternitatem habet, sicut linea se habet ad punctum, praesertim si fingere liceat ex quodam puncti motu procedere lineam punctumque produci. Putat vero Plotinus, sicut ex virtute cuiuslibet animae suo quandoque semini insita pullulat corpus proprium, sic ex naturali animae mundanae potentia intus afflante materiam corpus pullulare mundanum, idque in anima velut quodam mundi loco contineri regique, et moveri ad ipsum animae motum moverique temporaliter certisque temporum intervallis ad tempus ipsum motionis quae fit in anima et ad certa illius temporis intervalla, siquidem anima illa per intimum sui motum creavit in seipso tempus et una cum hoc motu simul et tempore produxit mundum in tempore mobilem. Unus vero est mundi locus anima mundi, unum et ubique tempus—siquidem et anima haec motum exercet ubique vitalem. Sed regitur interea motus quidem mundanus ab ipso animae suae motu: hic autem ab intellectu proprio et aeterno, ille tandem ab intellectu divino primaque ipsius aeternitate.

reason-principle, time also differs from motion in the same manner. The length of motion indeed differs from the motion, and moreover this length itself relates to eternity in the same way that the line relates to the point. This is especially so, if it is legitimate to imagine that a line proceeds from a certain motion of a point and that the point is protracted. Indeed, Plotinus thinks that, just as the individual body springs forth from the power of each and every soul that is implanted at some point in the seed, so does the world's body spring forth from the world-soul's natural power animating matter from within. The world's body is sustained and governed within the soul as though in a certain place of the world. Moreover, it is moved in relation to the movement of the soul, and is moved temporally and in definite intervals of time in relation to the very time of the motion occurring in the soul and to the definite intervals in the soul's time, given that soul creates time in itself through its inner motion, and simultaneously together with this motion and time has produced the world that is movable in time. The world's one place is the world-soul, and its one "everywhere" is time—given that this soul also performs its vital motion everywhere, However, the motion of the world is meanwhile governed by that very motion of its soul, this soul's motion by the intellect proper to it and eternal, and finally this intellect's motion by the divine intellect and its primal eternity.

[LIBER VIII]

ARGUMENTUM IN LIBRUM DE NATURA ET CONTEMPLATIONE ET UNO

Naturalia fiunt a vita quadam agente per rationes quasi contemplativas sibi infusas ab intellectu divino.

1 Philosophi quondam nonnulli simpliciter naturales putabant naturalia omnia a qualitate quadam elementali motuque generari ac talia provenire vel talia pro virtute qualitatis quae in agente vigeret et pro efficacia motus inde in materiam desinentis nec his praeesse rationem ullam modo intimae artis agentem. Plotinus autem corporales qualitates et motus duci vult ab incorporea forma non subiecta motibus sed praesidente quam vocat naturam universalem atque primam. Formam dico substantialem atque vitalem quae nec ulla sit corporum qualitas ut possit omnes pariter procreare nec solo impetu motus agat ut disponere possit omnia moderamine certo sed agat sua quadam ratione formali et naturali quadam arte, perinde ac si artificiosa ratio quae est accidens in artifice sit aliquid per se subsistens quamvis intra materiam atque ita suapte natura

[BOOK VIII]

ANALYSIS OF THE BOOK "ON NATURE, CONTEMPLATION AND THE ONE"

Natural things come to be from a certain life acting through reason-principles that are quasi-contemplative, these being infused into them from the divine intellect.

Some of the thinkers of the olden days who were simply philoso- 1
phers of nature thought that all natural things were generated
from a certain elemental quality and motion, and that one thing or
another came forth in accordance with the power of the quality
flourishing in the active principle and according to the efficacy of
the motion coming thence to cessation in matter. These philosophers did not think that there was any reason-principle having
agency in the manner of an inner art prior to that elemental quality and motion. However, Plotinus maintains that corporeal qualities and motions are derived from an incorporeal form, not subject
to motions but presiding over the latter, that he calls universal and
primary nature. I call a form substantial and vital that is not any
quality of bodies—in order that it might be able to produce all
qualities—and does not act solely by the force of motion—in order that it might distribute all things with unerring governance—,
but acts according to a certain formal reason-principle of its own
and a certain natural art. This substantial form acts in the following way: if a craftsmanlike reason-principle which is an accident in
the artificer is something self-subsistent, although it acts within
matter and thus in a craftsmanlike manner through its own nature, just as the artificer acts in a craftsmanlike manner through

agat artificiose ut artifex artificiose agit electione, immo sic naturali arte agat artificiose sicut ignis naturali calore naturaliter calefacit. Huic ergo vivae naturalique rationi parent qualitates et motus ut instrumenta, tametsi absque motu corporeo corporeum edit motum et sine qualitate ignis generat ignem, ac sine manifesto semine passim viventia genera, utpote quae essentiales in se habeat et vivas omnium rationes—quod satis in *Theologia* nostra probamus et ita in praesentia breviter confirmamus.

2   Super nutritionem et augmentum quae sunt generationes quaedam est ipsa simpliciter generatio quae et in his omnibus reservatur. Cum igitur hae generationes quaedam vitarum quarundam vel quorundam viventium opera sint, nimirum simpliciter et prima communisque generatio est opus simpliciter vitae vitaeque communis totum regentis mundum. Atque cum in mole mundi non sint certa ubique semina corporalium manifesta, profecto in[1] ipsa totius vita[2] sunt semina et propriae rationes seminum rerumque sensibus apparentium. Natura enim quae sine electione facit insita forma facit er certas ubique formas certis necessario formis: id est, rationibus seminalibus quibus sane tamquam principiis atque regulis motus omnes qui per se indeterminati sunt certo quodam tenore definiat et qualitates quae toto impetu agunt quicquid agunt et ⟨non⟩ cohibitae sunt naturaliter in angustum librata quadam moderatione ducat ad opus et id quidem multiforme uniformi tamen ordine. Nec aliter certum ubique finem spectet in his quae ipsa non vident finem quam ars soleat et consilium. Ars haec vivens atque naturalis omnes in se secundum actum naturales continet formas non aliter quam ars humana possideat artificia. Materia enim quae in potentia formabili semper est ad omnes non aliter

choice, by contrast, the substantial form that is the universal and primary nature acts in a craftsmanlike manner by natural art, just as fire naturally heats by natural heat. Qualities and motions obey this living and natural reason-principle as its instruments, even though it sends forth without corporeal motion the motion of bodies, generates fire without the quality of fire, and generates living things on all sides without apparent seed, being something that possesses the essential and vital reason-principles of all things in itself. We demonstrate this sufficiently in our *Theology*[1] and confirm it briefly in the following way here.

Above nutrition and growth, which are kinds of generation,   2 there is generation itself *simpliciter*, which is saved up also in all these things. Therefore, since these kinds of generation are the works of certain lives and certain living things, then assuredly the primal and universal generation *simpliciter* is the work of life *simpliciter*[2] and of the universal life that rules the entire world. And since in the bulk of the world definite seeds of corporeal things are not everywhere manifest, there are truly seeds in the life itself of the totality and proper reason-principles of seeds and things appearing to the senses. For nature, which makes without choice, makes by means of an innate form, everywhere making definite forms necessarily by using definite forms: that is, seminal reason-principles. By means of the latter which serve as principles and rules, it establishes a definite course for all motions that are in themselves indeterminate, and leads qualities that do whatever they do with total abandonment and are naturally unrestricted toward a narrowly defined work. With a certain balanced governance, accomplishes this multiform task with a uniform ordering. It always looks toward a definite end in those things that in themselves do not see that end, in a manner not unlike that in which art and planning are wont to do. This living and natural art contains in actuality all natural forms within itself, just as human art contains artificial forms. For the matter which is always in formable potentiality

ad actum perducitur omnium quam per vitam materiae quidem praesidentem sed cognatam in se omnes actu comprehendentem. Natura quidem haec artifex omnium neque materia quadam tali vel tali neque ipsa simpliciter materia ad suam indiget exsistentiam: ipsa enim materiam cottidie talem reddit atque talem materiamque expedito movet imperio. Iam vero nec qualitate hac vel illa materiae indiget ad suam simpliciter actionem. Potest enim qualitates absque qualitatibus generare quippe cum ipsa sit commune principium ad omnes pariter generandas. Ac si generat passim viva sine seminibus manifestis, magis potest qualitates elementales per semina sua tantum sine elementorum talium ministerio procreare. Quod si utitur materia qualitatibus certis affecta, non quidem necessitate eiusmodi qualitatibus utitur sed per accidens. Quod sane confirmatur ab illis qui in generatione resolutionem fieri usque ad primam materiam arbitrantur. Proinde memento naturam eiusmodi esse verum generationis ubique principium. Forma namque materialis, quia formarum est ultima, formale nihil proprie generat. Quid enim in aliquo genere postremum est nihil gignit in eo. Est ergo materialis forma non tam generationis principium quam affectio quaedam materiae inducta desuper ab occulto principio speciem generante.

3   Quod autem nihil generet confirmatur ex eo quia generatio ad vitam pertinet: haec autem vita caret. Vita vero carere constat ex eo quoniam oportet essentiam ulterius proficisci quam vitam, nec tamen usque ad materiam procedit essentiam, siquidem neque forma. In qualitate igitur essentia desinit et id quidem intrinsecus desinit, ergo vita in naturam similiter super materiae qualitatem. Natura quidem haec incorporea est. Quod enim corporeum est, si movet quicquam interea et movetur, movetur inquam etiam in

with respect to all forms is drawn toward the actuality of all forms not otherwise than through a certain life that presides over matter yet is related to it and embraces all forms in actuality. This nature-artificer of all things does not depend for its existence on this or that matter or even matter as such *simpliciter*, for it itself daily makes matter to be of one kind or another and moves matter with a ready command. Indeed, it depends on neither this nor that material quality for its own action *simpliciter*, being able to produce qualities without using qualities, since it itself is the universal principle with respect to the generation in like manner of all qualities. If it everywhere generates living things without manifest seeds, it is the more able to produce elemental qualities through its own seeds alone without the assistance of such elements. And if it employs a matter affected by definite qualities, it does not employ qualities of this kind in a necessary manner but only *per accidens* — indeed, this is confirmed by those who think that in generation a dissolution right down to primal matter occurs. Accordingly, you should remember that nature of this kind is everywhere the true principle of generation, since material form, being the last of forms, does not generate anything formal in the proper sense, for that which is the last in a certain genus does not generate anything within the latter. Therefore, material form is not so much the principle of generation as a certain affection of matter induced from above by the hidden principle that generates the form.

That the material form does not generate anything is confirmed 3 by the fact that generation pertains to life, whereas the material form lacks life. That the material form lacks life is proven from the following: Since it is necessary for being to proceed further than life,[3] and being does not proceed as far as matter, then neither does form. Being therefore ceases in quality, doing so internally. Life then ceases similarly in the nature that is above material quality. This nature is incorporeal. That which is corporeal, if it moves anything and is moved in the meantime, is also moved — and I

substantia. Primum vero movens est quod substantia permanet, ut
perpetuum continuare queat in motu tenorem. Si tamen est motor
intimus familiarisque velut forma quaedam, qualis est ipsa natura,
oportet dum movet, etiam quodam pacto moveri—per modum
quendam potius sui alium atque alium, non per essentiam aliquando declinantem. Denique sicut in quolibet animato non qualitas elementalis sed vitalis quaedam ratio principium est eorum
quae in corpore fiunt et super et contra qualitatum eiusmodi modum, sic in universo vivente: id est, mundo non elementalis qualitas aut motus tam pulchra tam diversa sed ratio quaedam viva
dispensat quam Plotinus ait in seipsa per essentiam permanere
quamvis in affectionem actu aliam vicissim ex affectione mutetur;
neque a materia dependere pariter et ab anima sicut et corporea
qualitas sed ab anima tantum velut perennem actum animae
vergentem erga materiam. Ideo qualitatem Plotinus corpoream
appellat accidens quoniam utrimque dependeat, vitam vero ab
anima communicatam corpori non accidens corporis neque rursum animae accidens sed essentialem actum animae quasi medium
inter verum accidens veramque substantiam. Quae usque ad intellectualem progreditur animam, siquidem virtutem aliquam habet
qua seipsam quodammodo sustineat et conservet et in seipsa pro-
ficiat—quo quidem munere omnes intellectuales essentiae per se
et ex se subsistere dici solent.

4   Sed ut ad naturam redeamus: id est, vitam ab anima dependentem, in hac sunt rationes omnes formarum naturalium produc-
trices ipsaque in ea ratio quaelibet non notio quaedam est ex

mean *moved*—in substance. The first mover is that which is stable in its substance, so that it may be able to maintain a perpetual course of motion.[4] However, if there is an internal and intimate mover in the manner of a certain form, as nature itself is, it is necessary that, when it moves, it is also in some way moved: this in a certain manner of an alteration of the thing itself in one way or another rather than through the falling away of being at some point. Finally, just as in any animated thing, it is not the elemental quality but a certain vital reason-principle that is the causal basis of those things that occur in the body, being itself both above and opposed to the measure of such qualities; similarly in the universal living thing: that is, the world, it is not the elemental quality or motion, as beautiful as it is diverse, that distributes living things but a certain living reason-principle. Plotinus says that this reason-principle is in itself stable in its substance, although it changes from one condition to another in a reciprocal process of actualization.[5] He further maintains that this reason-principle depends not on both matter and soul, as does a corporeal quality, but on soul alone, in the manner of a continual activity of soul inclining in the direction of matter.[6] Therefore, Plotinus calls corporeal quality an accident because it depends on both matter and soul, whereas he calls the life that is imparted to body by soul neither a bodily nor a psychic accident but an essential activity of soul, as though being a medium between a true accident and true substance. This life advances as far as the intellectual soul,[7] given that it has a certain power by means of which it may somehow sustain, preserve, and advance in itself. It is in terms of this same function that all intellectual beings are normally said to subsist through and from themselves.

But to return to nature: that is, the life depending on soul:— 4
All the reason-principles that are productive of natural forms are contained in it, and each and every reason-principle as such within nature is not some thought conceived at some point as a result of

argumento vel indagine quandoque concepta, sed essentialis proprietas atque actus essentiae non differens ab esse tali quodam atque tali. Est igitur in natura seminalis quaedam ratio eius quod
inde gignitur quae quamvis sit actus essentialis naturae ipsius, ip-
sumque suum esse tale, tamen translatione quadam nominatur
intuitus non acquisitus aliquando sed naturaliter illic affixus, non
quaerens aliquid sed ab initio possidens neque animadvertens in se
aliquid sed quasi stupidus qualis in attonitis esse solet ac forte talis
quidam sensus qualem nonnulli plantis attribuebant. Nam et haec
est communis universi planta per suum quendam quietum sub-
stantialemque sensum sua vita fruens naturaliaque concipiens atque hunc sine strepitu sensum: id est, sine distractione sui ad aliud
Orpheus naturae tribuit in hymno naturae. In natura quidem in-
tueri nihil aliud est quam esse tale et tale quiddam facere. Et quoniam quasi quodam intuitu et spectamine facit, ideo quod gignitur
in materia spectaculum dici potest, atque ita insuper spectamen
appellari naturae ut solemus in puero dicere: signum hoc huic
ingenitum est quaedam concupiscentia et imaginatio matris. Omnino vero neque in intellectu neque in natura est ulla cognitio vel
notio vel intuitus sic ab esse differens sicut differre solet intuitus
qui consideratio dicitur qualis est in illis qui rem ipsam spectant,
non possident naturaliter. Intellectus autem et natura quae a substantia[3] intellectuali dependet naturaliter possident, immo sunt,
illa ipsa quae intuentur et faciunt intuendo, quem quidem essentialem efficacemque intuitum appellat seminariam rationem.

5   Primam quidem rationem ponit in ipso simpliciter intellectu,
secundam in anima intellectuali quam primam nominat animam,

argument or investigation, but is rather an essential property and act of being not differing from being something of this or that kind. There is therefore in nature a certain seminal reason-principle of the thing that is generated from nature. And although it is an essential activity of nature itself and is the latter's determinate being, it is called an "intuition" by a certain metaphorical usage, this intuition being not acquired at some point but naturally fixed in nature. It does not seek something but possesses it from the start. It does not notice something in itself but is senseless, so to speak, as those who are astonished are wont to be senseless. Perhaps it is a sense of the kind that some writers attribute to plants, for it is the "plant" of the entire universe enjoying a life of its own and conceiving natural things by means of a certain quiescent and substantial sense that it has. Orpheus in his *Hymn to Nature* attributes to nature this noiseless sense: that is, this sense not distracted toward anything other than itself.[8] In nature, to "intuit" is nothing other than to be of such a kind and to do a certain thing of such a kind. And since it makes as though with a certain intuition and contemplation, that which is produced in matter can be described as a "contemplation." In addition, what is produced can be called a contemplation of nature, in the way that we are accustomed to say of a child that the mark engendered in it[9] is somehow the concupiscence and imagination of its mother. There is neither in intellect nor in nature any thought or concept or intuition whatsoever that differs from being in the way that that intuition is wont to differ from it that is called "consideration" and exists in things that observe the thing in itself but do not naturally possess it. The intellect that is prior and the nature dependent on the intellectual substance possess — indeed, *are* — those things that they intuit and make by intuiting. Plotinus calls this essential and efficacious intuition the "seminal reason-principle."

He places the first reason-principle in intellect *simpliciter*, the 5 second in the intellectual soul which he calls the first soul, the

tertiam in natura quam secundam animam nominat, quartam in materia: id est, materialem formam. Formae quidem rerum primae in ipso sunt intellectu, suntque ibi contemplationes vel contemplamina quaedam. Dicimus autem contemplamina vel spectamina notiones omnium sive conceptus ibidem resultantes interea, dum intellectus seipsum contemplatur et spectat. Secundae vero formae ab intellectu contemplante in animam intellectualem naturaliter exprimuntur: suntque hic etiam contemplamenta quaedam. Tertiae imprimuntur hinc in naturam quae, cum examussim ex contemplationibus exprimantur, sunt et ipsae contemplationes quaedam ne totiens dixerim contemplamina. Quartae tandem ex ipsis contemplativis naturae conceptibus concipiuntur in materia mundi. Et quoniam praedictas contemplationes sequuntur ordine quodam et imitantur ad unguem, contemplationes quaedam nominari possunt. Artificia sane ad visum spectantia dici solent intelligentiae quaedam ingeniaque artificis, multo magis soni musici, magis insuper cantus, — quoniam cogitationem expressiorem affectumque vivum secum ferunt — maxime verba sive prolata sive scripta. Formae igitur naturales in primis id habent ut et appellentur et sint intelligentiae quaedam conceptusque expressi ipsius intellectualis naturae sive naturalis intelligentiae.

6   Natura enim ipsa rerum artifex est potestas quaedam viva intellectualis animae figurans materiam non alienam ut ars sed suam, neque sicut ars extrinsecus sed intrinsecus, neque electione tali sed essentia[4] tali ac sine instrumento atque semper. Iam vero in hoc natura differt a geometria pulverem figurante quoniam haec et intus et sine instrumento[5] electioneque facit, perinde sicut geometria

third in nature which he calls the second soul, and the fourth in matter: that is, the material form.[10] The forms of things that are of the first rank are in Intellect itself, being there as certain contemplations or things contemplated: we call the notions or concepts of all things that spring up there in the very process where intellect contemplates and beholds itself things contemplated or things beheld. The forms of the second rank are impressed naturally on the intellectual soul by the contemplating intellect, these also being things contemplated of a certain kind. The forms of the third rank are impressed thence by the intellectual soul on nature. Since these are impressed precisely by contemplations, these are also contemplations of a certain kind — not to say "things contemplated" too often. Finally, the forms of the fourth rank are brought to conception in the matter of the world from the contemplative concepts themselves of nature: since these follow the aforesaid contemplations in a certain order and imitate the latter precisely, they can be called contemplations of a certain kind. Artifacts relating to vision are wont to be described as certain intellections and conceptions of the artificer. Musical sounds much more, songs even more, and — since these things carry with themselves a fuller conceptual expression and a vital condition — words most of all, whether pronounced or written, are so described. Therefore, natural forms primarily have as a characteristic that they are called and are "intelligences" of a certain kind and conceptual expressions of the intellectual nature or natural intelligence itself.

The nature that is itself the artificer of all things is a certain 6 living power of the intellectual soul, giving shapes to matter not as something other — in the manner of an art's operation — but as something of its own. However, it operates internally rather than externally as art does, by means of such and such a being rather than such and such a choice, without instrumentality, and always. Indeed, nature differs from the geometry that draws figures in the dust in that it operates internally and without instrumentality and

dum vehementer et affectu quodam figuras imaginatur, spiritum eius intimum imaginatione movet atque figurat. Fingit vero Plotinus quattuor haec: intellectum, animam intellectualem, naturam, materiam esse quasi vitra quattuor subinde disposita, ipsasque primi intellectus intelligentias inde velut a sole radios per animam, naturam, materiam pertransire, quasi continua quadam conformitate, ut quodammodo dici possint eidem radii eaedemque[6] intelligentiae in sequentibus et postremis qui et in praecedentibus esse sed deinceps gradatim a priori dignitate deficientes. Cum vero contemplatio intellectus primi atque deinceps contemplatio quaedam in anima et natura naturalium sit principium, nimirum et finis omnium est contemplatio quam et intellectualia perpetuo possident et in eiusmodi fine feliciter conquiescunt, quam et rationalia quaerunt ut in ea quandoque quiescant, quam et sensualia per actum continuum sentiendi pro viribus imitantur, quam et quae generant omnia tum in ordine motus tum in pulchra geniturae forma referre conantur. Denique divinae providentiae contemplatio ad exactissimam dirigit omnia pulchritudinem dum in tota dispositione rerum non minus, immo plus, ornamento quam necessitate consulitur. Ex quo quidem ornamento mirabili mentes excitat ad ipsam divinae mentis artem inveniendam et eiusdem pulchritudinem contemplandam.

choice, although it operates as geometry does when it imagines figures with a certain energetic affectivity, moving its inward spirit with imagination and shaping it. Plotinus envisions the following four terms: intellect, intellectual soul, nature, and matter, as four lenses placed in a row. The intelligences of the first intellect pass from there through soul, nature, and matter in a certain continuity of conformity as do the rays from the sun: this in order that one can somehow speak of the rays and of the intellections in the subsequent and last terms as being the same as they were in the previous terms albeit declining gradually and sequentially from their prior dignity.[11] Indeed, since the contemplation of the first intellect, being thereafter a certain contemplation in soul and nature, is the causal principle of natural things, then certainly contemplation is the end of all things. Intellectual things perpetually possess this and blessedly rest in an end of this kind; rational things seek it in order to come to rest in it at some time; sensible things through the continuous activity of sensation imitate it to the extent of their ability; and all generative things strive to reflect it both in the orderliness of motion and in the beautiful form of the nativity. Finally, the contemplation of divine providence steers all things toward the most exquisite beauty, when in the total disposition of things it has not less, but indeed more, concern for adornment than necessity. By means of this wonderful adornment, it excites minds toward the discovery of the very art of the divine mind, and toward the contemplation of its Beauty.

*De fine intellectualis naturae; et quod in cognitione vera idem
est cognoscens et cognitum; et de gradibus vitae et
intelligentiae; et quod intellectus primus est
omnia et perfecte totum.*

7 In capite libri quinto sextoque notabis vitae intellectualis finem
esse non simpliciter et quomodolibet habere bonum, sed bonum
habitum intelligere, nam et hoc ipsum ibi est habere: scilicet, intelligere. Haec enim est actio intellectualis naturae propria et praeci-
pua ratio possidendi. Item bonum nobis non sensibile quidem sed
intelligibile esse summum, quoniam hoc solum nobis est intimum,
maximeque quietum, idemque est tandem cum ipsa cognoscendi
potentia. Praeterea memento potentiam cognoscendi in ipso cognitionis actu unum quodammodo fieri cum obiecto. Et quo magis
fit unum, eo perfectiorem esse cognitionem atque vicissim, et ubi
perfectissima est, immo ubicumque vera, ibi unum idemque esse
re ipsa cognoscentem potentiam atque cognitum. Intellectus igitur
et intellectualis omnis essentia sicut est omnia semper actu, ita et
actu cuncta semper intelligit. Rationalis vero natura animae omnia
quidem est, sed non semper in actu omnia. Et quatenus actu se
confert in aliquam intra se latentium rationem, eatenus sit ipsa
ratio perque hanc intelligit quae in huius virtute comprehenduntur
et intelligendo fit illa. Summatim re vera cognoscere aliquid non
est aliud quam hoc ipsum esse vel fieri. Denique cum divinus artifex ipsa contemplatione sui faciat omnia et facta provocet ad seipsum pro viribus imitandum, nimirum omnia contemplativum vel

On the end of the intellectual nature; that in true knowledge, the knower and the thing known are the same; regarding the levels of life and intelligence; and that the first intellect is all things and is perfectly the whole.

In the fifth and sixth chapters of this book[12] you will note that the   7
end of the intellectual life is not to possess the Good *simpliciter* and in whatsoever manner but to understand the possession of the Good, for this itself—namely, understanding—is "having" there. This is the activity proper to the intellectual nature and also the primary reason-principle of possession. Moreover, that which is the Good *for us* is indeed not sensible but the highest intelligible, for this alone is most intimate to us and most at rest, being ultimately identical with the power of knowing itself. You should also remember that the power of knowing in the very activity of knowing becomes somehow one with its object. The more it becomes one, the more it is a more perfect knowing, and vice versa. Where it is most perfect or rather: everywhere true, there the knowing power and the thing known are, in reality, one and the same. Therefore, in the case of intellect—and the entire intellectual being—just as it is all things always in actuality, so it understands all things always in actuality. The rational nature of the soul is indeed all things, but not all things always in actuality. To the extent that it applies itself to some reason-principle of things concealed within it, to that extent it becomes the reason-principle itself, and understands through this the things that are comprehended in the latter's power, becoming those things in the process of understanding. In short, to know something is none other, in reality, than to be or become that thing. Finally, since the divine artificer makes all things through his very self-contemplation, and summons all things made toward imitation of himself to the extent of their

contemplabile aliquid appetunt atque moliuntur, sive intelligendo sive sentiendo seu etiam agendo atque generando.

8   Praeterea in capite septimo cognosces iterum omnem potentiam intellectualem esse idem cum re intellecta et in ea intelligere ab esse non discrepare quia in genere cognitionis est summa: potentiam vero rationalem fieri cum re cognita idem sed intuitum sensus exterioris atque naturae vergere ad[7] externum; item primam formam ob summam eius ad motum efficaciam esse primam vitam et ob efficaciam [esse][8] intimam suique ipsius compotem esse intelligentiam primam. Sicut ergo per omnes rerum gradus procedit forma a prima forma per essentiam facta, sic et vitam intelligentiamque procedere ut forma quaelibet dici queat vita et intelligentia quaedam.

9   Denique intellectum primum sicut uniformis est, propterea quod sit in eo genere primus, sic et omniformem fieri propterea quod contemplando seipsum propter fecunditatem intelligentiae sub variis sese formis concipiat: verumtamen in qualibet forma intra se concepta communem totius agnosci formam. Ideoque esse totum quiddam perfecta ratione totum, quia totum conservetur in singulis, idque habere quoniam sit unitissimum ex eo quod unitati divinae sit proximum a qua tamen degenerat. Quoniam in eo rationes[9] rerum formales discrepant inter se ratione formali perque gradus derivantur a superiori quodammodo ad inferius et a meliori similiter ad deterius, conclude in quolibet genere quod est primo totum esse perfecte, et ideo in qualibet sui parte totum, sic ens

capabilities, then certainly all things seek something that is contemplative or able to be contemplated, setting about it either by understanding, or by sensing, or by acting, or by generating.

Moreover, in chapter seven you will once again recognize that   8
every intellectual power is identical with the thing understood, and that understanding is not distinct from *being* in that thing.[13] For this is the highest point within the genus of knowledge: namely, that the rational power becomes identical with the thing known, although the intuition of the external sense and nature incline toward the exterior. You will also recognize that the primal Form, because of its highest power with respect to motion, is the first life, and because of its most inward and self-possessive power, the first intelligence. Therefore, just as the form that is made essentially by the first Form proceeds through all the ranks of things, so do life and intelligence proceed, with the result that each and every form can be described as a certain life and intelligence.

Finally, you should recognize that the first intellect, just as it is   9
uniform given that it is the first in that genus,[14] thus also becomes omniform given that, in the process of contemplating itself, it conceives itself thanks to the fertility of intelligence under a variety of Forms. Nevertheless, in each and every Form conceived internally the general Form of the totality can be recognized, and therefore a certain instance of totality is totality according to its perfect reason-principle, since the totality is preserved in the individuals: this happens because it is the most unified thing in being the closest thing to the divine unity relatively to which, however, it is deficient. Since the formal reason-principles of things within this totality differ among themselves according to a formal reason-principle, being distributed through a gradation of some kind from higher to lower, and similarly from better to worse, you should conclude that in each and every genus, that which *is* primarily is a totality in a perfect sense and accordingly a totality also in each and every part of itself.[15] Thus it is with being itself, life

ipsum, sic ipsa vita, sic intellectus. Quod vero sic est totum, non ita componitur ex suis velut quod[10] ex partibus essentiam mutuatur sed ipsa sui essentia esse dat partibus. Atqui eiusmodi totum quod se propagat in sua quodve in singulis conservatur totum dicitur infinitum. Nam infinite quicquid in eo acceperis, consequuntur et reliqua.

Intellectus etiam primus est necessario multiplex et est omnia;
igitur ante ipsum est principium omnium
quod non est omnia sed super omnia.

10   Haec in octavo capitulo consideranda videntur. Ratio namque intellectus haec ipsa est quod moveatur et illuminetur atque formetur: intelligibilis autem ipsius proprietates oppositae sunt. Item in ipsa intellectus ratione non necessario includitur ut sit ipsum intelligibile: nulla enim necessitas prohibet esse aliquem intellectum, etiam si intelligatur a nullo. Vicissim nec ad rationem intelligibilis necessario pertinet quod intellectus exsistat. Intellectualis namque potentia in ambitu obiecti sui comprehendit materialia simul et spiritualia, atque inter haec continet quae intelligunt et quae non intelligunt. Intellectus igitur atque intelligibile distinguuntur inter se quadam ratione formali. Eiusmodi vero distinctio distinctioni quae secundum rem appellatur proxima est — haec ipsa vero secundum rem distinctio postrema est. Illa itaque forma prima in qua intellectus cum intelligibili copulatur non est unitas simplicissima. Non est igitur primum universi principium quod simpliciter

itself, and intellect. In being such a primal totality, it is not put together from its own constituents — as is something deriving its essential nature from its parts — but rather gives subsistence to those parts through its own being. In any case, a totality of this kind which propagates itself into its constituents or preserves itself as a totality in each individual term is called infinite — for whatever you understand to be in the primary totality infinitely is attained also by the subsequent terms.

Even the first intellect is necessarily multiple, and is all things; therefore the causal principle of all things is prior to it, this principle being not all things but above all things.

These are the issues seemingly to be examined in the eighth chapter.[16] The reason-principle of intellect resides in its being moved and illuminated and formed as such, although of the intelligible itself there are opposite properties. It is not necessarily included within the reason-principle of intellect that it should itself be an intelligible, for nothing prohibits something from being an intellect even if it is not understood by anything. Conversely, it does not pertain to the reason-principle of the intelligible that an intellect must exist. The intellectual power comprehends, within the range of its objectivity, material and spiritual things simultaneously, containing among its objects both the things that understand and those that do not understand. Therefore, intellect and the intelligible are distinguished from one another according to a certain formal reason-principle, and this distinction is very close to the distinction that is called *secundum rem*. This *secundum rem* distinction itself is last in the series of distinctions. Therefore, that primal Form in which intellect and intelligible are joined is not the

unum est atque simplicissimum quemadmodum quicquid est in aliquo genere primum in eodem est necessario simplex.

11 Esse vero intellectum quadam necessitate multiplicem ideoque non primum sic etiam confirmatur: si intellectus est summa cognitio, habet secum intelligibile coniugatum: scilicet re ipsa idem quamvis non ratione idem. Item ipsum quod primo et secundum se intelligibile est, hoc habet et consequenter ut sic etiam intellectus: tale enim intelligibile est forma separata subsistens, ideoque et in se reflexa reportat intelligentiam. Res vero materialis si appellatur intelligibile, talis evadit quatenus transformatur in aliud vel per aliud intelligitur consequenter. Cum igitur intellectus atque intelligibile se invicem comitentur — adeo ut quod est alterutrum sit et alterum — atque haec different ratione formali, necessario intellectus primus est multiplex neque summum universi principium.

12 Dubitatur deinceps hunc in modum: principium ipsum quatenus est extra genus intelligentiae videtur esse sibimet ignotum et, quatenus super intelligibile genus exstat, cognosci nullo modo potest. Respondetur ad haec: ipsum praestantiore quadam ratione quam cognoscendo seipso frui atque animam eo frui excellentiore forsan cognitione quam intellectuali vel potius eminentiore quodam pacto quam cognoscendo. Non enim intellectus simpliciterque cognitio in nobis est summum sed unitas boniformis per quam prima fruimur unitate simul et bonitate, sicut et per luminosum sensum sensibili fruimur luminoso. Sicut ergo qui studet

simplest unity. It is therefore not the first principle of the universe which is one *simpliciter* and most simple in the way that whatever is first in a certain genus is necessarily simple in that genus.

That intellect is multiple, according to a certain necessity, and is 11 therefore not primal may also be confirmed as follows: If intellect is the highest knowledge, it has an intelligible conjoined with itself: that is, an intelligible identical with itself in reality if not identical according to the reason-principle.[17] Moreover, that which is an intelligible primarily and an intelligible in itself consequently has the characteristic of being also an intellect, for such an intelligible is a separately subsistent Form, and therefore acquires intelligence in turning back to itself: if a material thing is called intelligible, it is so to the extent that it is transformed into something else or is consequently understood through something else. Therefore, when intellect and the intelligible accompany one another— to such an extent that whatever is one of the two becomes the other of the two—and the intellect and the intelligible differ according to a formal reason-principle, the first intellect is necessarily multiple and is not the first causal principle of the universe.

A doubt is next raised as follows: the first causal principle itself, 12 to the extent that it is outside the genus of intelligence, might seem to be unknown to itself and, to the extent that it is above the genus of the intelligible, in no way able to be known. The reply to this is as follows:—This causal principle has enjoyment of itself in a certain relatedness (*ratio*) that is superior to knowing, and the soul enjoys the causal principle in a knowing perhaps more excellent than that of the intellectual kind, or rather a certain knowing that is somehow superior to knowing. For it is not intellect and knowing *simpliciter* that constitute the highest thing in us but the unity in the form of goodness through which we enjoy the first unity and first goodness simultaneously, just as we enjoy sensible luminosity through the luminous sense. Therefore, just as the one

vehementer imaginari a motu cessat[11] et sensu, et qui penitus intelligere imaginationem sedat, ita qui optat attingere quod super naturam intellectualem intelligibilemque exsistit omne prorsus intelligibile pertransire debet, et intellectum proprium posthabere, silentiumque intelligentiae prorsus imponere, redactus videlicet in aliquid sui primum per quod fruatur universi primo.

13   Conclude aliud atque aliud aliter atque aliter se ipso frui: corpus quidem animalis frui seipso per sensum, rationem vero non per sensum sed per melius aliquid semetipsa frui, intellectum quoque non per aliquem rationis discursum sed per aliquid eminentius sui ipsius fieri compotem, similiter unum ipsum atque bonum per aliquid intelligentia cognitioneque sublimius se ipso frui. Proinde si ab imperfectis ad perfecta gradatim est ascendendum, certe super imaginationem quae per aliqua rerum genera tantum et longo insuper tempore discurrere solet ponenda est ratio per omnia discurrens ac tempore ad hoc indigens breviore et, ubi est perfectissima, quam brevissimo. Super hanc intellectus omnia semper sine tempore consecutus qui, si perfecte habet in se videtque omnia, non habet illa confusa sed distincta sinceraque, non intuetur obscura sed clara discernit atque distincta.

14   Super hunc igitur hac necessitate multiplicem primum est universi principium quod neque est dumtaxat unum aliquid omnium. Alioquin non haberet ad omnia potestatem nec omnium principium esse posset. Neque etiam est ita omnia tantum ut non sit

who is keen to imagine more forcefully withdraws from motion and sensation, and the one who desires to understand thoroughly puts his imagination to rest; similarly the one who wishes to attain that which exists above the intellectual and intelligible nature must completely pass over the whole of the intelligible and put his own intellect after himself, absolutely imposing silence on his intelligence, namely by leading himself back to something primal in himself through which he can enjoy that which is first in the universe.

You should conclude that one can enjoy oneself as one thing and another and in one way and another. The body of an animate being enjoys itself through sense; reason enjoys itself not through sense but through something superior to itself; intellect also enjoys itself not through some discursiveness of reason but through something more elevated having control of its own coming to be. Similarly, the One itself and the Good enjoys itself through something more lofty than intelligence or cognition. Accordingly, if one ascends step by step from the imperfect to the perfect, then certainly above the imagination, which is accustomed to run discursively through certain kinds of things only and also in a lengthy span of time, one must place the reason that runs discursively through all things needing for the same purpose a shorter span of time and, where the reason is most perfect, the shortest span. Above this is the intellect, which achieves everything always and without time and, if it is in a perfect state and sees everything in itself, does not have these things as confused but as distinct and pure, and does not look at obscure things but discerns the clear and distinct. 13

Therefore, above this intellect, which is according to this necessity multiple, is the first causal principle of the universe.[18] This is not [I] something that is *merely a one among all things* — otherwise, it would not have power with respect to all things and could not be the causal principle of all. Again, it is not [II] *all things* only in 14

unum atque simplex. Hoc enim primum est; ubique vero prius est unitas multitudine et composito simplex. Neque rursum est et unum pariter atque omnia. Si enim hoc ab aliquo concedatur, ita distinguimus: aut est cuncta summatim, aut potius singulatim. Si summatim: id est, quod ibi sit una quaedam forma cum multitudine, aut haec una forma est ante multitudinem—atque ita haec ipsa dumtaxat principium est, neque opus est, ad[12] hoc ut sit principium ei multitudinem adhibere—aut una haec forma est cum multitudine simul—atque ita non est principium omnium quandoquidem ante omnia non exsistit—aut forma haec una post omnia ponitur quo nihil dictu videtur absurdius. Sin autem accipiatur alterum illud distinctionis membrum: scilicet quod principium illud omnium sit ita omnia, ut de unoquoque oculis demonstrato discurrendo per singula sit verum dicere, hoc est principium, sequetur ut quodlibet sit[13] principium. Cum vero[14] principium sit necessario unicum, unica res erit in universo vel vicissimim principia totidem quot res esse ponuntur.

Ipsum bonum est super essentiam, vitam, intellectum;
neque intellect potest attingi.

15   Cum in gradibus viventium videamus, consumatissimum vitae gradum esse tandem vitam intellectualem coniicere possumus, primam in toto rerum ordine simpliciter vitam esse ipsum simpliciter intellectum. Sive igitur ut vitam consideras, est motio quaedam ad

such a way that it is *not one and simple*—for this causal principle is the first; indeed, unity is everywhere prior with respect to multiplicity, and the simple prior with respect to the composite. Again, it is not [III] something that is *one and equally all*. If this were conceded by somebody, we make the following distinctions: The first is all things either [1] together, or else [2] singularly. If it is [1] all things together: that is, because there is a certain unitary form together with the multiplicity, then this one form is either [A] *prior to* the multiplicity—this form is thus the first causal principle alone, and there is no need to add a multiplicity to it in order for it to be this causal principle—; or else this one form is [B] *simultaneous with* the multiplicity—and thus it is not the causal principle of all things, since it does not exist before all things; or else this one form is [C] placed as *subsequent to* all things—and nothing seems to be more absurd than this. But if one accepts the other branch of this distinction: namely, that this causal principle of all things is all things in such a way that [2] by running discursively through individual things it is true to say of each and every thing pointed out to the eyes that "this is the causal principle," it will follow that each and every thing is the causal principle. And since the causal principle is necessarily one, there will [i] only be one thing in the universe, or else [ii] as many causal principles as things will be posited.

> *The Good itself is beyond being, life, intellect;*
> *and it cannot be attained through intellect.*

When we reflect upon the gradation of living things, we are able to   15
surmise that the most perfect grade of life is ultimately intellectual life, and that the first life in the entire order of things *simpliciter* is intellect itself *simpliciter*. If you consider this as life, it is a certain

terminum, ideoque ad aliud ut ad[15] bonum, sive ut intellectum accipis, est motus aliquis ad verum ut ad bonum. Utroque igitur pacto est dependens aliquid, neque contentum est[16] essentia sua cuius vita et intellectus exsistit, sed quaerit aliquid essentia melius: id est, ipsum bonum quod neque vita secundum formam neque intellectu indiget quo annitatur ad bonum, quandoquidem est ipsum bonum cui nec ulla opus est actione, siquidem omnis actio est ad bonum circa quod versatur. Quod quidem cum super intellectum et intelligibile prorsus exsistat, nomina vero ex intellectus conceptione imponi soleant, nullum proprium habet nomen. Appellatur autem bonum quoniam inde omnia efficiuntur et facta perficiuntur. Appellatur et unum quoniam interea supereminet omnibus neque movetur dum haec inde procedunt—alioquin nihil alicubi permaneret—neque dividitur in partes—alioquin cessaret unum ipsum quo sublato mox omnia perderentur—neque omnino multiplicatur in formis—alioquin admixtionem vel adiunctionem patiens, non esset amplius vera unitas et immensa simplicitas.

16   Si per arbores, per animalia, per animam, per mentem processeris, invenies quod in unoquoque horum simplicissimum est maximeque unum, esse omnium potentissimumm reliquorumque principium. Similiter universum ad unitatem rediges potentissimam de qua nihil ulterius praedicabis cum primum concepisti unitatem ipsam vel bonitatem—alioquin si quid praeterea praedicaveris, compones et minues componendo reddesque indigum et posterius. Noli ergo huic intellectionem addere. Alia enim est ratio intelligentiae, alia boni: non enim aeque utrumque convenit. Intelligentia igitur adiuncta bono congeriem conficit. Neque igitur illic

motion toward a limit, and therefore toward something else as its good; if you consider it as intellect, it is a certain motion toward the true as its good. Therefore, by either reckoning, it is something dependent, not satisfied with its own being consisting of life and intellect, and seeking something better than its being: that is, the Good itself. The latter has need neither of life according to form nor of intellect by means of which it might strive toward a good, given that it is the Good itself, having no need of action, since all action is toward a good around which it turns. Since this Good exists absolutely above intellect and the intelligible, and one is accustomed to apply names to it from our conception of intellect, it has no proper name. However, it is called "the Good" because all things are made by it and, having been made, perfected by it; it is called "the One" because it in the meantime transcends all things.[19] It is not moved, while all these things proceed from it: otherwise, nothing would anywhere be stable. It is not divided into parts: otherwise, it would cease to be the One itself and, with the latter removed, everything would be destroyed forthwith. It is absolutely not multiplied into forms: otherwise, being passive with respect to blending and addition, it would no longer be true unity and immeasurable simplicity.

If you advance your investigation through trees, animate beings, 16 soul, and mind, you will find that in each of these there is something that is the simplest and most unitary, and that this is the most powerful of all things and the causal principle of the other things. Similarly, you will lead back the universe to a most powerful unity of which you will predicate nothing further, as soon as you have conceived unity itself and goodness: otherwise, if you predicate anything else besides, you will compound it, diminish it by compounding, and render it deficient and secondary. Therefore, do not apply anything intellective to it. The reason-principle of intelligence is one thing and that of goodness something else, for these two terms are not equally applicable. Therefore intelligence

adhibebis ideas quas concipiuntur intelligentia differuntque inter se absolute ratione formali, praesertim contrariarum rerum oppositarumque ideae—quod patet ex ordine universi inde secundum essentiam formamque geniti. Quae enim in hoc opificio re ipsa differunt et subiecto, haec in opifice omnium intellectu absolute formalique differunt ratione—alioquin hic ordo formarum vel inordinato quodam casu consisteret vel ex materia prorsus informi procederet. Distinctiones vero formales at absolutas adhibere primo Platonici vetant, prohibent etiam post unitatem vel bonitatem adhibere vitam aut essentiam quorum nixus non quiescit in se sed contendit ad bonum. Iubent primum illud super essentiam atque esse ponere, sicut materiam quae ex opposito ultimum est sub essentia et esse iudicant collocandam. Ideoque sicut in attingenda materia descendendum est sub omnibus intelligentiae conceptionibus qui formales sunt, sic ad attingendum illud super omnes eiusmodi conceptus est ascendendum. Neque mobili vel multiplici vel formali intelligentiae actu attingi posse putandum quod super motum multitudinemque et formam mirabiliter exstat.

joined to goodness produces an accumulation. Therefore, you will not bring in at this point the Ideas, which are conceived by intelligence and differ among themselves absolutely according to a formal reason-principle.[20] You will especially not bring in the Ideas of contrary things and opposites: the order of the universe that is generated from that source according to being and form makes this point clear. For the things that differ in reality and according to subject in this work of creation differ in the intellect that creates all things absolutely and according to a formal reason-principle. Otherwise, this order of forms would either be constituted by a disorderly randomness of some kind or proceed from a completely formless matter. The Platonists forbid the application of formal and absolute distinctions to the First and also disallow—after unity and goodness—the application of life and being, for our travail[21] with respect to these does not repose in itself but strives toward the Good. They decree that this First should be placed above essence and being, just as they judge that matter—the last term and in opposition to the First—should be located below essence and being. Therefore, just as in touching upon matter, one should descend below all concepts of the intelligence that are formal, so in touching upon This, one should ascend above all concepts of such a kind. One should not think that one can, with any mobile or multiple or formal activity of intelligence, touch upon That[22] which stands above motion, multiplicity, and form in a wondrous[23] manner.

Ipsum bonum est pater cuius filius est intellectus semper a
patre plenus. Huius autem intellectus est imago mundus.

17 Quemadmodum aliud est visus, aliud vero lumen ad quod capiendum est oculus institutus—etiam si quis oculus fingatur ab aeterno lumine plenus—, sic aliud est intellectus, aliud vero verum
ipsum atque bonum ad quod naturaliter intellectus annititur,
differtque ab illo etiam intellectus ipse qui propter propinquitatem
boni semper bono plenissime fruitur. Ipsi itaque bono sicut et lumini nihil opus est visu. Iam vero si quis posset totius mundi visibilis ornatum totum uno simul intuitu contueri,[17] supra modum
admiraretur ac, velut ex imagine quadam, facilius mundum intelligibilem opficem huius suspicaretur sed admodum pulchriorem.
Rursum si quis conspiciat illum in quo nihil informe nihil deforme
nihil immoderatum vel vitae vel intellectus expers in quo totus
splendor et splendore purissimo totus ordo naturae, facilius coni-
ectaret quis pater eius et qua ratione tantum talemque genuerit
filium intellectum quidem purum et omnium plenitudinem pater
penes se generans ab aeterno, intellectu plenitudineque superior.

The Good itself is a father whose son is intellect, always filled by his father; the world is the image of this intellect.

Just as sight is one thing and light something else for the capturing 17 of which the eye has been constituted—even if some eye filled with eternal light could be imagined—, so is intellect one thing and the True itself and the Good something else toward which intellect naturally strives.[24] Intellect itself also differs from the Good in that it always, thanks to its proximity to the Good, enjoys it to the fullest. The Good itself, just like light, has no need of vision. Moreover, if anyone could contemplate the entire ordering of the entire visible world in a single simultaneous intuition, he would stand in amazement of it to an immeasurable degree, and would more easily—as though by means of an image—get an inkling of the intelligible world that is the creator of this world, albeit much more beautiful than the latter. Again, if anyone could perceive that world in which there is nothing unformed, nothing deformed, nothing unmeasured and devoid of life or intellect, and in which there is total splendor and, in the purest splendor, the entire order of nature, he would more readily surmise who its father is, and by what relationality (*ratio*) he has begotten a son of such greatness and of such a kind as this pure intellect and plenitude of all things, the father begetting eternally in himself and being superior to intellect and plenitude.[25]

[LIBER IX]

ARGUMENTUM IN LIBRUM DE OCTO CONSIDERATIONIBUS

Propositio prima: quod mundi auctor sit intellectus primus ipsius boni filius.

1 Novem praecipue in hoc libro considerationes apparent. Prima est de auctore mundi ubi, si quis viam Iamblichi Proculique sequatur, exponet Timaei dictum illud de opifice mundi—scilicet, quot[1] ideas intellectus intelligit in ipso vivente, totidem species cogitavit mundi opifex in mundo disponere—exponet id inquam ita: tres scilicet saltem esse divinas substantias inter principium primum: id est, ipsum bonum atque mundum, quarum prima secundum formam suam essentia sit boni particeps ac insuper vitae intellectusque causa; secunda vero secundum formam sit vita particeps quidem essentiae, intellectus autem formalis causa; tertia denique per formam sit intellectus vitae quidem particeps et causa mundi. Primum nominabit Caelium. secundum vero Saturnum, tertium denique Iovem, tantoque superiorem Saturno Caelium et Iove Saturnum existimabit, quanto superior priorque essentia est quam vita et vita quam intellectus—esse vero essentiam superiorem vita quatenus amplius se diffundit et vitam propter similem amplitudinem esse mente superiorem. Dicet itaque intellectum formalem Iovemque esse proximum mundi fabrum intellectuales ideas mundanarum rerum in se habentem, quas quidem ideas

[BOOK IX]

ANALYSIS OF THE BOOK "ON EIGHT CONSIDERATIONS"[1]

First proposition: that the founder of the world is the first intellect, the son of the Good itself.

Nine considerations appear primarily in this book. The first concerns the founder of the world. Here, if anybody follows the way of Iamblichus[2] and Proclus,[3] he will expound that well-known statement of the *Timaeus* regarding the artificer of the world[4] — namely, that intellect understands as many Ideas in the living creature as the artificer of the world thought to arrange in the world — doing so as follows:[5] — There are at least three divine substances between the first principle: that is, the Good itself, and the world. The first of these according to its form is being which participates in the Good and is also the cause of life and intellect. The second according to its form is life which participates in being, but is the formal cause of intellect. Lastly, the third through its form is intellect which participates in life and is the cause of the world. This expositor will name the first substance Caelius, the second Saturn, and lastly the third Jupiter. He will hold that Caelius is as much superior to Saturn and Saturn to Jupiter as being is prior to life and life to intellect. Being is superior to life to the extent that it diffuses itself further, and life is superior to mind on account of a similar greatness of diffusion. He will therefore say that the *formal* intellect and Jupiter is the proximate maker of the world, that he has in himself the intellectual Ideas of worldly things, that he has received these Ideas from the *vital* intellect: that is, from

acceperit ab intellectu vitali: scilicet, a Saturno in quo ideae sint intellectuales et intelligibiles aeque, quas Saturnus habeat ab intellectu essentiali:[2] scilicet, ab ipso Caelio in quo intelligibiles dumtaxat sint ideae. Sic igitur Timaeum interpretabitur: providentia Iovis excogitavit tot in mundo species fabricare quot animadvertit Saturnum intellectum ideas contemplari in ipso vivente: idest, in Caelio qui essentia sit causa vitae.

2   Apud Plotinum vero non tres substantiae sed una tantum substantia est illa quae nominatur essentia vitaque prima et intellectus primus. Vita enim prima nihil aliud est quam intimus perpetuusque vigor et actus essentiae formaeque primae efficacissimae omnium ad agendum. Primus quoque intellectus est reflexio quaedam in seipsam vitae primae potissimum se cum[3] ipsa constantis: illam ergo substantiam Plotinus appellat intelligibile primum quatenus viva est atque fecunda potestque in se ipsa concipere intellectum conceptumque movere penitusque formare; appellat item hanc substantiam intellectum quantum spectat ad vitalem eius actionem a se exortam in se reflexam; appellat rursum cogitativum aliquid quodammodo quoniam statuit quae vidit intus distribuere foras. Proinde putat in ordine rerum exoriri motum ante divisionem ideoque intellectum prorsus immobilem, motu inquam fluente, non posse in plures intellectus imparticipabiles propagari, genus autem animae suapte natura mobilis in animas plures multiplicari. Et quoniam genus hoc est intelligentiae particeps, ideo in hoc intellectum in plures intellectus participabiles propagari quatenus genus animae in plures animae species propagatur. Existimat quoque intellectum mundi opificem animam generare tum ipsam mundi animam tum reliquas communes sphaerarum stellarumque animas tum denique particulares animas: daemonum videlicet

Saturn in whom there are Ideas that are equally intellectual and intelligible, and that Saturn has these Ideas from the *essential* intellect: that is, from Caelius, in whom there are only intelligible Ideas. He will therefore interpret the *Timaeus* as saying that the providence of Jupiter thought to make as many species in the world as he perceived the intellect of Saturn to contemplate in the living creature itself: that is, in Caelius who is the being that is the cause of life.

In Plotinus however, there are not three substances but only 2 that one substance which is called first being, first life, and first intellect. For the first life is nothing other than the most inward and perpetual power, and also the activity of the first being and form that is most powerful of all things in its agency. Also, the first intellect is a certain turning back to itself of the first life that consolidates itself primarily in that turning back. Therefore, Plotinus calls this substance the first intelligible, to the extent that it is living and fertile, and able to conceive a thought in itself, move the thing conceived, and form it completely. He similarly calls this substance intellect, in so far as it looks toward its vital action that has arisen in itself as it is turned back to itself. Again, he calls it something capable of thinking[6] in some manner, since it has determined to distribute to the outside what it has seen within. Accordingly, Plotinus thinks that motion arises before division in the order of things, and therefore that a completely immovable intellect — motion being emanative — is not able to be propagated into a plurality of unparticipated intellects,[7] but that the genus of soul that is movable in its own nature is multiplied into many souls. Since this genus is a participant in intelligence, Intellect is propagated into many participated intellects[8] to this extent: namely, that the genus of soul is propagated into many species of soul. Plotinus also holds that intellect is the artificer of the world, and generates soul: both the world-soul itself and the other universal souls of the spheres and stars, and finally the particular souls: namely, those of

atque hominum. Et quoniam ad genus animae tamquam mobile atque multiplicabile distributio praecipue pertinet, idcirco vult intellectum illum aedificatorem mundi, per ipsam mundi animam primo creatam perque communes animas collegas eius, distributiones per gradus suos mundanorum animalium peregisse.

Propositio secunda: quomodo anima potest colligere se in proprium intellectum et per hunc intellectu formari divino. Sunt et in hoc capitulo tres aliae propositiones: duae de anima et una de Deo.

3　Hactenus consideratio prima quae intellectum mundi opificem declaravit; secunda vero consideratio tractat quomodo anima in universum hunc intellectum transferre se possit: videlicet si anima, quemadmodum multiplices sensus colligit in unum imaginationis sensum, sic imaginationes inter se longe diversas in unam colligat communem regulam rationis, deinde varios rationis nostrae discursus ad stabilem redigat intelligentiae normam, intellectu⟨que⟩ pro viribus tota formetur suo per quem universo formabitur intellectu totius opifice mundi—potest autem id in gradibus vitae fieri quandoquidem sit idem in ipsis scientiae gradibus. Propositionibus mille constat geometria et a priori posterior necessitate deducitur ideoque sequentes antecedentibus comprehenduntur omnesque continentur in prima. Anima quidem nostra per facultatem rationalem ex potentia transferrens se in actum atque vicissim. Si

daemons and men. And since distribution pertains primarily to the genus of soul that is as though capable of movement and multiplicity, for this reason he would have it that that intellect which is the builder of the world has accomplished, through the world-soul itself created first and through the universal souls that are its companions, the distributions of worldly living creatures through their levels.[9]

Second proposition: how the soul is able to gather itself into its own intellect and through this be formed by the divine intellect. There are also three other propositions in this chapter: two regarding the soul and one regarding God.

Thus far runs the first consideration which has declared intellect to be the maker of the world. The second consideration deals with the question how soul can transfer itself to this universal intellect: that is to say, whether the soul, in the way that it gathers the manifold senses into a single sensory imagination, can similarly gather imaginations that are very diverse among themselves into a unitary and general rule of reason, then reduce the various discursive motions of our reason to a stable norm of intelligence and then be formed as a whole and to the extent of its powers by its intellect through which it will be formed by the universal intellect that makes the entire world. This can come about in levels of life, given that the same thing occurs in the very levels of knowledge. Geometry consists of a thousand propositions. A posterior proposition is deduced from a prior according to necessity, and for this reason subsequent propositions are embraced in the preceding ones, and all propositions are contained in the first. Our soul transforms itself from potency to act and vice versa through its

3

totam geometriam habet, potest quidem habere propositiones omnes eius potentia quadam atque habitu dum aliquam earum habet in actu. Intellectus interea etiam noster in qualibet considerata secundum actum considerat per eundem actum et possidet omnes. Studendum est igitur ut rationalis nostra facultas pro viribus intellectui se conformet, quo in statu notiones omnes sequentes eodem actu quo et primam contueatur in prima.

4   In tertia consideratione Plotinus existimat mundi animam, quia semel atque potentissime animalem vitae formam in se complexa sit totam et inde totum corpus locumque penitus occupaverit, non posse vel in se mutare vitae formam vel extra se corpora permutare, similiterque se habere putat sphaerarum et stellarum omniumque caelestium animas quoniam universalem ab initio firmiter sortitae sint providentiam; animae vero particulares, particularem nactas providentiae modum, quales sunt daemonum plurimum atque hominum, vicissitudine quadam explere quodammodo perpetuam illam providentiam superiorum et, quatenus in seipsis de hac vitae forma mutantur in aliam, eatenus corpora sedesque mutare, unde videntur ad corpus locumque accedere, mutatione videlicet prius in se facta. At mundi corpus accedere videtur ad ipsam mundi animam. Illa enim in habitu suo firmiter permanente, corpus hoc ab initio sic affectum inde vivificatur, sicut aetheris pespicua regio semper illuminatur a sole. Dicuntur autem et particulares animae descendere quandoque ab anima: scilicet mundi, quoniam ab universali providentia formaque vitae quam

rational faculty and, if it possesses the whole of geometry, can possess all its propositions in a certain potency and condition, while it possesses one of these in act. Meanwhile, our intellect in the consideration of any proposition also through an act, considers and possesses all the propositions through this same act. Therefore, one should exert efforts so that our rational faculty may conform itself to intellect to the best of its abilities. In this state, all subsequent notions are in the same act in which that faculty beheld the initial proposition in its initial notion.

In the third consideration, Plotinus thinks that the world-soul, 4 because it is a whole having once and most powerfully embraced in itself the whole animate form of life, and has thus occupied the entire body and the whole of place, is unable either to change the form of life in itself or modify bodies outside of itself. He thinks that the souls of the spheres and stars and of all celestial things are in the same state, since they firmly obtained universal providence at the beginning. He thinks that particular souls—the souls of daemons for the most part and men—, having obtained a particular measure of providence, somehow fulfill—allowing for some change of status—that perpetual providence of the higher things. Moreover, to the extent that they are modified in themselves from this one form of life to another, to the same extent do they change their bodies and dwelling places: consequently, they seem to come to a body and place: that is, when a change has previously been made in themselves. But the world's body seems to come to the world-soul itself. With the world-soul remaining firmly in its own condition, the world's body, which is from the beginning affected in this way, obtains life from the same source, just as the transparent region of the aether is always illuminated by the sun. The particular souls are said to descend at times from the soul: that is, the world-soul, because they fall from the universal providence and form of life, which they possess at times together with the world-

simul cum mundi anima quandoque possident labuntur in propriam: non enim firmiter possederunt.

5   In quarta consideratione animam nostram in tres dividit formas: scilicet intellectualem et rationalem et ratione carentem,
putatque animam quandoque totam ad intellectualem sui trans-
ferri formam atque tunc habitare cum intellectu divino quandoque
illinc in se descendere: id est, in formam rationalem huius animae
propriam, quandoque vero hinc in formam ratione deteriorem,
unde simulacrum sui promit vitam videlicet communicatam corpori, cui quidem vitae subest et ultimum omnium simulacrum: id
est, materia quam anima per vegetalem sui potentiam prima pro-
pinquitate sua format corporea qualitate certaque figura, deinde
mox per hanc affectionem quasi escam allicitur naturaliter ad vivificandum corpus hoc certo iam modo dispositum.

6   In quinta consideratione ita notabis: sicut in circulo datur punctum in se ipso quod est centrum et punctum in toto ambitu et
qualibet eius parte, procedens ab eo quod in seipso est, immo
quasi ipsum, vel propagatio eius; item sicut est unitas in quolibet
numero eiusque parte fluens ab unitate quadam extra numerum in
se simpliciter cogitata; sic in tota rerum essentia est unitas quaedam essentiae fundamentum et cuiuslibet conservatio, procedens
ab unitate divina super essentiam[4] in se manente atque ita implente omnia quatenus praesentia ubique sua ex se procreat unitatem quandam in qualibet re creanda superessentialem cuiuslibet
essentiae productricem atque servatricem. Iam vero quia unitas
haec est praestantior quam essentia, coniicimus hanc, ubicumque
est, praesentia unitatis divinae fieri atque conservari.

soul, into their own providence, not having possessed the universal providence and form in a steadfast manner.

In the fourth consideration, Plotinus divides our soul into three 5 forms: namely, the intellectual, the rational, and the irrational. He thinks that the entire soul can sometimes be transferred into its intellectual form, at that time dwelling with the divine intellect; that it can sometimes descend from there to itself: that is, into the rational form proper to this soul, and that it can sometimes descend from there into the form inferior to reason. From that level, it brings forth a phantom of itself: namely, a life in communication with body, to which life in turn is subject the ultimate of all phantoms: that is, matter. The soul, through its life-giving power, and in its primal closeness, forms matter with bodily quality and a definite shape. Shortly after that, through this affecting that is like a bait, it is enticed naturally to the vivification of this body that is now arranged in a definite disposition.

In the fifth consideration you will note the following: Just as in 6 the case of a circle there is given a point in itself that is the center, and also a point on the entire circumference and any part of the circumference, the latter point proceeding from that central point in itself or rather as tough being that point or its prolongation; and again just as unity in any number and in its factor flows from a certain unity outside the number thought in itself *simpliciter*; similarly in the entire being of all things there is a certain unity that is the foundation of being and the source of preservation of anything, proceeding from the divine unity. This divine unity remains in itself above being and thus fills all things, to the extent that it produces from itself everywhere through its own presence a certain superessential unity in each thing to be created that is productive and preserving of each and every being. Moreover, since this unity is superior to being, we surmise that it comes to be and is maintained, wherever it is, by the presence of divine unity.

De intellectu etiam nostro: quomodo est semper in actu.

7 Sexta consideratio est de anima simul atque mente hunc in modum. Natura oculi diaphana: id est, translucida fit potissimum a natura solari et idcirco lumen naturaliter appetit facileque impletur lumine solis. Similiter diaphana in caelo natura proficiscitur a caelesti quodam lumine secundum ordinem universi antecedente diaphanum emananteque ab intellectuali lumine et confestim, dum emanat, diaphanum producente productumque implente — unde caelum fit quasi oculus caelestis animae hoc diaphano simul atque lumine cuncta providentis. Eodem pacto divina mens suo lumine rationalem generat animam quasi materiam sub illo diaphanam impletque illam perpetuo lumine quo anima semper tum seipsam intelligit a mente illuminatam tum mentem semper illuminantem. Id autem agit perpetuo intellectus noster animae caput. Rationalis vero facultas ad hunc quoque se habet, quasi visus ad lumen, non quidem semper sed aliquando rationabiliter intellectum. Quando igitur homo per rationem quodammodo seipsum intelligit, si modo perfecte intelligit, agnoscit interea se intelligentem esse, ergo et intellectualem qua sic intelligat se habere naturam. Haec ipsa (ut ita dixerim) intellectualitas est intelligentia quaedam non tam in motu posita manifesto quam in statu nobis occulto. Quin etiam per rationalem intelligentiam contemplator intelligit in se ipso ante intellectualitatem esse vitam atque essentiam ad quas intellectualitas ipsa posterius accedit ut actus, actus inquam ex quadam

Concerning our intellect also; and how it is always in act.

The sixth consideration, simultaneously regarding soul and mind, 7
is as follows: — The diaphanous: that is, transparent nature of the
eye arises primarily from its solar nature, and for that reason naturally seeks light and is easily filled by the light of the sun. Similarly, the diaphanous nature in the heaven comes forth from a
certain celestial light preceding the diaphanous according to the
order of the universe, this light emanating from the intellectual
light, and immediately—while it emanates—producing the diaphanous nature and filling it when produced: hence the heaven
becomes as though the eye of the celestial soul that provides for all
things simultaneously by means of this diaphanous nature and
light. By a similar arrangement, the divine mind generates by
means of its light the rational soul as though it were a diaphanous
matter below it, filling the latter with perpetual light by means of
which the soul always understands itself as illuminated by the
mind and the mind as always illuminating. Our intellect—the
summit of the soul—does this perpetually; our rational power
holds itself toward this intellect, as sight does toward light, not
always but sometimes, when the intellect is understood in reasoning. Therefore, when a man somehow understands himself
through his reason, provided that he understands himself perfectly, he recognizes in the meantime that he is in the process of
understanding and therefore also, to the degree that he understands himself thus, to have an intellectual nature. This very "intellectuality" (if I may coin a phrase) is a certain intelligence not so
much vested in a manifest motion as in a stability that is hidden
from us. Indeed, through his rational intelligence, the contemplator understands that there are in himself life and being before intellectuality, and that intellectuality itself comes after these as an

essentiae vitaeque fecunditate progenitus. Unde necesse est hanc ipsam essentiam atque vitam esse in se eminentiorem quandam intelligentiam. Probat quidem Plotinus hic animam ex intelligentia sui nova habere prius aeternam sui ipsius intelligentiam quae sit essentia vitaque fecunda ideoque habere in se intelligibilia firma actu ibi perpetuo intellecta, cuius intelligentiae imago quaedam sit discursio rationis quando pervenit ad summum unde et intelligentia nominatur.

8   Nos idem sic aliter confirmamus: tria sunt in ordine rerum ad cognitionem nostram pervenientia: singulare quiddam: id est, hic homo, et species communicata singulis: id est, homo, item idea hominis super singula. Quoniam vero tria haec essentiali quodam ordine a priori in posterius disposita differunt, vires quoque propriae cognoscentes haec similiter inter se differunt: singulare quidem imaginatio iudicat, speciem vero communem singulis ratio colligit et discernit, ideam autem intellectus agnoscit. Quoniam vero idea longius differt a specie extra quam exsistit quam species ab individuo in quo servatur, ideo intellectus a ratione longius quam ratio ab imaginatione distat. Verumtamen intellectus inest animae — alioquin non posset animus augurari ideas esse per rationem, nisi ratio id ageret per insitam nobis ab intellectu virtutem. Et quia ratio singula resolvit ad universale et corpus ad incorporeum sine imaginationis nostrae subsidio, immo ea invita quae retrahit ad oppositum, ideo intellectus absque motu argumentoque rationis semper intuetur ideas — semper inquam nam, si non pervenit ad illas imaginatione argumentationeque nova, aut numquam pervenit aut semper habet. Merito, cum anima sit media inter

act and, indeed, an act that is produced by a certain fertility on the part of being and life. For this reason, it is necessary that this being and this life in themselves constitute a certain higher intelligence. Plotinus here proves that the soul, from its newly acquired intelligence, possesses a prior eternal understanding of itself which is a fertile being and life, and that it therefore possesses the intelligibles in itself as understood steadfastly there in a perpetual act, the discursive motion of reason being a certain image of this intelligence when the motion arrives at that highest point from which it also is called intelligence.

We confirm this same point in another way. There are three 8 things in the order of reality that are accessible to our knowledge: a certain particular thing: that is, "this man," the species that is shared with the individual things: that is, "man," and the Idea of man above the particulars. Since these three differ, having been arranged in a certain essential order from prior to posterior, the proper powers which know them also differ among themselves. Imagination judges the particular thing; reason gathers and discriminates the species that is shared with the particulars; intellect recognizes the Idea. Since the Idea differs more from the species outside which it stands than does the species from the particular in which it is preserved, so does intellect stand further apart from reason than does reason from imagination. However, intellect is in the soul: the mind would not be able to divine the Ideas through the reason if the latter did not do this through a power implanted in us by intellect. And because reason resolves particulars into the universal and bodies into the incorporeal without the assistance of our imagination—indeed, in defiance of the latter which drags the reason back to its opposite—, therefore intellect will always, and I mean always, intuit the Ideas without motion or reason's argumentation. For given that it did not arrive at these with a new imagination and argumentation, either it never arrives or else it always has them. Rightly, since the soul is midway between eternity and

aeternitatem atque tempus—essentia enim eius fixa est et antecellit motum ab ea dependentem—, consentaneum est ut eius essentiae fixae, eo ipso signo quo praecedit motum, vis actioque insit prorsus immobilis et stabiliter intuens, quippe cum hic intuitus ab essentia et virtute stabili ad ideam omnino stabilem vergens utrimque stabilitatem sibi vindicet. Sicut ergo in anima ex eo quod sub aeternitate est convenit imaginatio mobilis, sic ex eo quod super tempus competit intellectus immobiliter agens. Actus quidem intellectus omnino immobilis[5] est, actus autem imaginationis omnino mobilis, actus denique rationis est mixtus; neque posset anima esse congruum universi medium nisi tria haec in se possideret.

Quomodo Deus est super motum et statum et cognitionem; item de eo quod in actu est et quod in potentia.

9   Septima consideratio probat in primo omnium principio nullum esse motum—nedum fluentem sed nec etiam metaphoricum—qui est actus tendens ad aliud: non enim tendit in aliud quod est primum penitus atque ultimum. Probat nec ibi esse statum: scilicet quietem ad quam tendit motus oppositam motioni—omnino vero nec quiescit in alio quod non movetur ad aliud, neque proprie quiescit in se quod est ipsa simplicitas: in ea enim[6] eiusmodi distinctio nulla cadit per quam distingui solet quiescens tum a quiete

time—for its substance is fixed and precedes the motion dependent on it—it is fitting that a power and activity that are completely immobile and stably intuiting should be present in the soul's fixed substance by the same token that the soul's substance precedes its motion.[10] This is the case inasmuch as this intuition, turning from a stable being and power toward the Idea that is altogether stable, claims stability for itself from both viewpoints. Therefore, just as in the soul, a mobile imagination is fitting, because of the fact that the soul is below eternity; there similarly an intellect acting immovably is appropriate, because of the fact that the intellect is above time. The act of intellect is altogether immovable; the act of imagination is entirely mobile; finally, the act of reason is mixed. Moreover, the soul could not be a harmonious mediation of the universe if it did not have these three in itself.

How God is above motion and rest and knowledge; also regarding that which is in act and that which is in potency.

The seventh consideration proves that there is in the first principle 9 of all things no motion—especially not emanative motion and not even a metaphorical motion. This is because motion is an activity tending toward another thing, and this principle, which is absolutely the first and the last, does not tend toward anything else. This consideration also proves that there is no rest there: that is, the repose toward which motion tends and which is the opposite of motion. That which is not moved toward another thing also does not rest in anything else, and that which is simplicity in itself does not in a proper sense rest in itself. For in this simplicity no distinction arises of the kind whereby that which is at rest is wont to be distinguished both from the rest and from the place in which

tum etiam a sede in qua quiescit. Iam vero motus a statu vim habet, dum a stabilitate motivae virtutis suum servat tenorem; status
autem ab unitate: stare enim nihil est aliud quam unitatem propriam conservare. Unitas igitur ipsa et motum antecedit et statum.
Antecedit igitur et actum intelligentiae qui motus quidam est a
potentia intelligendi ad verum intelligibile tamquam bonum. In
omni ergo intelligente, etiam si seipsam intelligat, distinctio talis
consideratur: in primo autem nulla est absoluta distinctio. Denique alia quidem ratio est exsistentiae alia prorsus intelligentiae:
non enim quicquid exsistit intelligit. Primo quidem principio ex-
sistentia concedetur. Si addatur intelligentia, tum compositio fiet
tum constabit exsistentiam ipsam sibimet ad perfectionem minime
suffecisse, quandoquidem intelligentia indiguerit per quam ten-
deret ad profectum.

10   In octava consideratione notabis condicionem actus formalis
potentiaeque formabilis inter se opponi adeo ut potentia haec accipiat actum, actus vero qua ratione actus est potentiam non reci-
piat. Ubi ergo actus est solus, ut in primo, sempiterna res est
quoniam nulla ibi ad aliam formam potentia latet. Item ubi potentia tota formabilis translata est in naturam formae adeo ut forma
illic nullo modo ad naturam potentiae retrahatur, res etiam est
sempiterna, praesertim quia potentia illic totum habet actum
quantumcumque potest cupitque habere. Quales sunt intellectuales essentiae ignisque caelestis. Ignis autem sub caelo inter inferiora perfectius est quatenus maxime est in actu: quod apparet
ex efficacia formae et ex motu perpetuo et quoniam non tolerat

it rests. Indeed, motion has its power from stability — while it maintains its course on the basis of the moving power's stability —, and stability has power from unity. To be stable is nothing other than to preserve one's proper unity. Therefore unity itself precedes both motion and rest. It therefore also precedes the act of intelligence which is a certain motion from the potency of understanding to the true intelligible that is its good, so to speak. In the case of everything that understands, even if it understands itself, a distinction of some kind is considered, whereas there is no "absolute distinction" in the first principle.[11] Finally, there is one reason-principle of existence and quite another of intelligence, for not everything that exists, understands. Now it will be granted that the first principle exists. But if intelligence is added to it, not only will it become a compound, but it will become clear that existence itself has not at all sufficed to make it perfect, given that it will have been in need of the intelligence through which it could make progress.

In the eighth consideration, you will note that the states of 10 formal act and of formable potency are mutually opposed to such an extent that this potency receives the act, although the act — to the extent that it is act — does not receive the potency. Where there is only act — as in the case of the first causal principle — a thing is everlasting, since no potency toward another form is latent there. Again, where the entire formable potency is transformed into the nature of form to such a degree that the form there is in no way drawn back toward the nature of potency, a thing is also everlasting: this being especially the case because the potency there possesses the entire act and wishes to possess it to the extent of its power. The intellectual beings and the celestial fire are things having such potency. However, the fire that is below the heaven is, among inferior things, the more perfect the more fully it is in act: something apparent from the efficacy of its form, from its perpetual motion, and from the fact that it does not tolerate blending.

mixtionem. Quoniam vero materiam habet sub actu nec eo contentam, non est semper.

11   Nona[7] consideratione memineris ipsam intelligentiam non esse bonum ipsum simpliciter primum atque ultimum, alioquin esset simpliciter expetenda—nunc autem condicione quadam eligitur: eligis enim cognoscere si modo cognoscas bene feliciterque et quod tibi tamquam bonum sit profuturum—item ipsum bonum non habere sui ipsius agnitionem, tum quia aliud haec est aliud ipsum bonum, tum quia, si ante agnitionem sibi sufficit, non est addenda, sin minus, non erat ipsum bonum. Quo autem pacto Deus neque caecus sit neque ignorans, etiam si ei cognitio non addatur—super quam Dionysius quoque Areopagita eum collocat—in quinta sextave *Enneade* opportunius explicabimus.

But this fire, having matter underlying its act and not being sustained by that act, is not everlasting.

In the ninth consideration, you will recall that intellect is not the Good itself *simpliciter* which is first and last: otherwise, the former would be something that is sought *simpliciter*. However, intellect is chosen upon a certain condition, for you choose to know, as long as you know well and happily, and know what is of advantage to you as a good. You should also recall that the Good itself has no knowledge of itself, both because knowledge is one thing and goodness itself another, and because, if the Good is self-sufficient before the knowledge, the latter should not be added to it, whereas if it is less than self-sufficient, it was not the Good itself. How it comes about that God is neither blind nor ignorant, even if knowledge (above which also Dionysius the Areopagite places him) is not added to him, we will explain at a more opportune time in conjunction with the *Fifth* or *Sixth Ennead*.[12]

Analytical Study of the
Commentary on Ennead IV

కులుత

SUMMARY

1. *Introduction*

It is in the *Commentary on the Fourth Ennead* that Ficino first fully implements a revised strategy with respect to commenting on the text of Plotinus. After a two-year hiatus in which he turned aside from his main project of commenting on the *Enneads* in order to translate various short treatises by post-Plotinian philosophical writers, Ficino had recommenced the work on Plotinus before

June or July 1489 with the commentary on the third treatise of the *Third Ennead*. However, by this time or shortly thereafter he seems to have decided to reduce the scope of his exegesis, since the commentaries on the later treatises of the *Third Ennead* according to the Porphyrian numbering are significantly shorter than those on the earlier essays. Indeed, by the time he had finished commenting on the *Third Ennead* and was some distance into his commentary on the third treatise of the *Fourth Ennead*, he had made a more drastic decision not only to reduce the scale of his commentary but to change its format entirely. He now explains that "if we pursue similarly lengthy analyses and indeed commentaries arranged separately from Plotinus' chapters themselves, a confused interpretation will arise and the project will expand to immense proportions. We have been sufficiently discursive and have now said sufficiently many things. Henceforth, it will be enough to insert certain brief notices between the chapters of Plotinus, as we have done in the case of Theophrastus."[1]

Now, the project that Ficino here promises of organizing a text as difficult as Plotinus' *Enneads* into chapters and providing accurate summaries would in itself represent a significant achievement in the field of Plotinian exegesis and, given the conventions of exegesis still prevailing at the beginning of the modern era, even this more modest project could be informative not only about Ficino's understanding of Plotinus' thought but also about the development of his own philosophical ideas. However, close inspection of the *Commentary on the Fourth Ennead* shows that the commentator is still not implementing the revised strategy on a consistent basis and can still treat the Plotinian text as a basis for the independent philosophical reflections that most interest the modern reader. The second two-thirds of the commentary on *Ennead* 4.3 is indeed very much reduced in scale, and from chapter fifteen to thirty-two we have little more than chapter headings, ranging from two to ten lines of text. However, *Ennead* 4.4 is equipped with a more

extensive commentary, although the material is arranged chapter by chapter rather than in the discursive manner of the commentaries on *Enneads* 1–3. The commentary on *Ennead* 4.5, which follows the format of the immediately preceding commentary, runs to approximately 50 percent of the length of the original Plotinian treatise. This means that most of Plotinus' important treatise "On Difficulties Concerning the Soul" — which Porphyry had divided into two major parts with a short appendix "On Vision" and comprises treatises twenty-seven to twenty-nine in the chronological order reported in the *Vita Plotini* — has something approaching a full Ficinian commentary.[2] Of course, it is unclear whether these facts indicate that Ficino had some lingering doubts about the viability of the revised strategy or had already written some of the later commentaries before the decision to modify his general approach was taken.[3]

1.1 Harmonic Structure

In our "Analytical Study" of Ficino's *Commentary on the Third Ennead of Plotinus*, we emphasized the function of a "deep structure" in Ficino's later metaphysics. This structure was formed by close relations of implication first, between various components of the general notion of the "harmonic," in particular the notions of ratio, mediation, and proportion (or analogy), and second, between these components and certain of their derivatives: for example, the notions of concord (or consonance) and attunement. We refer the reader to our earlier text for a detailed explanation of how this deep structure is constituted and would here simply call his or her attention to its continued significance for the *Commentary on the Fourth Ennead*.[4] Although the notion of the "harmonic" is not exploited in as systematic a manner here as it was in Ficino's discussions of the universal reason-principle in Plotinus' *Ennead* 3.2–3.3, harmonic thinking continues to play an important role in the com-

mentary on *Ennead* 4: the part of the Plotinian corpus in which Porphyry grouped the treatises on the soul, not least because the harmonic psychogony of Plato's *Timaeus* casts its shadow over both Plotinus and Ficino.

With respect to the notion of the "harmonic," there are nevertheless several important changes or shifts in emphasis between the commentaries on these respective *Enneads*. In particular, the notion of mediation becomes more important in the present commentary because of the mediate status of soul in the Ficinian universe, while the notion of proportion plays a more crucial role in the later commentary through its connection with the doctrines of cosmic sympathy and sense-perception. Conversely, the notion of ratio does not have the same importance in the commentary on *Ennead* 4 that it had in connection with the doctrines of reason-principle and daemon articulated in Ficino's earlier commentary. In addition to these changes, the notion of the harmonic in general appears in a more intensely dynamic form in the commentary on *Ennead* 4 because of the mobile or more precisely self-moving character of soul. For example, the relatively static notion of mediation is often converted here into the more dynamic notion of the complementarity of attraction—where a mediation is understood as present or inserted—and of repulsion—where the same mediation is treated as absent or removed.

1.1.1 MEDIATION

Ficino examines the status of "soul"—treating it here as a genus that would include universal soul, the world-soul, human souls, and other souls—at the beginning of his commentary on *Ennead* 4.1–2.[5] Having noted that the topic has been treated more extensively in his own earlier *Platonic Theology*, he provides a kind of summary, which has the advantage of showing the structural function of soul within the Ficinian architecture of the world.[6] Here, soul emerges in the first instance as the mediating term in a triad

in paragraphs 1–3 of the commentary — representing Ficino's notes on *Ennead* 4.2 — and then subsequently as the mediating term in a pentad in paragraphs 4–5 — being his notes on *Ennead* 4.1⁷ —, the larger structure being an expansion of the smaller one.[8]

Ficino recalls the teaching of Plato's *Timaeus* to the effect that soul is composed of a certain "indivisible substance" (*essentia individua*) and a substance "divisible around bodies" (*dividua circa corpora*). He notes Plotinus' view that the doctrine of soul stated here is that soul comprises two "powers or faculties" (*potestates . . . facultates*): namely, a power that understands intellectual being and never declines toward body and — as the second power — that "nature of the soul" (*animae natura*) which at the same time (*a*) completely accommodates itself to body and (*b*) remains indivisible. He also notes Plotinus' view that the doctrine of soul stated in the *Timaeus* is that the two powers or faculties of the soul mentioned "have this status" (*ita se habere*) relative to one another both in the case of the human soul and in that of the world-soul. That soul is being characterized here as a mediate term between two extremes emerges from the continuation of the argument in which Ficino explains the nature of the first power by comparing it with the next higher term in the hierarchy of being and that of the second power by comparing it with the next lower term. Thus, intellect — the next higher term — is indivisible, because it is present to every part of body but affects the body only through soul, whereas body — the next lower term — is divisible, because each of its parts is separated from each of its other parts.[9] Soul is similar to intellect in that it is present as a whole to each part of the body, but similar to body in that it performs one action in one part of the body and another action in another part. As an illustration of this final point, Ficino instances the adaptation by soul of sensation and motion to different parts of the body and to varying degrees, which might be thought to represent a quasi-divisibility of soul.[10]

Ficino has therefore shown that soul as a whole is a mediator between intellect and body in that it comprises—through a distinction of powers or faculties rather than in any spatial sense—one higher part, which is similar to intellect—the intellective faculty of soul—and another lower part, which is similar to body—the natural power of soul. The theory stated here should be compared with the account of the soul and the animate being in his commentary on *Ennead* 1.1. The latter text, which is seen by Ficino as providing a summary of and therefore an introduction to the psychological teaching of Plotinus' *Enneads* as a whole, divides "soul" (in the generic sense referred to in the commentary on treatises 4.1–2) into higher and lower parts or—in a certain sense—into higher and lower *souls*: the higher being the rational soul derived from intellect, and the lower the vital soul, which combines with body to constitute the animate being.[11] The relatively simple mediating function assigned to soul in the commentary on treatises 4.1–2 becomes more complicated in the commentary on treatise 1.1, because soul there is mediate not only in being between intellect and body but also in being combined with body, and also because the triadic structure of intellect, soul, and body is expanded with a triadic subdivision of the higher soul itself.[12]

Returning to the commentary on *Ennead* 4.1–2, we find Ficino treating soul as a mediator by comparing it no longer simply with the next higher term in the hierarchy of being but also with the next higher term and the term above that, and no longer with the next lower term but with the next lower term and the term below that.[13] First, he introduces two principles of division—divisibility and mobility—and establishes four terms by stating that the divine intellect is "indivisible and immobile" (*individuus . . . immobilis*), soul "indivisible and mobile in the proper sense" (*indivisibilis . . . proprie mobilis*), corporeal quality "divided and mobile" (*divisa . . . mobilis*),[14] and body "divided in the proper sense and mobile" (*divisum proprie . . . mobile*). The division is clarified with three

observations. Regarding divisibility, Ficino notes that any reference to soul as somehow divisible — as in the case of the earlier triadic analysis — means that it is not divided spatially among bodies as quality is divided but "adapted" (*accommodata*) to them. Regarding motion, he notes that the reference here to soul as mobile in the proper sense means that it is not moved externally as body is moved but "according to its accidents while remaining stable in its substance" (*secundum accidentia . . . tamen substantia permanere*). The commentator adds that because goodness begins from the highest and evil from the lowest term in the hierarchy, that which is mobile in the proper sense stands above that which is divided in the proper sense. Finally, Ficino introduces a further principle of division — multiplicity — and establishes five terms by noting that the Good is "one in itself" (*unum in se*), the divine mind "one-many" (*unum multa*), soul "one and many" (*unum atque multa*), corporeal quality "many and one" (*multa et unum*), and corporeal bulk "many in itself" (*multa in se*).[15]

If soul emerges as the mediator *par excellence* in Ficino's hierarchy of beings, the structural continuity of his system as a whole makes it possible for other principles also to exercise mediating functions. In fact, one further principle plays a particularly decisive role in Ficinian metaphysics by being placed between soul and body in such a way that it is assimilated in terms of its substance and function sometimes to the psychic and sometimes to the corporeal level. This ambiguous principle is "spirit" (*spiritus*).

One of the most striking discussions of the mediate status of spirit occurs in a passage where Ficino argues that all the parts of the world considered as a single animate being form a connective totality based on five foundations: namely, "matter" (*materia*), the "concord of qualities" (*concordia qualitatum*), "spirit" (*spiritus*), "nature" (*natura*), and the "world-soul" (*anima mundi*).[16] The connectedness produced by each of these foundations — specified variously as being a communion, contiguity, continuity, or union — is

based on the singleness and ubiquity of each foundation. Now since the world-soul is said to be "connected" (*coniungi*) through spirit to lower bodies while nature is held to be "bound" (*colligari*) through spirit to subsequent things, spirit clearly has not only a basic status as the third of the five connective foundations but also a supplementary function in connecting different connective foundations to one another. It is interesting to note the structural analogy between the position of spirit in this passage and that of the soul in the text considered above. Just as earlier soul mediated between, on the one hand, the divine mind as the next higher term and the Good as the higher term above that, and on the other hand, corporeal quality as the next lower term and corporeal bulk as the lower term below that, so here spirit mediates between, on the one hand, nature as the next higher term and the world-soul as the higher term above that, and on the other hand, the concord of qualities as the next lower term and matter as the lower term below that. In other words, a new fivefold structure as established within three of the terms forming the earlier fivefold structure.

So far, we have been considering mediation as static and as structure in Ficino's metaphysical system. However, its dynamic and processual counterpart, attraction, is an equally important component in his view of the world. That these are two aspects of a single underlying reality follows from his adoption from Neoplatonic sources of the emanative model of causation with only the necessary accommodations to Christian dogma.

Ficino places at the very beginning of the commentary on Plotinus, which now forms *De Vita* 3, a summary of the doctrine that he takes to be at the heart of the *Enneads*. He observes that if there were only two things in the universe—on one side intellect, and on the other body—neither would intellect be attracted to body nor body to intellect.[17] But if soul, which "conforms to both" (*utrique conformis*), is placed between them, an "attraction"

(*attractus*) from each side to the other will occur. This is for two reasons. First, soul is led most easily since it is the "first mobile thing" (*primum mobile*) and is self-moved; second, it is near to both sides since it is "the mediator of things" (*media rerum*). The writer expands on the second point by saying that soul "contains all things in itself after its own fashion" (*omnia suo in se modo continet*), is near to both sides "in a reason-principle" (*ratione*), and "is also connected equally with everything" (*conciliatur et omnibus etiam aequaliter*). Admittedly, Ficino does not at this point explain precisely why the static mediation corresponds to the dynamic attraction. However, the discussions of magic both in *On Life* 3 and in the *Commentary on the Fourth Ennead* provide elucidation. In short, the world is eternally permeated by processes that are both radiating on all sides and vibrating in two directions, these processes being advanced when the channels of communication are opened by the interpolation of mediators and inhibited when the channels are blocked by the removal of the same mediators.

1.1.2 ATTUNEMENT

Now if mediation is most frequently described in Ficino's texts as though it were primarily static, although, as we have just seen, it can reappear in a more dynamic form as attraction, the converse situation obtains in the present commentary with regard to the proportion representing the next stage of complexity in the deep structure of harmonic thinking.[18] According to this structure, mediation is to attraction as proportion is to attunement. Now, attunement is most often characterized in Ficino's writing as though it were primarily dynamic, although it can reappear in a more static form as proportion, these two approaches being expressed with vivid analogies drawn from the science of harmonics.[19]

In the first analogy, which he cites on several occasions and is actually a musical analogy drawn from Plotinus and combined with a medical analogy of his own, Ficino begins by comparing the

weaving together of nerves and veins in any complete animate being to the interconnection of natures and lives in the animate being that is the world.[20] The analogy then elaborates the notion of processes or motions occurring within the living creature, the most important features being (*a*) two-directionality (motion or passivity is transmitted between the neck and foot and vice-versa in the human being and between higher and lower things in the world),[21] and (*b*) the sharing of properties between things in separate locations within the human being and the world allowing motions to be transmitted and received instantaneously.[22] Ficino next merges this analogy with a second analogy, taking the processes or motions that have been described as occurring within the living creature and comparing these with those that occur within a musical instrument. Within this analogy, which is expressed in a more elliptical manner, the extension of nerves and veins in the human being and of natures and lives in the world is compared to the stretching of strings on a lyre, the most important features of this comparison being (*c*) the multiplicity of the strings, (*d*) the tension in the strings, (*e*) the vibration of the strings, (*f*) the sympathy between the different vibrating strings, and (*g*) the proportion or ratio making the sympathetic vibration possible.[23]

The dynamic aspect of attunement, which naturally predominates in Ficino's text, is set out clearly in the passage where the intellect of the world-soul and the higher reason-principle are identified as two aspects of the mythological Jupiter. Given that *ratio* means both "reason-principle" in the cosmological sense and "ratio" in the mathematical sense, and that ratio in the mathematical sense underlies the "consonance" of harmonic science, it is not surprising to find Ficino now envisioning the reciprocity of the cosmological process as a shifting pattern of dissonances and consonances. Here, Apollo as the mythological representation of the world-soul is said to pluck his lyre in heaven and sing in nature.[24] The perpetual arrangement of stars and their motions represented

by the former idea is said to be established "in perpetual harmony with" (*ad perpetuam concordiam*) the unfolding and enfolding of reason-principles represented by the latter notion.[25] Moreover, these reason-principles unfolding and enfolding at specific times themselves constitute a "universal harmony" (*universalis concentus*). Ficino adds that if anyone examines the continuity and arrangement of the Apollonian song in nature, he will thereby perceive the Apollonian sounds in heaven.[26] This is because human souls "attune" (*coaptant*) their descents, embodiment, and ascents to the song in nature and the sound in heaven and can be said to dance together with it "as though in a concordant step" (*quasi tripudio concordi*). Moreover, it is because we can hear the Apollonian sounds in heaven through the Apollonian song in nature that it is possible to make conjectures about the future course of human affairs, which is signified if not caused by the heavenly configurations.

The argument paraphrased above is further elaborated in a passage where Ficino uses the simile of a dancer in order to explain the processes of nature.[27] Plotinus had already exploited this simile at considerable length in *Ennead* 4.4, and the Florentine here responds to the work of his predecessor as he often does elsewhere by reducing the exploratory style of his model to a more overtly structured and systematic format. Ficino introduces the simile of the dancer by stating that the entire world is a single animate being "dancing according to a musical reason-principle" (*ratione musica saltans*) and changing all things together with itself by means of the dancing.

The detailed elaboration of the simile that follows can perhaps be summarized as having in the first instance several components, each of which comprises an attunement of some kind in the world itself.[28] Ficino describes attunement (1) as between [a] the "exemplary" (*exemplares*) reason-principles" and [b] the "seminal" (*seminales*) reason-principles; and attunement (2) as between [a] the intel-

lectual or rational phase of the world-soul and [b] its natural phase. The intellectual phase contemplates "from eternity" (*ab aevo*) the universe "in the series itself of the Ideas" (*in ipsa idearum serie*) and then chooses the course of worldly events "at once in a single general act of selection" (*una semel communi electione*). The natural phase then "transfixes without any selection" (*absque electione transfigit*) that course of worldly events. Finally, within the transfixing of the general act of selection, Ficino describes attunement (3) as between [a] the "cycles of the members of the world" (*membrorum mundanorum revolutiones*)—the spheres, parts of the spheres, and the stars—together with the "figures constituted by the stars' interrelations" (*figurae ex stellis invicem constitutae*) and [b] the "events below the heaven" (*eventus sub caelo*), which follow from these cycles or are indicated by them. The stars' figures are here associated with certain powers, both figures and powers being characterized as either of a stable or of a mobile kind.

Having established as a further component of the simile an attunement between [a] "a man dancing" (*tripudians*) and [b] "the animate being that is the entire world" (*totus mundus . . . animal*), Ficino clearly now intends to posit three attunements within the dancer corresponding to the three attunements described in the world, although these three correspondences are not presented very systematically in his text. He does clearly describe the attunement 1 between [a] "the art of the dancer" (*ars tripudiantis*) and [b] the "dance" (*saltandum*) itself. However, attunement 2 between [a] "the music implanted in him" (*insita sibi musica*) and [b] the unfolding progression of the dance can be extracted only from a passage where a further component is added to the original simile between dancer and world: the members of the dancer's audience, who are described as either spellbound by his movements or moving in synchronicity with them. Finally, within the transfixing of the implanted music, attunement 3 between [a] "the dancer's hand . . . the song and dance" (*saltantis manus . . . sonus choreaque*) and [b] the

sonic and gestural events that are predicted to follow in the choreographic sequence, is merely implied in a passage adding yet a further component to the original simile: a wise man foretelling worldly events from observation of astral figures.

The sheer complexity of the simile of the dancer in both Plotinus and Ficino has led to an uncharacteristically muddled exposition on the part of the Florentine.[29] However, the main ideas that the simile is intended to illuminate — the multi-layered process of the world conceived in harmonic terms and thereby permitting within limits the prediction of future events — do indeed come through the haze of details. It is worth noting in passing that the dancer's ability to articulate a rational sequence of figures without conscious reflection on the art implanted in him provides an excellent illustration of the unconscious activity of nature explained in the commentary on Ennead 3.2–3 and 3.8.

But consideration of attunement as dynamic and as process in Ficino's metaphysical system does not give us the whole story. In fact, its static and structural counterpart, proportion, is an equally important component in his view of the world. Again, his adoption from Neoplatonic sources of the emanative model of causation only modified to the extent required by Christian dogma shows that these are two aspects of a single underlying reality.

In an important passage near the beginning of his commentary on Ennead 4.1–2, Ficino explains that "intellectual souls" (*intellectuales animae*) are separated from one another in their embodied state but nonetheless present all together in intellect itself *simpliciter* through the intellectual faculties proper to them, just as "lines" (*lineae*) extended from the center as far as the circumference of a geometrical circle do not depart from the center and "rays" (*radii*) emitted by the sun toward earthly things in the sphere of the world do not depart from the sun.[30] The conjunction "just as" (*quemadmodum*) shows that Ficino is here introducing an analogy,

which, by representing not a merely conceptual comparison but a real state of affairs, is equivalent to a proportion. This mode of argumentation more than any other brings the deep structure of the harmonic to the surface of his writing, being paralleled in countless passages of the commentary on the *Enneads*. Another striking example can be found in a passage where Ficino establishes the principle of universal cosensation by arguing that the animate being of the world can look down toward all earthly things through the vitality, transparence, and luminosity of its "most extensive sphere" (*amplissima sphaera*) as it irradiates light, just as a human being can look up at celestial things through the vitality, transparence, and luminosity of its "eye" (*oculus*).[31]

1.1.3 Mediation and Attunement

Having discussed mediation — predominantly a static conception — with special reference to soul and attunement — predominantly a dynamic notion — with special reference to the world-animal, it is necessary to complete our account of the harmonic deep structure of Ficino's thought only by turning to the consideration of a doctrine that combines the ideas of mediation and attunement and maintains static and dynamic elements in a kind of equilibrium. This is the doctrine of sensation. Given that the results of Plotinus' account of sensation in *Ennead* 4.5, "On Vision," are indecisive even by his standards, Ficino's elaboration on the basis of his predecessor's tentative remarks can only be described as a notable achievement in the realm of philosophical systematization.[32]

Ficino's theory of sensation (or sense-perception)[33] may be said to take its starting point from his fundamental assumption of the lack of proportion between the sense and the object sensed, the latter in its turn resulting from the radical dualism of soul and body, which he espouses in line with Plotinus himself. Near the

beginning of the commentary on *Ennead* 4.6, he states that the soul is "more excellent than the things to be sensed without having proportionality to them" (*rebus sentiendis absque proportione excellentior*), and that it "does not communicate with them in matter or nature" (*neque cum eis in materia vel natura communicat*).[34] The content and phraseology of this passage calls to mind another text in which Ficino speaks of the world as a single animate being, arguing that there is "a certain communion" (*communio quaedam*) between all its constituents[35] based on "five foundations" (*quinque fundamenta*): (1) matter, (2) the concord of qualities, (3) spirit, (4) the generative nature, and (5) the world-soul.[36] Now, since communion in matter and nature between parts of the world-animal is clearly another aspect of the latter's internal attunement, and since the lack of proportion between sense and object sensed involves a lack of communication between the two in matter and nature, Ficino is clearly telling us something important through the combination of these two texts. This is, that the assumption of a radical dualism between soul and body — in itself not open to challenge — presents a problem not only for the theory of sensation but also for the theory of cosmic attunement.

The philosophical stakes are therefore extremely high for Ficino in discussing sensation, and at this point we will merely state in a preliminary way how he overcomes the lack of proportion between sense and object of sense by using the notions of mediation between sense and sensory object and attunement between the sense and the sensory object. The main features of his account of sensation are: [1] The soul operates on the microcosmic level. Because it exercises correct judgment in sensation, and passivity confuses sensation, the soul must be active.[37] [2] The process of sensation depends on the presence of what might be termed "vertical" and "horizontal" oppositional structures of higher and lower terms, which can be mediated in both dimensions. Thus, one must pos-

tulate ⟨2a⟩ a vertical structure consisting of soul — intellectual or sensitive — and body,[38] and ⟨2b⟩ a horizontal structure consisting of senses and sensible object.[39] One must postulate ⟨2c⟩ a mediator between the terms of the vertical structure: spirit; and consider ⟨2d⟩ a mediator or mediators between the terms of the horizontal structure: spirit or air. [3] The nature of spirit can be ⟨2a⟩ characterized as "spiritual Idea"[40] or as a kind of "form"[41] and ⟨2b⟩ contrasted with incorporeal light as a higher term and corporeal light as a lower term.[42] [4] The soul interacts on both the macrocosmic and microcosmic levels. The mediators on both the horizontal and vertical dimensions arise from the "living nature" of the world rather than from the subject or object.[43] When Ficino speaks of this living nature as "so attuning this sense with this sensible thing" (*sensum hunc cum hoc sensibili temperare*) that the former both acts upon and is acted upon by the latter, comparing this process to the vibration of one string of a lyre together with another string "attuned to it" (*contemperata*),[44] he is actually referring not only to the relation of macrocosm to microcosm but to the relations of the entire system of oppositions and mediators.

1.2 Platonism and Christianity

1.2.1 MAGIC AND DAEMONOLOGY

As always in Ficino, and either consciously or unconsciously, the deep structure of harmonic theory also grounds the notion of concord and discord between the Christian and non-Christian sources of his thought. Taking the discordant element first, it is worth noting that the commentary on Plotinus' *Enneads* contains very little overt criticism of their author — the Florentine's disagreement with him on the question of the human soul's possible transmigration into animal bodies being the most notable exception to this rule —, and Ficino always tries to bring out the Plotinian

doctrines that are most harmonious with Christianity and pass over rapidly or silently the teachings that are questionable according to such criteria.

In the *Commentary on the Fourth Ennead* Ficino reproves Plotinus for saying that a magician somehow ensnares daemons and acts through the world's totality on its parts and moves lower things through the higher.[45] The commentator is obviously not rejecting the notions that there are daemons in the world and that magicians can ensnare them. Rather, he seems to be taking exception to Plotinus' remarks for reasons that are both metaphysical and moral: metaphysical, because the inferior status of daemons means that action with their assistance could only be between the parts of the world and not between the totality and the parts; moral, because the daemonic world includes wicked spirits, who can deceive us by pretending to be attracted or repelled by certain magical contrivances. In effect, Ficino is criticizing Plotinus for advocating a doctrine that is both inconsistent with his own Platonic assumptions and subject to the traditional Christian objections against pagan daemonology.

Ficino's discussion of this Plotinian remark is noteworthy for introducing two further ideas in an intertextual manner. First, he informs us regarding the doctrine of Albumasar that it is possible to entice the daemons subject to Jupiter more effectively when that planet is in the constellation of the Dragon's Head or in aspect to it. He then contrasts this with a more laudable approach, whereby a man who strives for celestial goods will be more able to imbibe them through the beneficence of the planet itself when it occupies this same astrological position.[46] Second, Ficino reports that Porphyry and Iamblichus both condemn the superstitious practices that strive to flatter deceitful and troubled daemons. He then quotes with approval these same authorities' teaching that we have through God and the angels a position of authority over the dae-

mons that enables us to avoid the deception and harm that they can wreak.[47]

However, the most interesting component in Ficino's textual and hermeneutic encounter with Plotinus — leaving aside the original Ficinian philosophy that is somehow associated with the *Enneads* — is undoubtedly that in which the elements that are concordant and discordant with Christian thought are being sifted. In the *Commentary on the Fourth Ennead*, this thought process is best illustrated in Ficino's handling of three questions: that of the unity or multiplicity of soul, that of something that might be termed "two-directional" causality with respect to soul, and that of the descent of soul. The essential backdrop of all these discussions is provided by the division of soul in the generic sense in a twofold manner into (*a*) a higher part that — being derived from intellect — is termed the "rational soul" (*anima rationalis*)[48] and (*b*) a lower part that — in conjunction with body — comprises the "animate being" (*animal*), the higher part being subdivided into intellect, reason, and imagination (distinct)[49] and the lower part into imagination (confused),[50] exterior sense, and nature.[51] Indeed, this structuring, which is summarized at the beginning of Ficino's commentary on *Ennead* 1.1, is explicitly recalled at the beginning of his commentary on *Ennead* 4.1–2.1. Here, Ficino distinguishes: (1) the order of essential being in the eternal levels of the universe and (2) the order of essential being in the levels of generation, and states that the "intellectual soul" (elsewhere called "rational soul") is the highest limit of 2 and has the closest dependence on 1. Moreover, the intellectual or rational soul is not made in the realm of generation *simpliciter* but is rather adapted to body [*a* + *b* above] in order to complete the providence of the totality. One should note in connection with the arguments to be summarized and

discussed in the next three subsections that although Ficino for the most part refers to "soul" in a loose or generic sense, he is more specifically concerned with the intellectual or rational soul. It is for this reason especially that his treatment of the first of the three problems mentioned: that of the unity and multiplicity of soul in Plotinus, connects with his earlier critique of the doctrine of the unity of intellect in Averroes.

1.2.2.1 UNITY AND MULTIPLICITY OF SOUL

At the beginning of his commentary on *Ennead* 4.3, Ficino identifies seven *quaestiones* that will be examined in the treatise and states that the first "question" is whether our souls are derived from the world-soul either as being its parts or as being certain effects of it.[52] After noting that some have attempted to argue that our souls are parts of the world-soul on the basis of references in Plato and that he has elsewhere already criticized this theory in the form advocated by Averroes, he embarks on a detailed refutation "in conjunction with Plotinus" (*una cum Plotino*).[53] His initial argument is based on the notion of "world." Since the world is a totality of wholes and a totality of forms, its constituents must have their own substances and actions, although the world may be a "unity" in the sense of having a single order. It is therefore probable that the world contains a plurality of souls and animate beings.[54] There now follow six arguments based on the notion of "soul."[55] First, the world-soul is omnipresent, and self-identical. Therefore, it cannot be divided into parts. Second, since our souls can differ in their actions, opinions, affections, and conditions, they cannot exist as the same soul. Third, if the mind, which is part of my soul, were somehow a part of the world-soul, it would not have its own proper existence and its own proper action of turning toward itself in self-awareness, of surveying the world in thought, and of thinking of something above the world and its soul. Fourth, the human body is not a part of the world's body but

separate from it in its shape and its motion. Since the soul is superior to the body and the source of its shape and motion, *a fortiori* the human soul will not be part of the world-soul. Fifth, the world-soul endows the things that it makes with the exclusive characteristic of mobility. Since the human soul can resolve motion into rest and subject mobile things to immobility, it therefore cannot be part of the world-soul. Sixth, the mind, which is part of our soul, is *a certain* intellectual being. Therefore, it comes to be *simpliciter* from the same intellect from which the world-soul itself, which is also a kind of intellect, arises.[56]

In the same commentary, Ficino rejects various analogies proposed to explain the relation between the world-soul and individual souls,[57] these analogies being obviously designed to show how the latter can be *parts* of the former. Thus, certain "illegitimate" Platonists suggest that the world-soul can be divided into individual souls as a magnitude is divided into particles or a number into units. The argument against this is that the world-soul would perish by such a division. These Platonists also suggest that the world-soul is divided into individual souls as the whole warmth of the body is divided into the parts of warmth in the limbs. However, Ficino points out that the warmth is divided here only *per accidens*, whereas soul is present in an indivisible way to body.[58] The illegitimate Platonists next suggest that the world-soul is divided into individual souls as a complete science is divided into its concepts. The argument against this is that either the complete science is nothing beyond its concepts and the soul similarly not communal or else the complete science is something beyond its concepts and the soul similarly not adapted to the world. Finally, these Platonists suggest that the world-soul is divided into individual souls as the soul in our entire body is divided into soul as it is in the hand or the foot. Ficino counters that such a distribution fails to mark the distinction between the substantial omnipresence of soul and its localization through the instrumentality of bodily

organs. Later in the same commentary, Ficino rejects further analogies proposed by unidentified sources to explain the relation between the world-soul and individual souls.[59] These analogies seem designed to show how the latter can be at the same time *parts* and *effects* of the former in the sense of being multiplications of its unitary potency: an idea congenial to pagan Platonists in general, who hold an emanative view of causation. According to these unidentified sources, the relation between the world-soul and individual souls can be compared to the situation where the single light of the sun is distributed through the windows of many houses and then released back to its self-identity.[60] The argument against this is that visible light is dependent in the manner of an accident and does not maintain its own subsistence. According to the same sources, the relation between the world-soul and individual souls can be compared to the situation where the single root of a plant is distributed through the various stems propagated from it. However, Ficino points out that in this case an individual intellectual soul would cease to be after death when resolved back into the world-soul.

In the arguments considered so far, Ficino's approach to the main question under discussion has consisted of a negative response to certain positions. His positive view regarding the unity or plurality of souls can be determined on the basis of the following three passages:

(A) In the commentary on *Ennead* 4.9,[61] Plotinus is cited—here presumably with Ficino's approval—for rejecting the doctrines (1) that there is a universal soul that is one numerically in all things and (2) that there is a universal soul that is one specifically but multiple numerically in all things. His reasoning regarding the second point as reported by Ficino—that soul is not a continuous thing that can be distributed into parts, and that the multiplicity cannot be related to the unity as white qualities in things are related to whiteness or impressions in wax to a seal—shows that

universal soul is here being treated as a species in the Aristotelian rather than in the Platonic sense. Ficino next explains that "all souls are nonetheless a single soul in a certain sense" (*omnes tamen quodammodo una sunt anima*) first, because there presides over all things and there is present in all things "a single universal Idea of soul" (*una animarum generalis idea*); second, because each individual soul is "omniform" (*omniformis*)—this enables every soul to converge with every other soul in terms of its intellectual content, although each soul remains distinct in grasping that content in a different way—; third, because all souls can be in the same point without confusion as can lights and the images of colors.[62] Ficino's final point, that he has demonstrated sufficiently in the *Theology*, that there is not a single "soul or mind" (*anima aut mens*) in all things connects with the arguments of two further passages.

(B) A passage in the commentary on *Ennead* 4.1–2[63] explicitly treats the problem of the unity and multiplicity of soul as identical with that of the unity and multiplicity of *intellectual* soul.[64] Here, Ficino notes that intellect *simpliciter*—the principle that is most frequently called the divine intellect in his works—is everywhere as a whole, and that intellectual souls are "in it not only through the Ideas but also through their proper existences, so to speak" (*in eo non solum per ideas verum etiam per proprias* [*ut ita dixerim*] *exsistentias*): that is, through the intellectual faculty proper to them even while they are in the embodied state. Thus, souls within our world may be distinct in position according to their bodies but in the same place in the higher realm according to their intellects. In fact, the intellectual souls are "in" the divine intellect in the same way that radii can be projected to the circumference of a circle without departing from its center and the rays of the sun can attain to earthly things without leaving their source.

(C) A passage in the commentary on *Ennead* 4.3[65] again identifies the problem of the unity and multiplicity of soul with that of the unity and multiplicity of intellectual soul. Substances come

forth from the primal intellect in the first place as intellectual and in the second place as psychic. In the latter case one may also speak of many souls as "proceeding from the single ideal soul" (*prodire . . . ex una ideali anima*). Even though these souls represent distinct substances, they exhibit a certain unity among themselves in three respects: first, because they are "subject to the same Idea" (*sub eadem idea*); second, because they are minimally distinct with respect to places and times; and third, because they are formed by the same divine intellect "through their intellectual summits" (*per intellectuales suas . . . apices*) and everlastingly contemplate that same divine intellect. Ficino here passes over the further point that all the distinct souls exhibit a certain unity among themselves in contributing naturally to the end of universal providence.

Even though some of their details remain obscure, these three passages are clearly intended to prove the case that there is one world-soul *together with* a plurality of souls *existing independently of it*. At the beginning of the commentary on *Ennead* 4.9,[66] there is a brief summary of some further arguments to the same effect. The first argument is that the world must be a perfect and unitary composite and that individual souls must come together in an order. Neither would be possible without the presence of a single world-soul and a plurality of other souls. There follow three further arguments proving that, if there were not a plurality of independently existing souls,[67] (1) the affection, passion, and action of one animate being would immediately lead to all the affections, passions, and actions in the universe; (2) the mutual love of human beings signifying the union of souls would not be complemented by the mutual hatred indicated by the soul's diversity; and (3) magical seizure would not take place through the assemblage of disparate items as shown elsewhere. The final argument is that the world results from the unfolding of a single formal reason-principle into plurality. If the formal reason-principle of a nature, quality, or body can pass into many distinct natures, qualities, and bodies,[68]

so *a fortiori* must that formal reason-principle which governs souls that are superior to such things be similarly disposed.[69]

Having reached this point, we may perhaps state the main conclusions of Ficino's discussion of the unity and multiplicity of soul to be the following. Although it may be a unity as a purely abstract or notional genus, "soul" is not a unity in the metaphysically real sense. It is necessary to distinguish at least three types of soul: the Idea of soul in the divine intellect, the world-soul, and the other souls. There is a kind of metaphysically real unity underlying souls in the sense that they all depend on the unfolding of a formal reason-principle which is inherently one-and-many from the *Idea* of soul. Moreover, we may speak of soul as a kind of "unity" in that the world-soul and the other souls (*a*) depend on the single Idea of soul, (*b*) are characterized by omniformity, and (*c*) are "in" the divine intellect through the act of contemplation. However, we may not think of the relation between the other souls and the world-soul (and *a fortiori* the Idea of soul) in the sense of division of a spatial quantity or of multiplication of a unified potency of *soul*.[70]

As noted at the beginning of this section, Ficino in the present commentary announced his intention of refuting monopsychism "together with Plotinus" (*una cum Plotino*) since he had elsewhere already criticized this theory in the form advocated by Averroes. Indeed, he had explained in another of his Plotinian commentaries[71] that the position one should adopt regarding the unicity of soul depends on that taken regarding the unicity of intellect, given that intellect is the form of soul as soul is the form of the animate being and life the form of the body. At that point he argued that one must hold to the fundamental assumption that there is a single divine intellect and a multiplicity of intellects "inborn in souls" (*animabus ingeniti*). Concerning the divine intellect, one can say that it is "communal" (*communis*) to the extent that it is undivided and omnipresent, and "particular" (*proprius*) to the extent that it is

received by individual souls and in individual and particular ways. Concerning the multiple intellects, which are forms in souls, as both inborn in and presiding over the latter, it cannot be said that they are communal. However, it can be said that they are "a unity" (*unum*) [*a*] "according to the intellectual being" (*secundum esse intellectuale*) and [*b*] as "rendered intelligizing in act by the one light of that mind" (*redditum actu intelligens ab uno mentis illius lumine*).[72] This situation is explained by means of an analogy in which the *divine* intellect — presumably, the intellectual being and the mind just mentioned — is compared to the sun as source of visual rays and the multiple intellects to "the visual rays naturally implanted in the eyes" (*visuales radii oculis naturaliter insiti*). Ficino adds that, if we accept this interpretation, we can (1) agree with Alexander who "assigns to us besides the one intellect also a multiplicity of intellects" (*praeter unum intellectum multos quoque nobis attribuit*) while disagreeing with his view that these multiple intellects are mortal, and (2) disagree with Averroes who assigns a single intellect to us while agreeing with his view that "there is an immortal gift from the total intelligence" (*immortale omnis intelligentiae munus*). Moreover, by taking these positions one will have "the complete doctrine of our Plotinus" (*integra Plotini nostri sententia*).[73]

When judged entirely on the basis of these arguments presented in the first eight chapters of *Ennead* 4.3, Ficino's commentary on those chapters, and a few other passages from the commentary, the doctrines of Plotinus and Ficino concerning the unity or multiplicity of soul seem to be in agreement in terms of the general approach, although there are differences in terms of certain details. Plotinus and Ficino agree (1) that there is a universal soul that must be distinguished from the world-soul and other souls, (2) that the world-soul and the other souls all derive immediately from the universal soul. They disagree in that (*i*) for Plotinus, the universal soul is a third principle subsequent to universal intellect, whereas for Ficino, the universal soul is identical with the Idea of

soul in the divine mind; in that (*ii*) for Plotinus, there is an emanative continuity between the universal soul and subsequent souls, whereas for Ficino, a metaphysical distinction between creative and created being underlies the relation between the universal soul or Idea of soul and subsequent souls;[74] in that (*iii*) for Plotinus, the multiplicity of souls depends on a multiplicity of intellects contained within the universal intellect, whereas for Ficino, the multiplicity of souls depends on a multiplicity of intellects contained within the individual souls themselves.[75]

Of course, it is a fact of major importance that Ficino's interpretation of Plotinus' position with respect to the unity and multiplicity of soul allows him to bring that position into line with the orthodox Christian psychological doctrine, at least as understood since the time of Augustine. It is well known that Augustine had touched upon the notion of a unitary source-soul in his *On the Immortality of the Soul*, criticized it in *On the Quantity of the Soul*, and thereafter avoided it, probably on the grounds that the monopsychic metaphysical hypothesis was incompatible with the notion of individual moral responsibility.[76] Criticism of the doctrine along these lines runs like a thread through the medieval tradition of glossing works, such as Plato's *Timaeus*, Boethius' *On the Consolation of Philosophy*, and Macrobius' *Commentary on the Dream of Scipio*, that reported the doctrine, although it was partially rehabilitated with respect to philosophy of nature by twelfth-century French humanist philosophers. Indeed, the Averroistic doctrine of the unicity of intellect that was attacked by Latin scholastic writers such as Albert the Great and Thomas Aquinas should be seen to a large extent as a revival in a more overtly Aristotelian context of this older problem of Platonic philosophy.[77]

I.2.2.2 RATIO AND TWO-DIRECTIONAL CAUSALITY

If Ficino must choose carefully among various possible interpretations of Plotinus in order to avoid collision with Christian dogma

concerning the unity or multiplicity of soul, the same is true albeit to a lesser extent regarding the notion of "two-directional causality" in relation to the human soul. This second problem can be said to stem from an ambiguity in Plotinus' discussions in the *Fourth Ennead* as to whether the lower part of human soul is caused essentially by the higher part of the human soul, or by the world-soul, or by both.[78] Now, for Ficino, the necessity of maintaining the fundamental multiplicity of souls at the intellectual level in order to comply with the demands of Christian dogma is not complemented by any requirement to preserve the souls' fundamental multiplicity at the vegetative level. This point is stated almost in so many words near the beginning of his commentary on *Ennead* 4.9.[79] Therefore at least in principle, there is no reason why Ficino should be too concerned about choosing between the alternative solutions to the problem of the generation of the lower soul. Moreover for him, the problem is almost resolved in advance given two of his general philosophical assumptions. These are first, that primary causality is removed from intermediate principles to the first principle[80] and second, that the increased role of the world's reason-principle as instrument and analogue of divine action subsumes the causality of both the world-soul and the human soul.[81] Thus, two-directional causality with all its doubleness can easily be integrated within the sphere of God's action through the universal reason-principle.

In one passage, Ficino summarizes Plato's doctrine concerning the causal or productive relations between the divine craftsman, the world-soul, human souls, and bodies, taking his starting point from quotation of the *Philebus*.[82] Here, he states that the reason why "the intellect which is craftsman of the world" (*intellectus mundi faber*) in planning to give a soul to human beings must also have given a soul to the world was that the world-soul "was destined to prepare, through the universal emanation, seminal matters of animate beings for the reception of souls proper to them from all

quarters of the world" (*per universalem influxum praeparatura erat materias animalium seminales ad animas proprias undecumque suscipiendas*).[83] He continues by observing that the human body receives its intellectual soul from the craftsman of the world and its sensitive soul "for the most part" (*plurimum*) from its intellective soul but also from the world-soul "as a primary factor contributing to this" (*conferente ad hoc imprimis*). After some remarks about the descent of souls into bodies and their disengagement from the latter, he then notes that the part of us that resists bodily urges derives from somewhere higher than the world, whereas the life that is enslaved to bodily impulses "can depend also" (*etiam . . . posse pendere*) on the world-soul. In sum, the passage informs us that (1) the divine intellect produces the world-soul and the intellectual part of the human soul; (2) the world-soul produces the seminal nature and the life following the body and is coproducer of the sensitive part of the human soul, and produces by means of a universal emanation;[84] and (3) the intellectual part of the human soul produces the sensitive part.

The schematism with respect to causality and especially the notions of shared causality and two-directional causality are elaborated in more detail a few paragraphs later, where the authority is not so much Plato as the "Pythagoreans" as reported by Sextus Empiricus.[85] Here, Ficino argues that the world-soul "infuses by a general inspiration" (*universali instinctu infundere*) individual souls into things that have been produced, and that a general vegetative power coming from the world-soul "prepares" (*praeparet*) matters proper to living beings, "preserves" (*conservet*) them at a specific time, and "collects" (*conciliet*) them into a unity.[86] This unifying force is identifiable with "spirit" (*spiritus*). With this spirit "flourishing in the common domain" (*vigens communiter*), the rational soul is added to the embryo "in the human sphere" (*in nobis*). Moreover, the human soul "in subordination to this general light" (*sub hoc communi lumine*) thereupon "diffuses the light of its proper

and peculiar life" (*lumen propriae peculiarisque vitae diffundit*) into the body. Now we may assume that the craftsman of the world or intellect — not explicitly mentioned here — is responsible for any creative processes not assigned explicitly to the world-soul, its vegetative power here equivalent to spirit, or the human soul. The passage therefore shows Ficino's complete theory to be that (1) the divine intellect produces the world-soul, the other souls, the proper lives of living beings, and the rational soul for the embryo; (2) the world-soul infuses souls into generated things; (3) the vegetative power or spirit prepares, preserves, and unifies the matters underlying living beings and makes the entry of the rational soul into the embryo possible; and (4) the rational soul in collaboration with the vegetative power diffuses its life into the embryo.

1.2.2.3 THE "DESCENT" OF SOUL

The notion of a "descent" of the human soul represents another point at which Ficino must choose carefully between various possible interpretations of Plotinus in order to avoid a collision with Christian dogma.[87] This problem also can be said to stem from an ambiguity in Plotinus' discussions in the *Fourth Ennead*, although it might be more correct to speak here of an excess of subtlety rather than of an ambiguity. In one passage, Ficino states that the soul, although it is divine and often turns toward divine things even in the current life, is the last of divine things and comes into the body "through an inclination of a natural kind (*voluntate . . . scilicet naturali*),[88] in addition "by a certain choice" (*electione quadam*), and also "by necessity" (*necessitate*). He adds that it is necessary according to divine law that souls so affected and making such choices should "instantly" (*e vestigio*) reach a point — the exercise of the lower powers of the soul with respect to the experience of evil — where they come "willingly" (*sponte*) as though to a good while in the meantime falling "unwillingly" (*non sponte*) into an evil.[89] This

passage can be said to encapsulate Ficino's entire reading of the Plotinian theory of the soul's descent, for here we learn that the spatial motions of descent associated with the doctrine of transmigration derived from Plato's *Phaedrus* and *Timaeus* are to be understood primarily as allegorical descriptions of the dynamic relation of the soul to the body,[90] that this dynamic relation to the body[91] is based on a natural instinct toward bodily preoccupation, which can be intensified or counteracted by deliberate acts of will,[92] and that the entire instinctual and volitional relation to embodiment is comprehended within a necessity in the sense of a providential design regarding the soul's encounter with evil that we know from other Ficinian texts to derive from the higher or legislative reason-principle.[93]

Most of the aspects of the soul's descent stated briefly and abstractly in the text cited above are explained in more detail in a passage where Ficino expands on Plotinus' allusive introduction of the mythological account of the child Dionysus enjoying his reflection in a mirror as an allegory for the souls in the intelligible sphere being attracted by the sensible world.[94] The commentator explains that Dionysus represents the natural phase or vegetative power of the world-soul — equivalent to the lower reason-principle of the world[95] —, that the souls "look down at" (*prospicere*) the multiplicity of reason-principles contained in nature — characterized mythologically as the limbs of Dionysus divided by the Titans, who allegorically represent the daemons presiding over geniture —, and that the souls "fall in love with" (*amare*) those reason-principles and consequently descend into the lower world.[96] Given that Jupiter, who mythologically represents the intellect of the world-soul — here equivalent to the higher reason-principle of the world[97] — observes the play of Dionysus with the mirror,[98] the soul's relation to the body in terms of a natural instinct intensified by choice described allegorically here must also be situated within the realm of necessity. At any rate, Ficino goes on to parse the al-

legory by explaining that the souls in the intelligible sphere can be said to look down on the multiplicity of reason-principles with a kind of direct gaze into nature and then with a deflected gaze into matter because the soul's imagination turns itself toward the lower and then its reason turns itself away from intellect, that this "gazing" (*aspiciendum*) is also a "loving" (*amandum*), and that a love of this kind is the initiating cause not only of the descent to the lower but also of the remaining below after the descent.[99]

In the passages considered above, Ficino has interpreted the spatial motion of descent associated with the doctrine of transmigration as a figurative description of the dynamic relation of the soul to the body, which is founded on an instinctive tendency intensified by a subsequent act of volition. Such an interpretation can be contrasted with that occurring in one passage of the commentary on the *Fourth Ennead* where the descent of the soul is described as resulting *initially* from a willful act. Here, Ficino reports Porphyry's teaching that the soul falls toward the lower realm when, having been accustomed to bring out intellectual concepts, it now bears imaginary ones and when a vegetative act comes forth from the roots of the soul in the manner of a sprout that, when now extended through the body, cements itself to that body. Now if one accepts the view of Dionysius, Basil, and other Greek theologians that the daemons were ensouled beings, then the "fall" (*lapsus*) of souls described by Porphyry turns out to be similar to the "fall of daemons" (*casus daemonum*) mentioned by the Hebrews: that is, something produced by a defect of intelligence or will from which a mindless concupiscence will follow.[100] Ficino does not say precisely why he finds the Porphyrian approach to the interpretation of the soul's descent unsatisfactory. However, it would clearly represent a kind of Gnostic view of the reasons for the soul's embodiment and also of the relations between the higher and lower functions of the soul that is incompatible not only with Plotinus but with Ficino's more optimistic Augustinian psychology.

1.2.3 THE TRINITARIAN ANALOGUE

Returning to the notion of concord and discord between the Christian and non-Christian sources of his thought grounded by the deep structure of harmonic theory, we have finally to take account of the concordant element. In the case of the *Third Ennead*, the concord between Plotinus and Christianity emerges most fully in connection with the intimations of the Trinity that Ficino detects in Plotinus' account of the double derivation of the universal reason-principle and its characterization as spirit-and-word in *Ennead* 3.2 and also in that of the relation between the first Venus and the second Venus in *Ennead* 3.5.[101] Although we do not find any similarly overt presentations of trinitarian analogues in the commentary on the *Fourth Ennead*, the reader is undoubtedly meant to assume that the threefold structure of first intellect, intellectual soul, and reason-principle stated in *Ennead* 3 primarily as applicable to the world-soul is assumed to be applicable to the human soul as a threefold structure of intellect, intellectual soul (or rational soul or first soul), and animation (or vitalization or second soul) in *Ennead* 4.[102] The conceptual underpinning of this further application can perhaps be disclosed through a comparison of various passages elsewhere in the commentary on Plotinus. Thus, when Ficino states (*a*) in his commentary on *Ennead* 2.3 that each human being and the world as a whole consists of an intellectual soul separate from body and a life emanating from it to the body,[103] (*b*) in his commentary on *Ennead* 1.1 that there is an intellect inborn in each human soul that is a unity according to its illuminative relation to the divine intellect,[104] he is clearly recalling the statement (*c*) in his commentaries on *Ennead* 3.2 and 3.5 that there is a threefold structure of first intellect, intellectual soul, and reason-principle in the world-soul.[105] Now the second and third members of the threefold structure as stated in *c* are clearly assumed under *a*, and the first member of the threefold structure as

stated in *c* is clearly assumed under *b*. The difference in terminology associated with the third member of the threefold structure suggested by a comparison of statements *a* and *c* does not produce a problem. This is because both the reason-principle that is the third member of the threefold structure stated in *c* and the principle emanating from the intellectual soul under *a* embody the property of "life."[106]

Apart from the positing of the familiar trinitarian analogue as a general assumption underlying the relation between the world-soul and the human soul, perhaps the most overt application of trinitarian thinking in a particular instance in the commentary on the *Fourth Ennead* occurs in a passage where the relation between sensation and light is considered against the background of a further relation between the macrocosm and the microcosm.[107] Here, Ficino argues that the light employed in the process of vision is an image of the celestial light, and that the latter is itself an act of the celestial soul. Just as from the imagination of the human soul a "word" is sent forth as an act having the three components of air, motion, and meaning, so from the intellectual light of the celestial soul is poured forth an act having the three components of light, heat, and a hidden power.[108] The references to the "word" (*verbum*) and to the "intellectual light of the celestial soul" (*lux intellectualis caelestis animae*) suggest that Ficino is thinking of the third and second terms, respectively, in his usual trinitarian analogue.[109] In this case, the implicit first term would be the intellectual light *as such* or the intellectual light *in intellect*.

1.3 Intertexts

As we have reported elsewhere, the chronology of Ficino's work of commenting on Plotinus is sufficiently well established to show that he mostly followed the Porphyrian order of the treatises in writing his own exposition and that he digressed from this work

for two years after commenting on *Ennead* 3.2. This digression took the form of a project of translating and/or commenting briefly on works of various post-Plotinian thinkers, including Porphyry's *Orientations to the Intelligibles*, Iamblichus' *On the Mysteries*, Synesius' *On Dreams*, and Priscian of Lydia's *Interpretation of Theophrastus*.[110] Now, the intertextual preoccupation facilitated by this work of translation already apparent in Ficino's commentary on *Ennead* 3 is perhaps even more apparent in that on *Ennead* 4, given that the psychological, theurgic, and pneumatological subject matter of the works translated has especially provocative hermeneutic relations with the topics explored by Plotinus at this point. In the next three sections of this "Analytical Study," we will attempt to explore and evaluate the Florentine's intertextual strategy with reference to the writings of the later ancient Platonists and especially to those of Iamblichus, which seem to have a uniquely catalytic function with respect to Plotinian commentary.

1.3.1 SELF-CITATION

But before turning to his abundant citations of later ancient Platonists, it is worth noting that Ficino occasionally refers to his own earlier writings. When discussing Plotinus' remark that a magician may somehow ensnare daemons, he notes that he has examined the power of imagination, enchantments, and magic in the third book of his *On Life* and contrasted such practices—to be condemned—with the practice—to be recommended—of taking living drafts from the vitality of the world's body.[111] There are a few scattered references to the *Platonic Theology* mostly in connection with basic ideas concerning the number,[112] median status,[113] and immortality[114] of the soul,[115] which he does not wish to restate in detail in the Plotinus commentary, and one reference to *On Love* again in connection with the power of imagination, enchantments, and magic.[116] There are three references to his commentary on Priscian of Lydia's *Interpretation of Theophrastus* in connection with

sensation. One states that the forms of sensible objects are not imprinted in the soul as though by a seal in wax,[117] while two others argue that sensation occurs when spirit makes a proportion between the soul and the sensible object and when the communal life of the world attunes the soul to that object.[118]

1.3.2 Iamblichus as Source

The cross-references to the commentary on Priscian of Lydia are of particular importance in disclosing undoubtedly the most important intertextual feature of Ficino's commentary on *Ennead* 4: its dependence on Iamblichus, since Priscian declares himself to be following Iamblichus in several passages of the *Metaphrasis*, and Ficino seems to have concluded that the psychological doctrine of this treatise as a whole is Iamblichean.[119] If one combines the facts that Ficino decided to translate and comment upon Priscian's "Iamblichean" treatise while working on the Plotinus project, that by far the largest number of explicit citations of an author other than Plotinus in the commentary on *Ennead* 4 is to Iamblichus, that many of the overtly non-Plotinian ideas in this part of the Plotinus commentary are reminiscent of Iamblichus' thought, and that Ficino also found it useful to produce a Latin paraphrase of Iamblichus' *On the Mysteries* while working on the Plotinus project, then it becomes apparent that Iamblichus is a major guiding influence in much of Ficino's reading of Plotinus.[120]

Taking them simply according to their order of appearance in his commentary, we find Ficino explicitly citing Iamblichus either alone or in company with other Platonists for the following doctrines: (1) that the soul can exist at some point totally outside body;[121] (2) that our intellect can remain blessed in the divine sphere while our rational power is cast down to earth;[122] (3) that the spheres of the world have intellects inseparably joined to the divine mind, and that they receive intellectual gifts and divine gifts from the Ideas;[123] (4) that souls could be forever in the higher

realm through a certain choice;[124] (5) that soul in sensing stirs up through a spiritual form sensible forms hidden within it;[125] (6) that divine souls and the world-soul although omnipresent display their actions more in a certain place;[126] (7) that certain Platonists believe that we can connect our mind and spirit via prayer in order to receive emanations from the stars, and that some of these thinkers consequently worship at least the sun;[127] (8) that our prayers are anticipated and fulfilled by the celestial gods although we pray freely in the meantime, and that there are no concomitant changes in the divine will or order;[128] (9) that goods cannot be drawn off by quasi-magical attraction from the intellectual souls of spheres, and that will and choice are present there although this choice is not something persuaded by lower things but is of itself determined to imitate the supreme God and provide for subsequent things;[129] (10) that men even surpassing intellectual things also refer certain corporeal and external goods to the favor of intermediate spirits obeying the higher ones, and believe that they can avoid evils by acting through the protection of those spirits;[130] (11) that we have through God and angels a position of authority in opposition to lower deceiving spirits, and that we should avoid the superstition of flattering the deceiving daemons with choice enticements;[131] (12) that sensation is an activity in which we enliven the spirit and put forth the inborn forms of sensible things;[132] and (13) that souls who sin more grievously will be harassed by daemons in the afterlife.[133]

Now, all the main conceptual structures that we have already discovered as representing the deep structure of Ficinian thought in this part of his Plotinus commentary, or will examine below as constituting elaborations on the basis of that deep structure, have their counterparts somewhere in Iamblichus' writings.[134] It is therefore quite easy to demonstrate the importance of the notions of mediation, proportion, attraction, and attunement for Iamblichus using examples drawn from *On the Mysteries* and from *On the*

Soul: a work fragments or *testimonia* of which Ficino would have found in Priscian of Lydia's *Interpretation of Theophrastus*[135] and perhaps also in John Stobaeus' *Anthology.*[136]

The notions of mediation and proportion play an enormous role in the argument of *On the Mysteries* and especially in the first two books. At one point "Abamon"[137] answers Porphyry's question about the relation between the totally incorporeal gods and those possessing a celestial body by arguing that there is a unification among the gods based on their threefold structure of "beginning, middle, and end" (ἀρχή . . . μέσα . . . τέλη).[138] He has already explained that between the orders of gods and souls considered as extremes there is a fourfold order including two means: the order of heroes immediately above that of souls and the order of daemons distantly dependent on that of gods; that these two "means" (μέσα) produce a continuity and communion between the highest and the lowest, a "proportionate blending" (σύμμιξις σύμμετρος) of everything, and an equilibrium of descent and ascent between superior and inferior;[139] and that from the characteristics of the means one can deduce those of the extremes contiguous with them, the higher extreme being found to achieve its effects indivisibly and simultaneously, the lower divisibly and successively, and so forth.[140] Later in the text Iamblichus proposes a threefold division of the human sphere analogous to those of the divine and spiritual realms into men subject to the domination of nature, men employing an intellectual power beyond nature (the theurgists), and men "in the middle area" (περὶ τὰ μέσα) between nature and pure mind.[141] He also argues for a triple division of our visions of the higher orders of being, these visions revealing first, the order maintained by the objects of vision—the gods, archangels, angels, daemons, archons, and souls in a gradation of leadership; second, their functions of bestowing goods and administering punishment; and third, the regions to which they are assigned—celestial, aerial, and earthly—each of which is subdivided into beginning,

middle, and end.[142] Finally, one should note Iamblichus' obsession with mediative structure in the *De Anima*, where he insists — against what he sees as the wavering position of Plotinus and Amelius — that soul is a distinct level of being subsequent to intellect and "the middle term" (τὸ μέσον) of the indivisible and divisible and of the incorporeal and corporeal realms.[143]

Now, just as the static notion of mediation was complemented by the dynamic notion of attraction in Ficino's thought, so also was the static notion of proportion complemented there by the dynamic notion of attunement. We find these further aspects of the deep structure equally present in Iamblichus' works even if the terminology differs somewhat from Ficino's. Thus, in *On the Mysteries* the ancient Platonist argues that it is because the world is a single animate being in which there is a "force of cohesion," a "cause of blending," and a "tension extending" (συναγωγόν . . . τῆς συγκράσεως αἴτιον . . . διατεῖνον) through the totality that the gods are able to "hear" our prayers.[144] In the *De Anima* he states not only that "harmony" (ἁρμονία) can be understood as applying to the soul as a mean term of beings, as residing in the essentially preexisting reason-principles, and as interwoven in the world,[145] but that the entire cyclic process of souls between birth, death, and rebirth is determined according to a single "symmetry" (συμμετρία) akin to the Perfect Number.[146]

In addition to these parallels between Iamblichus and Ficino, we will discover in our further study of the present commentary many deviations from Plotinian thought — some more subtle than others — that seem to be in line with Iamblichus' own departures from the earlier Platonic tradition. In order to understand these tendencies in the Ficinian commentary without complicating our future analyses with a layer of *Quellenforschung*, it will be useful here to note Iamblichus' main teachings regarding the higher and the lower souls, the notions of *pneuma* and of cosmic sympathy, and the practice of theurgy.

Plotinus' distinction between a higher soul independent of body and a lower soul that combines with the latter to form the "animate being" takes on a more religious tone in Iamblichus. The author of *On the Mysteries*[147] reports the Hermetic doctrine that a human being has two souls: one deriving from the first intelligible and participating in the power of the Craftsman, the other contributed to us from the circuit of the heavenly bodies.[148] He also notes that daemons are assigned to preside not only over the higher souls but also over the combination of the lower soul with the body,[149] and that the distinction between the higher and the lower souls is most apparent when on the death of the solid body we are elevated to intellect and join the incorporeal gods,[150] and when with sleep loosening the chains binding us to that body we pursue a life free of generation.[151] However, the most important aspect of the twofold division of soul in *On the Mysteries* is its connection with a double mode of worship and sacrifice, the higher being simple, incorporeal, and purified and the other filled with bodies and bodily concerns.[152] It is exclusively the higher worship — the *theurgic* accomplished not by the soul's own activities but by the gods themselves[153] — that produces detachment from the bonds of fatal necessity resulting from the combination of the lower soul with the body.[154]

In his *On the Soul*, Iamblichus notes that there are different views concerning the relation between soul and body and that although some thinkers such as the majority of the Platonists join soul immediately to the organic body, others posit celestial, aetherial, and pneumatic wrappings as surrounding the intellectual life in order to serve as its vehicles, bring it into due proportion with the solid body, and join it to the latter with certain mediating and communal bonds.[155] The second view is obviously the one to which Iamblichus subscribes, and in his *On the Mysteries* there are extensive developments of the idea that there is a pneumatic sub-

stance between soul and body that joins the lower soul to the solid body or the higher soul to the animate compound or both.[156] This *pneuma* embodies the relation between macrocosm and microcosm in that it is diffused by the gods and breathed in by lower beings.[157] Although it has a nature in transition between something exhibiting the purity of aetherial fire when attached to a purer soul and something weighed down by material accretions when attached to a soul tending downward,[158] its predominantly luciform character is revealed when in the course of theurgic operations it illuminates the vehicle of the officiant and takes possession of the latter's imaginative power in order to reveal gods, heroes, and daemons.[159]

The notion of cosmic sympathy,[160] as already adapted from Stoic sources by Plotinus, especially in composing *Ennead* 4.4, plays an elevated role in Iamblichus' thought. According to the latter, the universe is a single living thing to such an extent that its individual parts exercise their powers not simply as parts but also as identical with the whole.[161] Moreover, the parts of the universe exercise their powers between distant things as though they were contiguous,[162] the basis of this exercise being similarity between the parts[163] or the fitness of the parts serving as patients to those serving as agents.[164] Sacrifices that exploit this structure correspond to a lower form of theurgic practice, although they reflect the form of higher theurgy by analogy.[165] In fact, there are three levels of sacrifice: one operating on the level of nature and exploiting cosmic sympathy, one operating on the level of daemons, and one operating on the level of demiurgic powers and exploiting their mediative structure.[166] Given the prevailing metaphysical assumptions, it is the lowest level of sacrifice that can be diverted toward maleficent ends.[167]

The *On the Mysteries* provides us with enough information to construct a technical definition or description of the highest level

of sacrifice.[168] According to Iamblichus, the ancient Egyptian priests believed that we should not just seek knowledge of the divine but ascend to the divine Craftsman through "sacred theurgy" (ἱερατικὴ θεουργία):[169] that is to say, theory must be supplemented by practice. This ascent has various stages: first, elevation to the daemon governing our soul's embodiment, and then ascension to a god controlling that daemon;[170] or first, purification of the soul, and then preparation of our reasoning-principle for participation and vision of the Good.[171] Viewed from the inside, theurgy is an activity of the divine sphere itself in the human practitioner[172] and involves a unification transcending intellection;[173] viewed from the outside, it imitates by ritual actions the order of the gods both intelligible and celestial by exploiting certain "tokens" (συνθήματα) or "symbols" (σύμβολα) implanted in the theurgist's soul by the divine Craftsman.[174] Iamblichus informs us that prayer is the element bringing completion to the theurgic process.[175] He divides prayer into three levels, of which a first, illuminative level produces contact with the divine, a second, progressive level establishes communion on the intellectual level, and a third, perfective level produces ineffable union with the gods. He notes that these prayers should be inserted at the beginning, in the middle, and at the end of the ritual, presumably in accordance with their level of elevation.[176]

The employment of the tokens or symbols in the theurgic ritual consists of the collecting together of these items in order to form a "receptacle" (ὑποδοχή) for the infusion of divine power.[177] Apparently, there are three levels of symbols corresponding to the three levels of sacrifice mentioned above: that is, material symbols such as animals, plants, minerals, and aromas[178] for theurgy operating on the natural level, intermediate symbols of a visible or audible nature such as the hieroglyphs[179] or certain chants[180]—together with the famous barbaric names[181]—for theurgy operating on the daemonic level, and presumably immaterial symbols of some kind

for theurgy operating on the demiurgic level.[182] The essentially *symbolic* character of the operations envisaged by Iamblichus should be underlined. Thus, even on the lowest level it is clearly a question of assimilating the external (physical) collection of tokens or symbols to its internal (psychic) counterpart[183] rather than of producing chemical operations of the medical or alchemical variety.[184]

The fact that we have already found some evidence, and will shortly find more, of Ficino's silent absorption of Iamblichean ideas into his commentary on *Ennead* 4 does not mean that the influence of other post-Plotinian thinkers should be ignored. One such thinker — exploited quite extensively in Ficino's commentary on *Ennead* 3 and also in his commentaries on the *Timaeus* and *Parmenides* of Plato — is Proclus, and he is cited on three occasions in the Ficinian commentary on *Ennead* 4: for the doctrine that the human soul always remains attached to some kind of body,[185] for his criticism of the Iamblichean notion that our intellect can remain blessed in the divine sphere while our rational power is cast down to earth,[186] and for the idea that the number of alternations of movement on the part of individual souls is not infinite.[187] Nevertheless, Iamblichus seems to be more important than Proclus in Ficino's commentary on *Ennead* 4, probably because of the psychotheurgic preoccupations, which the Florentine deems to be central to this segment of Plotinus' corpus and which can be reinforced on the basis of Iamblichus' *On the Mysteries* but not on that of any extant work of Proclus with the exception of the brief extract entitled *De Sacrificio et Magia* in Ficino's Latin translation.[188]

1.3.3 IAMBLICHUS AS INTERTEXTUAL NUCLEUS

Indeed, another reason for Ficino's resort to Iamblichus as a privileged authority is that the latter functions as a unique kind of junction point for various intertextual trajectories and in particular for a kind of double relation to Hermetic or Egyptian doctrine in

one direction and to Dionysian Christian teachings in the other, which fits in perfectly with his general conception of the history of *pia philosophia*. Ficino had obviously noted that the *On the Mysteries* explicitly refers to specific ancient Egyptian or Hermetic teachings in many passages.[189] The theological teaching that there is a first god above the intelligible sphere, a second god (Ikton) corresponding to the Good and the monad of the intelligible sphere,[190] and a third god (Kmeph) corresponding to intellect proper or the divine Craftsman[191] would have caught Ficino's attention because of the similarity to ideas that he had detected in his reading of Plotinus. The same could be said of the theological teaching that the divine Craftsman's intellect is called Osiris with reference to the goods that it produces and the life containing the reason-principles, and called Isis with respect to its undescended purity.[192] Moreover, the psychological doctrine that there are two souls in a human being, one derived from the primary intelligible and also participating in the Craftsman's power, and one contributed to us from the celestial circuit,[193] has obvious Plotinian echoes. At the same time, the Florentine would have been conscious of the numerous parallels between *De Mysteriis* and the Dionysian corpus. The theurgic doctrine of Iamblichus' treatise works in broadly the same manner as does the *hierurgic* teaching of Dionysius' *On the Ecclesiastical Hierarchy*.[194] Iamblichus' complex organization of the higher world into orders of gods, archangels, angels, daemons, archons, and souls together with their assignment to the supervision of specific regions[195] parallels similar ideas in *On the Celestial Hierarchy*, as does his association of specific properties with the substance, power, and activity of each member of the various higher orders[196] as revealed through their appearance in theurgic visions.[197] Finally, the symbolic doctrine of Iamblichus' work has its obvious counterpart in the exegetical practice and sacramental teaching of both the Dionysian hierarchies.[198]

1.3.3.1 HERMES AND DIONYSIUS

In commenting on Plotinus' *Fourth Ennead*, Ficino quotes Hermes for the doctrine that nature and the worldly Jupiter are both male and female in explaining the idea that the masculine and feminine powers are conjoined in the universal nature but separated in other things,[199] and again for the doctrine that those who sin grievously are punished not only by a change from a happy to an unhappy life but by being harassed by daemons.[200] However, these quotations only hint at the extent of the possible intertextual connections between Hermes, Plotinus, and Iamblichus seen by Ficino, for in the third book of *On Life*,[201] the author explains at length how a wise man who knows what sort of matters can receive a particular emanation from the heavens and then assembles these matters when that emanation is dominant can thereby obtain celestial gifts and that Plotinus "imitates Hermes" (*Mercurium imitatus*) in using almost the same examples when he says that the ancient priests or *magi* used to capture in statues something divine and wonderful.[202] After inserting a reference to Iamblichus' criticism of the Egyptians for treating daemons not just as steppingstones but worshipping them,[203] he returns to Hermes "or rather to Plotinus" (*immo ad Plotinum*). He notes how Hermes reports that the priests received a certain power from the nature of the world and then mixed it in the statues,[204] and how Plotinus follows him, albeit thinking that these things are accomplished rather through the mediation of the world-soul, since this soul generates and moves the forms of natural things through certain seminal reason-principles implanted in it from the divine.

Ficino quotes Dionysius—also perhaps in the light of Iamblichean parallels—once in commenting on *Ennead* 4.[205] At this point, the Florentine is considering the relation between the notion of a quasi-spatial descent of the soul from the higher part of

the universe and that of the unfolding of the soul's own lower part, and argues that the Platonic doctrine of the fall of souls — presumably to be understood in both these senses — is similar to the doctrine of the fall of daemons mentioned by the Hebrews. He notes that the latter doctrine is also stated by Dionysius[206] who in this context seems to postulate daemons as ensouled beings. Moreover, if John Damascene's statements that only the lowest angels fell and that these lowest angels turned into ensouled beings are true, then the fall of souls described by the Platonists will indeed be very similar to the fall of daemons mentioned by the Hebrews and the Christians.

Now, if Iamblichus is for Ficino a kind of junction point for intertextual trajectories in the direction of Hermetic or Egyptian doctrine on the one hand and in that of Dionysian Christian teachings on the other, he also forms to an equivalent degree a nucleus for the presentation of the doctrines of other late ancient Platonists and Pythagoreans. In a text that Ficino certainly knew well, Augustine mentions the name of Iamblichus in a list of eminent recent Platonists[207] and also reports some of Porphyry's questions to the Egyptian priest Anebo,[208] the combination of these references indicating that the church father had at least perused the De Mysteriis — presumably in a Latin translation that is no longer extant — and was aware of the two great Platonists' debate there concerning theurgy. That Ficino does see Iamblichus particularly in connection with Porphyry and sometimes in association with other late ancient Platonists and Pythagoreans can be shown by examining a number of other passages in the commentary on the Fourth Ennead.[209]

1.3.3.2 PORPHYRY

Taking them simply according to their order of appearance in his commentary, we find Ficino explicitly citing Porphyry either alone

or in company with other Platonists for the following doctrines: (1) that the soul can exist at some point totally outside body;[210] (2) that our intellect cannot remain blessed in the divine sphere while our rational power is cast down to earth;[211] (3) that the fall of the soul begins from intellect, that higher things act according to a certain measure of their power, that as the intensity of a lower power's acting is increased so is the intensity of a higher power's acting remitted and vice versa, and that intellect acts according to the measure of its power;[212] (4) that souls could be forever in the higher realm through a certain choice;[213] (5) that divine souls and the world-soul although omnipresent display their actions more in a certain place;[214] (6) that goods cannot be drawn off by quasi-magical attraction from the intellectual souls of spheres, and that will and choice are present there, although this choice is not something persuaded by lower things but is of itself determined to imitate the supreme God and provide for subsequent things;[215] (7) that men even surpassing intellectual things also refer certain corporeal and external goods to the favor of intermediate spirits that obey the higher ones, and believe that they can avoid evils by acting through the protection of those spirits;[216] (8) that we have through God and angels a position of authority in opposition to lower deceiving spirits, and that we should avoid the superstition of flattering the deceiving daemons with choice enticements;[217] and (9) that the soul falls toward the lower world when it is barren in the manner of a field that has produced wheat for many years but eventually yields darnel. Here, instead of intellectual concepts, the soul now brings in imaginary ones, and a vegetative act comes forth from roots of soul.[218]

1.3.3.3 PLATONISTS AND PYTHAGOREANS

Ficino's references to Platonists can be divided into those in which he speaks simply of Platonists (or of *certain* Platonists) and those

in which he speaks of "illegitimate" Platonists. Although it is not easy to identify precisely which Platonists are being cited in these instances, it is possible that the Platonists *tout court* correspond to various groups mentioned in doxographical works—including Christian writings such as Eusebius' *Preparation of the Gospel*—, while the illegitimate Platonists correspond to unidentified readers of Plato whose positions are attacked in the *Enneads* themselves. At any rate, Ficino refers to Platonists for the notions that souls differ somehow in species from the beginning,[219] that souls are everlasting according to substance,[220] that the rational soul cannot become the form of beast,[221] that the sun alone among celestial bodies is worthy of worship,[222] and that the Good stands above the divine intellect, the divine intellect above the pure intellects, and the pure intellects above the intellectual souls.[223] Conversely, the illegitimate Platonists are associated by Ficino with the notions that human souls are parts of the world-soul.[224]

Ficino's references to Pythagoreans are derived from a variety of intermediate sources. At one point the topic is the general vegetative power coming from the world-soul, which prepares the matters proper to living beings and then brings them into a unity, and Ficino quotes Sextus Empiricus' report that the Pythagoreans identify this unity with a spirit infused into all things in the manner of a soul and bringing humans into accord with other living beings.[225] From Philostratus, the Florentine quotes Apollonius of Tyana's view that corporeal sacrifices should be offered to the worldly gods, a detached sacrifice to the superior gods, and a most detached one to the primal god.[226] In another passage, Ficino cites among various views regarding the causes of the soul's descent its impulses and affectivity, an inclination of a natural kind together with a certain choice, and the necessity of divine law, noting apparently on the basis of a doxography at the beginning of *Ennead* 4.8 that the teachings of Empedocles, Heraclitus, and Plato agree on this question.[227]

1.3.3.4 PERIPATETICS

Of course, there are certain points at which Ficino introduces into his commentary on the *Fourth Ennead* material from sources not necessarily associated with the intertextual nucleus of Iamblichean doctrine. Near the beginning of the commentary, he notes that the Aristotelian doctrine that soul is the actuality of body[228] and also that the Peripatetic doctrine that there are separate and conjoined movers of celestial bodies[229] can both be understood to agree with Plotinus' teaching that the soul as form is at the same time separable and inseparable from the body. It is broadly within the context of Aristotelianism that we should also place Ficino's references to Averroes' doctrine—which he consistently rejects throughout the commentary on the *Enneads*, as he had done earlier in the *Platonic Theology*—that there is a single soul or single intellect in all human beings,[230] and also his occasional references to Arabic and Jewish astrological writers. Thus, Haly Abenrudian—whose work was translated by Hugh of Santalla and printed in 1484—is cited for an anecdote about a boy who spoke on the day he was born;[231] Abraham ibn Ezra—whose works were translated by Pietro d'Abano and printed in 1507—is cited for the important doctrine that religious souls by submitting to the supercelestial God can acquire power to increase goods and diminish evils occurring through fate;[232] and Albumasar—whose *Introductorium Maius* was translated by Hermann of Carinthia and printed in 1489—is cited for his conclusions regarding the most efficacious times for prayer.[233]

1.3.4 ECCLESIASTICAL AUTHORITY

It is perhaps obvious by now that most of the non-Plotinian sources introduced into Ficino's commentary on the *Fourth Ennead* are pagan. The only exception to this was the passage cited from the pseudo-Dionysius together with Basil and John Damascene

dealing with the fall of the daemons—to which we might now add the single citation from Boethius' *On the Consolation of Philosophy* emphasizing the important doctrine that sensation is active in nature.[234] Ficino was naturally aware that his textual practice was or might be seen as leading him into dangerous areas of religious controversy. At one point in this commentary he concludes an especially rich discussion of Platonic doctrine by saying, "Let these writers think whatever they like. It will be sufficient for us to have described these things, being rather prepared to accept that teaching which our theologians have primarily sanctioned."[235] That he did not say this kind of thing very often can be taken as a testimony to his philosophical integrity and independence.

2. Soul and Body

Having discussed these general methodological principles, it is now possible for us to turn to certain specific themes of Ficino's *Commentary on the Fourth Ennead* of Plotinus. We will organize this material under the rubrics of "higher soul" (§2.1), "embodied soul" (§2.2), "spirit" (§2.3), "magic and prayer" (§2.4), and "sensation" (§2.5). Ficino returns to these topics on numerous occasions in the course of his typically discursive commentary on this *Ennead*.[236] However, the first two blocks of the commentary material distinguished correspond most closely to the text of *Ennead* 4.1–4, the fourth to that of *Ennead* 4.4, and the fifth to that of *Ennead* 4.5–6. The third block of material corresponds partly to the text of *Ennead* 4.4 and partly to that of *On Life*, Book 3.[237]

As we have already noted,[238] the doctrine of soul elaborated by Ficino in his *Commentary on the Fourth Ennead* represents a more advanced and nuanced treatment of the doctrine set out in a more introductory and general manner in his earlier commentary on *Ennead* 1.1: "What is the animate being and what the man?" The

basic ideas presented in the earlier work are as follows: The "we" (*nos*) or the "man" (*homo*) is "an incorporeal rational substance deriving existence indeed from the divine intellect but truly subsisting in itself" (*substantia incorporea rationalis, ex divino quidem intellectu exsistens, in se vero consistens*), whereas the "animate being" (*animal*) is the "composite" (*compositum*) of this soul—"as it produces life in the body by its very presence" (*ipsa sui praesentia vitam . . . in corpore producens*)—and that body. We can speak of the incorporeal substance as the "rational soul" (*anima rationalis*) and of the life poured forth as "animation and vivification" (*animatio et vivificatio*). The rational soul is also a form that is mediate between the divine forms that are the primal acts of the divine intelligence and the natural forms, such as those of the elements or blended bodies. We can also follow popular usage and speak of the incorporeal substance as "first soul" (*anima prima*) and of the animation and vivification as the "second soul" (*anima secunda*).[239] The first soul has a threefold structure consisting of the powers of intellect, reason, and "distinct" imagination, whereas the second soul has a threefold structure consisting of the powers of "confused" imagination, exterior sense, and nature.[240]

2.1 The Higher Soul

As a general practice in his commentary on the *Fourth Ennead*, Ficino specifies that the higher soul is "the rational soul" (*anima rationalis*) and calls the latter either a "soul" (*anima*) or an "intellect" (*intellectus*).[241] A passage in which he argues that every *rational* soul "to the extent that it is intellectual" (*quatenus intellectualis*) contains all things in actuality and "to the extent that it is psychic" (*quatenus animalis*) contains all things in potentiality suggests that the higher soul is described as an intellect when considered in its dependence on the higher principle of intellect and as a soul when considered

simply in its own status.[242] Moreover, given that when subjected to an internal analysis the higher soul will turn out to be differentiated into the three faculties of "intellect, reason, and imagination" (*intellectus, ratio, imaginatio*),[243] calling the higher soul an intellect is simply to place the emphasis on its highest constituent power, whereas calling it a soul rather places the emphasis equally on its three constituent powers. At any rate, Ficino begins his commentary on *Ennead* 4.1–2 by underlining the median status of this intellect or soul. Here, in the course of distinguishing, on the one hand, the order of essential being in the eternal levels of the universe where intellect itself *simpliciter* holds the rank of a quasi-supreme principle, and on the other hand, the order of essential being in the realm of generation which strives toward being, life, and intellect, he explains that the "intellectual soul" (*anima intellectualis*) descends from the higher to the lower sphere and again that the "intellect of soul" (*intellectus animalis*), having descended, holds the highest rank and serves as the limit of the lower sphere.[244] Thus, the substitution of terminology brings out clearly the ambivalent status of the Ficinian higher soul.[245]

2.1.1 The "Descent" of the Higher Soul

A more detailed account of the "descent"[246] of the intellectual soul can be found in an important passage in the commentary on *Ennead* 4.3.[247] Here, Ficino asks us to engage in a kind of thought-experiment in imagining (1) the presence in the divine intellect of a multiplicity of intellects, (2) the presence in the divine intellect of a multiplicity of souls, (3) the procession of the Idea of soul into a multiplicity of souls, (4) the procession of the multiplicity of intellectual souls from the divine intellect, and (5) the procession of the multiplicity of intellectual souls from the Idea of soul, the language of thought-experiment being introduced in order to show that we are being asked to comprehend a complex dynamic relation between the intellectual and the psychic by distinguishing its

various conceptual components.[248] In this thought-experiment, Ficino urges us to "think of" (*cogitare*) the great soul [B1] in the divine mind [A1] as the generic Idea of intellectual souls and as a certain intellect. The species[249] of souls [B2] will also be contained there and will also be certain intellects [A2]. The ideal intellects of this kind [A2] will be distinguished from one another not by their different existences but by a certain reason-principle and a formal property when they are thought as being in the divine mind [A1]. However, these ideal intellects [A2] can be distinguished from one another by a difference of reason-principle *and* a difference of substance when they are thought as coming forth from the divine mind [A1]. The substances coming forth [A2/B2] from the primal intellect [A1] will be intellectual in the first instance [A2]. However, each one can put forth from itself as intellectual a certain specific characteristic which is now psychic [A2/B2]. The psychic is distinguished from the intellectual by its greater multiplicity. Moreover, the relation between the intellectual and psychic aspects of the emerging terms can be compared to that between a spark and a ray or that between an inner word and a word uttered. The most important thing to note about this thought-experiment is undoubtedly the statement that each of the many intellects "puts forth in itself *from its intellectuality* a certain specific characteristic which is now *psychic*" (*proprietatem quandam exprimit in se ipsa ex intellectuali iam animalem*), since Ficino is not attempting to explain the derivation of either a multiplicity of intellects from a single intellect or a multiplicity of souls from a single soul but a multiplicity of *intellectual* souls equivalent to intellects *of souls* from an Idea of soul which is actually an intellect.[250]

2.1.2 UNIFORMITY AND OMNIFORMITY

In the paragraph following the one containing the thought-experiment,[251] Ficino begins by explaining that the first principle is above all things in its simplicity but produces all things through

its power, and that "intellect, its son" (*intellectus eius filius*) is every-thing primally and perfectly in such a way that each of its Ideas is all the Ideas. Moreover, "soul" (*anima*) flowing forth from the Idea proper to it "contracts" (*contrahit*) all things in itself with the result that "each and every *intellectual* soul is the universe" (*quaelibet . . . intellectualis anima est universum*). Having explained that the intel-lectual soul is a contraction of the Idea of soul in somewhat Plo-tinian terms, he now attempts to prove the point by appealing to the general principle that the first member of each and every genus is both the most simple term and also contains all things,[252] the introduction of the first-person verb "I confirm" (*confirmo*) indicat-ing that Ficino is making an overt transition to his own doctrine. He therefore argues that intellect as the first form exists as "both uniform and omniform" (*et uniformis et omniformis*) and is all things in actuality, whereas every rational soul "to the extent that it is in-tellectual" (*quatenus intellectualis est*) is also a form having similar uniformity and omniformity and being all things in actuality, but "to the extent that it now emerges as not so much intellectual as psychic" (*quatenus . . . non tam intellectualis iam quam animalis evadit*) is now rather all things in potentiality.[253] This highly compressed statement seems to be an attempt to argue from the premise that (*a*) the *primal* intellect is the first in the genus and therefore both uniform and omniform to the conclusion that *every* rational soul *qua* intellectual is also both uniform and omniform, the intermedi-ate premises being (*b*) that the primal intellect is the totality of the Ideas, (*c*) that each intellect is the totality of the Ideas, (*d*) that soul is intellect in a certain sense, (*e*) that the Idea of soul is all the Ideas, and (*f*) that each soul is all the Ideas. As stated, this argu-ment seems to be problematic in transferring the uniformity and omniformity associated according to Ficino's usual criteria with the *first* member of a genus, here, the primal intellect, to *all* the members of another genus, here, the multiplicity of rational souls. The question is, how can this be understood in a manner that

does not force the Florentine into the theory of the unicity of intellect and soul that he elsewhere rejects as both Averroistic and
un-Plotinian?[254]

Ficino's answer is probably that one must distinguish as two
moments within the intellectual or rational soul its intellectual
quality per se—strictly speaking, the rational being's "intellect"—
and its intellectual-psychic quality—strictly speaking, the rational
being's "intellectual soul." The former moment—which alone embodies uniformity and omniformity in act—is that in which the
intellectual or rational souls "are formed by one and the same divine intellect through their intellectual summits" (*per intellectuales
suas . . . apices uno eodemque . . . formantur intellectu divino*)[255] or alternatively that in which they are in intellect *simpliciter* "through
their proper existences, so to speak, in accordance with the intellectual faculty proper to them" (*per proprias [ut ita dixerim] exsistentias . . . secundum intellectualem sibi propriam facultatem*).[256] On a certain level, one can illuminate the nature of these two moments by
saying that they correspond to the immanence of the divine intellect in each intellectual soul and the intellectual faculty of each
intellectual soul, respectively, which in turn correspond to the first
two members of the threefold structure forming the trinitarian
analogue in the soul as a whole.[257] However, given that Ficino's
anti-Averroistic position requires both the first *and* second moments to be genuinely multiple, further problems loom in understanding the nature of the first moment's multiplicity and the relation between the two moments. Apparently, his position on the
first question is that the multiplicity corresponds to that of the
limits of lines projected from a geometrical center and rays emitted
from the sun, these lines or rays being "distinct from one another"
(*inter se differentes*) although they "are in contact with" (*contingunt*)
the unitary center and sun.[258] On the second question, Ficino's
position seems to be that the irrational soul, which is imperfect in
the genus, can be referred back to the intellectual soul, which is

perfect in the genus and then to something—= presumably the intellectual summit—above the genus, the phrase "refer back" (*reducere*) indicating a purely dialectical or conceptual reduction.[259] In the end, the nature of the first moment's multiplicity and the relation between the two moments are seemingly to be explained only in terms of analogies and notional distinctions.[260]

In the remaining passages to be examined in this section, the precise status of the rational soul, intellectual soul, or intellect of soul to which Ficino refers must be understood either as applying to the intellectual soul without specifying the (purely notional) distinction between the individual intellect and the individual intellectual soul or else as applying specifically to the intellectual soul in distinction from the immanent divine intellect in the individual. The most important aspects of the intellectual soul thus understood that are mentioned in the commentary on *Ennead* 4—apart from the uniformity and omniformity considered above[261]—are undoubtedly its status as a transcendent-immanent form, its relation to temporality and atemporality, and its status as a nondiscursive thinker.

2.1.3 Transcendent and Immanent Form

It obviously follows from the arguments above that soul is itself a form. Ficino has already stated clearly near the beginning of this commentary that in Plotinus' second book on the soul—that is, *Ennead* 4.2—the famous Aristotelian doctrine of the "entelechy" can be understood as corresponding not only to the form and soul that is inseparable from the body but also to the form and soul that is separable from the body.[262] He has also rendered the same Aristotelian doctrine more precise by saying that this simultaneously separable and inseparable soul is the form of the animate being or composite of soul and body rather than of the body as such, whereas intellect is the form of the soul, and life is the form of the body.[263] Later on in the present commentary, Ficino states

along strictly Platonic lines that in combinations of form and matter the formal element can exist without the material one, although the opposite situation cannot occur, and that intellectual souls are included in the genus of such forms.[264] He adds that one must maintain that any form of this kind[265] is an "essential being" (*essentia*), which has its "being" (*esse*) and its "essential unity" (*essentialis unitas*) as one and the same and therefore has an indissoluble being by the same token that it has an indissoluble unity. Having at this point cited the various Plotinian arguments for the everlastingness of soul based on the above premises and his own evaluation of these arguments in the *Platonic Theology*,[266] Ficino goes on to argue that pure form has a "numerical and proper unity" (*unitas numeralis propriaque*), whereas composites of matter and form maintain "a perpetual unity of the specific form in succession" (*unitas speciei perpetua successione*), and also that intellectual soul should be placed in the former and corporeal things in the latter category.[267] Finally, he concludes that the simple form and the intellectual soul—whether it be that of the world or that of human beings—is "infinite" (*infinita*) not in the sense that it can be divided to infinity but because "it is vigorous without limitation and can act everywhere and always" (*sine fine vigeat et ubique semper agere possit*).[268]

The issue of soul's everlastingness touched upon here naturally reappears in Ficino's commentary on *Ennead* 4.7, which was devoted to this topic, and from the rather brief remarks added by the commentator we learn a few more things about soul as form, although the more precise nomenclature of "intellectual soul" is lacking. In particular, Ficino here develops the notion that the Plotinian soul—and on his view also the Aristotelian entelechy—is a form that is both inseparable and separable from the body by arguing that the soul has a twofold relation to the latter, on the one hand in being in relation to matter "as a certain substantial form" (*ut substantialis quaedam species*), and on the other in using the

body "as an instrument" (*ad instrumentum*).[269] Having added that the soul is not only separable but "in a sense separated now" (*et iam quodammodo separata*), he now expands on the two types of relation by noting that the presence of the substantial form produces a certain temperament of humors and a vital spirit in the body, and that the instrumental use of the body involves moving it according to choice. A few paragraphs later he expands on the twofold relation yet again by stating that the presence of the substantial form is responsible even for an accidental trace of life impressed on the body, and that soul can move itself contrary to the inclinations of the body toward incorporeal things.[270] Of course, the association of the soul with motion and life in these passages is important, because, for Ficino as it was for Plotinus, soul "preeminently" (*potissimum*) has the property of self-motion, which in its turn implies that soul has "life-through-itself" (*vita ex se*).[271]

2.1.4 ATEMPORALITY AND NONDISCURSIVITY

Now, in an important passage, Ficino characterizes the divine intellect immanent in the world-soul mythologically as Jupiter and describes it as effecting an infinite number of things through its omniform Form and as imprinting that same omniform Form in the human intellect.[272] In another passage, he elaborates some important further conceptual associations between omniformity, atemporality, and nondiscursivity with relevance to both the intellectual world-soul and the intellectual human soul.[273] Here, we learn that the innermost action of the world-soul is not accomplished in the successivity of time but "all at once in a moment" (*momento tota simul*), although its most external action—a procession of its power into the world and the action of the world itself—is carried out in temporal succession. Just as things that are spatially distinguished among themselves have only a formal distinction in the interiority of the world-soul, so things that are temporally prior or posterior to one another are differentiated in

that same interiority according to a certain order.[274] The world-soul through its omniform essential being is a stable exemplar and effector of the entire future order of the universe, which would be able to accomplish everything "in simultaneity" (*simul*) if matter were able to receive everything in this manner.[275] Ficino notes that the temporality of the external action of the world-soul[276] is confirmed by Plotinus in his book *On Time*—that is, *Ennead* 3.7—where he places time and motion not in the higher world-soul but only in the lower phase, where forms are not gained or lost in the course of time but awakened as though from a dream. However, although "changeable deliberation and temporal discursivity" (*ambigua consultatio temporalisque discursio*) are not present in the higher world-soul, because that which is best in it always dominates the other powers, these elements are present to the equivalent component of our soul, because different powers are dominant in us at different times, because we are deficient in respect to many things, and because passions befall us from the exterior.[277] Even if the rational power—the higher human soul—in us is not inherently weak in its nature, it is sometimes overcome by the irrational power—the lower human soul—, this occurring both because the former is tranquil and the latter disturbed and because the former is single and the latter multiple.[278]

2.2 Embodied Soul

Near the beginning of his commentary on the *Fourth Ennead*, Ficino had recalled the teaching of Plato's *Timaeus* to the effect that soul is composed of a certain indivisible substance and a substance divisible around bodies, and Plotinus' view that the doctrine of soul stated here is first, that soul comprises two powers or faculties: namely, the intellectual power which never declines toward body and that nature which at the same time (*a*) completely accommodates itself to body and (*b*) remains indivisible; and second,

that these two powers or faculties have this status relative to one another both in the human soul and in the world-soul.[279] Translated into more abstract terms, this means that the soul-form has a simultaneously transcendent and immanent relation to the body and that even within its "immanent" modality there is also a distinction between a transcendent and an immanent relation:[280] if this were not the case, the immanent form of soul would be indistinguishable from the immanent form of quality, and the mediate position of the soul-form as a whole between the indivisible and divisible substances of the *Timaeus* would be compromised. On this basis, it will be useful to consider the intersecting relations between soul and body that emerge in Ficino's reading of Plotinus and especially the relations between (*a*) the higher soul's distinction from the lower soul, (*b*) the lower soul's partial dependence on body,[281] and (*c*) the higher soul's partial dependence on body, this complex of relations being seemingly characterized as a "descent," where the quasi-bodily and therefore quasi-spatial aspect[282] of the various relations is being emphasized, and as an "inclination," where these aspects are given less emphasis.[283]

2.2.1 Modalities of the Soul-Body Relation

A simple statement of the higher soul's distinction from the lower soul and of the lower soul's partial dependence on body can be found in a passage where Ficino discusses the suggestion by Plotinus that the earth has a soul and has sensation.[284] That the earth has a soul follows from the fact that the earth is "an intellectual and divine animate being" (*animal intellectuale atque divinum*) and also "has sensation" (*habet sensum*), and that it has sensation from the fact that it has a "power of judgment" (*vis iudicaria*) which perceives things "connected with the body" (*coniuncta corpori*) and judges "the passions of its body" (*sui corporis passiones*).[285] However, when Ficino argues elsewhere that human souls have not only an intellect continually active in the intelligible world but also "reason"

(*ratio*), "imagination" (*imaginatio*), "sense" (*sensus*), and a "vegetative power" (*vis vegetalis*), that they must employ these powers in their proper functions at one time or another, that they use these powers "in the body" (*in corpore*), and that it is therefore proper for them to "descend" (*descendere*) into bodies from time to time, the situation becomes more complicated.[286] Since, reason is normally associated with the higher soul and imagination is associated with both the higher and the lower souls,[287] we seem to have here a reference not only to the higher soul's distinction from the lower soul and to the *lower* soul's partial dependence on the body but also to the *higher* soul's partial dependence on the body.

That the lower soul should be partially dependent on body is obviously required by the assumption of a distinction between a higher soul, which is indivisible, and a lower soul, which simultaneously remains indivisible and accommodates itself to bodies.[288] However, the suggestion in the last passage that the higher soul is also partially dependent on body would seem to make sense only on the assumption that the partial dependence of the lower soul can somehow affect the status of the higher.[289] Two passages in which Ficino follows very closely in the footsteps of his ancient philosophical sources consider some explanations of how precisely this situation arises.[290] In the first of these, he summarizes Plotinus' teaching that souls living in the divine world at some point survey the forms lying in the matter of the world through the imagination that is in them "the lowest phase" (*ultimum*), and that imagination "turns itself thus to that place" (*quorsum . . . se ita convertit*) while reason "turns itself away from intellect" (*se divertit ab intellectu*). The action of these two powers, which is not only gazing but loving, is the cause of the downward tendency,[291] although intellect "which such affectivity does not touch" (*quem non tangit affectus eiusmodi*) remains unmoved in the higher world.[292] In a second passage, Ficino reports Porphyry's doctrine that, since the soul cannot be inactive in all its faculties, whenever the intensity of

acting in a higher faculty is reduced, the intensity of acting in a lower power is increased proportionally. Therefore, the "fall" (*casus*) of the soul does not begin from the latter's imagination or nature as somehow "dragging" (*trahere*) its reason downward—as Plotinus seemed to suggest—but from the intellect and reason,[293] whose intensity of action is somehow "remitted" (*remitti*), while the intensity of action in imagination and nature is increased.[294] Now, these two passages interpret the relation between the higher and the lower souls and body as a descent or fall in the context of a discussion of transmigration, which Ficino could only endorse if understood in an allegorical sense.[295] Nevertheless, when corrected in terms of the Christian assumption that individual souls are created by God for individual bodies, they do provide explanations of how the lower soul's partial dependence on body could be seen to affect the status of the higher soul that the Florentine might have considered plausible.

2.2.2 Celestial, Daemonic, and Human Souls

The complex relation between the transcendence and immanence of soul, its partial dependence on body, and the relation between its higher and lower powers is further modified by the division into different classes of souls. In one of his discussions of the descent of souls, Ficino notes that among those natures that have a part that is intellectual and a part that is psychic there are three ranks, for in celestial souls the intellectual "prevails over" (*superat*) the psychic, in daemonic souls the two parts are in equilibrium, and in human souls the psychic prevails over the intellectual.[296] Elsewhere he explains that whereas celestial souls govern "with ease" (*facillime*) the bodies that are subject to them with the instinctiveness of nature and the assent of mind, human souls "depart from" (*abire*) the higher world in employing reason and imagination with respect to the administration of such bodies.[297] In

both these instances, Ficino summarizes the teaching of Plotinus' original text without demur.

2.2.3 The Faculties and Embodiment

As in Plotinus and ultimately as in Aristotle, the various modalities of the relation between soul and body give rise to an elaborate stratification of psychic faculties, which has already been set out in Ficino's commentary on *Ennead* 1.1.[298] The present commentary assumes the conclusions of this earlier treatment in presenting an organization of the faculties according to "harmonic" principles, although in this instance equal attention is now paid to the non-human souls.[299] Elaborating an obvious analogy between the internal structure of soul itself and soul's position in the structure of being as a whole, the fivefold articulation of the human soul into the faculties of (1) intelligence, (2) reason, (3) imagination, (4) sense, and (5) nature[300] furnishes the basic pattern for the psychological analysis.[301] With the assumption of this framework—which apparently applies equally to the world-soul, the souls of the stars and spheres, and the human soul—Ficino can argue in a passage laying down the underlying principles of all embodiment that the world-soul contains the faculties of intelligence (1), reason (2), and nature (5), comparing these to light, radiance, and heat, respectively. Here, the essential being of the world-soul is considered in two ways: first, as other than the three terms and "dark"; and second, as distinguished into the three and "light." In the former modality, the world-soul is the source of prime matter, whereas in the latter it is *qua* intelligence, *qua* reason, and *qua* nature, respectively, the source of the stable forms in matter, of forms moved in a stable manner, and of forms moved in a mobile way.[302] It should not be concluded that the intermediate faculties are missing on the macrocosmic level, since Ficino states in the passage comparing the animate being that is the world to a dancer

that the world-soul has delineated in its intelligence (1), thinking (2), imagination (3), and nature (5) all the future cycles of the world as though these are present,[303] and in a passage describing the process of natural production that the divine mind impresses its forms so strongly in the world-soul that this impression passes through its intelligence (1) to its imagination (3) and to its nature (5).[304] Moreover, Ficino notes that not only the world-soul but also the souls of the spheres and stars are endowed with sense (4) because they hearken to our prayers, although they are not conscious that they sense because their imagination (3) would have to be turned toward their sense for this to occur, whereas it is in fact always turned toward their intelligence (1).[305]

Especially given the principle of soul's omniformity,[306] one should not think of the highest power as corresponding strictly to the soul's transcendence, and the subsequent powers as corresponding strictly to its immanence, but rather of something like an unfolding of the sequence of these powers in accordance with the shift in the predominant modality from transcendence to immanence. Therefore, when Ficino speaks of the lowest member of the gradation of powers — described variously as nature, the vegetative power, or the vital power (5) — as being most closely dependent on body, he means us to understand that within the shifting modality of soul between transcendence and immanence the lowest member of the series has the greatest degree of immanence. Turning to Ficino's actual descriptions of the lowest phase, we find him establishing the fundamental premise for any discussion of this issue that, since it (a) has an equal relation to opposite qualities and motions in the body and (b) puts forth omniform motions through its vegetative power,[307] and since these functions cannot pertain to bulk or corporeal quality, the soul-form is neither "some definite body or corporeal thing" (certum aliquod corpus vel corporeum) nor "is dependent on a certain body or bodies" (ex corpore quodam corporibusve dependet).[308] On the basis of this reasoning, Ficino also argues

that the human soul emits first,[309] "something substantial and life-giving" (*substantiale aliquid et vivificum*) — to be called the "*idolum*" (*idolum*) of the soul — which has both sensitive and vegetative components; and second, "something accidental and quasi-vital" (*accidentale quiddam et quasi vitale*) — to be called the "image and shadow" (*imago . . . umbra*) of the soul — which corresponds to bodily quality.[310] The former is explicitly described as an act that is inseparable from the soul, while the latter seems from the context — it is later said to be the seat of *bodily* passions — to be a passivity quasi-separable from the soul.[311] He continues by stating that the soul is bound to the body "as though with two ligatures" (*duobus quasi nodis*): one of these a "tendency toward soul" (*vergere ad animam*) in the case of the life-giving act, and the other an "inclination toward body" (*declinare ad corpus*) in the case of the quasi-vital quality, and also that passions of a destructive or restorative nature falling upon the body in the case of the second ligature can be either avoided or pursued when *sensed* by the soul in that of the first ligature.[312]

2.2.4 Afterlife of the Soul

We will pass over the various further powers emerging in Ficino's discussion of the vegetative soul's impression of the "vital trace" (*vitale vestigium*) in the bodily humors,[313] and in his account of the quasi-mediate character of this trace between an act of deliberation and a combination of qualities,[314] both of these discussions transferring the theory summarized above to the macrocosmic level. It should simply be noted here that the complex relation between the transcendence and immanence of soul, its partial dependence on body, and the relation between its higher and lower powers is further modified by the distinction between the situation as it obtains in the present life and after physical death, respectively.[315] According to Ficino, the vital trace continues for a short time after death, the life-giving act survives much longer —

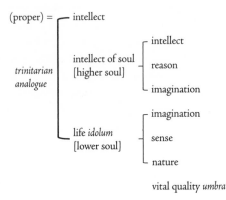

divine intellect
(communal)

(proper) = intellect

trinitarian analogue

intellect of soul
[higher soul]

- intellect
- reason
- imagination

life *idolum*
[lower soul]

- imagination
- sense
- nature

vital quality *umbra*

being sustained by soul as a coagulative principle of something that will be after death a kind of leaven for an aerial body—, and the higher part of the soul is obviously everlasting.[316]

The above diagram summarizes the arrangement of all the powers within the soul as stated in the passages considered in the last two sections.

2.3 Spirit

In order to trace the further development of the doctrine of the embodied soul, we must turn to the notion of "spirit" (*spiritus* = the Greek *pneuma*), which is for Ficino at the same time a most ambiguous[317] and a most fundamental[318] notion. In the *Enneads*, Plotinus makes scattered references to the notion of *pneuma*[319]— the most important being that to the spirit underlying the earth's exercise of its senses[320]—but it is Ficino alone who formulates a coherent doctrine by combining these.[321] Commenting ostensibly on Plotinus near the end of the third book of *On Life*, he states

that in the world's body "a spirit that is a certain body" (*spiritus corpus quoddam*) lies hidden, that in this spirit there flourishes a soul, and that in this soul there shines an intelligence. Just as in the sublunary realm, air is only blended with earth through water, and fire only with water through air, so in the universe it is the thing called spirit that functions as "a certain bait or kindling" (*esca quaedam sive fomes*) for connecting soul with body.[322] In characterizing this doctrine of spirit elsewhere as something he would defend as probable if not held back by the authority of great men,[323] he seems to suggest that he is going beyond the letter of the Plotinian text in elaborating a cherished thesis. As we will see especially in considering the handling of this notion in his commentary on Priscian of Lydia's *Interpretation of Theophrastus*, one major influence on this somewhat independent development was probably Iamblichus.[324]

2.3.1 SPIRIT AS MEDIATOR

Since the doctrine of spirit is developed most extensively in two works closely related to the commentary on Plotinus proper, the third book of *On Life* and the commentary on Priscian of Lydia, the briefer treatment in the Plotinus commentary being perhaps not totally comprehensible without reference to these other works, it will be necessary to study the doctrine in a combination of all these texts in order to understand adequately its function within Ficino's conception of the "Plotinian" metaphysical system. Such an approach to the notion of spirit should perhaps start by drawing attention to the fact that it is above all a "principle of mediation" (*medium*) with respect to the macrocosm, where it communicates life from the world's soul to its body,[325] to the microcosm, where it facilitates the individual soul's perception of external objects,[326] and between the macrocosm and the microcosm, where it permits celestial gifts to overflow from the sun into our soul and body.[327] Spirit can therefore be described in terms of all the other

notions associated with mediation in Ficinian thought. Thus, spirit is a principle of connection: a spirit is said to descend from the celestials in order to make things "coalesce" (*coalescere*) in vitality,[328] and a certain spirit is said to survive the death of the earthy body and act as a "coagulative principle" (*coagulum*) for the aery body.[329] A "Pythagorean" doctrine is also cited speaking of a spirit that prepares the matters proper to living beings, preserves them at a specific time, and brings together all living things into a unity.[330] Spirit is associated with proportion especially in the context of the human soul's sensitive powers, for example where Ficino argues that in order to discern the acts and qualities of external bodies the soul must have a certain "proportion" (*proportio*) to the latter that can be achieved only by its formation of a spirit.[331] Spirit is also a principle of attraction: ritual fumigations that are solar or Jovial in character are said to assist our spirit toward the "capturing" (*capiendum*) of the gifts of the sun or Jupiter when these stars are in the ascendant.[332] The "Zoroastrian magicians" are cited for their practice of whirling a golden ball engraved with the characters of the heavenly bodies and with a sapphire set in the middle in order to "call forth" (*evocare*) the spirit from Hecate,[333] and Proclus is quoted for his injunction to suspend the selenite gem set in silver from the neck by a silver thread in order to "insert" (*inserere*) the power derived through its lunar series into our spirit.[334] Spirit is associated with harmony in the context of the human soul's vital powers, for example where Ficino argues that "harmony" (*concentus*) through its numbers and proportions has a wonderful power to calm, move, and influence our spirit.[335] In addition to functioning as a principle of mediation, spirit often appears in contexts where other typical Ficinian mediators are also mentioned and where some analogy between spirit and the latter is implied. Spirit is associated with the sun through a shared property of mediacy when Ficino speaks of the world-soul as unfolding

its spirit or the quintessence through the medium of the sun.[336] Spirit will also be found to be analogous to or aligned with the world's reason-principle if one compares his statement that the heaven is the "the spirit, breath, and word" (*spiritus et flatus et verbum*) of the world-soul[337] with the assertion in his *Commentary on the Third Ennead* that the world's reason-principle comes forth from the perfect intellect and the intellect of the world-soul as the "spirit-and-word" (*spiritus verbumque*).[338] Finally, spirit is associated with daemons through a shared property of mediacy when Ficino speaks of the benefits accruing to our spirit from the stars and daemons, which themselves exist in and through spirit.[339]

2.3.2 BETWEEN SOUL AND BODY

The thread running through the various mediating functions assigned to spirit is a relation of some kind between soul and body, and Ficino summarizes this in Book 3 of *On Life* by arguing that just as between the soul and the body of the world, so between our soul and body there is everywhere a spirit.[340] To be more precise, spirit mediates between nature — the lower phase of soul — and body.[341] Therefore, the Florentine can elaborate on Plotinus' and Synesius' statements to the effect that nature is a sorceress by arguing that after conception nature prepares the human embryo in such a way that by means of this preparation, serving as a bait, she can lead down the spirit from the universe into the small body.[342] When thought through in the rigorous manner, the placing of spirit between soul and body would require spirit to mediate somehow between the incorporeal and the corporeal as such, and this is indeed exactly what we find in Ficino. Thus, he characterizes spirit in one passage as "a more excellent body as though not a body" (*excellentius corpus . . . quasi non corpus*),[343] in another as "a most tenuous body, as if not body but as though now soul, and again as if not soul but as though now body" (*corpus tenuissimum*

quasi non corpus et quasi iam anima, item quasi non anima et quasi iam corpus),[344] and in another as "a certain body escaping the capacity of fallen sense" (*corpus quoddam excedens caduci sensus capacitatem*),[345] its origin being explained differently from the viewpoint of its proximity to (full) incorporeality—where it appears as heaven or quintessence[346]—and from the viewpoint of its superiority to (mere) corporeality—where it appears as a hemal vapor.[347] He can therefore argue in the third book of *On Life* that spirit as heaven and quintessence is "almost the same" (*talis ferme . . . qualis*) in the world's and in the human body, the only difference being that the world-soul "gives birth to it from its own generative power" (*ex virtute sua procreat genitali*),[348] whereas our soul "draws it from the four elements as though being its humors" (*trahit ex quattuor elementis tamquam humoribus suis*).[349] The generation of the higher spirit is described in more detail in the *Commentary on the Second Ennead*, where Ficino can argue that this spirit is generated from the intellectual world-soul, is an image of the single act of intelligence in the intelligible world, and is a certain act of that intelligence proceeding to the exterior.[350] Now, if indeed rigorous thinking requires the placing of spirit between the incorporeal and the corporeal as such in the manner suggested, another feature of spirit implied in numerous texts acquires its justification. This is the *spatiality* of spirit, enabling it to mediate as incorporeal and spatial between soul as incorporeal and nonspatial, and body as corporeal and spatial.[351] For example, in the continuation of the passage cited above, Ficino speaks of the world-soul as breathing out the forms constituting its spirit and "extending them now in dimension" (*iam dimensione protendere*),[352] while in another text he speaks of the necessary "space" (*spatium*) between the sense-organ and the sense-object that is provided by the transparency[353] in its role of "spiritual medium" (*spiritale medium*),[354] and in another of the spirit comprised by song as acting powerfully not only on "its own" (*proprium*) but also on a "neighboring" (*propinquum*) body.[355]

2.3.3 Spirit's Relation to Soul

Many of the difficulties that arise in interpreting Ficino's discussions of spirit—in its mediative role within the macrocosm, the microcosm, and between the macrocosm and microcosm—can be resolved or at least mitigated by grasping the ambiguously incorporeal and corporeal nature of spirit and construing some of these accounts primarily in terms of its proximity to soul and others in terms of its proximity to body. With respect to its proximity to *soul*, spirit plays an important role in connection with the operation of the lowest faculty of the lower soul: namely, the vegetative function. Ficino explains that in the animated body there is not only soul and a life-giving act of soul—just as in a luminous body there is light shining forth into its body—; there is also a certain "vital trace" (*vitale vestigium*)—just as there is heat underneath the light shining forth into the body—, this last being "a spirit suitable for motions" (*spiritus motibus aptus*).[356] He also informs us that this spirit is born in the body together with a definite temperament of humors through the presence of soul as an immanent form in the body,[357] that it is through its mediation that soul is brought to bear on our bodily members,[358] and that this spirit survives for a short time after the physical death of the animate being.[359] Ficino further argues that the spirit underlying our vegetative life is in conformity with the rays emitted by the vegetative life subjoined to the intellect of the world-soul,[360] and can become more conformable and transferred into those rays[361] through prayer, a suitable disposition of life, and love.[362] Spirit also contributes significantly to the operation of the middle power constitutive of the lower soul: that is, the sensitive function.[363] Here, Ficino explains that soul is more excellent than things to be sensed, has neither proportionality nor passivity with respect to them, and cannot take on forms from them. Sensation takes place when it is the spirit that is "struck or affected" (*pulsatus vel affectus*) by external things

and is somehow "enlivened" (*vegetare*) in putting forth the inborn forms of sensible things.[364] Spirit also plays an important role in connection with the highest faculty of the lower soul: namely, the imaginative function. Here, Ficino observes that the power of a magical incantation proceeds to a distant thing not only as being propagated in a certain motion through the air. Rather, the imagination of the enchanter throws from a distance "the rays of his spirit" (*radii spiritus*), which, by suddenly proceeding into length, in themselves extend the powers of the one casting them.[365] Whether there is any association, in the eyes of Ficino, between spirit and any of the faculties of the higher soul is more uncertain. However, since imagination mediates between sense and reason[366] and imagination relies on spirit, it seems likely that spirit affects reason at least in an indirect manner.[367]

Given the rather ambiguous character of the Ficinian spirit, certain questions inevitably come to mind. First, what is the precise relation between spirit and the vital trace? Although the passage cited above seems simply to identify the vital trace with spirit, the situation must really be more complicated given that the vital trace is said to be destroyed a short time after the death of the earthy body, whereas spirit in the sense of the soul's vehicle remains attached to the immortal soul. Therefore, the epithet "suitable for motions" in the passage must indicate that the vital trace corresponds to spirit in a particular condition rather than spirit *tout court*. A second question is: does spirit exist in a stratified form? The association of spirit with the hierarchically ordered vegetative, sensitive, and imaginative faculties of the soul would seem to imply a corresponding structure within spirit. However, since soul is nonspatial whereas spirit is spatial, the internal articulation of the former — which is strictly according to a reason-principle — seems not to require a precisely equivalent organization in the latter. There are other questions arising in connection

with the nature of spirit that are, however, best answered by considering the Ficinian spirit as a whole from another viewpoint.

2.3.4 SPIRIT'S RELATION TO BODY

With respect to its proximity to *body*, Ficino broadly divides spirit into two levels. In an important passage of his commentary on the *Fourth Ennead*, he argues that the union or continuity within the animate being that is the world is based on five foundations.[368] The third and central foundation[369] is a spirit that is "everywhere single" (*ubique unus*), being (*a*) "the heaven on high" (*caelum . . . in excelsis*), and (*b*) "within the heaven" (*intra caelum*), infused into all things, and either "wholly celestial" (*caelestis omnino*) or "most similar to heaven" (*caelo simillimus*) in order that things might be governed from on high, that the world-soul might be joined to lower bodies, and that all things might coalesce in vitality.[370] He concludes by noting that this spirit — and presumably he is referring essentially to spirit *b* — is "similar to our own" (*nostro consimilis*). Now, what we have here is clearly a depiction of spirit as having something like a distinction between transcendent (= *a*) and immanent (= *b*) modalities, which is — because of the metaphysical ambivalence of spirit — combined with a spatial distribution. However, for more detailed information regarding these different modalities in the cosmic infusion of spirit, we must turn to other texts.

[*a*] The spirit equivalent to heaven on high — or possibly the combination of spirit *a* and spirit *b* with the emphasis placed on the former — is described in the commentary on *Ennead* 2.1 as the "breath" (*flatus*) and "word" (*verbum*) of the world-soul.[371] This principle is obviously equivalent to the spirit that doubly proceeds — as an analogue of the third person of the Trinity — from the divine intellect and the intellect of the world-soul according to Ficino's arguments elsewhere.[372] It is now said to be indicated in

Vergil's statement, "The spirit nourishes within," and in that of the book of *Genesis*, "The Spirit of God was borne above the waters."

[b] The spirit that is within the heaven and either wholly celestial or most similar to the heaven — or perhaps the combination of spirit *a* and spirit *b* with the emphasis placed on the latter — is also described in the same passage as the breath and word of the world-soul, although the word is "now expressed externally" (*iam extra prolatum*). The various features that it imparts to the visible heaven are said to reflect certain powers of the world-soul. Most importantly, because of the soul's intellect it emits "light" (*lumen*), because of the soul's greatness it puts forth "dimension" (*dimensio*), and because of the soul's intellectual Ideas it generates "forms" (*formae*).[373] Also because of the soul's intellect, the spirit is a translucid nature "as though tempered by the transparency and light" (*quasi ex diaphano et lumine temperata*) and emits heavenly light "to the extent that the light is in the transparent" (*quantum est in perspicuo*).[374] In other passages, Ficino expresses the nature of spirit *b* in quasi-elemental terms. At one point, an analogy is posited between [b1] the "quintessence" (*quinta essentia*), which spreads the power of the world-soul through all things, and [b2] the spirit that spreads the power of the human soul through the bodily members.[375] Regarding the macrocosmic spirit [b1], he continues by arguing that the world-soul gives birth to the four elements through this spirit "as though everything were contained in that spirit's power" (*quasi in illius spiritus virtute sint omnia*).[376] Elsewhere he explains that the multiplicity of souls following the world-soul produces the spatio-temporal structure of the world through the communal spirit by reducing the latter to "the form and shape of its intimate and proper circuit" (*intimi propriique circuitus forma et figura*) and by engendering a multiplicity of "spiritual spheres" (*spiritales orbes*) that are more quasi-rarefied toward the periphery and more quasi-condensed toward the center of the cosmos.[377] Regarding the microcosmic spirit [b2], Ficino argues that the hu-

man soul "draws this spirit out of the four elements serving as its humors" (*trahit ex quattuor elementis tamquam humoribus suis*).[378] With respect to both the macrocosm and the microcosm [b1, b2], degrees of rarefaction and condensation on the part of the spirit are associated with its corresponding quasi-fiery, airy, watery, and earthy manifestations.[379]

2.3.5 "Psychic" and "Corporeal" Spirit

The ambiguity in Ficino's notion of spirit — in its mediative role within the macrocosm, the microcosm, and between the macrocosm and microcosm — that is resolvable through its proximity either to soul or to body appears most clearly when he explicitly combines the more psychic with the more corporeal interpretation. Some good illustrations of this occur in the third book of *On Life*, where the author assumes a complex relation between psychic faculties, which are incorporeal, through the natural, vital, and animal spirits,[380] which are ambiguously incorporeal, and through the corporeal and planetary animate beings, which are combinations of the incorporeal and corporeal, to the bodily organs, which are corporeal.[381] In one passage Ficino also argues — connecting spirit with *body* through the planets — that Jupiter primarily "signifies" (*significare*) the natural spirit and the liver, the sun primarily the vital spirit and the heart, and Mercury primarily the animal spirit and the brain;[382] in another he argues — connecting spirit with *soul* through the same planets — both that the natural spirit is "properly assigned to" (*proprie dedicari*) Jupiter, the vital spirit to the sun, and the animal spirit to Mercury, and also that the Jovial spirit confers life, the solar spirit sense, and the Mercurial spirit imagination.[383] For technical medical and astrological reasons, the correlations are actually more complicated in Ficino's text — for instance, Jupiter also signifies the vital spirit and the heart — although our brief summary is perhaps enough to show the principles involved.[384]

2.4 Magic and Prayer

It is well known that Ficino found himself in agreement with late ancient Platonists such as Iamblichus and Proclus in advocating some combination of philosophical theory with the practice of "theurgy" ($\theta\epsilon o \upsilon\rho\gamma\iota a$), as long as the nature of that combination could be precisely regulated in accordance with Christian beliefs by avoiding purely superstitious elements and especially the risk of delusion by maleficent daemons. Ficino knew through his study of ancient and Byzantine sources that theurgy was a ritual involving the use of symbolic objects, prayers, chants, lights, and fumigations that was designed to channel the divine power — the "action of the god(s)" ($\theta\epsilon o\hat{\upsilon} + \check{\epsilon}\rho\gamma o\nu$) — down to the officiant and other participants. Augustine had described this set of ritual practices in Book 10 of *On the City of God*, arguing that, although under the general heading of "magic" (*magia*) a more honorable practice of "theurgy" (*theurgia*) could be distinguished from a more detestable one of "sorcery" (*goetia*), both should be rejected because of daemonic involvement and the perversion of the notion of "sacrifice" (*sacrificium*).[385] Now, an important section of *Ennead* 4.4 is devoted to questions concerning the operations of prayer and magic that Plotinus' successors comprehended under the rubric of theurgy,[386] and Ficino's main commentary on the ideas in this section was eventually separated by the author himself to form the third book of his treatise *On Life*.[387] However, the material that remained in the commentary on the *Fourth Ennead* is still very instructive concerning Ficino's understanding of the metaphysical principles underlying such ritual practices, this being especially true in the case of the detailed discussions that immediately precede and follow the famous analogy between the dancer and the world.[388] Here, the most important metaphysical principles are undoubtedly those involving the diffusion of emanative powers from the world-soul or spirit to the human soul or spirit, the systolic and diastolic mo-

tion of those emanative powers, and especially the possibility of intensifying those powers by human action in the form of prayer and magic.

2.4.1 EMANATIVE PRINCIPLES

Ficino lays the groundwork for his explanations of magic and prayer by distinguishing natural actions — those of the entire world toward its parts, or of the parts to the entire world, or of the parts to one another[389] — from artificial actions — either those involved in the completion of an artifact such as sculpture or those attending to the work of nature such as medicine, magic, rhetoric, and music. Regarding natural actions, he goes on to explain that the actions of the celestial bodies on lower things are not only through heat and quasi-elemental qualities but through "certain powers very different from qualities that are known" (*vires quaedam a notis qualitatibus longe diversae*).[390] These powers have an action of a mediate type between deliberative choosing and corporeal interaction.[391] Their source is the vegetative nature of the world-soul, which, as though being pregnant and tumescent with "innumerable and wonderful powers" (*innumerabiles mirabilesque virtutes*), overflows into the totality.[392] Moreover, the prayers and operation of magicians can adapt these powers for their use by implanting them or grafting them at various times.[393]

Although the powers under discussion are here traced back to the world-soul — more precisely to its lower vegetative phase or nature — they also have an important relation to light, spirit, and intelligence. Slightly later in the discussion, Ficino compares the "powers" (*vires*) emitted by Jupiter, Saturn, and Venus — that is, the bodies of these stars as enlivened by the vegetative power — to the "rays of the sun" (*solis radii*) collected in a mirror.[394] These rays have a particularly close relation with spirit, because Ficino goes on to speak of a man who by making himself receptive to a certain star and praying to it at an opportune moment "sends forth his

spirit into the rays" (*spiritum suum proiicit in radios*) emitted by the star and everywhere diffusive of life;[395] and again of the pronouncer of an incantation who by means of his powerful imagination and affection "casts from afar the rays of his spirit" (*radios spiritus . . . procul . . . iaculatur*) suddenly proceeding into length.[396] However, the rays emitted by the spirit originate not with the spirit of the world itself but with the intellect and intellectual soul that precede it, the spirit functioning more as a transparent medium for the projection of the rays in accordance with its level of purity. This latter point is suggested in *On Life*, Book 3, where Ficino explains how artificial figures and transparent objects suitably fashioned can immediately receive and transmit the light that is an activity of intelligence and passes through the celestial configurations and the "transparency" (*diaphanum*). Here, we are presumably intended to understand that our spirit's projection of the "harmonious rays" (*harmonici radii*) that it secretly receives from the intellect and intellectual soul is facilitated by the kinship between the celestial configurations and the artificial figures and between the transparency and the transparent objects.[397]

Now, a particularly important feature of these powers is their simultaneous motion in opposite directions: that is, between above and below on the vertical dimension — or between right and left[398] on the horizontal dimension, if we may be permitted to use a spatial metaphor. This simultaneity and multidirectionality results from the fact that the powers diffused from the world-soul are in themselves omnipresent and undiminished albeit constrained and inhibited to varying degrees by the lower things receiving them.[399] Therefore, if things on a lower level of reality can somehow increase their suitability to the reception of powers diffused from a higher level, in the present context especially by prayer, they can be said to "ascend" in the power through the very same action by which that power "descends" upon them. These processes are described in a passage where Ficino explains that from the intellec-

tual soul of the world and of each star and sphere through the subjoined vegetative soul associated with its body "something vital flows forth" (*profluit vitale*) toward lower things that is beneficial where the lesser things' matter is capable of receiving it, albeit less beneficial where that matter is not so capable.[400] Similar processes are described in another passage, where he reports Plotinus' teaching that a "wonderful power is present" (*mirabilis insit virtus*) in four things that are certain offshoots of the powers in the world's life: namely, hidden qualities, figures, chants and prayers. He goes on to define the last as "a certain strong motion of our soul toward the divinity that we implore" (*motus quidam animae nostrae vehemens erga numen quod obsecramus*) and to compare it to the action where one crumbles sulfur and throws it toward a fire and where the flame of the fire extends itself immediately to connect with the dust.[401]

A much more complicated account of the simultaneous motion of powers in opposite directions begins in the next paragraph of Ficino's discussion.[402] This begins by comparing the interconnection of nerves and veins in a human animate being with the interconnection of natures and lives in the animate being of the world. He notes that, just as in us the motion of the foot reaches back to the neck and that of the neck down to the foot, so in the world the motions of lower things go forth to the higher and vice versa, adding that every motion that comes from above is healthful as long as it is received in the way that it comes, and also that no separation in place prevents motions from coming forth in both directions when a lower thing has a property shared with the higher above the general interconnection. He ends by comparing the interconnection of the various components of the animate being to the motion of a string on a lyre which reaches another string separated from it but similarly tuned. Now this important passage combines two of Ficino's favorite similes. The neurological simile picks up the theme of the powers diffused through the world mentioned in the last paragraph, by explaining that the powers move

simultaneously in two directions between the whole represented by the animate being of the world and the part represented by a lesser animate being. However, the musical simile introduces a further element, by showing that the powers also move in two directions between one or more lesser animate beings seemingly separated from one another through the mediacy of the animate being of the world to which they are both connected. The combination of these two similes shows that simultaneous movement in two directions vertically may be seen as inseparable from simultaneous movement in two directions horizontally, the equivalence between the vertical and horizontal motions being grounded in the omnipresence of the animate being's ultimate source: the world-soul.[403] It is this structure that grounds the entire metaphysical notion of cosmic sympathy here underlying Ficino's theory of prayer and magic, just as elsewhere it underlies his theory of sensation.[404]

2.4.2 COLLECTION, ATTRACTION, AND ATTUNEMENT

As we have perhaps already seen in some of the passages quoted above, the factor that makes possible the *control* over the movement of powers in specific different directions in the ritual practices of prayer and magic—as opposed to the mere facticity of those movements—is the degree of natural suitability or artificial adaptation[405] on the part of the recipient of those powers. This degree of suitability or adaptation is connected with the general principle of harmony forming the deep structure of so much of Ficino's thought and is increased or modified—explicitly in the practice of magic[406]—in a three-stage process that might perhaps be loosely characterized as consisting of the collection, attraction, and attunement of various symbolic items.[407] The first stage of collection is indicated when Ficino speaks of the magician as "connecting" (*coniungere*) different powers that are "disconnected" (*disiuncta*) in the world-animal in order to produce a powerful effect,[408] as "laying out" (*exponere*) things suitable for the imbibing of

the vital force by using prayer or other actions,[409] or as "bringing to bear scattered things" (*adhibere sparsa*) in order to draw down a particular gift.[410] The next stage is the process of attraction, which, as always in Ficino, represents the dynamic form of mediation. As he explains, every bodily part of an animal has a "power for attracting its proper portion of nutriment" (*vis . . . ad portionem nutrimenti propriam attrahendam*)—for instance, the heart with respect to spices, the liver with respect to sweet things—so that a careful investigator will find the "bait for attracting all things" (*esca omnibus attrahendis*).[411] He further notes that magicians who know how to apply objects hidden all around "that are able to attract in emitting their power from a distance" (*quae vim suam eminus effundentia trahere valeant*) and also know how to apply objects "that can be attracted by such things" (*quae ab his trahi possint*) can bring a woman forcibly to a man.[412] The final stage of attunement—the dynamic form of proportion—is indicated when Ficino speaks of the magician's use of the power of connecting the bodily parts of the world-animal into one living being "in a tempered or untempered manner" (*temperate . . . intemperate*),[413] or of the manner in which the disposition of the stars confers a wonderful power on "blends of matters and qualities" (*materiarum qualitatumque mixtiones*),[414] or of the process by which those with the requisite knowledge can draw celestial things to themselves by means of lower things that are "attuned" (*consentanea*) to the higher.[415]

2.4.3 INTERNALITY AND EXTERNALITY

We have already noted that an important feature of the powers harnessed by the magician is their simultaneous motion in opposite directions: that is, between above and below on the vertical dimension or between right and left on the horizontal dimension. However, it is now necessary to take account of a further aspect of those powers by noting that the collection, attraction, and attunement of the various symbolic items used in the magical operation

must be understood as taking place first, *within* the practitioner, and second, both *within and outside* the practitioner. This is because the spirit that in its modality of imagination functions as a transparent medium for the projection of the rays originating in the intellect and intellectual soul of the world is not only dynamic but spatial. A passage already cited has described how the magician uses his "imagination and affection" (*imaginatio affectusque*) in order to cast the rays of his spirit from afar[416] — the quasi-incorporeal spirit here being characterized explicitly as spatial and *internal*—, and in the previous paragraph Ficino contrasts the power obtained by the blending of matters and qualities outside the magician's body with the couplings of words within his soul. These couplings are "conceived" (*conceptae*) within the soul but "expressed" (*prolatae*) outside it and are "living" (*vivae*) in both cases, their connection and procession "being stretched toward the object as though a directing and application of the inner power to the exterior" (*in obiectum intenta . . . quasi directio et applicatio virtutis intimae ad externum*).[417] Another passage already cited has described how a spirit that is "wholly celestial or most similar to the heaven" (*caelestis omnino vel caelo simillimus*) is infused into all things in order that they might coalesce into vitality[418] — the quasi-incorporeal spirit being here characterized explicitly as spatial and *external*—, and elsewhere Ficino explains how song in its composition of parts and in disposition of the imagination imitates these celestial things. Song indeed is "another spirit recently conceived in you in the power of your spirit" (*spiritus alter nuper penes spiritum tuum in te conceptus*) that acts not only on your body but on a neighboring one "when flowing out" (*profluens*), the process being similar to that in which spirit directed outward through the rays of the eyes can fascinate.[419]

The symbolic items that are arranged in the spirit both inside and outside the practitioner when he fashions magical utterances or songs — prayer being said to have a similar power if "suitably

and seasonably composed" (*apte et opportune composita*)[420]— are enumerated in several passages of the commentary on the *Fourth Ennead*[421] and systematically classified in the third book of *On Life*.[422] Taking the latter as our authoritative text, we find Ficino describing "seven levels on which attraction from the higher to the lower occurs" (*septem gradus per quos a superioribus ad inferiora fit attractus*):[423] (1) stones and metals; (2) composites of plants, of fruits, of saps, and of animals' members;[424] (3) the finest powders and vapors derived from the above, the odors of plants and flowers used as simples and those of ointments; (4) words, song, and sounds;[425] (5) strong concepts of the imagination, (6) discursive processes of human reason; (7) more secret and simple operations of intelligence as though separated from motion and joined to divine things.[426] We are clearly intended to associate[427] these seven levels with the planets along a double trajectory whereby — as stated in the present passage—, each level as a genus of items is associated with a specific planet[428] and also, — as stated in an earlier chapter[429]—, specific items from all levels can be associated with each planet.[430] Now, some problems of interpretation may be thought to arise in that the passage just summarized seems to be enumerating items on the first three levels that are simply *external* to the practitioner who fashions magical utterances or songs while also assigning strong concepts of the imagination *specifically to the fourth* level in the enumeration, whereas we have been arguing that spirit in its modality of imagination implies a certain *internalization* of the items and would be by implication the underlying factor in the utilization of items on *all seven* levels. In response to this, we have only to cite in connection with the question of externality or internality of the symbolic items Ficino's statement in the *Commentary on the Fourth Ennead* that things coming and going in our external world are at the very least delineated by the *world*-soul "in its imagination" (*in sua imaginatione*),[431] and in connection with the question concerning the generality of the imagination's function

his statement in the commentary on Priscian of Lydia's *Interpretation of Theophrastus "On Imagination"* that imagination "has an adoptive relation" (*est agnata*) to *all* the faculties of the soul and "transfers" (*traducit*) the forms from one power to another.[432]

2.4.4 ABUSIVE PRACTICES

Since he has so fully elaborated the metaphysical principles underlying magical rituals — and to some extent also prayers and chants —, it is reasonable to assume that Ficino believes in the efficacy of these practices with respect to the souls and spirits of those involved. The exception seems to be practices involving the fashioning of images in the sense of amulets or "characters," probably on the grounds that these are *artificial* and productions of the human imagination alone and not *natural* as productions of the world-soul's imagination, and consequently that any efficacy that such practices may have — and this possibility is by no means denied by Ficino — results from human delusion engendered by maleficent daemons.[433] Having adopted this stance, the Florentine has to make a careful interpretation of Plotinus' analogy between the ability of the statues made by the ancients to capture the gods — as reported in the Hermetic *Asclepius*[434] — and that of the corporeal totality suitably constructed to capture the world-soul.[435] According to Ficino's commentary on this passage, Plotinus "sports with" (*alludit*) the magicians who animate statues, because it is neither the souls of the statues nor of the stars who speak but only daemons led by the star under whose rule the statues were fashioned.[436] The philosophical issue involved becomes clearer in the more elaborate interpretation of the same passage in *On Life*, Book 3, where Ficino — who explicitly states that he is interpreting Plotinus at this point — argues first, that nothing higher than the vitality of the world-soul, of the celestial spheres' souls, and of the airy daemons can be captured in this way,[437] and second, that a magician can intensify connections only between reason-principles

and materiate forms that have already been implanted by the world-soul.[438] The position of Plotinus is to a certain degree acceptable to his commentator, in that the Greek thinker has avoided an excessively literalistic reading of the Hermetic doctrine by associating the statues only with the capturing of *vital* powers and by emphasizing the *natural* character of any effects produced through the statues. In other words, Ficino, as a Christian, endorses Plotinus' position in noting the dangers of subscribing to a belief that any *super*-natural power could be activated through such devices: a belief that he has already informed us to be tenable only to those suffering delusion induced by wicked daemons.

Apart from the need to avoid daemonic delusion,[439] Ficino also has a clear and consistent position in his *Commentary on the Fourth Ennead* regarding the distinction between acceptable und unacceptable magic—that is, between the theurgy and the sorcery distinguished by Augustine—and he states it by recalling the history of philosophy. The magicians of former days who were lovers of the present life contrived "corporeal sacrifices and prayers" (*corporea sacrificia votaque*) by which they were able to obtain goods only directed toward bodily things.[440] However, Platonists such as Porphyry and Iamblichus went beyond this in choosing with respect to the higher gods "a worship more select than any other and ultimately consecrated to the supreme God" (*adoratio prae ceteris . . . et supremo denique consecrata*).[441] In other words, the distinction between good and bad magic is vested not so much in any differences in the techniques involved but rather in the ultimate intentionality of the practitioner and the degree of his detachment from the disturbing influences of the corporeal world.[442]

2.5 Sensation

We have already learned that within "soul" in general Ficino distinguishes (*a*) a higher soul containing intellectual, rational, and

imaginative powers and separate from body from (*b*) a lower soul consisting of imaginative, sensitive, and vegetative faculties and joined to body. It is in his discussion of the central power of the lower soul — "sensation" (*sensus*) itself divided into the five faculties of sight, hearing, smell, taste, and touch — that the commentator on the *Enneads* departs to the greatest extent from the letter of the original.[443] This is for at least two reasons: first, because Plotinus' own doctrine especially as stated in *Ennead* 4.5 can be described as inchoate at best, and second, because Ficino can here introduce his own doctrine of *spirit* in such a manner as to produce truly dramatic results.[444]

2.5.1 GENERAL THEORY OF SENSATION

The Ficinian doctrine of sensation is stated most fully in three texts:[445]

(*A*) Ficino contrasts two processes to which the term "sensation" might be applied: one process in which the soul turns to the interior and another in which it turns to the exterior. In the first case the soul knows sensible things *simpliciter*. Here, to the extent that it is separated from the body, it turns toward the more divine forms inborn in it and by treating the latter "as though causal principles" (*velut principia*), also comes to know sensible things. However, since the soul has no proportion to sensible things through which "any impression or expression between it and them" (*impressio ulla vel expressio inter hanc et illa*) could come about, this is not true sensation. In the second case, the soul knows things in a genuinely sensitive manner. Here, to the extent that it is joined to the body, it employs the spirit that is "mediate between itself and external things" (*medium inter eam et externa*) in order to make "a proportion between the two" (*proportio inter utraque*). In this mediative spirit, qualities or passions coming from outside are converted into "a spiritual and pure form" (*species spiritalis puraque*), and

through this spiritual form the soul excites the forms of sensible things within itself.[446]

(B) Ficino argues that sensation does not take place when an extension of space is broken up or materially affected by some object. Rather, "a spiritual entity of some kind" (*nescio quid quodammodo spirituale*), which is "a certain formal act coming forth from the form of the thing sensed" (*actus quidam specialis ab ipsa speciei rei sentiendae proveniens*), acts on the sense over a great distance. The act is said to arise "from the form" not because it comes to be in matter but because "it depends on a spiritual and living Idea" (*a spirituali vivaque dependet idea*); the act is said to be "formal" and "spiritual" whether it arises (*a*) within the instrument of sense — as in the cases of touch and taste — or also (*b*) outside us in the air — as in the cases of sight, hearing, and smell — or also (*c*) comes forth from the instrument of sense itself — as in the case of sight. Moreover, this formal and spiritual act arises "amid the passion" (*inter passionem*), which in the case of the senses lower than sight is "also material" (*etiam materialis*), as being made in the air. It also arises opportunely "through a certain power of the general life" (*virtute quadam vitae communis*) that binds not only sense to the sensible but one conformed body to another.[447]

(C) Ficino begins by contrasting two hypothetical examples of the process of "sensation": one in which the process is unsuccessful and another in which it is successful. In the first case, a "material passion" (*materialis passio*) is borne from the thing sensed into the "intermediary" (*medium*) without the contribution of any additional factor. Since the cause of sensing is not adapted to the "incorporeal nature of the sense" (*incorporea natura sensus*), the result may be the overwhelming of the latter by the strength of the former. In the second case, the material passion is borne from the thing sensed into the intermediary together with "a certain spiritual entity" (*spiritale aliquid*), which rises up either in the interme-

diary or at least in the instrument of sense. Since this spiritual entity is "adapted to the sense" (*accommodatum sensui*), the cause of sensing does not overwhelm the sense by its strength. Ficino continues by providing further details of the successful example of sensation. He explains how that which "is everywhere and simultaneously perceived and signified as a whole" (*ubique totum . . . eodem momento percipitur significaturque*) by many people listening to a voice is an example of such a spiritual entity adapted to sense, and that it is not a corporeal cause that produces such a thing around each and every "subject that is at this point opportunely arranged" (*subiectum tunc opportune dispositum*) but rather the life of the world itself. He adds that the life of the world brings it about that the sense opportunely arranged is aroused to "act" (*actus*) not only in simultaneity with the act of the spiritual entity in relation to it but in simultaneity with the act of the sensible object, and that there is an "attunement" (*contemperare*) or "harmony" (*concentus*) between the sense, the spiritual entity, and the thing sensed.[448]

Ficino notes at the end of passage A that he states the whole of this matter "more carefully together with Priscian of Lydia and Iamblichus in his book concerning Theophrastus' *On the Soul*" (*diligentius in libro Theophrasti 'De Anima' una cum Prisciano et Iamblicho*), and at the end of passage B that he discusses the points mentioned above "in more detail in my *Commentaries on Theophrastus*" (*diligentius in 'Commentariis Theophrasti'*). Indeed, although all the essential points of the general theory of sensation can be recovered from the three passages if the reader is prepared to read them with sufficient attention, it is true that certain details of the theory emerge with greater clarity in the more extended and discursive treatment to which Ficino draws attention. Using the three passages cited above in conjunction with that additional material, we may summarize Ficino's theory of sensation as follows:

An initial problem is presented by the lack of proportion or attunement between the sense and the sensible object,[449] this prob-

lem being resolved by conceiving the process of sensation as consisting of several phases that occur in a very rapid succession approaching simultaneity.[450] Thus, (1) the form of the sensible object attempts to act emanatively on the sensible subject.[451] However, because the form is materiate, it cannot affect the sense of the perceiver, which is immaterial.[452] A mediation on the microcosmic level (sense to sensible object via spirit) must therefore be introduced. (2) The sense extends toward the sensible object a spirit,[453] which remains in continuity with the spirit in the instrument of sense.[454] This spirit can be passive.[455] (3) The form of the sensible object acts emanatively upon the spirit.[456] However, because the form remains materiate, it cannot affect the sense of the perceiver, which is immaterial. A mediation on the macrocosmic level (spirit to life of world via spiritual *Idea*) must therefore be introduced in addition. (4) The life of the world acts emanatively on the materiate form of the spirit[457] by means of the spiritual Idea.[458] Because the form is now rendered spiritual,[459] it can affect the sense of the perceiver despite the latter's immateriality.[460] The combined mediations on the microcosmic and macrocosmic levels represent the proportion or attunement of the sense to the sensible object originally sought.[461]

2.5.2 FICINO'S INNOVATIONS

The introduction of spirit as the mediating element into the Plotinian theory of sensation represents an innovation by Ficino when considered in comparison with the explicit teaching of the author of the *Enneads* himself. It even amounts to something of a departure from the doctrines of Iamblichus and Priscian of Lydia, who use the term *pneuma* only once in the *Interpretation of Theophrastus*,[462] whereas the Florentine employs *spiritus* lavishly in his commentary on the latter. However, Ficino follows these later Neoplatonic writers closely in connecting the bare act of sensation as described in the analysis above—for instance, awareness of a patch

of green color — with the activation of the soul's internal reason-principles in order to produce sensation coupled with judgment — for instance, the sensory judgment that "that is a green object."[463] Again, the emphasis on notions of attunement between sense and sense-object in developing Plotinus' doctrine of sensation also constitutes a Ficinian innovation, although a definite source of this idea can be found in another work that Ficino had recently translated: namely, Porphyry's *Orientations to the Intelligibles*.[464]

2.5.3 Vision

Now, in attempting to summarize Ficino's theory of sensation, we have so far concentrated on the passages referring to the process in rather abstract terms that are equally applicable to vision, hearing, smell, taste, and touch, this approach being adopted in order to present a very complicated issue in the simplest manner. However, in order to complete our exposition, certain further assumptions underlying Ficino's understanding of sensation with respect to the latter's particular modes of operation need to be considered. These assumptions are first, that vision is considered to be paradigmatic with respect to the process in general;[465] second, that sensation involves additional elements associated with the employment of specific bodily instruments; and third, that vision as dependent on the eye involves the additional factor of light.[466]

At the beginning of his commentary on *Ennead* 4.5, *On Vision* — the Plotinian essay that functions with respect to the main discussion of difficulties regarding the soul in *Ennead* 4.3–4 as a kind of appendix — Ficino states the essential features of the process of vision. He begins by noting that the soul must "through its vegetative power in a certain manner of its own" (*per vim vegetalem suo quodam pacto*) form a palpable body[467] or spirit in order that — through the instrumentality of the soul's own body — (*a*) the power and act of the body or spirit so formed may "stretch itself out" (*se porrigere*) to external things, and (*b*) the motions of exter-

nal things "may somehow seem to have reached the soul" (*quodam-modo videantur ad animam pervenisse*) in coming to this body or spirit.[468] Ficino continues by arguing that there must also be "light" (*lumen*) functioning as a medium between the vision and the visible. Thus, vision takes place either when (*a*) light "comes forth toward the visible object" (*proficiscitur ad visibile*) from the eye, or when (*b*) it "proceeds toward the sight" (*procedit ad visum*) from the visible object, or (*c*) when both these things occur. It also takes place because both the eye and the visible object are so arranged in the living nature of the world that they have in light "a property very much in conformity with both of them through which they are easily moved in a reciprocal manner" (*proprietas . . . invicem valde conformis per quam a se invicem facile moveantur*). However, a *bodily* medium such as air is not necessary for the accomplishment of vision.[469]

An obvious question arising in connection with Ficino's account of vision is, what is the relation between the formation of the spirit mentioned first and the reciprocal emission of light mentioned second in the passage above? It must be admitted that the commentary on the *Fourth Ennead* provides only certain hints toward a solution of this question, and that we must turn ultimately to the commentary on Priscian of Lydia's *Interpretation of Theophrastus* in order to complete something approaching an adequate reconstruction of Ficino's position.

The hints provided by the commentary on the *Fourth Ennead* have to do with the properties of light—especially its incorporeality and actuality[470]—and with the relations between light and "intellect" (*intellectus*) and between light and the "transparency" (*diaphanum*). Ficino states clearly that light is "incorporeal" (*incorporeum*) and an "action" (*actus*) as part of his argumentation to the effect that a bodily and passive medium between vision and the visible is not necessary.[471] It is because of these properties that light is present and absent in a moment, does not remain if the

illuminating substance is removed, and is everywhere as a whole.[472] Ficino also argues that Plotinus himself "labors everywhere" (*ubique molitur*) to prove that there is such conformity between vision and the visible that they interact without any passivity in a medium.[473] The relation between light and intellect is established in a passage where the Florentine argues that there pours forth from the "intellectual light" (*lux intellectualis*) of the celestial soul a most efficacious act, and that "every light" (*omne lumen*) is an image of the "celestial light" (*caeleste lumen*) corresponding to this act.[474] The continuation of this argument establishes the relation between light and the transparency. Thus, the emanation of the celestial light can be divided into three phases: the light that is internal to the sidereal body, the light that is partly internal and partly going forth to the exterior, and the heat that is internal to the air. The second phase—which is the light that mediates sensation in the present context—penetrates the transparency. Indeed, whenever something transparent is placed in front of a lucent body, a light of sufficient intensity while remaining in itself *simpliciter* immediately subsists and acts in this transparency.[475]

Now, the argument whereby the commentary on Priscian of Lydia's *Interpretation of Theophrastus* enables us to establish the connection between the formation of spirit and the reciprocal emission of light relies on the assumption that the transparency can be treated as broadly analogous to spirit: a position for which the authority of Plotinus himself can be cited.[476] Thus, lucent forms are said to be present in the transparency[477] as spiritual forms were elsewhere said to be present in the spirit,[478] while the transparency is characterized as the vehicle of light[479] as spirit was elsewhere characterized as the vehicle of soul.[480] The transparency is said to be both inside and outside the sensory instruments[481] as spirit was elsewhere said to have a similar status,[482] while light and the transparency are both characterized as forms situated between intelligible and sensible forms as spiritual forms[483] were elsewhere

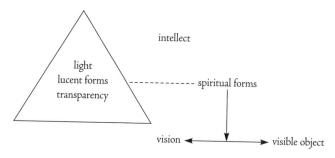

characterized similarly.[484] Perhaps most important of all is the association of the transparency with space.[485] Since light without the transparency is characterized by the nonspatiality of the incorporeal act that it essentially is, it is the relation between light and the transparency that produces the spatial extendedness of the illuminative act. Therefore both the transparency and the spirit have the same rather curious property: namely, extension prior to body. Now, the fact that the transparency is often treated as broadly analogous to spirit does not indicate that the formation of spirit and the reciprocal emission of light represent precisely synonymous depictions of the same phenomenon. The situation is rather that the process of vision relies on a complex interconnection or overlapping of the two structures, which might be presented diagrammatically as above.

Excursus 1: Further Trinitarian Analogues

We have noted that the concord between Plotinus and Christianity emerges most fully in connection with the intimations of the Trinity that Ficino detects in Plotinus' accounts of the double derivation of the universal reason-principle and its characterization as spirit-and-word in *Ennead* 3.2 and of the relation between the first Venus and the second Venus in *Ennead* 3.5.[486] We have also argued that Ficino assumes this doctrine as the general back-

ground of the various psychological discussions in his commentary on the *Fourth Ennead*, and that there is at least one instance of an overt trinitarian analogue in his reference to the ideas of intellectual light, the soul's intellectual light, and the expression of that light as light, heat, and the hidden power.[487] In addition to this, some brief allusions to a metaphysical triadism in the *cosmological* context are perhaps worth noting since these, at least to a reader familiar with the Florentine's program of Platonic-Christian philosophical syncretism, might seem like a distant echo of the divine mystery. A case in point is an argument appearing in two parallel passages where Ficino establishes a triad consisting of (A) the divine mind, (B) the intellect of the world-soul, and either (C1) the will of the world-soul or (C2) the general nature, concentrating his attention on the third member of the triad.[488] Here, he discusses the relation between, on the one hand, the unknowing associated with the moral evil resulting from human souls' freedom of choices[489] or the natural evil occasioned by their vegetative souls' encounter with matter,[490] and on the other hand, the hidden teleology inherent in the will of the world-soul (C1)[491] or the general nature (C2)[492] through the dependence on the higher intellectuality (A/B) in both cases. Moreover, Ficino compares the relation between the aspect of unknowing and the aspect of hidden teleology, in one passage, to the relation between the free movement of the interior sense and a magician's hidden enticement of that sense,[493] and in another passage, to the relation between our freedom of praying to the higher powers and the anticipatory fulfillment of those prayers by the latter.[494] Now the connection of references to the human *spirit* with the account of the third member of his triad in the second passage[495] shows that Ficino is presenting another version of his familiar trinitarian analogue. This fact confers special significance on his identification of the three terms with (A) the law, (B) the judgment, and (C) the justice of God, of which Orpheus sang and which Plato imitated in the *Laws*.[496]

Excursus 2: The Third Book On Life *and the*
Commentary on the Fourth Ennead

The question of determining the precise doctrinal relation between the *Commentary on Plotinus' Enneads* and the third book of
the treatise *On Life* as that doctrinal relation was intended to be
understood by the author of the works is a difficult one. It has led
to various controversies among modern scholars, which have been
difficult to resolve not least because of the absence of a modern
edition of the Plotinus commentary. On the basis of the present
edition and translation of the *Commentary on the Fourth Ennead*, the
section of the Plotinus commentary in which the connection with
the third book *On Life* was definitively made by Ficino, can some
further light be shed on this question?

First, we should recall precisely what Ficino tells us about his
Plotinus commentary in the treatise *On Life*. Already in chapter
twenty of Book 2, he states that he is composing a commentary on
Plotinus concerning images "in part" (*ex parte*) but concerning the
other aspects of celestial favor "especially" (*plurimum*), and that this
book should afterward be subjoined to the present book in the
same way that the latter should be inscribed after the one entitled
On Preserving the Health of Learned People.[497] However, most of the
references to Plotinus are in Book 3. In its proem addressed to
Matthias Corvinus, the king of Hungary, Ficino states that among
the books of Plotinus destined for Lorenzo de' Medici that he has
recently composed there is a commentary on Plotinus' book "concerning the drawing of favor from the heaven" (*de favore caelitus
hauriendo*) and numbered among his other commentaries on that
author, and that he has now decided to extract this commentary and — indeed, with the approval of Lorenzo himself — dedicate it to the king.[498] The *Ad lectorem* prefixed to Book 3 concludes by stating that the author has at this point addressed the
reader enough, partly in order to obtain his goodwill and partly in

order to encourage him, and that henceforth author and reader should "converse with Plotinus" (*cum Plotino loqui*) — indeed, in such a manner as to promote the care of the reader even more.[499] The title and subtitle of Book 3 read, "The book 'On Obtaining Life from the Heaven' by Marsilio Ficino of Florence being composed by him among his *Commentaries on Plotinus* . . . in what, according to Plotinus, the power that attracts favor from the heaven consists: namely, the fact that the world-soul and the souls of the stars and daemons are easily allured through the forms of bodies adapted to them."[500] In chapter fifteen of Book 3, Ficino notes that he will next briefly adduce that which can be alleged from the opinion of magicians and astrologers on behalf of images "in order to interpret Plotinus" (*ad Plotinum interpretandum*),[501] and in the final chapter of the same book he observes that one should review the matters at hand briefly in order not to digress too far "from the original starting point of our discussion: the interpretation of Plotinus" (*ab eo quod interpretantes Plotinum instituimus ab initio*),[502] and again that he will discuss that which here concerns religion in another context where Plotinus raises the issue.[503] In the longest passage of Book 3 referring to the Greek author, Ficino notes that Plotinus himself uses almost the same examples in the passage where "in imitation of Hermes" (*Mercurium imitatus*) he says that the ancient priests or *magi* used to capture in statues and sensible sacrifices something divine and wonderful, and that Plotinus also maintains "in agreement with Trismegistus" (*una cum Trismegisto*) that the priests captured through these materials not divinities totally separate from matter but only those that pertain to the world.[504] Ficino adds that he has said from the beginning and in agreement with Synesius that by "pertaining to the world" in this context is meant a certain life or something vital stemming from the world-soul and the souls of the spheres and stars, or even a certain motion or vital presence deriving from the daemons. He adds that the Hermes "whom Plotinus follows"

(*quem Plotinus sequitur*) also holds that such daemons are themselves sometimes present in the materials — these being airy and not celestial daemons, let alone more elevated ones — and that Hermes himself has from plants, trees, stones, and spices fashioned certain statues that contain within themselves — according to his own report — a natural power of divinity.[505] After a digression, Ficino urges his reader to return to Hermes "or rather to Plotinus" (*immo ad Plotinum*). He notes that Hermes was of the opinion that the priests received an appropriate power from the nature of the world and formed a blend from it, that Plotinus follows him in holding that all of this can be easily accomplished through the harmonious activity of the world-soul to the extent that the latter generates and moves the forms of natural things through certain seminal reason-principles implanted in it from the divine, and that Plotinus even calls these reason-principles gods since they are never cut off from the Ideas in the supreme mind.[506] Finally in the *Apologia* forming a postscript to the third book *On Life*, Ficino addresses his friend Piero Guicciardini and urges him to rise up and reply to certain unnamed meddlesome academics by stating that magic and images are not being approved by the author of the book but recounted by him "in interpreting Plotinus himself" (*Plotinum ipsum interpretante*), and that Ficino's own writings will make this perfectly clear if they are read in a fair-minded way.[507]

We can perhaps extract the following basic facts from these passages: (1) Ficino's aims in one or more of his Plotinian commentaries were to study primarily the gaining of favor from the heaven and secondarily the nature and function of images; (2) in connection with the secondary issue, Ficino was reporting the teaching of Plotinus rather than actively endorsing it; and (3) Plotinus in at least one of his works had followed the teaching of Hermes Trismegistus regarding the gaining of favor from the heaven through the fabrication of statues. Because of its placing in

the MS Firenze, Pluteus 82.11,[508] we know that the text eventually published as De Vita 3 was intended as an extended comment on Ennead 4.3.11, such digressive materials being found elsewhere — albeit without actual detachment and not on an equivalent scale — in the Plotinus commentary: for instance, in the summa following the more basic analysis of Ennead 3.1. However, despite the known facts, certain problems of interpretation remain, including the following: (1) The discussion of the employment of natural and artificial images that looms large in De Vita 3 relates more closely to Plotinus' explanation of the metaphysical basis of magic in terms of cosmic sympathy at Ennead 4.4.30–45 than to anything stated in the specified lemma of the commentary;[509] (2) it is unclear how Ficino's claim to be reporting the doctrine of Plotinus in the present context rather than endorsing any of it relates to the hermeneutical approach that he on other evidence takes in the same connection.

Now, it seems possible to take account of these facts and resolve these questions with a careful study of the broader context surrounding Plotinus' remarks in Ennead 4.3.9, especially if the original Plotinian argument is translated into more Ficinian terms and given a more Ficinian emphasis. With the implementation of such a strategy, the doctrine stated in Ennead 4.3.9–14 might be construed somewhat along the following lines.

The main philosophical issue in these chapters is that of the soul's entry into the body. At the beginning of chapter nine,[510] Plotinus asks the question, what is the soul's manner of entering the body? This entry can be considered in terms of two possibilities: that whereby the soul changes one body for another, and that whereby the soul goes from the bodiless to the embodied state. Plotinus decides to concentrate on the latter, starting from the world-soul. Since there is no temporally prior disembodied state, the notion of "entry" into body in the case of the world-soul is metaphorical. However, even with this qualification, it is clear that

the soul could not go forth from the intellectual sphere unless body already existed. Therefore, the world-soul must produce a body for itself, this process being compared to light's informing of darkness and the architect's production of a house. Moreover, the world-soul produces by means of the reason-principle that comes forth from it, the body produced thereby being coextensive with this reason-principle. In chapter ten,[511] Plotinus considers in more detail how the world-soul produces body for itself by means of its reason-principle, which is equivalent to nature, and explains that this process of formation involves no planning or consideration. Moreover, the production of a body for itself by the world-soul can be compared to the construction of shrines for gods and dwellings of men. In chapter eleven Plotinus notes that the ancients made statues in order to make gods present to them, since they realized that the nature of soul is easy to attract. This formation by universal nature represents a first instance of the attraction of soul to body and may be compared with a second instance of the attraction of soul to body represented by the descent of particular souls. Thus in chapter twelve,[512] Plotinus shifts from the consideration of the world-soul to that of particular souls, and explains how these souls descend into bodies while their highest parts remain undescended. One cause of this descent is necessity, since the descents and subsequent ascents of souls and the exchange of one body for another are required to complete the order of the cosmos. Plotinus speaks here mythologically of the "dispensation of Zeus," who is equivalent to the divine craftsman, the intellectual soul, and the higher reason-principle. Another cause of the descent is attraction, since the particular souls see their images below them in that which may be mythologically characterized as the "mirror of Dionysus." The souls are instinctively moved toward these images. Moreover, given that the images toward which the particular souls are attracted have been prepared for them by the world-soul together with the lower reason-principle or nature, the

descents of the world-soul and of particular souls are seen to be mutually interdependent. Chapter thirteen[513] explains that the second cause of descent, attraction — now identified with spontaneity — is consistent with the first cause of descent, necessity, and that this combination is exemplified in magical powers and sexual desire. Finally, in chapter fourteen,[514] Plotinus explains all the processes hitherto described by means of an allegory: namely, the story of Prometheus, Epimetheus, and Pandora. Here, Zeus corresponds to the intellectual soul or the higher phase of the world's reason-principle, Prometheus to nature or the lower phase of the world's reason-principle, and Pandora to the animate beings produced. Since Pandora receives gifts from Aphrodite and the other divinities and is given voice, she clearly corresponds to the shrines and statues mentioned near the beginning of the discussion.

The conclusion to be drawn from all this is that the statue making mentioned at the beginning of *Ennead* 4.3.11 is important to Plotinus and Ficino primarily because it represents a *metaphor* — together with the making of shrines and dwellings in general and the fashioning of Pandora — for the complex metaphysical process of the world-soul's and particular souls' embodiment, which grounds the possibility of extracting favor from the heaven.[515] The metaphysical process of the world-soul's and particular souls' embodiment can be compared by the two authors in this manner to the magical practice of statue making[516] apparently because of the element of instinctive attraction, which together with the element of necessity brings both the world-soul and the particular souls into conjunction with body and allows the world-soul to ground the particular souls' embodiment. Now, it is because the significance of the statue making is primarily *nonliteral* that the problems of interpretation mentioned earlier can be resolved. For this reason, Plotinus' report of the ancient religious practice at the beginning of *Ennead* 4.3.11 can be seen by his commentator as forming a valid introduction to the explanation of the

metaphysical basis of magic in terms of cosmic sympathy at 4.4.30–45. Accordingly, Ficino's commentary inserted after *Ennead* 4.3.11 — that is, Book 3, *On Life*, in its entirety — can be viewed as a legitimate expansion of the lemma provided by this Plotinian text. It is also because the primary significance of the statue making is *nonliteral* that Ficino as commentator can be seen as having a subtle and complicated relation to the text on which he is commenting, where he is neither simply committed to nor simply detached from the material at hand. Thus, he is fully committed as a philosopher to the general theory of attracting favor from heaven that is represented by the *metaphorical* understanding of the statue making, being simultaneously more or less detached on religious or ethical grounds from the particular magical practices that are represented by the *literal* understanding of the same phenomenon.

NOTES

1. Ficino, *In Enneadem* 4.3.33: *Si enim longa similiter argumenta immo et commentaria seorsumque ab ipsis Plotini capitibus disposita prosequamur, et confusa continget interpretatio et opus excrescet in immensum. Satis evagati sumus; satis multa iam diximus. Sat igitur erit deinceps breves quasdam annotationes, ut in Theophrasto fecimus, Plotini capitibus interserere.*

2. On the Plotinian doctrine of soul in general, see especially the various publications of Henry J. Blumenthal: "Plotinus *Ennead* IV. 3. 20–21 and Its Sources"; *Plotinus' Psychology*; "Soul, World-Soul and Individual Soul in Plotinus"; "Plotinus' Psychology"; "Nous and Soul in Plotinus"; "Plotinus' Adaptation of Aristotle's Psychology"; *Soul and Intellect*; and "On Soul and Intellect." Among more recent publications, see especially the collected volumes: Chiaradonna, *Studi sull'anima in Plotino*; Barbanti and Iozzia, *Anima e libertà in Plotino*; and Corcilius and Perler, *Partitioning the Soul*. Karfík, "Parts of the Soul in Plotinus," provides an accurate summary of the Plotinian psychological doctrine as a whole.

3. Another complicating element with respect to the *Commentary on the Fourth Ennead* is the fact that part of the commentary as originally

planned was later removed, revised, and utilized as the third book of the treatise *De Vita*. On the relation between the Plotinian commentary as it now stands and the latter work, see our *Excursus 2*.

4. See Gersh (ed. and trans.), *Marsilio Ficino, Commentary on Plotinus: The Third Ennead*, "Analytical Study," §§1 and 1.1–1.2.

5. For convenience of -exposition at this point, the "genus" comprising soul can be understood n an Aristotelian sense (as a notion of soul abstracted from various real instances). However, Ficino's Aristotelian (immanent) forms are ultimately to be understood as Platonic (transcendent-immanent) forms, and this rule applies especially in the case of soul. On the Ficinian "Idea" of soul see below.

6. As usual in Ficino's summaries of the basic Plotinian ontology, the unitary self-subsistent first principles, or hypostases, of the original are silently transformed into generic terms within which a number of self-subsistent principles are notionally comprehended.

7. There is a disagreement in the scholarly tradition regarding the order of the first two treatises of the *Fourth Ennead*, Although most of the MSS place second the short note numbered as 21 in the historical order of composition reported by Porphyry—thereby making it 4.2 in the enneadic ordering—Ficino places it first before the slightly longer essay numbered as 4 in the historical order—accordingly making it 4.1 in the enneadic sequence—no doubt reasoning on philological grounds that in his MSS the note had already appeared at the end of treatise 3.9 without any break in the text and was afterward perhaps accidentally repeated after the longer essay, and also on methodological grounds that the short note provided to a greater extent a summary of the doctrine worked out in the *Fourth Ennead* as a whole. On the problem of ordering, see Henry and Schwyzer (eds.), *Plotini Opera*, vol. 1, pp. ix–x, and vol. 2, pp. 3, 10.

8. Kristeller in his seminal *The Philosophy of Marsilio Ficino*, pp. 106–8, stated that the "theory of five substances" that looms large in the early books of Ficino's *Platonic Theology* was derived from Plotinus, arguing the point on the basis of Plotinus' explanation of the different levels of divisibility and indivisibility and the introduction of quality as the second level between body and soul in *Ennead* 2.1–2. The present Ficinian com-

mentary gives some support to Kristeller's interpretation. For further details of the scheme, see also Kristeller, pp. 266, 400–401. However, given the Florentine's tendency to synthesize doctrine derived from many sources, the argument of Allen, "Ficino's Theory of the Five Substances," that Ficino's approach was also influenced by post-Plotinian interpretations of the hypotheses in the second part of Plato's *Parmenides* may also be valid.

9. Ficino shows that he is thinking of intellect here — as he thinks of soul and body in the same context — in a generic sense, since he goes on to specify that "intellect" can refer to the intellect in the human soul, the intellect of the world-soul, and the divine intellect.

10. Ficino, *In Enneadem* 4.1–2.**1–3**.

11. Ficino, *In Enneadem* 1.1 [ch. 1] (Basel 1580, sign. γ4r–v).

12. Ficino, *In Enneadem* 1.1 [ch. 8] (Basel 1580, sign. γ5v).

13. Less complete enumerations of the levels of reality can be found at Ficino, *In Enneadem* 4.3.**12**, **25**; 4.4.**16**; 4.6.3. It is perhaps important to note that in setting out two hierarchical structures rather than one Ficino does not encourage his reader simply to correlate the first structure with the second. This is indicated by the fact that the lower phase of soul — nature — that appears in conjunction with the first structure cannot simply be equated with the fourth term — quality — in the second structure. Indeed, in other passages of his commentary on the *Fourth Ennead* — see §2.2.3 below — Ficino maintains a clear distinction between the *idolum* of the soul, which includes nature, and the soul's *umbra* corresponding to bodily quality. Schwyzer, "Zu Plotins Interpretation von Platons *Timaeus* 35a," pp. 364–66, maintains that a structure with *four* levels of being in addition to the One or Good and with nature as the third level is intended by Plotinus in *Ennead* 4.2 and elsewhere.

14. Although justifiable on the basis of Plotinus' reference at *Ennead* 4.2.1.29–40 to "another nature" (ἄλλη φύσις), which is not primarily divisible in the way that bodies are divisible but becomes divisible in bodies: namely, "colors, all qualities, and every shape" (χροιαὶ καὶ ποιότητες πᾶσαι καὶ ἑκάστη μορφή), the introduction of quality as one of the five terms renders a structure that is only implicit in the original more

explicit. It is important to note that the type of quality that is comprehended within this term of Ficino's classification is quite distinct from the Aristotelian categorial quality, being rather (*a*) equivalent to accidental form in general (as opposed to *species* or specific form), and (*b*) conceived as an active power. See the important remarks of Kristeller, *The Philosophy of Marsilio Ficino*, p. 42.

15. Ficino, *In Enneadem* 4.1–2.**4–5**. There are extensive developments of the notion of soul as a mediator or mean within a pentadic structure in Ficino's *Compendium in Timaeum*. At *Compendium in Timaeum*, ch. 28 (*Opera* 2:1447), he says that the number 5 agrees with the structure of soul for three reasons: (1) as five consists of the first even number and the first odd number, so soul consists of the divisible nature and the indivisible nature; (2) the natures by which God composes everything are five in number: being, same, different, rest, motion; (3) since soul is the mediator of the universe, it is naturally associated with the number five, which is the mean of universal number. Later in the same chapter Ficino notes that according to the followers of Plato — a phrase that seems to allude to Proclus' commentary on the *Timaeus* — soul consists of five natures: its essential being subdivided into substance, harmony, and type, its power, and its activity. Moreover, soul is composed in five ways: (*a*) from being, same, different, rest, motion; (*b*) from numbers; (*c*) from rhythmical harmonies; (*d*) from the rudiments of shapes; (*e*) from the beginnings of movements, being related to the divine according to *a* and *b*, to the natural according to *d* and *e*, and to itself as mean according to *c*. These developments are more closely associated with the *Timaeus* than with the *Enneads* and clearly reveal the influence of Proclus and Macrobius.

16. Ficino, *In Enneadem* 4.4.**26**.

17. Ficino, *De Vita* 3.1.1–12 (ed. Kaske-Clark, p. 242).

18. See our "Analytical Study" of the *Third Ennead*, §1.1 and especially pp. xiv–xv.

19. The relation between a static system of proportions and a dynamic system of attunement, even if not explicitly stated, also underlies Ficino's discussion of law. See Ficino, *In Enneadem* 4.3.**31**, 4.4.**40**, 4.8.**6**.

20. Ficino, *In Enneadem* 4.4.**44**.

21. The two-directional motion had traditionally been associated with the "spirit" ($\pi\nu\epsilon\hat{u}\mu\alpha$/*spiritus*), which also plays an unstated role in the development of Ficino's medical analogy. On this point see further §2.3.

22. This sharing of properties corresponds to the mediation discussed in the passage from *De Vita* 3 mentioned above. For a more detailed discussion of this association of ideas and its role in Ficino's notions of magic and sensation, see §§2.4.2 and 2.5.

23. Ficino undoubtedly thought long and hard about the phenomenon of sympathetic vibration since it grounds much of his thinking both in the commentary on the *Fourth Ennead* and in *De Vita* 3. The notion of sympathetic action was discussed in the pseudo-Aristotelian *Problemata*, which is one of the major sources of *De Vita*. See *Problemata* 7.1–9.886a–87b. Moreover, the commentary of Pietro d'Abano—an author much admired by Ficino—had been published in 1475, and d'Abano had made considerable strides in associating the vibration of strings with a similar agitation of air. However, the precise connection between sympathetic vibration and the movement of air was first explained by Girolamo Fracastoro in 1546. On the physics of sound in pseudo-Aristotle and Pietro d'Abano, see Palisca, *Music and Ideas in the Sixteenth and Seventeenth Centuries*, pp. 135–38, and on sympathetic vibration in particular, see p. 158.

24. Ficino, *In Enneadem* 4.3.**28**. As argued earlier, since Jupiter represents the normal Ficinian higher reason-principle (life), the two actions of Apollo represent a subdivision within the normal lower reason-principle (nature) rather than the normal higher and lower reason-principles (life and nature).

25. That is, the lower subdivision of the seminal reason-principles. See the present author's "Analytical Study" of the *Commentary on the Third Ennead*, §4.4.

26. Ficino's further comment here: "if I may speak for myself" (*ut proprie loquar*) could mean either that he is expressing his personal viewpoint or that he is himself hearing the sounds, or (as is most likely) both of these ideas.

27. Ficino, *In Enneadem* 4.4.**33–35**.

28. The entire passage is full of references to music. For instance, there are "musical proportions" (*musicae proportiones*) in the cycles of the world, the cosmic processes are "as though a melody and harmonies of sounds" (*quasi cantilena sonorumqe concentus*), and these processes are followed by a wise man "as though a musician" (*quasi musicus*) according to the argument of the first paragraph alone.

29. To the present author at least, the further attunements suggested at Ficino, *In Enneadem* 4.4.**33**, where the dancer is said, after contemplating the music implanted in him, to gaze at the cycles of the members of the world and the events following the cycles (which substitute for 2*b* and 3*b* in our summary), confuse rather than clarify the issue. Although this suggestion reinforces the analogy between the dancer and the world and shows that the whole analogy is not just *about* attunement but *is* also a proportion or analogy (a perfectly reasonable idea in the Ficinian context), the conflation of metaphorizer and metaphorized at this point leaves a somewhat unsatisfactory impression in the reader's mind.

30. Ficino, *In Enneadem* 4.1-2.**1**.

31. Ficino, *In Enneadem* 4.4.**24**. Other examples of such proportions or analogies can be found at Ficino, *In Enneadem* 4.3.3, **9**, **11**, **31**; 4.4.4, **13**, **28**, **42**; 4.8.8. The most important examples tend to involve proportions or analogies between microcosm and macrocosm (as in the case of the "eye") or between the divine Trinity and created things. Occasionally, Ficino's analogies expand into mythological allegories: see Ficino, *In Enneadem* 4.3.**27**.

32. Ficino refers several times in his *Compendium on the Timaeus* to the treatment of this doctrine in his commentary on Plotinus, thereby indicating perhaps the weight that he himself placed on it. See Ficino, *Compendium in Timaeum*, ch. 41 [incorrectly numbered 42] and summa 30 (*Opera* 2:1462, 1470-71).

33. Ficino's use of the term *sensus* often rather loosely embraces the notion of both "sensation" (bare reception of sensory data) and "sense-perception" (sensation together with an element of judgment), although he is aware of, and sometimes makes some effort to exploit, the difference

between the two. Plotinus proceeds in exactly the same way with reference to the Greek term αἴσθησις.

34. Ficino, *In Enneadem* 4.6.**2**. At *In Enneadem* 4.5.**6**, Ficino states the problem in a slightly different way, by speaking of the incommensurability between the incorporeal sense and the materiality of the passion in the sense-organ. However, the underlying problem — the incommensurability between soul and body — is the same. For more detail regarding these formulations, see §2.5.

35. Or: "contiguity, continuity, union" (*contiguitas . . . continuitas . . . unio*).

36. Ficino, *In Enneadem* 4.4.**26**.

37. Ficino, *In Enneadem* 4.6.**2**.

38. Ficino, *In Enneadem* 4.5.**2–3**.

39. Ficino, *In Enneadem* 4.5.**1**, 4.6.**2**.

40. Ficino, *In Enneadem* 4.5.**1** and **4**.

41. Ficino, *In Enneadem* 4.5.**4**.

42. Ficino, *In Enneadem* 4.5.**1–2**, 4.6.**2**.

43. Ficino, *In Enneadem* 4.5.**2–4** and **6**.

44. Ficino, *In Enneadem* 4.5.**4**. Cf. *In Enneadem* 4.5.**6**. A further important element in this complex process — which we will simply note at this point — is the identification between the reason-principles in the subject and the object, which, in effect, transforms bare sensation into sensory judgment (see Ficino, *In Enneadem* 4.6.**1**). Moreover, the implicit understanding of the relation between sense and sense-object is an analogue, albeit distant, of the divine Trinity (see Ficino, *In Enneadem* 4.5.**10–12**).

45. Ficino, *In Enneadem* 4.4.**53**. The passage to which he refers is Plotinus, *Ennead* 4.4.43.12–16.

46. Ficino, *In Enneadem* 4.4.**51–52**.

47. Ficino, *In Enneadem* 4.4.**53**.

48. Or "intellectual soul" (*anima intellectualis*).

49. Sometimes this is also called "sensation."

50. Sometimes this is identified with the "common sense."

51. This performs the functions of reproduction, growth, and vitality.

52. Ficino, *In Enneadem* 4.3.**1**. For a detailed analysis of the Plotinian text giving rise to Ficino's *quaestio*, see Helleman-Elgersma, *Soul-Sisters*, especially at pp. 63–78. Modern interpreters have been divided regarding the correct interpretation of the relation between universal and individual souls in Plotinus' thought. Earlier scholars such as Eduard Zeller and William R. Inge had maintained that the universal soul is equivalent to the world-soul and that individual souls are derived from this higher soul, this derivation being understood in the manner of nineteenth-century Idealism. However, Henry J. Blumenthal argued decisively for the distinction between universal soul and world-soul and for the generation of the world-soul as well as individual souls from the universal soul. For a thorough review of this history of interpretation, see Helleman-Elgersma, *Soul Sisters*, pp. 89–103. As we will see in the discussion that follows, Ficino endorses the second interpretation — as do most modern writers, including Helleman-Elgersma — although he states the position more clearly and introduces many arguments not in the original Plotinian text.

53. Ficino, *In Enneadem* 4.3.**2**.

54. Ficino, *In Enneadem* 4.3.**3**. Helleman-Elgersma, *Soul-Sisters*, pp. 65–67, points out that the foundation of Plotinus' argument in *Ennead* 4.3 is twofold, being based in the first instance on the attribution of (1) the genus-species relationship and (2) the potency-actuality relationship to soul.

55. Ficino, *In Enneadem* 4.3.**4**.

56. He notes that *nonintellectual* souls could arise directly from the world-soul.

57. Ficino, *In Enneadem* 4.3.**6**.

58. Ficino later adds a variant of this argument based on the omnipresence of the judging faculty of the soul.

59. Ficino, *In Enneadem* 4.3.**9**.

60. Ficino himself accepts an analogy that is subtly to be distinguished from this one. See note 62.

61. Ficino, *In Enneadem* 4.9.**3**.

62. This analogy that Ficino accepts should be compared and contrasted with the similar analogy that he rejects. See note 60.

63. Ficino, *In Enneadem* 4.1–2.**1**.

64. See above.

65. Ficino, *In Enneadem* 4.3.**11**.

66. Ficino, *In Enneadem* 4.9.**3**.

67. By which he means: souls existing independently of the world-soul.

68. That is to say: while remaining a unity.

69. The argument based on the unity and plurality of the reason-principle also appears at Ficino, *In Enneadem* 4.3.**15**. Here, there is also an interesting statement of how the differences between souls are explained by Plotinus and other Platonists, the assumption being that this differs from Ficino's argument about the reason-principle. According to Plotinus, the differences are caused by two factors: (*a*) the differences of bodies having various motions according to differences of blood, bile, and spirit; and (*b*) differences of the choices regarding types of life made in previous incarnations. Certain other Platonists trace the differences between souls back to (*c*) differences of species distributed through various degrees of being within the genus soul that have existed from the beginning; and (*d*) differences in the free motions according to which souls although equivalent to the universe as a whole select this or that kind of life.

70. If Ficino can be said to have established in the foregoing the existence of a multiplicity of individual souls, he has not explained precisely how their individuality is established. Some light on this question is cast by his commentary on *Ennead* 5.7 (Basel 1580, pp. 538–41). Here, he argues that the "entire arrangement of individual things" (*tota singularum rerum dispositio*) is preestablished in nature, in the mind of the world-soul, and in the divine mind, and that the multiplicity of things produced is

equal to the multiplicity of "reason-principles" (*rationes*) and virtually equivalent to the multiplicity of "Ideas" (*ideae*) precontained. The commentator contrasts the great year (i.e., the present world) with the subsequent year (i.e., the world to come) and argues that, since the number of reason-principles is finite, the same things will be reconstituted from the same reason-principles, here using the Plotinian discussion as an argument for the Christian resurrection. Ficino further argues that each soul and nature also contains the "seminal reason-principles" (*rationes seminales*) of a limited number of "lives" (*vitae*), that these reason-principles govern the proper forms, shapes, and modes of nativity, that the reason-principles have an absolute distinction from one another, and that the formal differences of things generated are equivalent to the reason-principles. Although certain further differences among things produced may arise through defect of form, chance, and quantitative division, the reason-principles contained in each soul (and also in the nature, the mind of the world-soul, and the divine mind) govern *individual* unities and not just *specific* ones. This is indicated by Ficino's wording quoted at the beginning of this note and by his later comment that the many things produced are distinguished according to the reason-principles even "if they are enumerated together in the same specific form" (*si in eadem communiter specie computentur*) (ch. 2, Basel 1580, p. 539). Certain modern interpreters of Plotinus — for example, Blumenthal, "Soul, World-Soul, and Individual Soul in Plotinus," at pp. 59–61 — have erred in arguing that the Plotinian doctrine of soul ultimately does not ground individuality except through modes of embodiment. This conclusion may be true with respect to the doctrine of soul considered in the narrow sense. However, Ficino was undoubtedly more correct in understanding the grounds of individuality as being provided by the doctrine of *Logos*, especially as elaborated in *Ennead* 3.2–3.

71. Ficino, *In Enneadem* 1.1 [ch. 8] (Basel 1580, sign. γ5v).

72. This kind of intellect appears only occasionally (and somewhat allusively) in the commentary on the *Fourth Ennead* and represents either the agent intellect or a combination of the agent and possible intellects as understood by the Peripatetics. In the *Commentary on the First Ennead*, the Aristotelian distinction between the agent and possible intellects is often

identified with that between the intellect (nondiscursive) and reason (discursive) of Plotinus-Ficino. Therefore Kristeller, *The Philosophy of Marsilio Ficino*, p. 238 n. 25, was wrong to suggest that "the theory of the *intellectus agens* has no significance whatsoever for Ficino." The clearest reference to such an intellect in the present commentary is perhaps that at Ficino, *In Enneadem* 4.8.9, where it is said to be "at least probable" (*probabile . . . saltem*) that our intellect, like the intellects of celestial souls, "always acts around divine things" (*circa divina semper agere*). The intellect referred to here is further associated by Ficino with the undescended intellect mentioned in similarly circumspect language at Plotinus, *Ennead* 4.8.8.1–4, and representing something of an innovation with respect to traditional Platonism. See Ficino, *In Enneadem* 4.8.**5**.

73. Ficino establishes this compromise position at great length in the course of *Platonic Theology* 15. Copenhaver, "Ten Arguments in Search of a Philosopher," at pp. 444, 468–79, has shown convincingly that the arguments attributed to Averroes or "the Averroists" by Ficino are derived from Thomas Aquinas' *Summa contra gentiles* rather than from Averroes directly. For a briefer summary of the "Averroistic" doctrine of the unity of both the agent and the possible intellects as criticized by Ficino, see Allen, "Marsilio Ficino on Saturn," at pp. 89–94.

74. On this distinction between Plotinus and Ficino, see our "Analytical Study" of Ficino's *Commentary on the Third Ennead*, §§2.2.2 and 2.2.2.1–2.2.2.3.

75. Plotinus, *Ennead* 4.3.5.6–18, provides a good summary of Plotinus' position.

76. See Augustine, *De Immortalitate Animae* 15.24 and *De Quantitate Animae* 32.69.

77. In response to the recent scholarship that has become wary of the earlier view that Ficino was combating a contemporary group of doctrinaire Averroists in formulating his critique, Allen, "Marsilio Ficino on Saturn," at pp. 90, 95–96, suggests that Ficino's main motivation for attacking the Averroistic doctrine of the unicity of the intellect in the *Platonic Theology* was to prepare the ground for a defense of Plotinus' doctrine of intellect. On Ficino and contemporary Averroism, see Monfasani,

"The Averroism of John Argyropoulos," and Copenhaver, "Ten Arguments in Search of a Philosopher," at pp. 462–64.

78. On this ambivalence see Helleman-Elgersma, *Soul-Sisters*, pp. 60–61, who notes that Plotinus sometimes considers our body a product of our soul (e.g., in *Ennead* 4.4.28) and sometimes says that our body is preformed by the world-soul for our use (e.g., at ibid. 4.9.3.15–18, 6.7.7.8–16). According to Karfik, "Parts of the Soul in Plotinus," at pp. 127–28, the human vegetative soul comes from the world-soul (see *Ennead* 4.9.3.25–29; cf. 4.3.27.1–3), the individual human soul grafting its own power onto that which is given by nature. Blumenthal, "Soul, World-Soul, and Individual Soul in Plotinus," at p. 63 suggests that the world-soul and individual souls are for Plotinus united closely at the highest levels, diverge in the middle range, and are reunited at the lower levels in a kind of circular configuration.

79. See Ficino, *In Enneadem* 4.9.**2**.

80. See the present author's "Analytical Study" of the *Commentary on the Third Ennead*, §2.2.2.2.

81. See the present author's "Analytical Study" of the *Commentary on the Third Ennead*, §4 and its subsections (especially §4.4).

82. Ficino, *In Enneadem* 4.3.**14**. He continues by citing the *Phaedrus* and "Timaeus."

83. For a detailed explanation of the various lower phases of soul discussed in this passage and the next, see §2.2.

84. Ficino in agreement with Plotinus also allows the world-soul to be productive of matter. Thus, at *In Enneadem* 4.3.**22–24** he argues that the world-soul operating in terms of its intellectual, rational, and vegetative powers produces (*a*) as darkness, primal matter, and (*b*) as light, forms in matter. The latter consist of stable forms (produced by the world-soul's intellectual power), stably moved forms (produced by its rational power), and mobily moved forms (produced by its vegetative power).

85. Ficino, *In Enneadem* 4.3.**20**. The immediate starting point of the discussion is criticism of those who interpret Plotinus as holding that the soul in animals and plants generated from putrefaction is the world-soul

only. Ficino notes that this idea is contradicted in Plotinus' treatise *On the Immortality of the Soul*.

86. At *In Enneadem* 4.3.**32** Ficino says that this vegetative power — described mythologically as "Prometheus" — makes natural things (as "statues") from matter (as "mud").

87. It may well be that Ficino has more trouble in accepting the Platonists' accounts of the descent of the soul than he does in accepting their accounts of its ascent, perhaps because of the complexity of established church doctrine regarding the fall, original sin, and redemption. The relatively limited discussion of the souls' descent in the myth of Plato's *Phaedrus* is noted by Allen, *The Platonism of Marsilio Ficino*, pp. 181–82 (à propos summae 23–25 of the commentary).

88. On the important theme of the soul's natural inclination to body in Ficino, see Kristeller, *The Philosophy of Marsilio Ficino*, pp. 359–60, 388–94.

89. Ficino, *In Enneadem* 4.8.**7**. According to Ficino, there are three main reasons for the descent of the soul: namely, (1) instinct, (2) choice, and (3) necessity. This undoubtedly represents a correct interpretation of Plotinus, who at *Ennead* 4.8.2.5–6 says that soul dwells in the world "either willingly or under compulsion or in some other way" (ἑκοῦσα εἴτε ἀναγκασθεῖσα εἴτε τις ἄλλος τρόπος) and that it is possible to harmonize the teachings of Heraclitus, Empedocles, and Plato in the *Phaedrus* and the *Timaeus* regarding this topic. For reasons that we will explore below, although Ficino accepts all three reasons, he actually pays the greatest attention to reason 1. The issue is important because there has been a tendency among modern interpreters of Plotinus to postulate only reasons 2 and 3 and to argue that there is an inconsistency in his thought between these two. For instance, see Schuhl, "Descente métaphysique et ascension de l'âme," at pp. 71, 81–82. Dodds, *Pagan and Christian in the Age of Anxiety*, pp. 24–26, had gone as far as to argue that the disparity represented two phases in the evolution of Plotinus' thought. For a correction of this erroneous view, see the careful study of O'Brien, "Le volontaire et la nécessité."

90. For the connection between the descent of souls and their transmigration, see Ficino, *In Enneadem* 4.3.**29–30**; Ficino describes the descent

in straightforward Plotinian terms at ibid. 4.4.**3–4**. A clear statement that the descent of souls, although described as taking place through space, is not to be understood literally in this manner can be found at Ficino, *Platonic Theology* 18.5.2. Here, Ficino comments regarding the Platonists' doctrine that souls descend into generation through the tropic of Cancer and ascend from generation through the tropic of Capricorn that "nobody should be so much deceived as to accept the descent or ascent here as referring to place" (*nemo vero adeo falli debet ut descensum ascensumve hic accipiat secundum situm*). Descent through Cancer means that the soul is attached to body through an instinct that is lunar and vegetative — the moon being the mistress of Cancer — and detached from body through an instinct that is saturnian and intellectual — Saturn being the lord of Capricorn. Cf. 17.4.1.

91. This dynamic relation to the body is stated explictly at Ficino, *In Enneadem* 4.7.**13**, where the Florentine follows Plotinus in mentioning three ranks of souls: the celestial, the daemonic, and the human, adding that the human soul although divine descends into a mortal body "when it descends *in itself* to a third level" (*quando in seipsa descendit ad tertia*): that is, in descending below intellect or reason and imagination to the vegetative power.

92. The dynamic relation of the soul to the body in Ficino is of course strictly to be understood as that of a nonspatial principle to something in space. On the basis of passages such as *Ennead* 6.4.16.22–35 one could argue that this is also Plotinus' view, although the literal doctrine of transmigration embraced by the latter requires also a spatial movement of descent. Passages such as *Ennead* 4.8.4.5–7, which speak of the first stage of soul's descent as being "in heaven" (ἐν οὐρανῷ), are therefore ambiguous. In post-Plotinian writers, the association of souls with various kinds of pneumatic vehicle somewhat reconfigures the relation between nonspatial souls and spatial bodies, since the pneumatic vehicles are spatial in nature and move locally: see Porphyry, *Sententiae ad intelligibilia ducentes* 29, and Macrobius, *Commentarius in Somnium Scipionis* 1.12, the role of *pneuma* being specified in the former text. As we shall see in §2.3, Ficino also assigns an important role to spirit, albeit with slightly different results.

93. See the present author's "Analytical Study" of the *Commentary on the Third Ennead*, §4.4.

94. Plotinus, *Ennead* 4.3.12.1–4. This passage in Plotinus is discussed in a useful article by Pépin, "Plotin et le miroir de Dionysos."

95. The reason-principle is identified in the subsequent paragraph.

96. Ficino, *In Enneadem* 4.3.**27**.

97. As indicated in the subsequent paragraph.

98. Jupiter is mentioned in the headnote preceding the present passage and again at Ficino, *In Enneadem* 4.3.**28**.

99. For further references to the instinctive phase of the soul's descent, see Ficino, *In Enneadem* 4.4.**19**, where he follows Plotinus in speaking of the double ligature of the human soul to the body consisting on the one hand of "its life-giving act springing forth toward body" (*vivificans eius actus emicans erga corpus*) and on the other of an "inclination toward body" (*declinare ad corpus*), and 4.7.**11**, where Ficino argues that the soul's ability to move itself is proven when it moves "against the inclinations" (*contra inclinationes*) of the body and "transfers itself" (*se transfert*) to incorporeal things. At 4.4.**32** Ficino assigns a kind of instinctive phase to the world-soul by arguing that the heaven acts on lower things by means of certain powers of the vegetative soul that are "as though mediate terms between deliberation and corporeal qualities" (*inter consilium et corporeas qualitates quasi media*). For a further reference to the overarching context of necessity, see 4.8.**7**.

100. Ficino, *In Enneadem* 4.8.**2–3**.

101. See the present author's "Analytical Study" of the *Commentary on the Third Ennead*, §§2.3 and 2.3.1–2.3.2. In interpreting Ficino's use of these analogues, it is important to note two potential causes of confusion: (1) Some of the analogues are more "Arian" (with hierarchical arrangement of the three terms) and some more "Catholic" (including consubstantiality of the first two terms); (2) *Ratio* can appear sometimes as the second term (where the analogue is more "Christian") and sometimes as the third term (where the analogue is more "Platonic"). For further examples of trinitarian analogues in Ficino's works, see the recent discussions of

Allen, "Sending Archedemus," at p. 416; "Prometheus among the Florentines," at pp. 37–40; and "*Ratio omnium divinissima*," at pp. 483–89.

102. For further details of this argument, see §2.2.3.

103. Ficino, *In Enneadem* 2.3 [ch. 9] (Basel 1580, pp. 127–28). The passage also states two further important points: (1) that the twofold structure also applies to the souls of celestial bodies and spheres; and (2) that the intellectual souls can be associated with good angels and the emanating life with angels and daemons that have fallen into bodies.

104. Ficino, *In Enneadem* 1.1 [ch. 8] (Basel 1580, sign. γ5ν).

105. See above.

106. See the present author's "Analytical Study" of the *Commentary on the Third Ennead*, §4.4.

107. Ficino's finding of a trinitarian analogue in sensation has an excellent precedent in Augustine's *De Trinitate*, Book 11.

108. Ficino, *In Enneadem* 4.5.**10**.

109. The "word" would here be the third term thinking "Platonically" (*Platonice*), as he often notes. Of course, thinking in the Christian or Johannine manner, the "word" would be the second term.

110. Ficino's commentary on Priscian of Lydia's *Interpretation* (*Metaphrasis*) *of Theophrastus* is divided into two sections, entitled *Super Theophrastum* (*Opera* 2:1801–24) — dealing with sensation — and *Super Theophrastum de phantasia et intellectu* (*Opera* 2:1824–35).

111. Ficino, *In Enneadem* 4.4.**53**. On the relationship between the third book of *De Vita* and the *Enneads* commentary, see our *Excursus* 2.

112. Ficino, *In Enneadem* 4.3.**7**, 4.9.**5**.

113. Ficino, *In Enneadem* 4.3.**7**.

114. Ficino, *In Enneadem* 4.3.**17**; 4.7.**2** and **16**.

115. Ficino, *In Enneadem* 4.1–2.**1** (reference specifically to Books 1, 3, 7 of the *Platonic Theology*).

116. Ficino, *In Enneadem* 4.4.**53**.

117. Ficino, *In Enneadem* 4.6.**1**.

118. Ficino, *In Enneadem* 4.4.**23**, 4.5.**4**.

119. The proof of this is that in commenting on certain passages where the original Greek text simply states a doctrine on the part of Priscian himself Ficino notes that it stems from Iamblichus. For instance see Ficino, *Super Theophrastum*, ch. 15 (*Opera* 2:1808). On Iamblichus as a source of Priscian of Lydia's *Metaphrasis*, see Steel, *The Changing Self*, pp. 10–20, and Huby, "Priscian of Lydia as Evidence for Iamblichus." Iamblichus was also a source of the pseudo-Simplicius' *De Anima*, and modern scholars interested in finding traces of Iamblichus in later works tend to study Priscian and pseudo-Simplicius in tandem. See Steel and Bossier, "Priscianus Lydus en de *In De Anima* van Pseudo (?)-Simplicius," and Blumenthal, "The Psychology of (?) Simplicius' Commentary on the *De Anima*."

120. On the doctrine of soul in Iamblichus and on the reconstruction of his *De Anima*, see Blumenthal, "Neoplatonic Elements in the *De Anima* Commentaries"; Steel, *The Changing Self*, pp. 23–75; Finamore, *Iamblichus and the Theory of the Vehicle of the Soul*; Zintzen, "Bemerkungen zum Aufstiegsweg der Seele in Jamblichs 'de mysteriis'"; Shaw, *Theurgy and the Soul*; Blumenthal, *Aristotle and Neoplatonism in Late Antiquity*, pp. 36–37, 55–56, and *passim*; García Bazán, "Jámblico y el descenso del alma"; Finamore, "The Rational Soul in Iamblichus' Philosophy"; Finamore and John Dillon (eds.), *Iamblichus, 'De Anima,'* pp. 10–18; and Helmig, "Iamblichus, Proclus and Philoponus on Parts, Capacities, and *ousiai* of the Soul."

121. Ficino, *In Enneadem* 4.3.**21** (together with Plato, Plotinus, and Porphyry and opposed to Proclus). Cf. 4.3.**37**.

122. Ficino, *In Enneadem* 4.3.**29**. Ficino is somewhat hesitant about the "Iamblichean" nature of this doctrine, which, as he also observes, was rejected by Porphyry and Proclus.

123. Ficino, *In Enneadem* 4.3.**32** (together with Plotinus).

124. Ficino, *In Enneadem* 4.4.**5** (together with Porphyry and Julian).

125. Ficino, *In Enneadem* 4.4.**23** (together with Priscian of Lydia).

126. Ficino, *In Enneadem* 4.4.**26** (together with Plotinus and Porphyry).

127. Ficino, *In Enneadem* 4.4.**30** (together with Julian). It may be that Ficino is attributing only the last idea to the two thinkers mentioned.

128. Ficino, *In Enneadem* 4.4.**39.**

129. Ficino, *In Enneadem* 4.4.**46** (together with Porphyry) .

130. Ficino, *In Enneadem* 4.4.**47** (together with Porphyry). Here, Ficino notes that one may read more about these topics in the works of Iamblichus and Porphyry, which he has recently translated.

131. Ficino, *In Enneadem* 4.4.**53** (together with Porphyry) .

132. Ficino, *In Enneadem* 4.6.**2.**

133. Ficino, *In Enneadem* 4.8.**7** (together with "Hermes" and "Orpheus"). Together with the citations of Iamblichus himself, we should draw the reader's attention to a few passages in which Iamblichus' followers are quoted. For Julian see notes 124 and 127 above, and for Priscian of Lydia note 125 above.

134. In this area, Ficino was especially influenced by Iamblichus' writings on Pythagorean mathematics, which he had translated or paraphrased in his early years; these writings are examined in detail by O'Meara, *Pythagoras Revived*, pp. 30–105. On the rediscovery of Ficino's *Iamblichi De Secta Pythagorica libri iv*, see Kristeller, *SF*, 1:cxlv–cxlvi — there being also a transcription of some of Ficino's annotations at Kristeller, *SF*, 2:98–103 — and Gentile, "Sulle prime traduzioni dal greco di Marsilio Ficino." On the broader issue of Ficino's "Pythagoreanism," see Celenza, "Pythagoras in the Renaissance," and Allen, "Eurydice in Hades," at pp. 22–25.

135. The *testimonia* in Priscian of Lydia — together with similar ones in ps.-Simplicius — are collected in Finamore and Dillon (eds.), *Iamblichus' 'De Anima,'* appendix, pp. 230–51.

136. It cannot be established with certainty that Ficino had access to the Stobaeus material. Although there is one fourteenth-century Florentine MS, it is defective and does not preserve all the Iamblichus fragments. For details see Finamore and Dillon (eds.), *Iamblichus' 'De Anima,'* pp. 24–25.

137. The work is a fictional dialogue between an Egyptian priest called "Abamon" (representing Iamblichus) and Porphyry. For a wide-ranging

study of Ficino's version of this text, see Giglioni, "Theurgy and Philosophy in Marsilio Ficino's Paraphrase of Iamblichus's *De Mysteriis Aegyptiorum*." The author considers Ficino's use of the term *theurgia*, the combination of translation, paraphrase, and commentary in the Florentine's *versio*, and the relation between Ficino's understanding of Iamblichus' notion of theurgy and his own project of securing the favor of the celestials.

138. Iamblichus, *De Mysteriis* 1.19.9.1–60.5 [citations according to the edition of Clarke, Dillon, and Hershbell, which reproduces Parthey's (1857) pagination together with a new line-division].

139. Iamblichus, *De Mysteriis* 1.5.16.5–17.15.

140. Iamblichus, *De Mysteriis* 1.6.19.6–1.7.23.7.

141. Iamblichus, *De Mysteriis* 5.18.223.8–224.4.

142. Iamblichus, *De Mysteriis* 2.7.83.8–86.3.

143. Iamblichus, *De Anima* 7. Iamblichus criticizes Plotinus' position from many angles in his *De Anima*, and in most cases the criticism is based on his predecessor's failure to maintain in a consistent manner the mediative status of soul. For the basic criticism see also *De Anima* 17–19. Further repercussions emerge at *De Anima* 13, 15, 37, 39, 46–47.

144. Iamblichus, *De Mysteriis* 4.11.195.1–4.12.196.10. The same principle is said to underlie the possibility of divination at *De Mysteriis* 3.16.138.1–5. Cf. also 1.12.42.5–14.

145. Iamblichus, *De Anima* 5.

146. Iamblichus, *De Anima* 25.

147. On the doctrine of the double soul, see also Iamblichus, *De Anima* 10.

148. Iamblichus, *De Mysteriis* 8.6.268.12–269.4.

149. Iamblichus, *De Mysteriis* 9.6.280.1–281.4.

150. Iamblichus, *De Mysteriis* 5.15.219.1–5.

151. Iamblichus, *De Mysteriis* 3.3.106.3–11, reading with Ficino, *Versio Iamblichi de mysteriis* (*Opera* 2:1882), *a generatione* (i.e., τῆς γενέσεως in place of Des Places' τῆς γνώσεως in the Greek).

152. Iamblichus, *De Mysteriis* 5.15.219.1–220.1.

153. Iamblichus, *De Mysteriis* 3.20.149.10–12.

154. Iamblichus, *De Mysteriis* 10.5.290.5–291.10.

155. Iamblichus, *De Anima* 38.

156. In the passage quoted above from the *De Anima*, the *pneuma* is said to surround the intellectual life (i.e., the higher part of the soul). However, in most of the passages in *De Mysteriis*, it seems rather to link soul (i.e., the higher and lower parts of the soul) and body. Presumably, the two positions can be reconciled on the assumption that there are various levels and layers in the *pneuma*.

157. Iamblichus, *De Mysteriis* 2.8.86.7–87.10. On this "inspiration" (ἐπί-πνοια), see *De Mysteriis* 3.7.114.5–6, 3.8.117.1–4, 3.21.150.9–12. A parallel "Orphic" doctrine of drawing breaths from the cosmos is suggested at Iamblichus, *De Anima* 8 and 32.

158. Iamblichus, *De Mysteriis* 2.7.84.11–14. For the contrast of two levels, see also Iamblichus, *De Anima* 21. That the lowest level is identifiable with the medical *pneuma* seems to be suggested at *De Mysteriis* 3.8.116.4–9. For the latter see also Iamblichus, *De Anima* 11.

159. Iamblichus, *De Mysteriis* 3.14.132.7–14. For the vehicles of heroes and daemons respectively, see Iamblichus, *De Mysteriis* 2.5.80.4–7 and 5.12.215.6–8. The term *pneuma* is associated with "spirits" in general at Iamblichus, *De Mysteriis* 2.10.92.2–3.

160. On the relation between audible music and cosmic sympathy, see Iamblichus, *De Mysteriis* 3.9.120.3–10.

161. Iamblichus, *De Mysteriis* 4.8.191.9–4.9.193.9.

162. Iamblichus, *De Mysteriis* 4.10.194.2–3, 5.7.207.11–12.

163. Iamblichus, *De Mysteriis* 4.8.191.13–192.2, 4.10.193.13–194.1, 5.7.207.8–11.

164. Iamblichus, *De Mysteriis* 4.8.191.14–192.8. Iamblichus' doctrine of cosmic sympathy also includes the notion that nature — within which sympathy in the strict sense operates — consists of a multiplicity of reason-principles. See *De Mysteriis* 3.28.169.6–8 (seminal reason-principles), ibid. 5.8.208.6–8 (natural reason-principles), and *De Anima* 7 (the soul as totality of reason-principles).

165. Iamblichus, *De Mysteriis* 5.7.207.6–5.8.209.8.

166. Iamblichus, *De Mysteriis* 5.10.210.11–211.5.For a description of the same three levels from a slightly different viewpoint, see *De Mysteriis* 5.18.223.8–5.19.226.14. Cf. 9.1.272.14–273.9 (two levels). At ibid. 5.22.231.4–12 Iamblichus stresses that religious cult should operate on all the levels in order to reflect the articulated structure of the higher world.

167. Iamblichus, *De Mysteriis* 4.10.193.10–4.12.197.9.

168. On theurgy as the highest form of "sacrifice" (θυσία), see Iamblichus, *De Mysteriis* 5.13.216.7–5.15.220.14.

169. Iamblichus, *De Mysteriis* 8.4.267.6–7. For the theurgic aim of conjunction with the divine Craftsman, see also 5.26.239.11–240.2. At 10.5.291.10–11 the theurgic gift of well-being is said to be the portal to the divine Craftsman and the courtyard of the Good.

170. Iamblichus, *De Mysteriis* 9.6.280.1–281.4.

171. Iamblichus, *De Mysteriis* 10.5.291.11–12. Iamblichus differs from his teacher Porphyry in holding that theurgic purification affects the higher part of the soul (at least the reasoning part) as well as the lower, whereas Porphyry confined its efficacy to the lower part. See Iamblichus, *De Anima* 39 and 46.

172. Iamblichus, *De Mysteriis* 3.20.149.4–14. See also 6.6.246.12–247.5.

173. Iamblichus, *De Mysteriis* 2.11.96.9–97.2.

174. Iamblichus, *De Mysteriis* 1.21.65.3–11. Iamblichus goes on to note that these tokens or symbols function as eternal measures that confer forms and images on the things transcendinng form and image: i.e., make ineffable and incomprehensible things available to us. Cf. 4.2.184.1–6. At 3.28.167.8–11 Iamblichus explains that we grasp the true forms of the gods in this way, and at 3.26.163.4–164.4 that this represents the highest type of divination.

175. At *De Mysteriis* 1.15.46.12–47.3 Iamblichus explains that the gods can be said to "hear" our prayers because the primary causes know and precontain in unity all subsequent things.

176. Iamblichus, *De Mysteriis* 5.26.238.9–11. On Iamblichus' theory of prayer — also explained in the surviving fragments of his *Commentary on*

the Timaeus — see Dillon (ed.), *Iamblichi Chalcidensis in Platonis dialogos commentariorum fragmenta*, pp. 407–11.

177. Iamblichus, *De Mysteriis* 5.23.233.12. For an excellent account of the levels of symbols and their uses, see Shaw, *Theurgy and the Soul*, p. 162ff.

178. Iamblichus, *De Mysteriis* 5.23.233.10–13.

179. Iamblichus, *De Mysteriis* 7.2.250.10–253.1.

180. Iamblichus, *De Mysteriis* 3.9.118.13–120.10.

181. Iamblichus, *De Mysteriis* 7.5.257.5–14.

182. In actual fact, Iamblichus says nothing in *De Mysteriis* about the highest level of symbols, undoubtedly because — according to the Neopythagorean approach — such things cannot and should not be expressed. Shaw, *Theurgy and the Soul*, p. 189, makes some plausible suggestions about their nature but is forced to cite *Ficino* as evidence.

183. This would even be true of that which is for Iamblichus the highest natural token: the sun. See *De Mysteriis* 7.3.253.9–254.8, where the diffusion of the sun's rays is an Egyptian symbol of the unitary God grasped in many forms.

184. See Iamblichus, *De Mysteriis* 4.13.197.10–198.2, where he comes close to stating this point explicitly. Cf. his criticism of the use of fumigations at 5.4.204.11–205.2, of standing on characters at 3.13.129.12–132.2, and of making images at 3.28.167.8–3.30.175.11.

185. Ficino, *In Enneadem* 4.3.**21**.

186. Ficino, *In Enneadem* 4.3.**29**.

187. Ficino, *In Enneadem* 4.8.**4** (together with Plotinus).

188. The ancient title was *On the Hieratic Art* (Περὶ τῆς ἱερατικῆς τέχνης). On the use of this text in Ficino's commentary on the *Third Ennead*, see the present author's "Analytical Study" of the *Commentary on the Third Ennead*, §3.2.3.

189. These "Egyptian" elements include the persona of "Abamon" adopted by Iamblichus in his reply to Porphyry's questions, together with the references to the attribution to Hermes of all the priestly writings of the Egyptians (Iamblichus, *De Mysteriis* 1.1.1.1–3), to Pythagoras' and Plato's

dependence on the "stelae of Hermes" (1.1.2.8–1.1.3.3), to the enormous number of books attributed to "Hermes" by Seleucus and Manetho (8.1.260.12–261.3), and to the "Hermetic" book inscribed in hieroglyphs and interpreted by Bitys (8.5.267.11–268.2). Copenhaver, *Magic in Western Culture*, pp. 76–81, draws attention to some passages in Ficino (especially *De Vita* 3.26.93–98 [ed. Kaske-Clark, p. 388] = *Versio Iamblichi de mysteriis* [*Opera* 2:1901]) in which he contrasts "Chaldaean" favorably with "Egyptian" doctrine. Ficino is however here referring to the specific issue of constructing statues and enticing daemons into them — reading this passage in conjunction with *Asclepius* 24.326.9–20 — and in any case somewhat mitigates the Chaldaean "preference" toward the end of the passage quoted. There is no doubt that Ficino sees Iamblichus' *De Mysteriis* as a repository of "Egyptian" doctrine, which he generally approves, especially in relation to the theological ideas stated in Book 8.

190. Iamblichus, *De Mysteriis* 8.2.261.7–262.7.

191. Iamblichus, *De Mysteriis* 8.3.263.1–6. At the end of his epitome of *Republic* 6 (*Opera* 2:1408), Ficino suggests that Iamblichus' Hermetic formulations had been influenced by Christian sources into stating the consubstantiality of the first two "gods." This interpretation seems to have resulted from corrupt readings in the MS of *De Mysteriis* available to him. On this point see Allen, "*Ratio omnium divinissima*," at pp. 487–88.

192. Iamblichus, *De Mysteriis* 8.3.263.7–264.3, 6.7.248.1–6.

193. Iamblichus, *De Mysteriis* 8.6.269.4–9.

194. The doctrine of theurgy is associated with the Egyptians at *De Mysteriis* 8.4.267.6–10. For possible connections in Ficino's mind between Iamblichean theurgy and Christian sacramentalism (mediated by shared terminology), see Giglioni, "Theurgy and Philosophy in Marsilio Ficino's Paraphrase of Iamblichus's *De Mysteriis Aegyptiorum*," at pp. 7–8.

195. Iamblichus, *De Mysteriis* 2.7.83.8–86.3. Cf. 2.3.70.7–2.4.79.5.

196. Iamblichus, *De Mysteriis* 1.4.11.6–1.6.20.14.

197. Iamblichus, *De Mysteriis* 2.3.70.7–2.9.90.5.

198. The symbolic doctrine is associated with the Egyptians at *De Mysteriis* 7.1.249.9ff.

199. Ficino, *In Enneadem* 4.4.**27** (together with "Orpheus"). In Ficino, the notion of Hermes as writer sometimes overlaps with that of "Hermes" as metaphysical principle. For the latter, see Ficino, *In Enneadem* 3.6.**13**.

200. Ficino, *In Enneadem* 4.8.**7** (together with "Orpheus" and Iamblichus). Orpheus alone is quoted by Ficino at *In Enneadem* 4.3.**31** (application of the doctrine in his three hymns regarding law, judgment, justice to the divine mind, the intellect of the world-soul, and will of world-soul), and *In Enneadem* 4.4.**38** (our vegetative life and spirit are receptive to vegetative life of intellectual soul).

201. Ficino, *De Vita* 3.26.64–76 (ed. Kaske-Clark, pp. 386–88).

202. Ficino, *De Vita* 3.26.77 (ed. Kaske-Clark, p. 388).

203. Ficino, *De Vita* 3.26.93–95 (ed. Kaske-Clark, p. 388).

204. Ficino, *De Vita* 3.26.122–24 (ed. Kaske-Clark, p. 390).

205. Ficino, *In Enneadem* 4.8.**3**.

206. Ficino adds that Basil and other Greek theologians agree with this interpretation.

207. Augustine, *De Civitate Dei* 8.12.

208. Augustine, *De Civitate Dei* 10.11.

209. As we have seen in the case of the commentary on *Ennead* 3, Augustinian ideas are often operating on a kind of subliminal level in Ficino. A good illustration of this from the commentary on *Ennead* 4 can be found at Ficino, *In Enneadem* 4.6.**2**, where the topic is the active theory of sensation. There is here no reference to the church father in connection with a doctrine that is quite prominent in the latter's work. However, exactly the same doctrine is expounded more fully at Ficino, *Platonic Theology* 7.6.3 together with a verbatim quotation from Augustine, *De Musica* 6.5.

210. Ficino, *In Enneadem* 4.3.**21** (together with Plato, Plotinus, and Iamblichus but rejected by Proclus.

211. Ficino, *In Enneadem* 4.3.**29** (agreement with Proclus in rejecting an Iamblichean doctrine).

212. Ficino, *In Enneadem* 4.3.**30**.

213. Ficino, *In Enneadem* 4.4.**5** (together with Iamblichus and Julian).

214. Ficino, *In Enneadem* 4.4.**26** (together with Plotinus and Iamblichus).

215. Ficino, *In Enneadem* 4.4.**46** (together with Iamblichus).

216. Ficino, *In Enneadem* 4.4.**47** (together with Iamblichus). See note 129.

217. Ficino, *In Enneadem* 4.4.**53** (together with Iamblichus).

218. Ficino, *In Enneadem* 4.8.**3**.

219. Ficino, *In Enneadem* 4.3.**15**.

220. Ficino, *In Enneadem* 4.3.**20**.

221. Ficino, *In Enneadem* 4.3.**29**.

222. Ficino, *In Enneadem* 4.4.**30**. Ficino notes here that Iamblichus and Julian also composed orations to the sun.

223. Ficino, *In Enneadem* 4.4.**47**.

224. Ficino, *In Enneadem* 4.3.**6**.

225. Ficino, *In Enneadem* 4.3.**20**.

226. Ficino, *In Enneadem* 4.4.**47**.

227. See Ficino, *In Enneadem* 4.8.**6** [headnote]. On the background of this doxography, see Burkert, "Plotin, Plutarch und die Platonisierende Interpretation von Heraklit und Empedokles."

228. Ficino, *In Enneadem* 4.1–2.**4**.

229. Ficino, *In Enneadem* 4.3.**5**.

230. See Ficino, *In Enneadem* 4.3.**2** and **8**.

231. Ficino, *In Enneadem* 4.3.**33** (possibly a citation through Pietro d'Abano).

232. Ficino, *In Enneadem* 4.4.**47**.

233. Ficino, *In Enneadem* 4.4.**51** (possibly a citation through Pietro d'Abano).

234. Ficino, *In Enneadem* 4.6.**1**.

235. Ficino, *In Enneadem* 4.3.**30**. There are several passages composed with similar intent in Ficino, *De Vita* 3 where he appeals especially to the teaching of Thomas Aquinas.

236. We will assume in the discussion to follow that Ficino, in the absence of explicit statements to the contrary, finds the Plotinian account of the relation between soul and body broadly acceptable. There are passages in the *Platonic Theology* that express caution with regard to some of the doctrines that reappear in the *Commentary on the Enneads*, a good example of this being at *Platonic Theology* 17.2.5–6, where the unfolding of the soul's faculties in relation to body, later to be treated at length in the Plotinus commentary, is the main issue. Cf. 15.12.4. Even without taking account of the fact that Ficino might have changed his views in the decade or more intervening between the composition of the two works, the question of determining the degree of the Florentine's personal commitment is a delicate one, since there is a large gray area between outright rejection and outright acceptance represented by the combination of rejection with acceptance facilitated by allegorization. This is especially true with respect to accounts of the "descent" of the soul, which were probably understood nonliterally by Plotinus and certainly so by Ficino: see Ficino, *Platonic Theology* 17.4.1 on the "poetic" (*poetica*) character of such doctrines.

237. In order to make a comparison between Ficino's analysis of the structure of soul in the commentary on the *Fourth Ennead* and in his earlier *Platonic Theology*—a project we will touch upon only at a few notable points of contention—an excellent starting point is the discussion of "the empirical functions of consciousness" at Kristeller, *The Philosophy of Marsilio Ficino*, pp. 364–410. See especially pp. 364–74 (the internal stratification of soul), pp. 374–85 (the pivotal role of reason as "principle of actuosity"), and pp. 384–88 (relation between human and cosmic souls).

238. See p. 147 above.

239. This would accord with the usage of Iamblichus. See p. 180 above. At *In Enneadem* 4.3.**36** Ficino notes that this formulation also represents the "somewhat poetic view" (*opinio quasi poetica*) that Plotinus states in his

interpretation of the myth of Heracles seeing his shadow in Hades at *Ennead* 4.3.27.13–17. On the Plotinian passage, see Pépin, "Héraclès et son reflet dans le Néoplatonisme." For Ficino's development of this theme see Allen, "Eurydice in Hades," at pp. 35–36.

240. See Ficino, *In Enneadem* 1.1 [ch. 1] (Basel 1580, sign. γ4r–v). The internal structure of the soul is explored in more detail, especially at ch. 8 (Basel 1580, sign. γ5v). An even more complicated picture emerges from Ficino's commentary on *Ennead* 6.7, where Plotinus' theory of Forms with special reference to the Form of "man" is explained. The most important conclusions are: (1) There are three levels of "man": (*a*) the divine Idea, (*b*) the rational soul, (*c*) the animate being (*In Enneadem* 6.7 [chs. 5–6 (Basel 1580, pp. 697–98)]); (2) One can also speak of $a + b$ as the formal reason-principle of "man," and by implication of $a + b + c$ as the formal reason-principle of "animate being" (chs. 4, 10 [Basel 1580, pp. 696, 702]); (3) The precise nature of the interrelation between these terms depends on our level of understanding. Thus, according to reason *a, b, c* are distinct but related, whereas according to intellect $a = b = c$ (ch. 2 [Basel 1580, p. 694]); (4) The relations between *a, b, c* must be understood as holding (*i*) in the universe as a whole and (*ii*) in each of us individually (ch. 6 [Basel 1580, p. 698]). Ficino himself presumably agrees with this theory to the extent that one substitutes an "illuminative" for an "emanative" relation between "man" *a* and "man" *b*. It is worth noting that in advocating point 4, Ficino has neatly resolved the doubts raised by modern interpreters regarding the question whether Plotinus really believed in Ideas of individuals. See Armstrong, "Form, Individual and Person in Plotinus," and Helleman-Elgersma, *Soul Sisters*, pp. 73–74, 77–78.

241. In subsequent sections of this study and in order to simplify some very complicated discussions, we will use the term "higher soul" as a general designation for the principle that Ficino himself calls variously, "intellectual soul" (*anima intellectualis*), "rational soul" (*anima rationalis*), and (albeit less frequently) "first soul" (*anima prima*). To a certain extent, Ficino's variation in terminology represents a careful exegetical and philosophical response to Plotinus, who maintains simultaneously that soul in its highest phase is (*a*) "rational" — i.e., it exercises discursive reason — (as

at Plotinus, *Ennead* 4.3.18.1–13) and (*b*) "intellectual" — i.e., it exercises intuitive reason — (as at Plotinus, *Ennead* 5.3.3.1–45). In the second passage Plotinus attempts to reconcile the two positions by saying that the presence of "pure intellect" (νοῦς καθαρός) in the soul does not undermine the soul's essential character of being "in reasonings" (ἐν λογισμοῖς) because the intellect is "ours and not ours" (ἡμέτερος καὶ οὐχ ἡμέτερος) depending on whether we are "bringing it into use" (προσχρῆσθαι) or not. A similar set of problems underlies the interpretation of the ruling-principle of the world at Plotinus, *Ennead* 4.4.12.1–49.

242. Ficino, *In Enneadem* 4.3.**12**. In this discussion, Ficino is reflecting a problem that recurs in Plotinus' depictions of the hypostases of intellect and soul: namely, that certain characteristics of intellect are sometimes transferred to soul in such a way that it becomes difficult to distinguish the two hypostases. On this point see Blumenthal, "*Nous* and Soul in Plotinus," pp. 203–19. Blumenthal here notes that one of the main differences between the two hypostases — that intellect exercises timeless intuition, whereas soul unfolds a temporal discursus — is often suppressed by assigning a nondiscursive mode of thinking to soul (for instance, at Plotinus, *Ennead* 4.4.1.1–16, 4.4.6.5–17, 4.4.15.1–20) (pp. 209–11). Blumenthal suggests quite plausibly that the reason for this is that Plotinus sometimes wishes to contrast the intelligible and sensible spheres as a whole (with soul as a whole being placed in the former) — as in *Ennead* 6.4–5 — and sometimes wishes to emphasize the impassivity of the soul in contrast to the passivity of the body (with the intellectual part of soul providing the clearest example of impassivity) — as in the first part of *Ennead* 3.6 (pp. 212–13, 215). He also notes that there are shifts in the depiction of soul from contrast with intellect to assimilation to intellect and back to contrast with intellect in the course of the long discussion in *Ennead* 4.3–4, as the investigation alternates between the topics of the relation between universal and particular souls, of the embodiment of soul, of the soul's existence as a transcendent principle, and so forth (pp. 213–14). In Ficino, many of the ambiguities in the Plotinian doctrine are reduced. The fundamental premises for the Florentine are: (*a*) that soul as hypostasis is identified with the Idea of soul (in the divine intellect), (*b*) that the distinctions between the primal intellect and the many intellects

and between the primal soul and the many souls are underpinned by the radical disjunction between creator and created. This means that the only remaining problem of demarcation between intellect and soul is on the level of *individual* intellects and souls. Here, perhaps mainly because of his further assumption of a trinitarian analogue in the soul consisting of intellect, intellectual soul, and vegetative principle, Ficino postulates (1) a clear distinction between an *intellect* and an *intellectual soul*, and (2) a clear distinction between these and the individual rational being. Texts such as *Ennead* 1.1.8.3–6 and 5.3.4.20ff. would provide the main Plotinian textual warrant for holding this position.

243. See below.

244. Ficino, *In Enneadem* 4.1–2.**1**. Accordingly, Ficino maintains that the soul is the last divine thing. See Ficino, *In Enneadem* 4.7.**8**.

245. This ambivalent status explains how this principle of intellect or soul can be considered as a force of attraction between intellect proper and body. See Ficino, *De Vita* 3.1.1–12 (ed. Kaske-Clark, p. 242), and our discussion on pp. 149–50.

246. This descent is not at all to be understood spatially with respect to intellect and only spatially in a qualified sense with respect to soul. See §2.1.1.

247. Ficino, *In Enneadem* 4.3.**10–11**.

248. For a simpler statement of the relation between the primal intellect and the many intellects and the primal soul and the many souls, see Ficino, *In Enneadem* 4.8.**4–5**.

249. "Species" is here used in the standard Ficinian sense as denoting transcendent Forms in their *cognitive* aspect within the divine intellect and not as representing conceptual-real classes in the Aristotelian sense. The species here will therefore correspond to individual soul-forms.

250. On the distinction between the multiplicity of intellectual souls — as discussed here — and the multiplicity of *intellects*, see notes 241–42.

251. Ficino, *In Enneadem* 4.3.**12**.

252. On this important Ficinian metaphysical principle, see the present author's "Analytical Study" of the *Commentary on the Third Ennead*,

§2.2.2.3. Kristeller, *The Philosophy of Marsilio Ficino*, pp. 151–52, argues that the important Ficinian principle of "the first term in any genus" (*primum in aliquo genere*) is derived from Plotinus and especially from the latter's treatment of quality as quasi-substantial in passages of *Enneads* 1.2.1 and 2.6.1–2. The present author must confess to not following Kristeller's usually persuasive arguments at this point and therefore proposes another likely source: namely, the treatment of the "unparticipated term" in Proclus' *Elementatio Theologica*. See the present author's "Analytical Study" of the *Commentary on the Third Ennead*, Excursus 3.

253. At *In Enneadem* 6.7 [ch. 13] (Basel 1580, p. 705), Ficino explains how a higher principle can have the properties of uniformity and omniformity by using the image of a cone. He argues that, just as each ray of light leaps forth from the broad orb of the sun into a cone and embraces all the powers of the sun that it previously had in the broadness albeit emitting one power in the cone primarily, so each intellectual act proceeds internally from the first intellect and embraces all the Ideas where it originates although each one of these acts terminates in precisely one Idea.

254. On this position see Ficino's remarks at *In Enneadem* 1.1 [ch. 8] (Basel 1580 sign. γ5*v*), discussed on pp. 165–67 above.

255. Ficino, *In Enneadem* 4.3.**11**.

256. Ficino, *In Enneadem* 4.1–2.**1**.

257. For a discussion of these questions, see the present author's analysis of Ficino's commentary on the *Third Ennead*, §§2.3 and 2.3.1–2.3.2.

258. Ficino, *In Enneadem* 4.1–2.**1**. For a similar idea see 4.9.**3**.

259. Ficino, *In Enneadem* 4.3.**5**.

260. Hence, Ficino's resort to "thought-experiments" to explain the doctrine.

261. In other passages, Ficino provides some less problematic examples of the uniformity and omniformity of the divine intellect. At *In Enneadem* 4.4.**9** he speaks of Jupiter, who rules the world—meaning here and elsewhere in the commentary the divine intellect immanent in the world-soul—as effecting through "his single, simple, and omniform Form" (*per*

unam simplicemque sui formam omniformem) an infinite number of things. Cf. 4.4.**12**. At 4.8.**5**, he explains how this same divine intellect has imprinted the "omniform Form of the universe" (*omniformis universi forma*) into the human intellect, from where it passes its glimmer into the human reason.

262. Ficino, *In Enneadem* 4.1–2.**4**. On this style of interpreting Aristotle, see Giardina, "Se l'anima sia entelechia del corpo alla maniera di un nocchiero rispetto all nave."

263. See Ficino, *In Enneadem* 1.1 [ch. 8] (Basel 1580, sign. γ5*v*).

264. Ficino, *In Enneadem* 4.3.**16**.

265. The restriction to form "of this kind" (*eiusmodi forma*) is probably an allusion to the fact that for Ficino there are at least three levels of form: namely, divine, psychic, and natural. See Ficino, *In Enneadem* 1.1 [ch. 1] (Basel 1580, sign. γ5r–v).

266. Ficino, *In Enneadem* 4.3.**16–17**.

267. Ficino, *In Enneadem* 4.3.**18**. Ficino makes two further important points here: (*a*) that the soul-form is a numerical and not a specific unity — therefore, our soul cannot be blended into a certain generic soul with our personal properties discarded; (*b*) that corporeal things only preserve their specific unity in succession because they depend on the world-soul.

268. Ficino, *In Enneadem* 4.3.**19**. For the important points regarding the soul-form's omnipresence made by Ficino here, see our discussion of embodied soul in the next section.

269. Ficino, *In Enneadem* 4.7.**1**.

270. Ficino, *In Enneadem* 4.7.**4**.

271. However, soul is not preeminently self-living, since the latter is one of the characteristics of intellect.

272. See note 261.

273. Ficino, *In Enneadem* 4.4.**15–17**. In the passage to be considered here, Ficino only briefly touches upon the complex question of the relation between the world-soul, eternity, and time (and the corresponding question with respect to the individual soul). For a full discussion of his

doctrine—which requires consideration of the world-soul's relation to higher and lower reason-principles)—see the present author's "Analytical Study" of the *Commentary on the Third Ennead*, §4.6.

274. In this order, "each thing yields to another" (*aliis alia cedunt*) rather than "takes its place" (*succedant*). Ficino probably intends to agree with Plotinus, *Ennead* 4.4.12.1–22, that the world's ruling-principle is somehow both atemporally intuitive and temporally discursive. See above, note 242. On the philosophical problem of nondiscursivity and discursivity in the highest phase of soul in Plotinus, see Blumenthal, *Plotinus' Psychology*, pp. 102–9; Lavaud, "La dianoia mediatrice entre le sensible et l'intelligible"; Chiaradonna, "La conoscenza dell'anima discorsiva."

275. On the connection between omniformity and motion, see also Ficino, *In Enneadem* 4.7.**2**.

276. As Ficino is also careful to note, the world revolves for Plotinus not so much "around" (*circa*) the soul in time as it does "within" (*intra*) the soul in time.

277. For a more detailed explanation of the relation between the various faculties of the human soul, see Ficino, *In Enneadem* 1.1 [ch. 9] (Basel 1580, sign. γ5v–γ6r).

278. The analogy just stated between the world-soul and the human soul shows that, although the terminology has become more specific, Ficino is here contrasting the higher and the lower phases of the latter as a whole.

279. Ficino, *In Enneadem* 4.1–2.**3**.

280. The conscious application of the distinction between transcendent and immanent modalities to soul is indicated especially by Ficino's elaboration of the analogy between the relation between the divine intellect and the soul's intellect and that between the higher and the lower souls.

281. The dependence must be partial, for otherwise some component in soul would be totally immanent in the latter, and the simultaneous transcendence and immanence of the soul-form as a whole could not be maintained.

282. The prefix *quasi* is of great importance here, since for Ficino (as for Plotinus) no aspect of the soul—even of the lower soul—is really bodily

or spatial. However, soul does acquire in its "descent" a kind of bodily *relatedness* (or *relation to* body) and a kind of spatial *relatedness* (or *relation to* space). In Ficino's case, this relatedness on the part of soul is exactly what is produced by the "spirit" (*spiritus*) that emerges as a mediate term between soul and body as a whole. On the notion of spirit, see §2.3.

283. On the notion of "descent" in Plotinus, Porphyry, and Ficino, see §2.1.1.

284. Since sensation here is said to involve an element of judgment, it corresponds more precisely to "perception" in modern English philosophical parlance.

285. Ficino, *In Enneadem* 4.4.**22**.

286. Ficino, *In Enneadem* 4.8.**5**.

287. See below.

288. As stated at Ficino, *In Enneadem* 4.1–2.**3**.

289. For an account of how this takes place in Plotinus, see Blumenthal, *Plotinus' Psychology*, pp. 54–57, 65–66.

290. Ficino holds as a general rule that the lower faculties of the soul receive influences from the higher faculties and *vice versa* to the extent that there is not an obstruction of some kind to the transmission. Thus at *In Enneadem* 4.8.**10** he argues that both vegetative (in the lower soul) and intellectual (in the higher soul) actions are hidden from us. Thus, any concupiscent motion in sensation is not apparent to us unless — in the upward direction — it passes to the imagination and through the latter to reason. Similarly, any act of intelligence does not reveal itself to us until — in the downward direction — it passes to the reason and through the latter to imagination.

291. More precisely, of "descending (*descendendum*) and of a "fall" (*casus*).

292. Ficino, *In Enneadem* 4.3.**27**.

293. Although Ficino mentions only intellect here, the reason must be included because of the contrast with the lower powers of imagination and nature that follows.

294. Ficino, *In Enneadem* 4.3.**30**.

295. This point is underlined by his cautionary remark at the end of the Porphyry citation to the effect that he himself only accepts teachings that "our theologians" (*theologi nostri*) have sanctioned.

296. Ficino, *In Enneadem* 4.7.**13**.

297. Ficino, *In Enneadem* 4.8.**10**.

298. See especially Ficino's discussion at *In Enneadem* 1.1 [ch. 8] (Basel 1580, sign. γ5v), where he considers how soul relates to higher and lower things. Here, (A) the One or Good has no relations; (B) intellect has two relations: (1) to the One, and (2) to itself; (C) soul has three relations: (1) to intellect (*qua* intellect) it has understanding of all things divinely, (2) to intellect (*qua* soul) it has reason, thinking, discursus, and deals with universals, (3) to intellect (*qua* part of animate being) it has imagination, and deals with particulars); and (D) the life of the animate being has four relations: (1) to soul, yielding imagination, (2) to itself, yielding the five senses, (3) to body in governance, yielding vitality, (4) to body in adherence, yielding the passions.

299. Another distinction between the treatment of embodiment in the two discussions is that in the commentary on *Ennead* 1.1, chs. 9 and 11, there is a sixfold articulation of soul into intellect, reason, imagination (determinate) = the higher soul, and into imagination (indeterminate), sense, and nature = lower soul, whereas in the commentaries on *Ennead* 4 we find a fivefold articulation into intellect, reason = higher soul, and into sense and nature = lower soul, with a single imagination as a kind of pivotal element. Allowing for a slight shift in emphasis in the role of imagination, the two schemes are basically in agreement with one another. At *Compendium in Timaeum*, ch. 34 (*Opera* 2:1456), there is a sevenfold articulation of soul introducing more overtly "harmonic" notions. Here, the faculties of soul are arranged in the form of the lambda diagram with essential being at the apex, will (= 1), imagination (= 2), and the generative power (= 3) descending on the left, and intelligence (= 2), reason (= 3), and the connective power (= 4 — presumably equivalent to sensation) descending on the right. There will be a *duple* (2:1) ratio between intelligence and will, a *sesquialteral* ratio (3:2) between reason and imagination, and a *sesquitertial* ratio (4:3) between the sensitive and gen-

erative powers. By assigning the *sesquioctaval* ratio (9:8) to the essential being, Ficino is able to find analogues between all the intervals of the diatonic scale (with the exception of the troublesome semitone) and the psychic faculties or relations between those faculties. For a recent discussion of this chapter, see Prins, *Echoes of an Invisible World*, pp. 154, 161–65.

300. Or "the vegetative power."

301. Ficino, *In Enneadem* 4.8.**5**.

302. Ficino, *In Enneadem* 4.3.**22**.

303. Ficino, *In Enneadem* 4.4.**33**.

304. Ficino, *In Enneadem* 4.4.**13**. The three faculties are here described explicitly as the highest, the middle, and the lowest parts of the soul: that is, viewed in terms of the pentadic structure.

305. Ficino, *In Enneadem* 4.4.**25**. On the elaborate organization of faculties with respect to the embodied soul elaborated by Plotinus, see Blumenthal, *Plotinus' Psychology*. Blumenthal notes that the tripartite division of Plato is not seriously considered by Plotinus, who prefers the Aristotelian faculty division (pp. 21–24), and that there is no complete list of faculties, because we are really dealing with an indivisible continuum (pp. 25–26). He also provides a useful diagram that summarizes the results of his analysis (p. 44). In general, Ficino follows Plotinus, albeit elevating the doctrine into a more systematic form.

306. See Ficino, *In Enneadem* 4.3.**11**.

307. He also argues (*c*) that soul is not a (totally) immanent form.

308. Ficino, *In Enneadem* 4.7.**4–5**. Ficino really means that no aspect of the soul-form is *totally* dependent on body, since a *partial* dependence is unavoidable given its relatedness (requiring *two* terms) or its reason-principle with respect to body. The discussion preceding the passages paraphrased shows that the Florentine's aim is (1) to emphasize that transcendence is a necessary aspect of soul's relation to body, and (2) to show that soul does not result from some blending of bodies.

309. The first and second moments discussed here are, of course, not temporally distinguishable phases.

310. Ficino, *In Enneadem* 4.4.**18**. The whole passage is pervaded by the imagery of light (= life-giving act) and heat (= quasi-vital quality).

311. On the passivity of the soul-body composite in Plotinus, see Blumenthal, *Plotinus' Psychology*, pp. 46–54; O'Meara, "Plotinus on How Soul Acts on Body"; and Caluori, "Plotin."

312. Ficino, *In Enneadem* 4.4.**19** — the passage contains Ficino's fullest discussion of the emotions. This account of the structure of the lower soul should be compared with that utilized by Ficino at *Platonic Theology* 13.2.9–23, where the writer in dialogue with certain Platonists elaborates an interpretation of providence, fate, and nature. Here, Ficino argues that rational souls have not only the power of understanding but also a "life-giving" (*vivifica*) power that rules the body by "nourishing" (*alere*) the body in the body, "sensing corporeal things" (*sentire corporalia*), and "moving" (*movere*) the body in space. The Platonists call this life-giving power — which also contains the "seeds" (*semina*) of all the motions and qualities that are unfolded by the soul in the body — the "idolum" (*idolum*) or the "semblance" (*simulacrum*) of the soul. Ficino goes on to state that subsequent to this in the lower soul's structure comes "nature" (*natura*), which is "a certain definite effective and vital affection or complexion" (*certa quaedam affectio sive complexio efficax atque vitalis*) of the body given by the life-giving power to the body, and which is characterized by the Platonists as "a certain vestige of the soul in the body or a shadow" (*quoddam vestigium animae in corpore sive umbra*). At first sight there seems to be a slight doctrinal conflict, since the analysis presented here situates nature as subsequent to the vegetative power (i.e., outside the idolum), whereas that set out in the Plotinus commentary identifies nature with the vegetative power (i.e., inside the idolum). The reason for the disparity seems to be (1) that the account in the *Theology* follows Proclus (who is cited explicitly for the teaching at 13.2.12), whereas in the commentary the Plotinian version naturally prevails, and (2) Ficino is working out a broader doctrine in this part of the *Theology*, where a triad of providence, fate, and nature is fundamental, and the psychic structure as a whole needs to be aligned with the second term. On the "Proclean" theory of the idolum, see Kristeller, *The Philosophy of Marsilio Ficino*, pp. 369–70 and 373–77, and Allen, *The Platonism of Marsilio Ficino*, pp. 219–22.

313. Ficino, *In Enneadem* 4.4.**28**. Cf. 4.4.**23**. The vital trace is, of course, equivalent to the quasi-vital quality mentioned above.

314. Ficino, *In Enneadem* 4.4.**32**.

315. Ficino reports details of Plotinian eschatology (to which, given his rejection of literal transmigration theory, he cannot subscribe) at *In Enneadem* 4.4.**3–7**. On the human soul's existence at some point totally outside body — which Plotinus admits but Ficino in agreement with Proclus rejects — see Ficino, *In Enneadem* 4.3.**21**.

316. Ficino, *In Enneadem* 4.4.**29**. This passage also is pervaded by the imagery of light (= life-giving act) and heat (= vital trace).

317. The ambiguity is shown at *In Enneadem* 4.7.**3** [headnote], where Ficino notes both that soul is a spirit with a definite property and that according to the Epicureans and the Stoics spirit is a most subtle body either of a more fiery or of a more airy nature. At *Super Theophrastum de phantasia et intellectu*, ch. 2 (*Opera* 2:1825), he says of imagination (one of the primary manifestations of spirit) that it is "Proteus" and a chameleon.

318. At *In Enneadem* 2.1 [ch. 3] (Basel 1580, p. 87), he cites references to spirit in two works having considerable authority and prestige: the book of Genesis and Vergil's *Aeneid*. The Vergil citation also appears in a similar context at Ficino, *De Vita* 3.3.36–37 (ed. Kaske-Clark, p. 256).

319. For a list of these passages, see the present author's "Analytical Study" of the *Commentary on the Third Ennead*, §3.2.2, notes 264–65.

320. Plotinus, *Ennead* 4.4.26.5–31. On the significance of this passage in the development of Ficino's theory of sensation, see §2.5.1.

321. Ficino seems to have held the doctrine of spirit at he develops at length in the commentary on the *Enneads* and in *De Vita* 3 from his earlier years onward. For spirit as mediator between soul and body, as a vapor produced from blood, and as diffusing the powers of the soul through the body, see Ficino, *De Amore* 6.6 (ed. Laurens, pp. 141–43). It is especially significant that this passage also contains *in nuce* the theory developed in Ficino, *In Enneadem* 4.5, whereby spirit grounds the process of sensation because of the inherent impassibility of soul itself. See the next section of the present work.

322. Ficino, *De Vita* 3.26.1–10 (ed. Kaske-Clark, p. 384).

323. Ficino, *In Enneadem* 2.1 [ch. 3] (Basel 1580, p. 88).

324. Iamblichus provides the best key to the structural handling of *spiritus* within Ficino's Plotinian commentary, although separate components of the doctrine can be found in a vast array of late ancient sources, from Aristotle, through the Galenic, Hermetic, Stoic, and Neopythagorean traditions, to Porphyry and the later Platonists. Apart from Iamblichus, particularly important channels for the transmission of the notion of spirit as used in the cosmological (as opposed to the medical) context were the Hermetic *Asclepius* (see *Asclepius* 14.313.3–23, 17.316.3–4) and Firmicus Maternus (see *Mathesis* 4.1.1, 4.1.6, 5.pr.3, etc.). The Arabic-Latin treatise *Picatrix*, which was a major source for Ficino's *De Vita*, makes extensive use of the notion of spirit, especially in the sense of the multiplicity of planetary spirits. See *Picatrix* 1.5.35–46 and 4, *de proprietatibus spirituum*. On spirit in the first two sources, see Gersh, *Middle Platonism and Neoplatonism*, vol. 1, pp. 361–63, and vol. 2, p. 731, and in the last source Garin, *Astrology in the Renaissance*, pp. 46–55, and Kaske and Clarke (eds.), *Marsilio Ficino, Three Books of Life*, pp. 45–47. On Iamblichus' notion of spirit, see pp. 180–81 in the present volume.

325. Ficino, *De Vita* 3.3.4–9 (ed. Kaske-Clark, p. 254).

326. Ficino, *In Enneadem* 4.4.**23**.

327. Ficino, *De Vita* 3.4.21–26 (ed. Kaske-Clark, p. 258). Cf. 3.2.91–94 (ed. Kaske-Clark, p. 254). Perhaps the most striking elaboration of the connection between spirit and mediation occurs in Ficino, *Compendium in Timaeum*, ch. 27 [incorrectly numbered 26] (*Opera* 2:1445–46), where "the world's spirit" is established as a mediator between two extremes here characterized as "pure spirit" and "the world's substance." Since the divine craftsman had differentiated the world's substance into the four elements of fire, water, air, and earth, he also compounded the world's spirit from intellect (the ruler of the sphere), soul (moving the sphere through its own self-motion), intelligence (implanted into the world-soul by God and the intellect), and nature (the vital or seminal power infused into matter) — the four components of the world's substance being images of the four components of the world's spirit. In this passage, spirit becomes

a principle that establishes a structural analogy — specifically by means of the notion of quadruplicity — between the higher intellectual and psychic and the lower bodily realm, and might perhaps even be understood as the structural analogy itself. A similar argument using slightly different components occurs at ibid. ch. 39.

328. Ficino, *In Enneadem* 4.4.**26**.

329. Ficino, *In Enneadem* 4.4.**29**.

330. Ficino *In Enneadem* 4.3.**20**. On spirit as connection see also Ficino, *De Vita* 3.26.9–10 (ed. Kaske-Clark, p. 384).

331. Ficino, *In Enneadem* 4.5.**1**. The same idea is restated at *In Enneadem* 4.4.**23**, 4.5.**6**, 4.6.**2**, and at *Super Theophrastum*, chs. 34, 49 (*Opera* 2:1817, 1824).

332. Ficino, *De Vita* 3.20.42–48 (ed. Kaske-Clark, p. 352).

333. Ficino, *De Vita* 3.13.19–22 (ed. Kaske-Clark, p. 306). The mode of citation shows that Ficino is here citing Plethon's commentary on the *Chaldaean Oracles*.

334. Ficino, *De Vita* 3.15.1–10 (ed. Kaske-Clark, p. 314). Ficino is here citing Proclus' *De sacrificio et magia*, which he had himself translated.

335. Ficino, *De Vita* 3.17.28–32 (ed. Kaske-Clark, p. 330). Cf. 3.21.74–142 (ed. Kaske-Clark, pp. 358–62) for a more extensive elaboration of this idea. On spirit as harmony see also Ficino, *Super Theophrastum*, ch. 44 (*Opera* 2:1821). For the association between spirit and harmony, see also note 330.

336. Ficino, *De Vita* 3.1.75–90 (ed. Kaske-Clark, p. 246). Cf. 3.4.21–26 (ed. Kaske-Clark, p. 258). On spirit as quintessence see below.

337. Ficino, *In Enneadem* 2.1 [ch. 3] (Basel 1580, p. 87).

338. Ficino, *In Enneadem* 3.2.**43**. The passage also shows that spirit as much as reason-principle is analogous to the third person of the Trinity.

339. Ficino, *De Vita* 3.4.1–5 (ed. Kaske-Clark, p. 258). Cf. 3.23.27–31 (ed. Kaske-Clark, pp. 370–72) for a more extensive elaboration of this idea. Of course, daemons are described as themselves spirits by Ficino (following traditional usage). See Ficino, *In Enneadem* 4.4.**43**, **53**, etc.

340. Ficino, *De Vita* 3.3.4–7 (ed. Kaske-Clark, p. 254).

341. See Ficino, *In Enneadem* 4.4.**26**.

342. Ficino, *De Vita* 3.26.21–33 (ed. Kaske-Clark, pp. 384–86).

343. Ficino, *De Vita* 3.3.11–12 (ed. Kaske-Clark, p. 256).

344. Ficino, *De Vita* 3.3.32–33 (ed. Kaske-Clark, p. 256).

345. Ficino, *De Vita* 3.26.6. The closest thing to spirit that we can sense in the normal way is (as the etymology would suggest) "breath." On spirit as breath see Ficino, *De Vita* 3.4.7–8 (ed. Kaske-Clark, p. 258); *In Enneadem* 2.1 [ch. 3] (Basel 1580, p. 87).

346. For fuller discussion of these notions, see below.

347. See also Ficino, *Super Theophrastum*, ch. 44 (*Opera* 2:1821); *Compendium in Timaeum*, summa 66 (*Opera* 2:1477). For fuller discussion of this notion, see below.

348. He adds here "to speak Platonically or rather Plotinically" (*ut Platonice sive Plotinice loquar*). The quasi-identification between spirit and quintessence leads to an interesting discussion of the relation between these two notions and harmony at Ficino *Compendium in Timaeum*, ch. 31 (*Opera* 2:1451–52). The author here explains that just as the four elemental qualities combine into one essence — the quintessence (being subordinate to a special, hidden, and heavenly power) — so numerous voices properly blended produce a consonance that has a new and wonderful power, the production of one note from a number of notes sounding in a certain proportion — as though a form common to them all — being here also compared to the vibration of one plucked string passing to a second string that has been similarly tuned.

349. Ficino, *De Vita* 3.3.26–31 (ed. Kaske-Clark, p. 256). In this passage, Ficino is clearly not positing a simple opposition between a (higher) spirit not constituted by the four elements and a (lower) spirit so constituted, since he goes on immediately to state that the world-soul "gives birth to" (*parit*) the four elements and that the latter are "in the power of that spirit" (*in illius spiritus virtute*). Presumably, he is really establishing something like a continuum of spirit and arguing that in the higher state of the spirit the elements are present in a form approaching

ideality, whereas in the spirit's lower state, they are more corporeally subsistent.

350. Ficino, *In Enneadem* 2.1 [ch. 3] (Basel 1580, p. 88). The passage also establishes a close association between spirit and the transparency. See note 353.

351. The concomitant temporal aspect is not relevant to this mediating structure, since soul, spirit, and body are all temporal. On the notion of preparing our spirit to receive celestial influences at opportune astrological times, see Ficino, *De Vita* 3.4.21–26, 3.11.52–89, 3.21.95–99 (ed. Kaske-Clark, pp. 258, 292–94, 358), etc.

352. Ficino, *In Enneadem* 2.1 [ch. 3] (Basel 1580, p. 88). Ficino sometimes speaks of spirit as omnipresent, although this omnipresence must presumably not be thought in the manner of soul's omnipresence. In the case of spirit, there is a presence of something *spatial* in all of space, whereas in the case of soul, the presence is of something *nonspatial* in all of space. For the omnipresence of spirit, see Ficino, ibid. 4.4.**26**.

353. This is our first reference to the notion of "transparency/the transparent" (*diaphanum* = τὸ διαφανές), which will play an increasingly important role in Ficino's doctrines of spirit, magic, and vision. In §2.3 (and subsections), the transparency appears either as simply equivalent to spirit—primarily understood in its macrocosmic sense—or as closely associated with spirit. Transparency is actualized by light, since spirit is the third member of the triad of intellect, intellectual soul, and spirit, while intellect emits (intellectual) "light." In §2.4 (and subsections), the same doctrine appears—with more emphasis on the microcosm—in connection with magic. Here, Ficino considers such issues as the the projection of light rays and the use of the transparency in objects by the magician. In §2.5 (and subsections), we find the most complete account of the relations between transparency, light, and spirit. Ultimately, Ficino's exploitation of this complex of notions can be traced back to two passages in Aristotle's *De Anima*: namely, *De Anima* 2.7.418a–19b, 3.5.430a. In the first passage, Aristotle explains how vision occurs when a transparency is activated by phosphorescence and color, and that "light" is the presence of fire or aether in the transparency. In the second, he compares the relation

between the active and the passive intellects to that between light and colors in order to explain the process of intellection. In short, Ficino's theory of transparency, light, and spirit combines ideas from the two Aristotelian texts by (1) establishing a metaphysical continuum between intellectual and physical light, and (2) utilizing the ambivalently incorporeal and corporeal *spiritus* as the analogue of the transparency activated by the metaphysical *continuum* of light. This combination also permits something of a *rapprochement* between Aristotle's incorporealist and Plato's corporealist theories of light. Between Aristotle and Ficino there are various intermediate stages of development, including Plotinus' identification of *pneuma* and the transparency at *Ennead* 4.4.26.23–28, and especially certain ideas in Iamblichus. Regarding the Iamblichean contribution, see the useful discussion of Finamore, "Iamblichus on Light and the Transparent." Iamblichus' doctrine can be reconstructed from Julian, *Oratio ad Solem* 132c–34b, and its main features are the interpretation of light (*a*) as an emanative activity in the transparency (rather than an actualization of the transparency) and (*b*) as a continuum between the incorporeal and the corporeal (rather than as something purely incorporeal or as purely corporeal). Both these features recur in Ficino. Apart from the uses of the doctrine of spirit/transparency in the commentaries on Plotinus' *Enneads* and on Priscian of Lydia, which will be discussed in more detail below, Ficino particularly develops the theme of the transparency in his short treatise of 1492, *De Lumine* (*Opera* 2:999–1009). On the latter see Vasiliu, "Les limites du Diaphane chez Marsile Ficin," at pp. 108–12.

354. Ficino, *Super Theophrastum*, chs. 23, 32 (*Opera* 2:1812, 1816).

355. Ficino, *De Vita* 3.21.95–98 (ed. Kaske-Clark, p. 358). Cf. Ficino, *In Enneadem* 4.4.**50**, on the magician's imagination as affecting distant things through the rays emitted by his spirit. For Ficino also, daemonic possession is understood as the *spatial* occupation of an individual's body by the daemons and their spiritual vehicles. See *De Vita* 3.23.100–103 (ed. Kaske-Clark, p. 376). On Ficino's view of the Arabic and Egyptian beliefs regarding the spatial introduction into statues of stellar spirits and daemons, see 3.20.21–35 (ed. Kaske-Clark, p. 350).

356. Ficino, *In Enneadem* 4.4.**29**. On the connection between spirit and the vital trace, see also Ficino, *Compendium in Timaeum*, summae 71, 86 (*Opera* 2:1478, 1480–81).

357. Ficino, *In Enneadem* 4.7.**1**.

358. Ficino, *De Vita* 3.1.75–76 (ed. Kaske-Clark, p. 246).

359. Ficino, *In Enneadem* 4.4.**29**.

360. And also by the vegetative lives subjoined to the intellects of the spheres' and stars' souls. On the diffusion of life from the celestial, see p. 210.

361. At Ficino, *In Enneadem* 4.4.**26**, a spirit is said to descend from the celestials.

362. Ficino, *In Enneadem* 4.4.**38**. On the process associated with prayer, see 4.4.**43** and **45**

363. For a fuller discussion of sensation, see below.

364. Ficino, *In Enneadem* 4.6.**2**.

365. Ficino, *In Enneadem* 4.4.**50**. For a more detailed account of this process attributed to "the Arabs," see Ficino, *De Vita* 3.20.36–42 (ed. Kaske-Clark, p. 350–52).

366. See Ficino, *Super Theophrastum de phantasia et intellectu*, ch. 1 (*Opera* 2:1824). In his commentary on *Ennead* 1.1 especially, Ficino explores the nature of this mediation by distinguishing two levels of imagination: one forming the lowest term in the higher soul triadically subdivided into intellect, reason, and imagination, and one forming the highest term in the lower soul's triadic subdivision into imagination, sensation, and vitality. See *In Enneadem* 1.1 [ch. 8] (Basel 1580, sign. γ5v).

367. Some of Ficino's references to the operation of prayer also lend support to this thesis. Hankins, "Ficino, Avicenna and the Occult Powers of the Rational Soul," argues especially on the basis of the epitomes of Plato's *Leges* and passages of *Platonic Theology* 13 that Ficino, under the influence of Avicenna, and in order to explain Christian prophetic visions and miracles, had at one point extended the role of magic above the level of

spirit considered strictly as inferior to soul. This argument is clearly valid. Indeed, when the Ficinian spirit is understood in terms of its more general mediative function and its indirect affect on the reason, the later doctrine of *De Vita* interpreted in conjunction with that of the *Commentarius in Plotinum* is not inconsistent with the earlier position suggested in the epitomes and the *Platonic Theology*. For a salient example of the extended notion of spirit, see note 327.

368. Ficino, *In Enneadem* 4.4.**26**.

369. The other foundations in ascending order are (1) matter, (2) the concord of qualities, (4) nature, and (5) the world-soul.

370. On the relation between spirit and heaven, see Ficino, *Compendium in Timaeum*, ch. 27 [incorrectly numbered 26] (*Opera* 2:1445–46). The quasi-identification is here based on proportion or analogy because, just as the heaven is a mediator between the world's soul and body, so is spirit a mean between our soul and body.

371. Ficino, *In Enneadem* 2.1 [ch. 3] (Basel 1580, p. 88). He adds that it is a word "speaking in the Platonic manner" (*quantum Platonice loqui*), because he is establishing an analogy for the *third* person of the Trinity in which the word—speaking in the Christian manner—would be the *second* person.

372. See the present author's "Analytical Study" of the *Commentary on the Third Ennead*, §§2.3 and 2.3.1–2.3.2.

373. Cf. Ficino, *De Vita* 3.21.114–17 (ed. Kaske-Clark, p. 360), where he reports the doctrine of the Pythagoreans and Platonists that the heaven is a spirit arranging all things through motions and tones.

374. Ficino, *In Enneadem* 2.1 [ch. 3] (Basel 1580, p. 88). See note 353.

375. Ficino, *De Vita* 3.1.75–79 (ed. Kaske-Clark, p. 246). He adds that this quintessence flourishes everywhere "as though a spirit inside the world's body" (*tamquam spiritus intra corpus mundanum*) and instills the world-soul's power especially into those things that have absorbed the most of "this kind of spirit" (*eiusmodi spiritus*).

376. Ficino, *De Vita* 3.3.29–31 (ed. Kaske-Clark, p. 256).

377. Ficino, *In Enneadem* 2.1 [ch. 3] (Basel 1580, p. 88). We are probably to understand the processes as quasi-condensation and rarefaction, because Ficino is here describing the spirit in terms of its proximity to body, whereas elsewhere he describes it in terms of its proximity to soul. Only bodies as such (inhabited and sustained by the spirit) have *real* condensation and rarefaction.

378. Ficino, *De Vita* 3.3.27–28 (ed. Kaske-Clark, p. 256). Cf. *In Enneadem* 4.4.**29** and **42**.

379. See Ficino, *In Enneadem* 2.1 [ch. 3] (Basel 1580, p. 88), *In Enneadem* 4.7.**2**, *De Vita* 3.24.23–29 (ed. Kaske-Clark, p. 378), etc. The *quasi*-elemental (rather than *really* elemental) character of spirit is shown by numerous passages in which Ficino explains how the elements are more volatile when full of spirit, that gems and elements do not generate, because the spirit is *inhibited by* the grosser matter, that spirit can be separated in order to make it more generative (as in the case of the alchemists' elixir) (*De Vita* 3.3.1–23 [ed. Kaske-Clark, pp. 254–56]), and that spirit can be separated from beclouding vapors by medicines (3.4.19–21 [ed. Kaske-Clark, p. 258]; cf. 3.11.90–91 [ed. Kaske-Clark, p. 294]).

380. On the relation between these three types of spirit and the bodily organs, see also Ficino, *Compendium in Timaeum*, summa 71 (*Opera* 2:1478). The three kinds of spirit are discussed in connection with *De Vita* by Kaske and Clark (eds.), *Marsilio Ficino, Three Books of Life*, pp. 412 n. 1, 454 n. 14. These editors tend to treat the "medical" spirit as something that is quite isolated from the other more "theological" sense of spirit, thereby obscuring the unifying or mediating function of spirit in general within Ficino's metaphysical system as a whole. For a comparison of Galen's and Plato's doctrine regarding spirit as breath, see Ficino, *Compendium in Timaeum*, ch. 45 [numbered incorrectly as continuation of 42] (*Opera* 2:1465).

381. On the relation between spirit and the planets, see also Ficino, *De Vita* 3.20.63–65, 3.23.27–32 (ed. Kaske-Clark, pp. 352, 370–72).

382. Ficino, *De Vita* 3.6.1–16 (ed. Kaske-Clark, p. 264). Further correlations are also possible. At Ficino, *Super Theophrastum*, ch. 44 (*Opera*

2:1821), the natural spirit is associated with the liver and air, the vital spirit with the heart and fire, and the animal spirit with the brain and fire and water.

383. Ficino, *De Vita* 3.11.61–65 and 72–74 (ed. Kaske-Clark, p. 288). The "signifying" and "dedication" do of course here reflect real analogies in the structure of things.

384. There is a brief allusion to the doctrine of natural, vital, and animal spirit also at Ficino, *In Enneadem* 4.4.**29**.

385. See especially Augustine, *De Civitate Dei* 10.4, 10.9.

386. On this part of Plotinus' work, see Merlan, "Plotinus and Magic." Merlan studies the three passages associating Plotinus with magic in Porphyry's *Vita Plotini*, also providing a useful summary of Plotinus' philosophical theory of magic as stated in *Ennead* 4.4.40–44 (pp. 344–46). The doctrine of Plotinus regarding the processes underlying magic, its efficacy, and the philosopher's relation to it turns out according to Merlan's reconstruction to be remarkably similar to that which we find later in Ficino. Armstong, "Was Plotinus a Magician?," attacks Merlan's position. However, this critique depends on the unwarranted assumption that much of Porphyry's evidence about Plotinus' interest in magic is the result of the latter's superstitious misunderstanding of his master's true opinions and/or as having a purely metaphorical significance.

387. On the relation beween *De Vita* 3 and the ideas developed in the *Commentary on the Fourth Ennead*, see our *Excursus* 2.

388. Ficino, *In Enneadem* 4.4.**33–34**.

389. For a similar analysis of the components of cosmic sympathy in Iamblichus, see p. 181.

390. Ficino, *In Enneadem* 4.4.**31**.

391. Ficino, *In Enneadem* 4.4.**32**.

392. Ficino, *In Enneadem* 4.4.**36** cf. 4.4.**32**. Ficino also stresses the analogy between the vegetative life in the world-soul and that in the human soul.

393. Ficino, *In Enneadem* 4.4.**36**. In the next paragraph, Ficino goes on to argue that "the marvelous actions above their elemental nature" (*mira-*

biles supra naturam elementarem actiones) in gems, metals, and herbs proves the existence of a world-soul filling everything with its "powers" (*vires*).

394. Ficino, *In Enneadem* 4.4.**41**. On the powers inherent in light rays, see also Ficino, *De Vita* 3.1.36–42 (ed. Kaske-Clark, p. 244) (on daemons and stars), and 3.18.16–29 (ed. Kaske-Clark, p. 334) (on the figure of the cross).

395. Ficino, *In Enneadem* 4.4.**43**.

396. Ficino, *In Enneadem* 4.4.**50**. The connection between rays and the spirit is explored in more detail at Ficino, *De Vita* 3.16.32–55 (ed. Kaske-Clark, pp. 322–24), where he explains that the rays of the stars bring down gifts from the imaginations and minds of the celestials, acting to the greatest extent on the spirit, which is "most similar to the celestial rays" (*caelestibus radiis simillimum*). He continues by noting that diverse powers arise from the combinations of rays at one time or another, and that they act more quickly than do mixtures of elemental qualities or combinations of musical tones and rhythms.

397. Ficino, *De Vita* 3.17.24–72 (ed. Kaske-Clark, pp. 330–32). See note 353.

398. Or: before and behind.

399. In some respects, the easiest way to imagine the simultaneity and multidirectionality of these motions is to think of them as centrifugal and centripetal within a sphere. However, Ficino does seem to think of these motions in most cases as having more specifically an up-down and in others more specifically a right-left (or before-behind) trajectory. These more limited views would presumably be seen by him as consistent with the inhibition and constraint placed on the ubquitous powers by the limited capacities of the recipients.

400. Ficino, *In Enneadem* 4.4.**38**.

401. Ficino, *In Enneadem* 4.4.**43**. For a briefer allusion to the same theory, see 4.4.**30**.

402. Ficino, *In Enneadem* 4.4.**44**.

403. On the simultaneous motions and magical theory, see also Ficino, *De Vita* 3.15.12–16, 3.21.74–80, 3.26.20–29 (ed. Kaske-Clark, pp. 314, 358, 384).

404. See §2.5 on the corresponding mechanism underlying sensation.

405. The artificial adaptation must, to be effective, intensify natural processes (as in the case of agriculture, medicine, etc.). For this reason Ficino favors the metaphor of "grafting" (*insitio*) at *In Enneadem* 4.4.**36** and elsewhere. See below, concerning degrees of magical efficacy, and concerning good and bad magic.

406. And perhaps implicitly also in the practice of prayer.

407. All the processes described in this paragraph must be performed at astrologically suitable moments, therefore exhibiting a special sense of the third stage of attunement. On this aspect see the remarks at Ficino, *In Enneadem* 4.4.**30**, **45**, and **49**. For a more detailed account see Ficino, *De Vita* 3.1.32–62 (ed. Kaske-Clark, pp. 244–46) and *passim* in that work.

408. Ficino, *In Enneadem* 4.4.**42**. As he notes in the previous paragraph with respect to the collection of rays from Venus, the power can sometimes be overwhelming.

409. Ficino, *In Enneadem* 4.4.**45**.

410. Ficino, *De Vita* 3.1.19–23 (ed. Kaske-Clark, p. 242).

411. Ficino, *In Enneadem* 4.4.**42**.

412. Ficino, *In Enneadem* 4.4.**48**. Ficino also notes that the reverse process — of repulsion — can also be accomplished by these magicians. For more information about the magical use of attraction, see Ficino, *De Vita* 3.1.23–25, 3.26.30–32 (ed. Kaske-Clark, pp. 242, 384–86).

413. Ficino, *In Enneadem* 4.4.**42**

414. Ficino, *In Enneadem* 4.4.**49**

415. Ficino, *De Vita* 3.15.85–89 (ed. Kaske-Clark, p. 318).

416. Ficino, *In Enneadem* 4.4.**50**. See p. 210 and n. 355.

417. Ficino, *In Enneadem* 4.4.**49**. Ficino compares this to the situation where a finger marking the thigh of a pregnant woman who is lustful is the sign of a thing desired to excess. This curious example is intended to

illustrate the spatial projection of the imaginative spirit, i.e., where the imaginative (interior) aspect is continuous with the physical (exterior) aspect.

418. Ficino, *In Enneadem* 4.4.**26**.

419. Ficino, *De Vita* 3.21.105–17 (ed. Kaske-Clark, p. 360).

420. Ficino, *De Vita* 3.21.144–45 (ed. Kaske-Clark, p. 362).

421. See Ficino, *In Enneadem* 4.4.**43**, on hidden qualities, figures, chants, and prayers. Cf. 4.4.**49**, where images, words, songs, and incantations are associated with specific planets.

422. For Iamblichus' corresponding doctrine of theurgic σύμβολα, see p. 182 above.

423. These are said to be listed "in ascending order" (*in ascensu*).

424. Cf. Ficino, *In Enneadem* 4.4.**42**.

425. Cf. Ficino, *In Enneadem* 4.4.**49–50**.

426. Ficino, *De Vita* 3.21.24–38 (ed. Kaske-Clark, pp. 354–56).

427. Various terms indicate this "association." Ficino speaks of "referring to" (*referre*), "corresponding to" (*respondere*), "pertaining to" (*pertinere*), etc. The basic idea is of a cognitive notion of similarity that, however, reflects a real metaphysical connection of some kind.

428. The order is: the moon, Mercury, Venus, the sun (or Apollo), Mars, Jupiter, Saturn.

429. See Ficino, *De Vita* 3.14.1–15.89 (ed. Kaske-Clark, pp. 308–18).

430. This is according to the principle of the "series" (σειρά — *ordo*) explained by Proclus in his *De Sacrificio et Magia*. Ficino cites this author explicitly for the doctrine at *De Vita* 3.15.4–15 (ed. Kaske-Clark, p. 314).

431. Ficino, *In Enneadem* 4.4.**33**. In other words, things that seem external and objective to us are still rooted in imagination. It is because of this that Ficino the medical practitioner can argue — in company with Hippocrates, Galen, and Avicenna — that even the *individual* imagination of a patient plays a role in the effectiveness of the medicines that he swallows. See Ficino, *De Vita* 3.20.57–75 (ed. Kaske-Clark, pp. 352–54).

432. Ficino, *Super Theophrastum de phantasia et intellectu*, ch. 1 (*Opera* 2:1824).

433. This is argued by Ficino, *De Vita* 3.18.141–83 (ed. Kaske-Clark, pp. 340–42), who approvingly cites Thomas Aquinas' views that if any such images have power, it is because of the materials in which they are engraved, and that if any effects are produced beyond the purely natural ones, this is through the cooperation of deceiving daemons. He adds that even certain Platonists such as Iamblichus think that those who place too much faith in such magical techniques are the likely victims of daemonic manipulation.

434. *Asclepius* 24.326.9–20, 37.347.3–38.349.8.

435. Plotinus, *Ennead* 4.3.11.1–8.

436. Ficino, *In Enneadem* 4.3.**33**. Here, Ficino combines the reading of the Plotinian passage cited in the previous note with that of Plotinus, *Ennead* 4.3.14.1–19, explaining the myth of Prometheus and Epimetheus.

437. Ficino, *De Vita* 3.26.77–93 (ed. Kaske-Clark, p. 388).

438. Ficino, *De Vita* 3.26.122–39 (ed. Kaske-Clark, pp. 390–92). One must remember also that Ficino is much taken with Plotinus' idea that nature can be personified as a "sorceress" (*maga*). See Ficino, *In Enneadem* 4.4.**54**.

439. On the role of daemons in magic, see also Ficino, *In Enneadem* 4.4.**51** (with citation of Plato).

440. Ficino, *In Enneadem* 4.4.**45**.

441. Ficino, *In Enneadem* 4.4.**47**. Ficino refers to his recent translations of these authors for detail on this topic. For Iamblichus' similar account of the distinction between higher theurgy and vulgar magic, see pp. 182–83 above.

442. See Ficino's account of two contrasting ways in which one can approach Jupiter's star at *In Enneadem* 4.4.**51–52**.

443. On the life-giving *idolum* of the soul that includes sensation, see also Ficino, *In Enneadem* 4.4.**18–19**. Kristeller, *The Philosophy of Marsilio*

Ficino, p. 234, makes somewhat disparaging remarks about Ficino's theory of sensation, suggesting that the latter was only interested in sensation to the extent of determining the soul's ability to detach from it. Although this may be true with respect to the *Platonic Theology*—the focus of Kristeller's study—it is certainly not the case with respect to the *Commentary on the Enneads*—as we will demonstrate at some length in the present section.

444. On Plotinus' theory of sensation, see in the first instance Blumenthal, *Plotinus' Psychology*, pp. 67–79. Among those topics most relevant to the Ficinian developments with which we are concerned, Blumenthal considers the distinction between sensation and sense-perception (p. 68); the notion of sensation as a kind of instrumentality of the body allowing the premise of the impassivity of soul as a whole to be maintained (p. 70); the notions that soul is not impressed but receives a kind of "translation," that sensation is not directed to objects but to impressions produced in the "living being," that the latter are already intelligible entities, and that sensation directed outside is an image of this truer perception (pp. 71–72); the theory of "transmission" considered in relation to Galen's neurology (pp. 74–75); the notion that similarity is necessary for sensation and that this similarity is provided by the notion of universal sympathy (pp. 76–78); the necessity of positing a third thing between sense and sense-object, having an affection between sensible and intelligible, and being a proportional mean (pp. 77–78); the various senses, some of which require a medium and some do not (p. 78); and the need for sympathy rather than continuity to explain sensation (p. 78). For a more detailed account, see Emilsson, *Plotinus on Sense-Perception*, pp. 36–62.

445. There is also a brief summary of the theory at Ficino, *In Enneadem* 4.6.**1-2**. It is important to remember that although Ficino concentrates on the sensation exercised by an individual human soul in the passages summarized below, he does also maintain that the world-soul and the souls of the celestial animate beings also have a faculty of sensation. See especially Ficino, *In Enneadem* 4.4.**24**. Here, it is argued that the souls of celestial spheres have sensation—including hearing and vision—and

where an analogy is established between the celestial "eye" — the outer-most sphere — and the human eye. The celestial eye projects its rays to-ward the center of the world, whereas the human eye sends its rays to-ward the periphery. Cf. also Ficino, *De Vita* 3.11.6–14, 3.16.68–70 (ed. Kaske-Clark, pp. 288–90, 324); *Super Theophrastum*, ch. 22 (*Opera* 2:1812) on the Orphic "eye." Cf. ch. 13 (*Opera* 2:1806).

446. Ficino, *In Enneadem* 4.4.**23**. At 4.6.3 Ficino contrasts the soul's pos-session of internal reason-principles with a view to sensation with its possession of seminal reason-principles with respect to its bodily parts.

447. Ficino, *In Enneadem* 4.5.**4**. This text shows that Ficino is advocating something that modern scholars label the "active" theory of sensation and find most famously in authors such as Plotinus and Augustine (who fol-lows Plotinus on this point especially in *De Musica*, Book 6). In the Ficin-ian version of the active theory, both the sense and the sensible object — *qua* formal — exhibit activity, whereas the spirit functioning as the intermediary of sensation is simultaneously active and passive. That something can be simultaneously active and passive results from the ema-native character of the Aristotelian act *understood in the Neoplatonic manner*. On the background to Ficino's doctrine, see Gannon, "The Active The-ory of Sensation in St. Augustine," and Wagner, "Sense Experience and the Active Soul."

448. Ficino, *In Enneadem* 4.5.**6**. Cf. 4.5.**12**.

449. Cf. Ficino, *Super Theophrastum*, chs. 34, 45, 49 (*Opera* 2:1817, 1822, 1824) proportion. Cf. ch. 40 (*Opera* 2:1819–20).

450. Emilsson, *Plotinus on Sense-Perception*, p. 37, notes that the main question of Plotinus' *Ennead* 4.5 (on which Ficino is commenting) is whether a medium plays a causal role in vision and whether this happens by progressive affection of a medium, Plotinus' own position being that there is no such medium and that the visual transmission takes place somehow by means of "sympathy" (συμπάθεια). The passages most relevant to this topic in Plotinus are (1) *Ennead* 4.4.23.1–28, raising the question whether the soul senses the sensible object "by itself" (ἐφ' ἑαυτῆς) or "together with something else" (μετ' ἄλλου), and answering

by saying that there cannot just be two things: the sensible object and the soul, since that would leave no room for any passivity. There must be a third thing that is affected, receives the form, and is of one matter with the sensible object. Moreover, this third thing must have an affection that is "between the sensible and the intelligible, as a proportional mean" (μεταξὺ αἰσθητοῦ καὶ νοητοῦ . . . μέσον ἀνάλογον); (2) 4.5.3.15–18, arguing that the absence of a physical intermediary between the sense and the sensible object does not imply the absence of "the sympathy of the living being with itself and of its parts with one another which depends on being one thing" (συμπάθεια τοῦ ζῴου . . . πρὸς αὐτὸ καὶ ἡ πρὸς ἄλληλα τῶν μερῶν τῷ ἓν εἶναι); (3) 4.5.5.29–31, concluding that the sense of hearing—as much as the sense of sight—is "a certain common awareness of the kind that occurs within a living-being" (συναισθή-σεώς τινος ὡς ἐν ζῴῳ). Emilsson rightly observes that, having provided some tantalizing suggestions in passages such as those quoted above, Plotinus explains neither what the third mediating term is nor how this relates to sympathy (47–54, 57–59). He then suggests that Galen's interpretation of the Platonic theory of vision in the *Timaeus* (Galen, *De Placitis Hippocratis et Platonis* 7.5.5–19, 32–33) may operate in a "conceptually kindred" manner to the theory that Plotinus seems to propose albeit rather tentatively. Galen postulates a certain relation between the outgoing visual ray, sunlight, and the air, in which the intermediate air becomes sensitive through the presence of the outgoing pneuma in the sunlight, and in which the intermediate air has the same relation to the eye as the nerve leading from the eye has to the brain, the main difference between Galen's and Plotinus' theories being that Galen does not take the organic unity that grounds sensation to be a permanent condition, as Plotinus seems to suggest, but as something brought about by the temporary condition of the visual pneuma (59–62). Now Emilsson's perceptive analysis of Plotinus' doctrine of sensation is broadly in line with Ficino's, although—as we shall see—the Plotinian theory needs to be completed with a more carefully articulated doctrine of *pneuma/spiritus*. However, having suggested something similar to the Ficinian interpretation, Emilsson—perhaps suspecting that he has diverged too far from

the letter of the *Enneads* — subsequently reverts to the notion that the mysterious third term is the sense-organ (67–70).

451. Cf. Ficino, *Super Theophrastum*, ch. 30 (*Opera* 2:1815), formal activity of sensible object. A more recent interpretation by Gurtler, *Plotinus, Ennead IV. 4. 30–45 and IV. 5*, pp. 231, 238–39, 245, 254, maintains the role of the third thing in Plotinus' theory of sensation, albeit seeing it as a body of some kind (as opposed to the Ficinian semi-incorporeal *spiritus*).

452. Cf. Ficino, *Super Theophrastum*, chs. 16, 32 (*Opera* 2:1808–9, 1816), materiality of sensible object versus spirituality of sense. Cf. chs. 27–28 (*Opera* 2:1814), material and immaterial aspects of the process of sensation.

453. Cf. Ficino, *Super Theophrastum*, ch. 13 (*Opera* 2:1806), spatial extension of spirit. Cf. ch. 44 (*Opera* 2:1821–22) for a general definition of spirit.

454. Ficino, *Super Theophrastum*, chs. 3, 27, 34, 40, 45 (*Opera* 2:1802, 1814, 1817, 1819, 1822), spirit in instrument of sense.

455. Cf. Ficino, *Super Theophrastum*, chs. 3, 40 (*Opera* 2:1802, 1819), spirit as passive.

456. Cf. Ficino, *Super Theophrastum*, chs. 15, 32 (*Opera* 2:1808, 1816), activity and passivity in sensation.

457. Cf. Ficino, *Super Theophrastum*, ch. 30 (*Opera* 2:1815), necessity for the life of the world to complete the process. See also chs. 26–27, 32 (*Opera* 2:1814, 1816).

458. Cf. Ficino, *Super Theophrastum*, ch. 29 (*Opera* 2:1815), spiritual form in dependence on Idea.

459. Cf. Ficino, *Super Theophrastum*, chs. 15, 28–30 (*Opera* 2:1808, 1814–15), spiritual form. Cf. ch. 13 (*Opera* 2:1806), spiritual reason-principle.

460. Cf. Ficino, *Super Theophrastum*, chs. 3, 27, 32 (*Opera* 2:1802, 1814, 1816), the spiritual form as active.

461. For a summary of the entire process, see Ficino, *Super Theophrastum*, ch. 30 (*Opera* 2:1815).

462. Priscianus Lydus, *Metaphrasis* 4.3.

463. This phase is mentioned at the end of passage *A* quoted above. It is discussed in more detail at Ficino, *In Enneadem* 4.6.**1–2**. Cf. Ficino, *Super Theophrastum*, chs. 4–5 (*Opera* 2:1803), reason-principle as the active element in sensation; chs. 9, 27 (*Opera* 2:1805, 1814), reason-principle and sensory judgment.

464. Porphyry, *Sententiae ad intelligibilia ducentes* 18.9.3–13.

465. On vision as the most perfect sense, see Ficino, *Super Theophrastum de sensu*, ch. 21 (*Opera* 2:1811). The mechanism of vision is discussed at considerable length at Ficino, *Compendium in Timaeum*, summa 30 (*Opera* 2:1472–74), where it is Plato's theory (of which Plotinus was himself somewhat critical) that forms the starting point. The account is less metaphysical than that in the commentary on *Ennead* 4.5 but provides more detail regarding the physical side of the process. In particular, Ficino discusses the emission of visual rays through the eyes, the mingling with external light, and reflection back to the eyes; the seeing of objects in perspective; the relation between multiplicity and unity of rays in the shape of a cone; the vibratory character of the rays emitted by the eyes and reflected back to them; and the formation of images by the rays. An important function is assigned to spirit here, as it was in the case of the more "Plotinian" theory, the spirit in this case being specified as "animal" and "solar" in nature.

466. An extensive discussion of sound and hearing can be found at Ficino, *Compendium in Timaeum*, ch. 31 (*Opera* 2:1451–52). These are considered in more detail there because the *Timaeus* is very much concerned with the harmonic structure of the soul, and because such a harmonic structure is more closely associated with the phenomena of sound than with those of vision. See also summa 62 (*Opera* 2:1477).

467. "Palpable body" (*corpus manifestum*). On Ficino's notion of spirit as a kind of body, see §§2.3.4–5.

468. Ficino, *In Enneadem* 4.5.**1**.

469. Ficino, *In Enneadem* 4.5.**1–2**. In 4.5.**2–3** Ficino gives a number of reasons why a bodily medium is not necessary. These include: (*i*) the light-ray flows naturally from the eye to the visible object in a straight line without a support; (*ii*) the exposure of the vision and the visible ob-

ject to a mutual passivity is a sufficient connection between the two; (iii) the necessity of turning the eye to the visible object shows that the giving of color and shape to the medium of air is not sufficient to produce vision; (iv) the form of the visible object is not imprinted in the eye by coming in sequence through parts of the air; (v) the light involved in the process of vision can become neither a property of air nor itself corporeal.

470. On the incorporeality of light, see also Ficino, *Compendium in Timaeum*, ch. 37 [incorrectly numbered 38] (*Opera* 2:1459). In this chapter two levels of light are distinguished: (a) the light that is visible to the eyes, (b) the light hidden in the fabric of the heaven. Both lights depend on the intellect of the world-soul (and are presumably incorporeal). However, a depends on it in so far as it is an image of intellect, whereas b depends on it in so far as it has become intellect; moreover a pervades all things having come from the sun, whereas b pervades all things having come from the firmament.

471. Ficino, *In Enneadem* 4.5.**5** and **7–8**. Cf. 4.5.**11**. On the doctrine of light, spirit, and transparency, see note 353.

472. Ficino, *In Enneadem* 4.5.**3**. Cf. Ficino, *Super Theophrastum*, ch. 20 (*Opera* 2:1811).

473. Ficino, *In Enneadem* 4.5.**5**. He means, of course, a *bodily* medium.

474. Ficino, *In Enneadem* 4.5.**10**. Cf. Ficino, *Super Theophrastum*, ch. 44 (*Opera* 2:1821).

475. Ficino, *In Enneadem* 4.5.**11**. Cf. 4.5.**9**; Ficino, *Super Theophrastum*, chs. 18–19 (*Opera* 2:1810).

476. See Plotinus, *Ennead* 4.4.26.26–28, where Plotinus concludes regarding the underlying principle of sensation that "if it is *pneuma*, then it is also the transparent" (εἴπερ πνεῦμα, καὶ διαφανές). This is the main (perhaps the only) passage on the basis of which Ficino could maintain that his theory of *spiritus* is "Plotinian." See note 353.

477. Ficino, *Super Theophrastum*, ch. 25 (*Opera* 2:1813). On the association between light and spirit, see further Ficino, *Compendium in Timaeum*, ch. 37 (*Opera* 2:1459–60).

478. See pp. 226–28.

479. Ficino, *Super Theophrastum*, chs. 17, 26 (*Opera* 2:1809, 1814).

480. See pp. 211–12.

481. Ficino, *Super Theophrastum*, chs. 24, 34 (*Opera* 2:1813, 1817).

482. See pp. 222–23.

483. Ficino, *Super Theophrastum*, chs. 17, 37 (*Opera* 2:1809, 1818).

484. See pp. 228–29.

485. Ficino, *Super Theophrastum*, chs. 14, 23 (*Opera* 2:1807, 1812).

486. See the present author's "Analytical Study" of the *Commentary on the Third Ennead*, §§2.3 and 2.3.1–2.3.2.

487. See above, §1.2.3.

488. Ficino, *In Enneadem* 4.3.**31**, 4.4.**38–40**. Another faint echo is perhaps the triad of hidden power, light, and heat that Ficino attributes to the celestial bodies at 4.5.**10–11**.

489. Ficino, *In Enneadem* 4.3.**31**.

490. Ficino, *In Enneadem* 4.4.**39**.

491. Ficino, *In Enneadem* 4.3.**31**.

492. Ficino, *In Enneadem* 4.4.**38–39**.

493. Ficino, *In Enneadem* 4.3.**31**.

494. Ficino, *In Enneadem* 4.4.**39**. Iamblichus is quoted as authority for this idea.

495. Ficino, *In Enneadem* 4.3.**38**.

496. Ficino, *In Enneadem* 4.3.**31**, 4.4.**40**. In actual fact, Ficino establishes an intertextual connection in the second passage not only between Plato and Orpheus but between Plato's *Statesman*, *Laws*, *Timaeus*, and *Phaedrus*. In other words, the authority for the Plotinian doctrine is very compelling.

497. Ficino, *De Vita* 2.20.34–36 (ed. Kaske-Clark, p. 350).

498. Ficino, *De Vita* 3.pr.24–28 (ed. Kaske-Clark, pp. 236–38).

499. Ficino, *De Vita* 3, *Ad lectorem* 32–34 (ed. Kaske-Clark, p. 240).

500. Ficino, *De Vita* 3.1 (ed. Kaske-Clark, p. 242): MARSILII FICINI
FLORENTINI LIBER DE VITA CAELITUS COMPARANDA COMPOSITUS
AB EO INTER COMMENTARIA EIUSDEM IN PLOTINUM . . . *in quo consistat secundum Plotinum virtus favorem caelitus attrahens, scilicet in eo quod
anima mundi et stellarum daemonumque animae facile alliciuntur corporum formis accommodatis.*

501. Ficino, *De Vita* 3.15.109–10 (ed. Kaske-Clark, p. 320).

502. Ficino, *De Vita* 3.26.1–2 (ed. Kaske-Clark, p. 384).

503. Ficino, *De Vita* 3.26.20–21 (ed. Kaske-Clark, p. 384).

504. The reference is to *Asclepius* 37.347.3–38.349.8. Cf. 24.326.9–20.

505. Ficino, *De Vita* 3.26.77–88 (ed. Kaske-Clark, p. 388).

506. Ficino, *De Vita* 3.26.122–27 (ed. Kaske-Clark, p. 390).

507. Ficino, *Apologia* 55–58.

508. This fact is, of course, decisive. However, Kaske and Clark, *Marsilio
Ficino, Three Books on Life*, pp. 25–26, further argue that the title of Ficino's commentary on *Ennead* 4.3.11 — occurring only in the MS — is an
earlier version of the title of *De Vita* 3.1; that in Ficino's translation of
Plotinus the marginal title of *Ennead* 4.3.11 points similarly to phraseology in *De Vita* 3.1; and that at *De Vita* 3.26.77–88 (ed. Kaske-Clark,
p. 388) Plotinus is said to have imitated the statue-animating process: a
point arising only at *Ennead* 4.3.11.

509. See Kaske and Clark, *Marsilio Ficino, Three Books on Life*, pp. 26–27
and p. 73 n. 8.

510. Cf. Ficino, *In Enneadem* 4.3.**21–24**.

511. Cf. Ficino, *In Enneadem* 4.3.**25–26**.

512. Cf. Ficino, *In Enneadem* 4.3.**27–30**.

513. Cf. Ficino, *In Enneadem* 4.3.**31**.

514. Cf. Ficino, *In Enneadem* 4.3.**32–33**.

515. There is another striking instance of Ficino's metaphorical interpretation of statue making in his *Commentary on Dionysius' Mystical Theology*
18.1–2, where the inspiration is a passage from Dionysius himself. Since
the world here is compared to statue of God, the metaphysical meaning

of the metaphor is identical with that in the *Commentary on the Fourth Ennead*. On statue making in Ficino, see Allen, "To Gaze Upon the Face of God Again."

516. Nature is explicitly compared to a sorceress at Plotinus, *Ennead* 4.4.44.29–30.

[ENNEADIS QUARTAE]
CAPITULA

[LIBRI I ET II]
ARGUMENTUM DE ANIMA

Intellectus primus est essentia prima a quo et in quo sunt semper intellectus alii. Item quomodo anima sit individua simul atque dividua.

[LIBER III]
ARGUMENTUM DE DUBIIS ANIMAE

CHAPTER HEADINGS OF ENNEAD IV

[BOOKS I AND II]
ANALYSIS OF "ON THE SOUL"

The first intellect is the first essential being from which and in which the other intellects always are; also how the soul is simultaneously undivisible and divisible.

[BOOK III]
ANALYSIS OF "ON DIFFICULTIES CONCERNING THE SOUL" [FIRST BOOK]

Chapter I   That our souls are different from the world-soul and are not derived from it.

Chapter II   On the twofold soul; and that our souls are not parts of the world-soul.

Chapter III   There are besides the world-soul many intellectual souls which are distinguished among themselves not by external but by internal boundaries.

Chapter IV   Intellectual souls are distinguished among themselves not through accidental but through essential properties; and how the many souls are said to be one and from one.

Cap V   Quomodo anima quaelibet rationalis est omnia; et
          quomodo differant inter se species rationalium
          animarum.

Cap VI   Respondetur ad dubia et probatur rationales animas
          non esse ex anima mundi.

Cap. VII Quomodo animae differant et quomodo sint
          immortales in propria forma restantes et quomodo
          anima mundi ubique praesens omnibus conducat ad
          vitam.

Cap. VIII Quot modis insinuetur anima corpori; et qualis sit
           anima mundi, et quomodo faciat mundum et
           dimensionem eius, et quomodo sit ubique.

Cap. IX   Quomodo anima mundi agit in se ipsa atque ita
          naturaliter gignit mundum sic omniformem sicut
          omniformis est ipsa.

Cap. X   De descensu animae, Dionysio, Iove, curriculis
          vitarum, ordine mundi, consonantia universi.

Cap. XI   Lex iudicium iustitia universi ducit intrinsecus ani-
          mos tum sponte, tum necessitate ad suum quemque
          terminum.

Cap. XII De connexione huius mundi ad superiorem et
          Prometheo statuisque loquentibus.

Capp. XIII–XXX [Tituli horum capitulorum desunt]

[LIBER IV]
DE DUBIIS ANIMAE

Capp. I–XLII [tituli horum capitulorum desunt]

Cap. XLIII Magica fascinatio nititur viribus naturalibus tam caelestium quam inferiorum rerum, scilicet atque verborum. Attingit igitur proxime spiritum nostrum et per hunc non solum humores sed etiam vitam irrationalem dependentem etiam ab ipso mundo. Animam vero rationalem natura vitaque corporea mundi superiorem et solum a mente divina pendentem nequit attingere, nisi quatenus cum vita inferiore consentit.

Cap. XLIV Vita contemplativa libera est, activa ministra actionum et rerum atque fortunae, voluptuosa serva corporis.

Cap. XLV Homo non solum tamquam mundi pars quaedam fataliter agit patiturque multa, sed etiam substantiam habet propriam naturaliter quidem partim superioribus, partim inferioribus cognatam. Ac libero motu potest insuper affectionem et habitum induere tam cum superioribus quam cum inferioribus congruentem.

[LIBER V]
DE DUBIIS ANIMAE VEL
DE VISIONE

Capp. I–VIII [tituli horum capitulorum desunt]

[LIBER VI]
DE SENSU ET MEMORIA

Cap. I   [titulus deest]

Cap. II   Sentire non est pati a rebus sentiendis sed agere circa
illas.

Cap. III Meminisse et reminisci non est conservare atque
repetere rerum formas aliquando impressas animo.

[LIBER VII]
DE ANIMI IMMORTALITE

Cap. I   Unusquisque nostrum totus est immortalis, siquidem
est ipse animus immortalis.

Cap. II   Nullum corpus qua ratione corpus propriam et
insitam habet vitam; anima vero habet. Igitur anima

non est corpus; ergo neque fit ex corpore vel corporibus cum sit natura praestantior.

Cap. III   Omne corpus efficit distantia partium ut parte alia patiente non statim compatiantur et aliae. Per ipsam vero animam corpus vivum habet ut ad partis unius motionem passionemque cunctae statim commoveantur. Anima igitur nec est corpus neque forma distenta per corpus.

Cap. IV   Stoici et Epicurei animam esse spiritum suspicabantur: id est, subtilissimum corpus. Illi quidem potius igneum, hi vero magis aerium; et utrique non quemlibet spiritum sed certa quadam proprietate affectum animam nominabant.

Cap. V   Anima motus effectusque omniformes tam vegetali virtute per rationes seminales quam electione profert; et corpus certo quodam ordine ad certum auget terminum, permanetque ipsa interea eadem. Item tota anima est in qualibet — vel ficta portione animae vel vera corporis portione — ; totaque virtus animae in qualibet seminis gutta servatur.

also, it does not come to be from body or
bodies, since it is superior in nature.

Chapter III Every body brings it about, through separation
of parts, that when one part suffers an affect the
other parts do not immediately suffer together
with it. It is through the soul that a living body
has the wherewithal to bring it about that all
parts are immediately moved in response to the
motion and passion of a single part. Therefore,
the soul is neither a body nor a form extended
through body.

Chapter IV The Stoics and the Epicureans surmised that
the soul was a spirit: that is to say, a most subtle
body. The Stoics thought of the spirit more as
fiery, the Epicureans more as airy. Both groups
named as soul not any kind of spirit but the one
bestowed with a certain definite property.

Chapter V The soul puts forth its omniform motions and
effects as much using the vegetative power
operating through seminal rational-principles as
using choice. It increases the body according to a
certain definite order toward a definite limit,
while in the meantime remaining the same.
Moreover, the soul is entire in each and every
thing—either an imagined "part" of the soul or a
true part of the body. The entire power of the
soul is preserved in each and every drop of
semen.

Cap. VI   Necesse est diversa per sensus varios influentia ad intimum et unum individuumque sensum redigi omnia inter se comparantem.

Cap. VII   Principalis sensus passionum iudex passiones cuiuslibet membri subito percipit; in qua particula membri sint distincte discernit; huc oculos manusque statim admovet.

Cap. VIII Intelligentia frequenter attingit et penetrat incorporea, formasque separat a corporibus. Fit igitur absque corpore; intellectus ergo non est corporeus.

Cap. IX   Essentia corporea tamquam imperfecta dependet ab incorporea perfecta; quae quidem cum ex seipsa primoque sit et vivat, semper est et vivit: in cuius genere anima continetur.

Cap. X   Duae sunt mentium divinarum dotes: una quidem claritas intellectus omnia cernens, altera vero optimus vitae habitus. Eiusmodi dotes maxime consequitur animus quando seipsum ab omni labe corporea segregans revertitur in seipsum. Ex quo apparet eum esse divinis mentibus natura cognatum.

Cap. XI   Corpus animatum ipsius animae beneficio habet ut ex se quodammodo moveatur. Igitur anima

potissimum habet idem; igitur et vitam ex se habet; igitur et in se a corpore non dependentem: semper ergo vivit etiam a corpore separata.

Cap. XII   Anima nostra mundi animam motu rerumque intelligentia imitans sempiterna est, sicut et illa, praesertim quoniam, dum revocando se ad intima sui res intelligit, declarat absolutas rerum formas sibi ingenitas se habere.

Cap. XIII   Anima nostra, etsi est in genere divinorum, tamen quia in eo genere ultimum tenet gradum, merito descendit in corpus — et id quidem caducum — ad divinum gradum iterum reversura.

Cap. XIV   Omnes animae proprias immortalesque vitas habent.

Cap. XV   Animae defunctorum nostra haec memoriter tenent sentiunt curant malefaciunt benefaciunt.

Marsilii epilogus.

[LIBER VIII]
DE ANIMAE DESCENSU
IN CORPORA

Cap. I   Animae nostrae intellectuales in corpus descendunt
per naturam vivificam intelligentiae suae subiunctam
et corpus naturaliter asciscentem sicut flamma sulfur;
similiter et caelestium intellectuales animae
corporibus suis per eiusmodi medium copulantur.

Cap. II   Coniunctio animae cum corpore, etsi est secundum
quandam animae naturam atque etiam ad universi
perfectionem, tamen duplici ratione animis nostris
obest, quia et intelligentiam quodammodo impedit et
animum perturbationibus implet; animis vero
caelestibus haec impedimenta non accidunt.

Cap. III   Quoniam omnis natura praeter primam
simplicissimam infinitam multiplicabilis est, ideo in
genere intellectuali multi sunt intellectus, in genere
animali multae sunt animae. In ordine animarum
multae sunt intellectuales quales sunt caelestes,
daemonicae, nostrae.

Cap. IV   Intellectus divinus impressit intellectui nostro
omniformem universi formam quae facile in rationem

[BOOK VIII]
ON THE SOUL'S DESCENT
INTO BODIES

vacantem inde surrutilat. Quando igitur ratio ad eam
penitus se convertit secumque rapit imaginationem,
in eodem statu quo et mundi anima permanet.

Cap. V   De animae descensu Empedoclis Heracliti Platonis
dicta consentiunt.

Cap. VI   Anima venit in corpus non solum infirmitate quadam in divinis ultra consistere non valente, sed etiam
potestate naturae fecundae pullulantis in germen;
forma namque corporea est animae fecundae
propago.

Cap. VII   Sicut aer inter ignem aquamve medius, illinc quidem
igneus, hinc vero fit aquaeus, ac vicissim ad utraque
fertur; sic animus ad divina se habet atque caduca.

Cap. VIII   Cum animus noster vires et actus caelestibus animis
consimiles habeat, probabile est saltem intellectum
nostrum, sicut et illorum, circa divina semper agere,
sicut natura vegetalis in nobis circa corporea versatur
assidue.

there, this Form readily casts its glimmer into the reason which is free to receive it. Therefore, when the reason completely turns itself toward the Form and snatches away the imagination, it remains in the same status as that of the world-soul.

[LIBER IX]
UTRUM OMNES ANIMAE
UNA SINT ANIMA

Cap. I   Plotini sententia est mundum unam habere propriam sibi animam et animalia omnia suas propriasque habere.

Cap. II   Concessurus revera Plotinus animas esse distinctas, non facile cedit rationi iam dictae: scilicet, passionem animalis unius mox in aliud universumque transituras.

Cap. III   Ludit adhuc Plotinus noster.

Cap. IV   Opinionem dicentem cunctis inesse animam numero unam iam respuit; tangit vero dicentem esse unam specie distinctam numero, atque singulas esse derivatas ex una divisa.

Cap. V   Animae, quamvis per essentias inter se distinctae sint, omnes tamen quodammodo una sunt anima tribus videlicet modis.

[BOOK IX]
WHETHER ALL SOULS ARE
ONE SOUL

LIBRI PLOTINI PHILOSOPHI
EXCELLENTISSIMI
INTERPRETE MARSILIO FICINO
PLATONICO
QUARTA ENNEAS

FOURTH ENNEAD OF THE BOOK
BY PLOTINUS
A MOST EXCELLENT
PHILOSOPHER
TRANSLATED BY THE
PLATONIST MARSILIO FICINO

[LIBRI I ET II]

ARGUMENTUM DE ANIMA

Intellectus primus est essentia prima a quo et in quo sunt
semper intellectus alii. Item quomodo anima sit individua
simul atque dividua.

1 Quoniam quae hic Plotinus de anima disserit alibi latius pertracta-
vimus, praesertim in primo et tertio et septimo *Theologiae* libro,
ideo hic breviter attingemus. Generatio semper contendit ad esse:
primo quidem ad esse nudum, deinde ad esse vivum, post haec ad
esse quod dicitur sensuale, denique ad esse intellectuale tamquam
summum ubi anima intellectualis ad corporis descendit commercium. Eiusmodi vero est ordo essentiae vel essendi in generationis
gradibus acquisitus; super hunc ordinem exstat ordo essentiae in
aeternis gradibus universi in quo summum tenet velut principium
ipse simpliciter intellectus. A quo intellectus animalis in generatione descendens summum tenet in toto generationis ordine tamquam finis, non quidem simpliciter generatione factus sed accom-
modatus corpori ad providentiam totius explendam. Est autem
ipse simpliciter intellectus ubique totus. Sunt et in eo non solum
per ideas verum etiam per proprias (ut ita dixerim) exsistentias
intellectuales animae secundum intellectualem sibi propriam facultatem etiam dum sunt in corpore. Quemadmodum lineae a centro

[BOOKS I AND II]¹

ANALYSIS OF "ON THE SOUL"

The first intellect is the first essential being from which and in which the other intellects always are; also how the soul is simultaneously undivisible and divisible.

Since we have elsewhere examined in more detail what Plotinus   ₁
says here about the soul, having done so especially in the first, third, and seventh books of the *Theology*,² we will therefore here touch upon these issues briefly. The realm of generation always strives toward being: first toward being in the bare sense, next toward being alive, after that toward the being that is called sensitive, and finally toward intellectual being as though the highest being where the intellectual soul descends to dealings with the body. In this manner, indeed, is the order of essential being or of essential act in the levels of generation something acquired. Above this order there stands the order of essential being in the eternal levels of the universe in which intellect itself *simpliciter* holds the rank of a quasi-supreme principle. From this the intellect of soul descending into the realm of generation holds the highest rank, being as though a limit in the entire order of generation. This is not made in the realm of generation *simpliciter*, but rather adapted to body in order to complete the providence of the totality. The intellect itself *simpliciter* is everywhere as a whole. The intellectual souls are in it not only through the Ideas but also through their proper "existences," if one may put it thus, in accordance with the intellectual faculty proper to them, even while they are in an embodied state. Just as lines extended from a center as far as a circumference do not depart from the center while reaching the circumference, or as

ad circumferentiam usque productae non discedunt a centro dum attingunt circumferentiam et radii non relinquentes solem interim terrena contingunt, atque sicut lineae radiique extra prominentes inter se loco distant, in ipso tamen principio sunt loco simul; sic animae apud nos secundum corpora situ distantes ibidem sunt omnes secundum intellectum in mente divina: secundum intellectus inquam suos illic inter se differentes, sicut et linearum radiorumque termini inter se sunt alii etiam ubi centrum solemque contingunt.

2   Hinc effici vult Plotinus ut intellectus prophetae hominisque abstracti, etsi in oriente tantum videatur esse, prospiciat tamen quae fiunt in occidente atque ex uno quodam loco miraculosum aliquid agat in alio et cogitatione affectioneque sua clam moveat alios — quia videlicet intellectus omnes in se invicem et ubique sunt, quandoquidem sunt semper in simplici mente divina tota semper ubique praesente. Qua quidem praesentia et Deus percipiat preces et homines cum Deo familiarissime colloquantur. Esse quoque vult intellectus eiusmodi familiares hominum daemones assiduosque duces singulis singulos attributos, nam externi daemones forte non adeo possunt singuli hominibus singulis adhiberi.

3   Censet Platonem, ubi ait in *Timaeo* animam componi ex essentia quadam individua[1] itemque dividua circa corpora, primam essentiam intellexisse intellectualem animae potestatem numquam ad corpora declinantem, secundam vero illam animae naturam quae corpori se prorsus accommodat. Quae tamen interim individua dicitur, quoniam et anima corpori copulata quantumcumque

rays without leaving the sun in the meantime attain to earthly things, and just as the lines and the rays on coming forth to the exterior are separated spatially from one another but are all together spatially in their causal principle itself, so similarly the souls within our world which are distinct in position according to bodies are within the divine mind all in the same place according to intellect: according to their intellects, that is, which differ there among themselves as the limits of lines and rays are distinct from one another even where they are in contact with the center and the sun.

Plotinus holds that it is because of this that the intellect of a prophetic and disengaged man, even if it seems to be only in the east, can nevertheless observe things taking place in the west, and can in some particular place accomplish something miraculous in another place, secretly moving other men with its own thinking and affectivity—this presumably because all intellects are reciprocally in one another and everywhere, given that they are always in the simple divine mind which is present everywhere as a whole. Moreover, he thinks that it is through this presence both that God perceives our prayers and that men can converse with God most intimately. Plotinus also holds that intellects of this kind are the personal daemons of men, these daemons being individually assigned to individual men as their assiduous guides, since external daemons are perhaps not sufficient to be assigned individually to individual men.

Plotinus maintains that, when Plato says in the *Timaeus* that the soul is composed of a certain indivisible substance and a substance divisible around bodies,[3] his opinion is that the first power of the soul has understood intellectual being and never declines toward body, and that the second power of the soul is that nature which completely accommodates itself to body but is in the meantime said to be indivisible: even when coupled with the body; however much the parts of the body are separated from one

membra corporis inter se distent, ipsa a seipsa non distat quippe cum eadem in quolibet membro sit tota. Ita vero se habere utramque (ut diximus) animae facultatem tum in anima nostra tum etiam[2] in anima mundi. Ceterum cum dicat intellectum et mundi et hominis omnibus sui corporis membris esse praesentem itemque divinum intellectum partibus mundi cunctis adesse, cur non ex hoc saltem dicitur ita per corpus esse divisus ut anima? Quia videlicet intellectus quilibet sua praesentia nihil tribuit corpori nisi per animam: ut videatur adesse potius quam inesse. Praeterea intellectus aeque se habet in qualibet corporis portione ut videatur penitus indivisus; anima vero aliam sui vim actionemque in hoc membro aliam in alio exercet, vitamque et sensum atque motum per diversos gradus corporis sui membris accommodat: itaque divisa quodammodo videtur in corpore.

4   In secundo hic de anima libro notabis entelechiam[3] illam Aristotelicam qua anima dicitur actus et perfectio corporis accipi posse etiam apud Aristotelem non solum pro forma et anima a corpore inseparabili sed etiam pro ea quae sit a corpore separabilis. Proinde considerabis quod proprie dividitur id in substantia dividi, quod vero movetur posse moveri quidem proprie secundum accidentia eius et qualitates atque modos, interim tamen substantia permanere, ideoque divisione potius quam motu attingi substantiam atque laedi. Cum vero in ipso rerum descensu bonum quidem exordiatur a summo malumve a minimo, merito descendendo rem proprie mobilem prius quam proprie divisibilem reperimus.

another, soul is itself not separated from itself, being self-identical and as a whole in each and every part of the body. Plotinus also maintains that Plato's view is that the two faculties of the soul (as we have called them) have this status both in our soul and also in the world-soul. But when Plato says that the intellect both of the world and of man is present to all the parts of the body, and similarly that the divine intellect is present to all parts of the world, why is intellect not therefore said to be divided through body at least in the manner in which soul is divided? This is presumably because each and every intellect does not, through its presence, confer anything on the body except through the mediacy of soul—making it seem to be present *to* rather than present *in* body. Moreover, intellect subsists equally in each and every part of the body in such a way that it might seem to be completely undivided. However, soul exercises one of its powers and performs one action in this one part of the body and another of its powers and actions in another part. It adapts its life, sensation, and motion to different parts of the body and to various degrees, and therefore seems somehow to be divided in body.

Here in the second book concerning the soul, you will note that 4 the famous Aristotelian doctrine of the "entelechy" whereby the soul is said to be the actuality and perfection of the body[4] can be understood, even on Aristotle's terms, as corresponding not only to the form and soul that is inseparable from the body but also to that which is separable from the body. Therefore, you will consider that that which is divided in a proper sense is divided in its substance, but that that which is moved can be moved in a proper sense according to its accidents and qualities and modalities, albeit being meanwhile stable in its substance, and that therefore its substance is affected and damaged more by division than by motion. Indeed, since in the descent itself of things goodness begins from the highest or evil from the lowest, we rightly find in descending a thing that is mobile in the proper sense before a thing that is in

Igitur sub intellectu divino qui et individuus est penitus et immobilis invenimus animam indivisibilem quidem quamvis proprie mobilem, deinde formam qualitatemque corpoream undique mobilem atque divisam, demum corpus quod et huius divisionis origo est ac velut iners aliunde movetur. Quando vero animam divisibilem dicimus, non proprie ut de corpore atque etiam qualitate sed improprie loquimur, intelligentes non quidem sectam secundum corporis sectiones ut qualitas sed accommodatam corpori mobili divisoque viresque suas et actus et dona aliis membris aliter distribuere.

5   Notabis interea molem formamque corpoream natura sua penitus dissipabilem tum in nobis tum in mundo non posse aliter colligari quam ab anima quae non sit aeque divisa sed in qualibet parte sit tota; item mundi animam quatenus in se multitudinem habet virium atque formarum quodammodo mobilem esse accommodatam ad corpus mundi vivificandum—accommodatam inquam ab ipsa mente divina immobili quidem omnino, habente tamen multitudinem in se formarum, quamvis non usque ad minima differentium ibi sicut in anima differunt—; item quatenus et in mente divina primum et deinde in anima mundi regnat unitas vigetque simplicitas eminens, inde ratione quadam intellectuali sapienterque omnia regi. Conclude quinque hic rerum gradus: ipsum bonum unum in se tantum est; divina mens unum multa; anima tum mundi tum nostra unum in se est atque multa; qualitas formaque corporea quaelibet multa in se est et unum; corporis ipsa moles non unum iam secundum se sed multa censetur. Relique in *Theologia* (ut diximus) exponuntur.

the proper sense divisible. Therefore, below the divine intellect which is altogether indivisible and immobile we find the soul that is indivisible although mobile in the proper sense, after that the corporeal form and quality that is everywhere mobile and divided, and finally body which is both the source of this division and is moved externally as though it were something inert. When we say that the soul is divisible, we speak of this divisibility not in the proper sense as we would in the case of body and also quality but in an improper sense, understanding the soul not as cut according to corporeal segmentation as quality is cut but rather as adapted to the mobile and divided body and as distributing its various powers, acts, and gifts to different parts of the body.

In the meantime, you will note that the corporeal bulk and 5 form is altogether naturally capable of dispersal and that, both in us and in the world, it cannot be bound together otherwise than by soul which is not divided in like manner but is a whole in each and every part. Furthermore, you will note that the world-soul, to the extent that it has in itself a multiplicity of powers and forms, is somehow mobile and adapted to the enlivening of the world's body, being adapted indeed by the divine mind itself that is altogether immobile but having in itself a multitude of forms, although these forms are there not differentiated down to the lowest level as forms in the soul are differentiated. Again, you will note that, to the extent that unity rules first in the divine mind and then in the world-soul and also that overriding simplicity prevails, so are all things governed by a certain intellectual reason-principle and governed wisely. You should conclude that there are here five levels of things. The Good itself is one alone in itself; the divine mind is the one-many; the soul—both the world-soul and our soul—is one in itself and also many; each and every corporeal quality and form is many in itself and also one; and the corporeal bulk itself is judged to be not one but many in itself. The other matters are expounded (as we have said) in the *Theology*.

[LIBER III]

ARGUMENTUM DE
DUBIIS ANIMAE

: I :

*Quod animae nostrae differant ab anima mundi
neque sint ab ea.*

1 Primus de dubiis animae liber septem praecipuas continet quaestiones. Prima quaerit utrum animae nostrae sint ex anima mundi sive ut partes eius sive ut quidam effectus ab ea; secunda, quomodo anima insinuetur corpori: scilicet qua proprietate, quo ordine differenti, qua lege iustitiae; tertia, utrum anima extra corpus vivens discursu quodam rationis utatur; quarta, quo pacto in anima dicatur impartibile aliquid simul atque partibile; quinta, utrum anima aliquo modo sit in loco et qua conditione sit in corpore; sexta, ubi sit anima quando seorsum est a corpore; septima, utrum animae hinc seiunctae humanarum rerum reminiscantur et simpliciter de memoria atque reminiscentia.

2 Suspicabitur forte aliquis animas nostras esse quasdam mundanae animae partes, idque ex tribus Platonis[1] dictis asseverabit: primo quidem quod et in *Philebo* videtur innuere: quemadmodum corpora nostra mundani corporis partes sunt, sic et animae animas; deinde et quod in *Republica* et in *Phaedro* pariter et in *Timaeo*

[BOOK III]

ANALYSIS OF "ON DIFFICULTIES CONCERNING THE SOUL" [FIRST BOOK]

: I :

That our souls are different from the world-soul and are not derived from it.

The first book on difficulties concerning the soul contains seven 1
primary investigations. The first inquires whether our souls are
derived from the world-soul either as being its parts or as being
certain effects of it; the second, how the soul is introduced into the
body: that is to say, according with what property, with what differentiation of order, and with what law of justice; the third,
whether the soul, when living outside the body, employs a certain
discursiveness of reason; the fourth, in what sense there is said to
be simultaneously something indivisible and something divisible;
the fifth, whether the soul is somehow in place and on what basis
it is in the body; the sixth, where the soul is when it is separated
from the body; and the seventh, whether souls separated from
here remember human affairs — treating, in simple terms, of memory and reminiscence.

Someone perhaps will surmise that our souls are certain parts 2
of the world-soul, and will affirm this on the basis of three statements by Plato. First, as he seems to suggest in the *Philebus*,[1] that,
just as our bodies are parts of the world's body, so are our souls
parts of the world-soul; second, as seems to be Plato's opinion in
the *Republic* and the *Phaedrus*[2] and likewise in the *Timaeus*,[3] that

sentire videtur: animas nostras sequi totius mundi circuitum et inde mores fortunasque accipere; postremo quod in *Phaedro* dicit: animam quoque nostram totius inanimati curam habere. Videtur autem communis haec cura dumtaxat ad mundi animam pertinere. Videtur insuper verisimile homines intra mundum genitos vitam a mundo sortiri et quasdam totius vitae portiones habere. Hanc equidem suspicionem in *Theologia* ubi contra Averroem agitur pro viribus e medio sustuli. Atque hic ad eandem similiter exstirpandam imprimis una cum Plotino sic agamus.

3   Praestantior est forma quam materia et totum partibus. Igitur, si datur totum materiale, datur et formale totum. Item si totum ex partibus, ergo et totum ex totis. Cum enim universum summa ratione optimeque sit constructum, merito quicquid optime se habere ratio vera concludit iam exstat in universo, nam et inde ratio id coniectat. Totum materiale dicitur sicut lignum nam et, si multiplicatur in partes materiali divisione, non tamen multiplicatur in formas. Totum formale est arbor: in multas enim dividitur formas inter se perspicue differentes. In hoc quoque toto formali verum inest materiale totum, nam ex eo quod in formas particulares distinguitur differentes etiam in materias quodammodo differentes, formis scilicet propriis differentibus. Cum igitur mundus sit totum absolutissimum, certe et formale totum est totumque ex totis. Non erit autem totum ex totis nisi multa sint in eo non solum differentia formis, sicut in arbore, sed etiam secundum exsistentiam quoque disiuncta et actionibus segregata, sicut cantores in choro ubi unusquisque et communi officio cum ceteris ad idem congruit et interea proprius est et sui iuris exsistit. Oportere

our souls follow the circuit of the entire world and thence derive their habits and fortunes; and finally, as he says in the *Phaedrus*, that our soul also has care of the inanimate totality. However, this universal care seems to pertain only to the world-soul. Moreover, it seems probable that men born within the world are allotted their life from the world and have certain portions of the universal life. I have put this surmise about our souls out of court in the *Theology* where the case against Averroes is pursued energetically.[4] And let us here primarily apply ourselves similarly to rooting out such a belief in company with Plotinus.

Form has priority over matter and whole over parts. Therefore, 3 if a material totality is conceded, then a formal totality is also assumed. Again, if a totality consisting of parts is conceded, then a totality consisting of wholes is also admitted. For since the universe is constructed by a supreme reason-principle and in the best way possible, then rightly whatever true reason concludes to exist in the best way now exists in the universe, for it is a reason derived from there that makes this surmise. The material totality is said to be like wood, for even if it is multiplied into parts in a material division, it is however not multiplied into forms. The formal totality is the tree, for it is divided into forms that are clearly different among themselves. In this formal totality there is also a true material totality, for from the fact that it is distinguished into particular forms, the formal totality is also divided somehow into matters: that is, matters differing according to proper forms. Therefore, since the world is a totality in the most absolute sense, then it is also a formal totality and a totality consisting of wholes. However, it will not be a totality consisting of wholes unless the many things in it not only differ according to their forms — as in the case of the tree — but are also distinct according to their existence and separated according to their actions — like the singers in a choir where each member both comes together with the others in a shared function and in the meantime exists as his own individual and

autem mundum hunc esse verum totum ex rebus vere totis non solum eius perfectio postulat sed etiam exemplaris imitatio exigit nam et illud totum est ex totis. Illic enim in unoquoque aliter aliterque sunt omnia, sed in hoc insuper mundo localem quoque rerum disiunctionem adducit operis huius condicio dimensioni locoque et motui temporique subiecta. Denique ubi perfectiores sunt partes, perfectius est et totum. Partes vero perfectiores sunt quae exsistentiam propriam propriumque habent officium. Sic ergo et totum magis formale est ubi partes magis sunt formales. Hae vero ibi formales magis ubi formis atque exsistentiis sive substantiis et actionibus distinguuntur. Ad hoc autem ut totum sit vere unum satis profecto facit ordo cunctorum unus ab uno pariter et ad unum. Ex his apparet non esse probabile hanc mundi machinam unicam dumtaxat habere animam, sed probabilius esse plures adesse animas et animalia plura praeter mundanam animam animalque mundanum.

4   Atqui et in nobis esse propriam animae nostrae substantiam ab ipsa mundi anima differentem inde coniicimus quod proprium noster animus liberumque possidet arbitrii motum. Qua de re in *Theologia* de libero disputantes arbitrio satis egimus. Alioquin si pars totius foret, subito totius impetu raperetur neque foret discursionis rationalis et consilii compos neque aberrare posset quandoquidem anima mundi errare non potest. Liberum vero in nobis arbitrium Plato in decimo de *Republica* et in *Phaedro* atque *Timaeo* absque dubio ponit et Aristoteles ubique confirmat. Omnino vero ponere nostras esse partes animae mundi nihil alius est quam dicere hanc animam tuam esse ipsam totam mundi animam

with his own rights. That it is necessary for this world to be a true totality consisting of true wholes is something which is not only demanded by the world's perfection but also required by its imitation of an exemplar which is itself a totality consisting of wholes. For within the latter each thing is in each other thing in one way or another, whereas in this world the condition of this work subjected to dimension and space, and to motion and time introduces a spatial differentiation of things in addition. Finally, where there are more perfect parts, there also is a more perfect whole, those parts being more perfect that have a proper existence and a proper function. Therefore, a whole is more formal where its parts are more formal, and these parts are more formal where they are more differentiated in their forms, in their existences or substances, and in their actions. The order of all things, certainly, is sufficient to bring it about that the totality should truly be a unity,[5] this order being equally from one and to one. On this basis it seems improbable that this contrivance of the world would have only one soul, and more probable that there are present in it a plurality of souls and animate beings in addition to the soul and animate being of the world.

But we surmise that there is in us a proper substance of our 4 soul that differs from the world-soul itself from the fact that our mind has a motion of free choice which is its own — a question we have dealt with sufficiently in the *Theology*[6] when discussing freedom of choice. Otherwise, if our soul were part of a whole, it would suddenly be seized at the impulse of the whole, it would not be in control of its discursive reason and deliberation, and it would not be able to go astray since the world-soul is incapable of error. Plato asserts without doubt that there is free choice in us in the tenth book of the *Republic*,[7] in the *Phaedrus*,[8] and in the *Timaeus*,[9] Aristotle everywhere confirming this point. Indeed, to posit that our souls are parts of the world-soul is altogether nothing other than to say that this soul of yours is the entire

meamque similiter. Illa enim dividi nequit in varias portiones sed tota individuaque et eadem prorsus est simul ubique. Cum vero mea nunc et tua inter se omnino repugnent actionibus opinionibusque et affectibus et habitibus, non possunt eadem anima eademque mens exsistere. Praeterea si animus meus est quoquomodo pars animae mundi, non habet propriam exsistentiam nec insuper propriam actionem. Non igitur reflectitur in seipsum neque seipsum potest animadvertere. Immo et tamquam pars quaepiam angustissima non poterit mundum totum cogitatione complecti neque percurrere neque super hunc mundum animamque ipsius aliquid cogitare. Considera corpus humanum: non est hoc continua quaedam portio machinae sed secundum propriam seiunctum est figuram simul et motionem. Cum vero anima et praestantior sit quam corpus et figurae huius motionisque origo, nimirum non quasi continua est mundanae animae portio sed substantiam possidet propriam. Iam vero neque facta est ab ipsa mundani corporis anima: quod enim ipsa facit, mobili facit proprietate, ideoque mutabilem adeo facit essentiam ut nequeat immutabile quicquam attingere. Animus vero noster et motum resolvit in statum et mobilia subicit immobilibus. Denique cum animus noster sit quaedam intellectualis essentia, merito fit proprie ab ipso simpliciter intellectu a quo nascitur et anima mundi quae et ipsa similiter intellectus quidam est scilicet animalis. Hinc efficitur ut anima nostra possit similiter atque anima mundi fieri compos intelligentiae et ad illa quae super mundum sunt aeterna consurgere. Reliquae autem animae praeter intellectuales vel exoriri vel pendere a mundi anima possunt.

world-soul itself, and my soul likewise. The world-soul cannot be divided into various portions but is absolutely everywhere simultaneously as total, undivided, and self-identical. But since my soul and yours are at some point wholly at odds with one another in actions, opinions, affections, and conditions, they cannot exist as the same soul or the same mind. Moreover, if my mind is in some way or other a part of the world-soul, it does not have its own existence and also an action proper to it. Therefore, it does not turn back toward itself or have awareness of itself. Furthermore, it will not be able—as though some most restricted part of the world—to take hold of and run through the latter in thinking, and will not be able to have any thought of something above this world and its soul. Consider the human body. This is not some portion of the world's contrivance in continuity with it, but is separate from it according to both its own shape and motion. Since the soul is superior to the body and the source of its shape and motion, surely it is not a portion of the world-soul as though in continuity with it, but rather possesses its own specific substance. What is more—it is not made by the soul of the world's body, for that which this soul makes, it makes with the specific characteristic of mobility. Consequently, it makes the latter's essential being as mobile to such an extent that it is unable to attain to anything immutable. However, our soul both resolves motion into rest and subjects mobile things to the immobile. Finally, since our mind is a certain intellectual being, rightly it comes to be from the intellect itself *simpliciter* from which the world-soul is also born, the world-soul itself being similarly a kind of intellect: namely, a psychic intellect. Hence it comes about that our soul and the world-soul similarly are able to become possessors of intelligence and to rise up to those eternal things that are above the world. However, the remaining souls that are in addition to the intellectual ones *are* able to come forth from or depend upon the world-soul.

: II :

De duplici anima; et quod animae nostrae
non sunt partes animae mundi.

5   In capite secundo notabis imperfectum quodlibet in quovis genere
reducendum esse ad perfectum aliquid in eodem genere positum
per quod reducatur ad perfectum aliquid supra genus; ideoque
animam ratione carentem velut imperfectam quae et pars compositi est et instrumentis addicta corporeis reducendam esse ad
rationalem intellectualemque animam sui iuris et in se perpetuo
consistentem; idque faciendum esse tum in nobis tum in daemonibus et stellis sphaerisque et mundo. Quae opinio valde consonat
cum Peripateticis duos in caelis motores rite locantibus quorum
alter corpori mobili sit coniunctus ut forma mobilisque sit motor,
alter autem sit motor quodammodo separatus immutabilisque et
primum motionis principium atque finis.

6   Proinde Platonici quidam non legitimi qui dicebant hominum
animas esse partes animae mundi, interea fatebantur ipsam mundi
animam esse substantiam individuam sempiternam unam simpli-
cem ubique totam, et propterea consequenter addebant quamlibet
hominis animam esse animae mundanae conformem totamque simul et eadem attingentem quae tangit et anima mundi. His utique
positis non possunt animam mundi in nostras ita secare sicut vel
magnitudo quaedam in particulas vel numerus in unitates dividi
solet: sic enim illa quae dicitur totius anima eiusmodi divisione
periret neque restaret una. Non possunt insuper illam in has divi-
dere sicut calor totius corporis in partes caloris membrorum dividi

: II :

*On the twofold soul; and that our souls are
not parts of the world-soul.*

In the second chapter you will note that anything imperfect in any   5
genus is to be referred back to something perfect placed in the
same genus through which it is referred back to something perfect
above the genus. Therefore, an irrational soul which, being as
though imperfect, is both a part of a composite and also given over
to corporeal instruments should be referred back to a rational and
intellectual soul that is perpetually established in its own right and
in itself. The irrational soul should be handled in this way equally
when it is understood in us, in the daemons, in the stars, in the
spheres, and in the world. This doctrine is very much in agreement with the Peripatetics[10] who rightly place in the heavens two
movers of which one is conjoined to a mobile body in order that it
might be a form and a moved mover, the other a mover that is
somehow separate und unmoved, being the first beginning and
end of motion.

Accordingly, certain illegitimate Platonists[11] who maintained   6
that mens' souls were parts of the world-soul declared nevertheless
that the world-soul itself was an indivisible, everlasting, unitary,
simple, and omnipresent substance. For those reasons, they further concluded that each and every human soul was in conformity
with the world-soul, simultaneously attaining as a whole to all
those things to which the world-soul also attains. Having established these positions, they are certainly not able to dissect the
world-soul into our souls, as a given magnitude is wont to be divided into particles, or a number into unities, for that which is
called the soul of the totality would perish by such a division, and
would not remain a unity. In addition, the illegitimate Platonists[12]

videtur, nam animam illi substantiam esse volunt in corpore non extensam. Atqui calor ipse non proprie secatur sed dimensio in qua est calor, ideoque cuiuslibet membri calor[2] ipse communis potius est calor in parte corporis quam pars caloris. Veruntamen divisionem per accidens quodammodo patitur quatenus per extensionem corporis aequaliter est extensus. Anima vero non ita, nam absque ulla extensione sua dimensioneque dimensionibus astat ut divisibilia quaeque distantiaque perfecte connectat in unum. Neque possunt rursum distribuere mundi animam sic in nostras ut scientia tota in suas distribuitur notiones, nam sive nulla sit praeter notiones tota quaedam scientia — ita non erit usquam una communis anima — sive sit praeter illas una quaedam — non erit accommodata mundo sed eminens. Asserent denique sic nostras animas dici animae mundanae partes perinde ac si quis dicat animam nostram in manu vel pede esse partem totius animae nostrae. Sic itaque dividentes nihil dividunt et omnino divisionis vocabulo abutuntur: una enim eademque anima membro cuilibet[3] adest ubique tota simul quae cunctas in se animales potentias habet ubique, quamvis alias per alia membra velut instrumenta actiones exerceat. Passiones quidem sunt in membris: index autem sensibilium passionum tandem unus est, unum exhibens de diversis comparando iudicium tum imaginatione tum etiam ratione. Sic inquam fit in nobis: non potest autem omnino similiter fieri et in mundo in

are not able to divide the world-soul into our souls in the way that the warmth of an entire body seems to be divisible into the parts of warmth in the limbs, for these men hold that the soul is a substance not extended in the body. Moreover, warmth itself is not dissected in a proper sense, but only the dimension in which the warmth resides, and for this reason the warmth itself of any limb is more the shared warmth in part of the body than a part of the warmth. Nevertheless, warmth does undergo division *per accidens* in a certain manner to the extent that it is equally extended through the extension of the body. This is certainly not the case with soul, for the latter stands adjacent to the dimensions without any extension or dimension of its own in order that it might perfectly connect all divisible and separated things into a unity. Again, the illegitimate Platonists are not able to distribute the world-soul into our souls in such a way that a complete science is distributed into its own concepts, for either the certain complete science is nothing over and above its concepts—in which case, there will nowhere be a one shared soul—or else the complete science is one certain thing beyond its concepts—in which case the soul will not be adapted to the world but standing above it. Finally, these men will assert that our souls are said to be parts of the world-soul in the way that somebody might say that our soul in the hand or foot is part of the whole of our soul. But if they divide it thus, they are dividing nothing and totally abusing the term "division," for one and the same soul is everywhere present all at once to each and every limb, having all the animating powers everywhere in itself, although it performs actions in one way or another in this or that limb which is as though its instrument. Its passions are in the limbs, the judge of sensible passions however being ultimately one and delivering a single judgment in the comparison of different things sometimes in the imagination and sometimes also in the reason. This is, indeed, how it comes about in us. However, it is altogether impossible for this to come about similarly also in a

quo,[4] si unica singulorum esse fingatur anima, poterunt quidem diversi homines diversa pati sicut nunc in quolibet nostrum instrumenta diversa sed unicum denique iudicium adhibebitur. Eadem opinio intelligentia eadem: haec enim ad iudicem pertinent passionis expertem — si modo verus sit passionum rerumque iudex — et ideo exstat in se a patientibus quodammodo segregatus ideoque unicus neque propter varia instrumenta diversus. At vero cum contraria in hominibus inter se iudicia sint, proprie nimirum intelligentiae sunt. Propriae quoque substantiae sunt animarum, siquidem non per instrumenta sed per intimam substantiae facultatem officium rationale peragitur.

: III :

Multae[5] sunt praeter mundi animam intellectuales animae
quae non externis terminis
sed internis[6] inter se distinguuntur.

7 In capite tertio atque deinceps quod iterum reperitur: non posse fieri ut anima in mundo sit unica, rursus ita confirmo. Providentia summa totius ad summum[7] universi decorem in ordine consistentem varia rerum genera fore constituit et innumerabilia iterum individua. Inter haec vero velut valde distantia diversas in quolibet genere species esse voluit, amans prae ceteris copiam specierum velut rerum admodum perfectarum. Quod si in generibus inferioribus anima ordinem quamplurimum digessit in gradibus specierum, cur non et in natura genereque animae parem copiam

world where, if it is imagined that there is a single soul of individual things, different men will be able to suffer different things. It will be as though in each one of us there is now a different instrument, but finally a single judgment applied. The same opinion is the same understanding, for the latter pertains to a judge free of passivity — if ever there were a true judge of passions and realities — and this judge consequently exists in himself somehow separated from the passions, and therefore also as single and not differentiated on account of the various instruments. But since there are judgments in men that are contrary to one another, there are surely proper understandings and also proper substances of souls, given that the rational function is exercised not through instruments but through the inner capability of a substance.

: III :

There are besides the world-soul many intellectual souls which are distinguished among themselves not by external but by internal boundaries.

The point repeated in the third chapter and thereafter: that it is 7 not possible that the soul in the world should be unique, this I also confirm as follows. The highest providence of the totality has established that there should be, with a view to the highest embellishment of the universe that resides in order, various genera of thing and also innumerable individuals. Among these as though very disparate things, providence wished there to be different species in each and every genus, desiring before all else that there should be an abundance of species as though very perfect things. But if providence has distributed into levels of species the very extensive order in genera lower than soul, why has it not striven

affectaverit similemque graduum ordinem per differentes animarum species disposuerit, quandoquidem et animae ipsius natura
propter conditionem eius quodammodo compositam mobilemque
accommodatamque corporibus multiplicabilis sit propagabilisque
per corpora et ipsa quin etiam natura mentis quae compositionem
aliquam non excludit, immo et includit aliquam, in mentes valeat
plurimas derivari? Sed de mirabili mentium numero in primo
Theologiae satis est dictum per quem confirmatus sit et numerus
animarum. Denique solum primum ipsum universi principium
propter summam primi simplicitatem naturarum in se numerum
non admittit. Reliqua sub hoc genera rerum: scilicet mentis animae naturae corporis et recipiunt numerum specialem et iam habent tamquam ad commune totius bonum maxime pertinentem.
Non potest autem animae ipsius natura primum tenere in rerum
ordine gradum neque secundum sed necessario tertium—quod
nostra satis *Theologia* probat. Non cogitur itaque esse unica neque
debet rursum neque denique potest. Praeterea cum Plato animam
mundi asserat esse semper in corpore eandemque semper agere
vitam, nostras autem aliquando a corporibus separari atque separatas in diversa proprietate subsistere et differenti inter se condicione vivere et secundum electiones proprias sortiri rursum differentia corpora ac denique pro arbitrio dissimiliter vivere et pro
vitae dissimilitudine discrepantes post obitum sortiri vivendi gradus, quisnam Platonicus animam poterit unicam suspicari?

8   Enimvero si quis aliquando suspicetur more Averrois esse unicum in cunctis hominibus intellectum, nos utique non similiter
adversus eum sicut de anima dubitabimus. Nec principaliter

for an equivalent abundance in the nature and genus of soul, and arranged a similar order of levels through the different species of souls? Why has it not done this, given that the nature of soul itself is, on account of its condition which is somehow composite, mobile, and adapted to body, capable of multiplication and propagation through bodies and indeed, the nature itself of mind, which does not exclude some compositeness but rather includes the latter, is able to be dispersed into a multiplicity of minds? But enough has been said regarding the wonderful numerosity of minds in the first book of the *Theology*, and the numerosity of souls is also confirmed thereby. Finally, it is only the first cause of the universe itself that, on account of the utmost simplicity of the first, does not admit any numerosity of natures into itself. The remaining kinds of thing below this: that is, mind, soul, nature, body, are both receptive of specific numerosity and already have the latter as though pertaining to the common good of the totality to the maximal degree. However, the nature of soul cannot hold the first or second rank in the order of things, but necessarily holds the third — a point of which our *Theology* gives sufficient proof.[13] Therefore, the soul is neither compelled, nor obliged, nor finally able to be unique. Moreover, when Plato asserts that the world-soul is always in body and always leads a life of sameness, whereas our souls are at some point separated from bodies, subsist in different conditions when separated, live in a condition of differentiation from one another, are again assigned different bodies according to their specific choices, in the end living in different ways according to their choice, and after death being differently assigned levels of living in accordance with the dissimilarity of their life, what Platonist will surmise that soul is unique?

Indeed, if someone ever supposes in the manner of Averroes 8 that there is a single intellect in all men,[14] we will certainly not raise doubts against him as we have done with respect to soul. Nor will we primarily make objection against him by asking in what

obiciemus quonam pacto alius quidem intellectus sit in corpore,
alius autem extra corpus, item quomodo in corporibus tam diversis possint esse omnino consimiles intellectus ut modo de anima
dicebamus. Animae namque tamquam declinantes ad corpora
praeter intimas inter se differentias differunt quoque per actiones
varias circa varia corpora perque corporum ipsorum diversitatem.
At si quando intellectus qui separatiores sunt quam animae actio-
nesque proprias absque corporeis peragunt instrumentis probaturi
simus inter se differre, non ad corporum actionumque eiusmodi
varietatem confugiemus sed ad diversas potius intelligentiae species modosque intelligendi admodum discrepantes intellectio-
nesque et habitus in eodem tempore inter se repugnantes quae
unico simul intellectui inesse[8] non possint. Sicut enim in primo
intellectu differentiam inter multas notiones eius non aliter as-
signamus quam ex formalium intus proprietatum diversitate, sic
assignaturi intellectuum aliorum inter se differentias eas ex intimis
proprietatibus afferemus. Decet enim multas esse mentium et intelligentiae species, si tam dives est natura corporum mentibusque
longe deterior, ut multae sint[9] species metallorum plures plantarum plurimae animalium, unde appareat et daemonum et[10] mentium qualescumque sint esse complurimas. Quin etiam animae
ipsius naturam quae indivisibilis substantia est perpetuoque in
seipsa subsistens non decet ita in plures animas distribuere iterumque plures in unam quandoqe confundere, sicut aquam mul-
tam partimur in partes[11] easque rursus confundimus in eandem.

9   Neque debemus iterum sic unam in plures animas derivare,
sicut lumen a sole unum in plura domicilia per fenestras quodam-

manner there is one intellect in the body and another outside the body, or again by asking how it is possible for there to be altogether similar intellects in bodies that are so diverse, as we have just now done in connection with soul. For souls as though inclining toward bodies, in addition to their internal differences among themselves, also differ through their various actions around various bodies and through the diversity of the bodies themselves. But if ever we are intent on proving that intellects, which are more separate than are souls and perform their proper actions without corporeal instruments, differ among themselves, we will resort not to such variety of bodies and actions but rather to the different forms of intelligence and the very disparate modes of understanding, and also to the intellections and conditions simultaneously in conflict with one another that are not able to be present in intellect at the same time. For just as in the case of the primal intellect, we assign the difference between its many concepts not otherwise than on the basis of the diversity of formal characteristics within it, so being intent on assigning the differences among themselves of the other intellects, we adduce these on the basis of internal characteristics. For it is fitting that there should be many species of minds and intelligences, if the nature of bodies that is far inferior to minds is so abundant, in order that there might be many species of metals, more species of plants, and even more species of animals — from which it appears that there is a large number both of daemons and of minds, of whatever nature these are. Indeed, it is not fitting that the nature of soul itself, which is an indivisible substance subsisting everlastingly in itself, should be distributed into a multiplicity of souls and at some point bringing back together the many souls into a single soul, in the way that we divide a large amount of water into portions and then bring these together again into the same amount.

We must also not disperse one soul into many souls in the way that we somehow distribute the single light of the sun to many

9

modo distribuimus paulo post in idem penitus resolvendum. Lumen enim visibile accidentis more dependet omnino nec propriam retinet subsistentiam. Longe vero diversum est ab hoc luminis intelligibilis intellectualisque genus, non accidens quidem sed substantia prorsus absolutissima. Ideoque si differentes inter se gradus habet, eos non extrinsecus accipit, sicut accidentales formae, sed intrinsecus, proque differentibus proprietatibus eius multas admittit (ut ita dixerim) subsistentias easque specie distinctas in eodem genere servat confusionis expertes. In hoc sane intellectualis substantialisque luminis genere rationales animas collocabis et quomodo differant inter se cognosces neque umquam confundantur in unam viliorum more liquorum. Cognosces necesse tales ad mundi vitam qualia sunt vestigia quaedam vitae in animalibus ex planta nascentibus, siquidem et vitam universi actione percurrunt affectuque transcendunt. Neque finges eas nihilo ab anima mundi differre quasi sint quaedam propagines eius per mundi corpus, nec aliter anima mea a tua differat quam quia differunt inter se corpora per quae facta fuerit propagatio, nec aliter utraque differat ab anima mundi quam quia illa quidem sit radix plantave prima, hae vero sint ex illa propagines. Sic enim intellectualis ipsa Socratis anima post obitum in mundi animam (ut fingitur) resolvenda, dum propriam perdiderit exsistentiam, esse omnino desinet quando accesserit ad esse perfectum. Quod quidem intellectualis natura non patitur non externis ad distinctionem suam terminis indigens, ut liquores atque lumen, sed velut exactior intimis in

houses through their windows and then a little later completely release it back into its self-identity. For visible light is wholly dependent in the manner of an accident and does not maintain its own subsistence. Far different from this is the genus of intelligible and intellectual light, being not an accident but a fully independent substance. For that reason, if it has levels differentiated among themselves, it receives these not externally—as do accidental forms—but internally. It admits many "subsistences" (if I may put it thus) in proportion to its different characteristics, and it preserves these subsistences distinct in species without confusion in the selfsame genus. Of course, you will place rational souls in this genus of intellectual and substantial light, and you will recognize how they differ among themselves and are never blended together into a single soul in the manner of the baser liquids. You will recognize that such souls are as necessary to the life of the world as are traces of a certain kind of the life in animate things born from a plant, given that they pass through the life of the universe in their action and transcend it in their desire. And you will not imagine that these differ in no way from the world-soul, as though being certain things propagated from the latter through the world's body; and that my soul and yours differ in a manner not dissimilar to that in which our bodies—through which the propagation will have taken place—differ among themselves; and that both these souls differ from the world-soul in a manner not otherwise than where the world-soul is the root or the primal plant and the individual souls are the things propagated from it. For thus the intellectual soul of Socrates after his death will (as it is imagined) be resolved into the world-soul as long as it has lost its proper existence, and will cease to be altogether when it has acceded to perfect being. But the intellectual nature does not suffer this. It does not need external boundaries in order to have its own distinctiveness, as do liquids and light, but—as though something more precise—is distributed into its

species suas et exsistentias terminis distributa. Probatum satis in *Theologia* fuerit rationalem animam quatenus intellectualis est tanto perfectius se habere quanto longius seipsam a corpore separaverit—perfectius inquam se habere ad propriam sui substantiam peculiaremque proprietatem. Cum vero summopere a corpore separetur in obitu, tunc sane necesse est propriam huius animae substantiam esse perfectam. Unde fingere liceat nemini mentes singulas in unam quandoque confundi subitoque disperdi.

: IV :

Intellectuales animae non per accidentalia sed per essentialia propria inter se distinguuntur; et quomodo multae animae dicuntur esse una atque ab una.

10 Cum enim primus intellectus et essentia prima sit idem, merito intellectus omnes sunt essentiae verae ideoque veris inter se differentiis distributae: id est, non per accidens nec terminis acceptis extrinecus, ut divisae continui partes et ipsae inter se moles et plurimum materiales formae, sed pro dignitate essentiarum suarum in se subsistentium propriis intimisque differentiis et terminis distinguuntur. Verius enim distinguitur hoc ab illo si discrepet proprietate formali quam si materiali divisione vel accidente vel loco. Quilibet igitur intellectus essentiam suam et esse possidet in sua quadam intima prorsus identitate et (ut ita loquor) alteritate: identitate inquam prout est simplicissima forma a sua simplicitate

forms and existences by inner boundaries. It has been proven sufficiently in the *Theology* that the rational soul, to the extent that it is intellectual, is in a condition so much the more perfect as it has separated itself more from the body, the more perfect condition being indeed relative to its proper substance and special characteristics. When it is separated from body to the greatest extent at death, then certainly it is necessary that the proper substance of this soul should be most perfect. Hence, let nobody be allowed to imagine that individual minds will ever be blended into one or suddenly destroyed.

: IV :

Intellectual souls are distinguished among themselves not through accidental but through essential properties; and how the many souls are said to be one and from one.

Since the primal intellect and the primal being are the same, then   10
rightly all intellects are true beings and therefore divided among themselves by true differentiae: that is to say, they are distinguished neither accidentally nor having received their boundaries from outside—as is the case with the divided parts of a continuum, with masses that are themselves divided from one another, and especially with material forms—but through their proper and internal differentiae and boundaries in accordance with the dignity of their essences subsisting in themselves. For this thing is distinguished more truly from that thing, if it is distinct in a formal property than if it is distinct in material division, accident, or place. Therefore, each and every intellect possesses its essence and being in a certain wholly internal sameness and (if I may put it thus) otherness of its own. It possesses its essence and being in

numquam cadens, alteritate rursum prout eiusmodi forma per seipsam talem velut per suam proprietatem a re qualibet alia et a quolibet alio distinguitur intellectu. Quod si primo et per se distinguitur, permanet semper procul a confusione discretus. Cogita in mente divina magnam animam: id est ideam animarum intellectualium generalem, in qua conceptae sint et species animarum. Et illa idea quidam intellectus est ibi, et hae species ibi quidem sunt intellectus. Distinguuntur autem illic inter se ideales intellectus eiusmodi, non quidem exsistentiis differentibus (unica enim hactenus substantia est) sed ratione quadam et proprietate formali. Essentiales autem eiusmodi proprietates si cogitantur extra prodire, distinguuntur subito magis: distinguuntur igitur exsistentiis. Adeo enim intus sunt efficaces ut foras agant non accidentale aliquid sed substantiam substantiasque diversas pro rationum diversitate formalium.

11   Substantiae quidem eiusmodi e proximo prodeuntes ab intellectu primo intellectuales imprimis exsistunt. Quoniam vero et ipsae sunt admodum efficaces ad conceptum videlicet intimum, ideo unaquaeque proprietatem quandam exprimit in se ipsa ex intellectuali iam animalem magisque in plura distinctam — sicut vel a scintilla radius emicat vel ab intimo imaginationis verbo simpliciore verbum in prolatione multiplicius iam mobiliusque producitur. Prodeunt igitur ex una ideali anima foras animae multae tum mundi tum etiam aliorum. Quae etsi differentes substantiae sunt, sunt tamen inter se quodammodo unum triplici potissimum ratione: tum quia sub eadem idea cunctae, tum quia locis et

"sameness" to the extent that it is a most simple form which never falls away from its simplicity, and in "otherness" in so far as a form of this kind is distinguished through itself as such a form—as though through its own specific property—from each and every other thing and from each and every other intellect. And if it is distinguished primally and through itself, it always remains discrete and far from confusion. You should *think of* the great soul in the divine mind: that is, the generic Idea of intellectual souls, in which the species of souls are also conceived. This Idea in the divine mind is a certain intellect, and these species there are also certain intellects. However, the ideal intellects of this kind are distinguished from one another there not by their different existences—for so far there is a single substance—but by a certain reason-principle and formal property. But if essential properties of this kind *are thought of* as proceeding to the exterior, they are suddenly distinguished to a greater extent, being therefore distinguished by their existences. These properties are so powerful internally that they produce on the exterior not something accidental but substance and different substances according to the diversity of their formal reason-principles.

Substances of this kind coming forth proximally from the primal intellect exist as intellectual in the first instance. But since they are very powerful with regard to that inner conceptuality of theirs, each one of them in itself puts forth in itself from its intellectuality a certain specific characteristic which is now psychic and distinguished into greater multiplicity—just as a ray shines forth from a spark, or just as from the inner more simple word of the imagination a more multiple and mobile word is put forth in utterance. Therefore, there proceed to the exterior from the single ideal soul many souls, both that of the world and also those of other things. Even though these souls are different substances, they are somehow a unity among themselves primarily for a threefold reason: namely, because all are subject to the same Idea,

11

temporibus minime distinguuntur, tum etiam quoniam per intellectuales suos quaelibet apices uno eodemque secundum actum formantur intellectu divino eundemque cunctae perpetuo contuentur. Mitto quod ad eundem naturaliter omnes conferunt universalis providentiae finem.

: V :

Quomodo anima quaelibet rationalis est omnia; et quomodo differant inter se species rationalium animarum.

12 Summum omnium principium propter summam tum simplicitatem est super omnia, tum potestatem mox efficit omnia. Intellectus igitur eius filius est primum omne, ideoque est omne perfecte et idcirco quaelibet eius idea est omnes ideae. Anima igitur ab idea propria naturaliter et proxime profluens secum contrahit omnia: quaelibet igitur intellectualis anima est universum. Id totum rursus confirmo: primum in quolibet genere et simplicissimum ibi est et ibidem continet omnia. Cum igitur intellectus ipse primus sit prima forma, merito et uniformis est et omniformis[12] exsistit. Itaque omnis rationalis anima, quatenus intellectualis est, non solum forma simplicissima est, sed etiam est omniformis et omnia: omnia inquam actu, sicut et intellectus ipse est actu omnia. Quatenus autem anima non tam intellectualis iam quam animalis evadit, retinet quidem munus idem quo sit adhuc omnia, sed minus perfecte retinens est iam in potentia universum—et merito,

because they are minimally distinct with respect to places and times, and also because all of them through their intellectual summits are formed by one and the same divine intellect according to its actuality and all of them everlastingly contemplate that same divine intellect. I pass over the fact that all these souls contribute naturally to the end of universal providence.

: V :

How each and every rational soul is all things; and how the species of rational souls differ among themselves.

The supreme principle of all things is above all things because of its supreme simplicity and at the same time produces all things immediately because of its supreme power. Therefore intellect, its son, is everything primally and thus everything perfectly, each and every one of its Ideas consequently being all the Ideas. Therefore soul, flowing forth naturally and proximately from the Idea proper to it, contracts all things in itself with the result that each and every intellectual soul is the universe. I confirm the whole of this again as follows. The first member of each and every genus is both the most simple term there and there also contains all things. Therefore, since the first intellect is the first Form, it rightly exists as uniform and as omniform. Consequently, every rational soul, to the extent that it is intellectual, is not only a most simple Form, but also omniform and all things. Indeed, such a soul is all things in actuality, just as intellect itself is all things in actuality. However, to the extent that the soul now emerges as not so much intellectual as psychic, it retains the same function through which it is still all things, but in retaining this function in a less perfect manner, it is now the universe potentially. This is rightly so, since

12

quando deus eam rerum mediam collocavit, eam ex omnibus temperavit.

13   Temperavit autem ita diversas species animarum ut anima quae mundi universalis vita fovet ad intellectum semper converteretur universalem atque universaliter insuper et insuper attentissime. Unde factum est ut universalem semper totius gereret providentiam atque hanc potestate mirabili ideoque et facilitate mirifica, siquidem potestas omnis venit ex alto; animae vero reliquae post hanc caelestes ad intellectum quidem universum converterentur, nec tamen adeo universaliter nec attentione pari. Ideo providentiam neque tam universalem agunt neque etiam tam potentem. Inferiores tandem his animae ita constitutae sunt ut aliquando ad intellectum se verterent universum atque tunc sive magis sive minus universaliter vel attente ideoque alias cum universali magis concurrerent providentia alias vero minus — minus quoque potenter —; item ut aliquando non tam ad universum quam ad proprium se flecterent intellectum minusque perfectae forent, quandoque ad rationem ubi et perfectae minus, interdum ad imaginationem quamplurimum laberentur deterrimaeque evaderent. Denique rationalis anima quando in se explicat universum, ad universalem animae mundi admittitur providentiam; quando vero in se gradatim ab universo munere cadens ad partem muneris sese dirigit, particularem gradatim subit curam corpusque proprium magis induit magisque laborat.

God has placed it in the middle of things and has blended its proportionality from all things.

However, he proportionately blended the different species of souls in such a way that the soul which nourishes as the universal life of the world always undergoes reversion to the universal intellect, reverting additionally in a universal manner and most attentively to boot. Hence, it has been brought about that this soul should always manage the providence of the totality, doing this with a marvelous power and therefore also a wonderful facility, given that all power comes from on high. It has also been brought about that the remaining heavenly souls subsequent to this are reverted to the universal intellect, but without such universality or equal attentiveness. Accordingly, they enact a providence that is neither so universal nor indeed so powerful. Finally, the souls below these have been so established that they sometimes turn themselves to the universal intellect: on these occasions they are either more or less universal and attentive, being at one time more in agreement with universal providence, and at another time less in agreement and also less powerfully so. Moreover, in order that at some point they might be turned not so much toward the universal as toward their own particular intellect and be less perfect, these souls have been so established that they sometimes sink down toward reason when they are less perfect and occasionally slide right down to the imagination and turn out in the worst condition. Finally, when the rational soul unfolds the universe in itself, it enters into the universal providence of the world-soul, but when it gradually lapses from its universal function and directs itself toward a part of that function, it gradually assumes a particular charge, becoming more embroiled in its own body, and enduring more troubles.

: VI :

Respondetur ad dubia et probatur rationales animas
non esse ex anima mundi.

14 Plato probaturus in *Philebo* mundum esse animatum inquit: 'Unde
nam haberet corpus nostrum quod ex partibus elementorum componitur animam nisi mundus qui ex totis componitur elementis
animam possideret?': id est, intellectus mundi faber non adeo fuit
imprudens ut nobis daturus animam non daret et mundo, praesertim quia mundi anima per universalem influxum praeparatura erat
materias animalium seminales ad animas proprias undecumque
suscipiendas. Ideo corpus nostrum habet et animam intellectualem
non aliunde quam mundus: id est, ab eodem mundi fabro, et animam sensualem plurimum ab anima intellectuali nostra, conferente[13] ad hoc imprimis anima mundi. Timaeus quoque rationales
animas non ab anima mundi sed ab eodem auctore a quo et illam
et ex generibus consimilibus asserit constitutas; neque has esse vel
illam vel partes vel vires illius, sed esse a Deo in diversis speciebus
gradibusque dispositas: unde et has labentes in corpora erran-
tesque introducit et exeuntes, quod animae mundi contingere nequit. Ait autem in *Phaedro*, quotiens particularis anima quae et
universum est in potentia extra corpus hoc ad universalem se
formam actu cogitando amandoque converterit, hanc quoque ad
universalem mundi providentiam ammittendam, caelesti videlicet

: VI :

*He replies to difficulties; and it is proven that rational souls
are not derived from the world-soul.*

When Plato sets out to prove in the *Philebus*[15] that the world is an   14
animate being, he says: "From which source could our body, which
is composed of parts of the elements, have its soul, if the world,
which is composed of whole elements, did not have a soul?" That
is to say, the intellect which is the craftsman of the world was not
so imprudent that, in setting out to give us a soul, he would not
also give it to the world, especially since the world-soul was destined to prepare, through the universal emanation, seminal matters of animate things for the reception of souls proper to them
from all quarters of the world. Therefore, our body even has its
intellectual soul from no other source than does the world: that is,
from one and the same craftsman of the world, and has its sensitive soul for the most part from our intellectual soul, the world-
soul as a primary factor contributing to this derivation. Timaeus
also asserts that rational souls are constituted not by the world-
soul but by the same creator by whom that world-soul was constituted and from similar kinds. He also maintains that rational
souls are neither the world-soul, nor its parts, nor its powers, and
that they have been arranged by God in various species and levels.
For this reason, he makes reference to them as falling into bodies,
as having vagaries, and as coming out of bodies—things which
cannot happen to the world-soul. Moreover, Plato says in the
Phaedrus[16] that a particular soul which is also potentially the universe outside this body, whenever it has turned itself toward the
universal form in actuality by thinking and loving: this soul also is
to be admitted into the universal providence of the world, presumably as having been endowed from the start with a body of

corpore ab initio praeditam, siquidem et in corpore caduco philosophus contemplator civilisque idem pro viribus experitur. Proinde sicubi Plato videtur innuere animas sequi caelestem motum, ibidem atque alibi subdit etiam posse non sequi. Probatum est quin etiam posse prudentia arte moribus caelestium influxibus repugnare: ex quo apparet, si qua in nobis est vita pedissequa corporis perque hoc fato serviens, hanc ab anima etiam mundani corporis posse pendere, sed eam in nobis animam quae corporeis incitamentis mundanisque resistit impulsibus altius quam a mundo descendere. Atqui etsi intra mundum geniti sumus, aliunde tamen animam habemus superiorem quae metitur et mundum. Nam et foetus in alvo aliam accipit animam praeter matris animam et aliunde habet animam quam a matre.

: VII :

Quomodo animae differant et quomodo sint immortales in propria forma restantes et quomodo anima mundi ubique praesens omnibus conducat ad vitam.

15   In octavo capite haec imprimis considerabis: ad hoc ipsum ut animae nostrae tum invicem tum etiam cum anima mundi adeo consentiant, quod consimili saepe afficiantur instinctu et impulsus aliquis facile ab aliis fluat in alias et particulares animae clam moveantur ab universali, non est utique necessarium animas nostras

heavenly nature. This is because a philosopher is a contemplator even in this mortal body, and a politician has the same experience to the limit of his powers. Accordingly, if Plato anywhere seems to suggest that souls follow the heavenly motion, he there and elsewhere adds that they are able not to follow it. Moreover, it is proven that one can fight against the emanations of the heavenly realm with sagacity, art, and habits, and from this it appears that, if there is anywhere in us a life that slavishly follows the body and thereby is subservient to fate, this can depend also on the soul of the world's body. But that soul in us which resists bodily urges and worldly impulses descends from somewhere higher than the world. In any case, even if we are born within the world, we have our higher soul — which also measures the world — from somewhere else, for the embryo in the womb receives a soul other than its mother's soul and has this soul from a source other than its mother.

: VII :

How souls differ; and how they remain immortal in their proper form; and how the world-soul which is everywhere present contributes to the life of all things.

In the eighth chapter[17] you will consider these matters primarily: namely, that in order to bring it about that our souls should be so much in harmony both with one another and also with the world-soul that they could often be affected with a similar instinct, that a certain impulse could easily flow from one to another, and that particular souls could be moved by the universal soul in a hidden manner, it is by no means necessary that our souls be generated by

15

esse ab anima mundi progenitas. Satis enim ad hanc consensionem et quasi compassionem facit communis ipsa tum animae mundanae tum aliarum ex eadem mente divina eademque generali animarum idea similisque processio. Proinde quattuor praecipue sunt humanarum differentiae animarum: differunt quodammodo secundum corporum differentias quando motus magis minusve concitatos pro differentia sanguinis bilisve et spiritus habere videntur; differre dicuntur ex praecedenti vita — si verum sit hanc animam ad actiones, illam ad contemplationem nunc promptiorem exsistere quoniam haec quidem ante ortum negotiosissimam egit vitam, haec vero prorsus contemplativam — ; differre quoque Platonici putant quodammodo specie naturaliter ab initio, siquidem sub eodem genere proximo humanae sint animae, differant autem inter se specialibus quibusdam — etsi quam minimis potest fieri differentiis — quibus a summo quodam gradu per secundum tertiumve et quartum distribuantur; differre denique putant quod, quamvis quaelibet rationalis anima sit universum, potest tamen libero quodam motu aliter atque aliter se[14] afficere prout alia se vertit ad vitam contemplativam, alia ad activam, alia ad voluptuosam. Et quae ad contemplandum se conferunt aliae hanc formam contemplationis eligunt, aliae prae ceteris illam, et quam elegerunt mox induunt quasi naturam. Quamquam vero anima quaevis est omnia, eiusmodi tamen quasi paritas non efficit animas inter se sine ullo discrimine pares. Est enim in mente prima communis idealisque animarum ratio non individualis quidem dumtaxat sed admodum generalis varios inter se possidens animarum idealium gradus quorum numerum sequitur par numerus animarum et similis ordo. Et quemadmodum in mente divina haec quidem idea

the world-soul. The communal and similar procession itself of both the world-soul and the other souls from the same divine mind and the generic Idea of souls is sufficient explanation of this accord and sympathy, so to speak. Hence, there are primarily four differentiations of human souls: they differ somehow according to the differences of bodies when they seem to have more or less energetic motions in accordance with their differences of blood, bile, and spirit. They are said to differ as a consequence of a previous life, if it be true that this soul is more disposed toward actions but that soul more toward contemplation on the grounds that this soul led a most commercially orientated life before birth but that one a thoroughly contemplative one. The Platonists[18] think that souls also differ somehow naturally in species from the beginning, given that the souls are human as subsumed under the same proximate genus, although they differ among themselves according to certain specific properties — even if this can come about with the most minute differentiation —, and that it is in accordance with these same properties that they are distributed from a certain highest level through a second, third, and fourth degree. Finally, they think that although each and every rational soul is the universe, it can nevertheless affect itself in one way or another with a certain free motion according to whether it turns in one case to the life of contemplation, in another to the active life, and in another to the life of pleasure. Among those souls that devote themselves to contemplation, some choose this form of contemplation and others prefer that form, these souls soon taking on as though naturally the form chosen. Although each and every soul is all things, a quasi-equality of this kind does not make the souls equal without any differentiation from one another. For there is in the primal mind a communal and ideal reason-principle of souls which is not only individual but very generic and possessing various gradations among ideal souls, an equal number and similar order of souls following this ideal gradation. And just as in the divine mind

est aliter omnia et aliter illa, sic anima haec omnia aliter est quam illa et aliter suo utitur universo.

16   Rationi praeterea consentaneum est composita ex quattuor elementis posse in elementa pura resolvi, ac si elementa deteriora nequeant omnino seorsum a praestantioribus esse, saltem alicubi praestantiora seorsum a deterioribus in sua puritate consistere, similiter compositum ex materia formaque tamquam geminis elementis resolvi quodammodo in materiam puram et omnino redigi ad formam aliquam per se puram quae per se et in se consistat absque materia, quamvis materia nequeat procul ab omni forma consistere. Sicut elementum (ut dixi) formale a materiali procul exsistit, quamvis e converso non accidat, in genere formarum eiusmodi intellectuales animae numerantur. Eiusmodi quidem forma est essentia simplex esse suum per se possidens in seipsa in qua et esse suum idem est atque essentialis unitas eius. Contra vero compositorum essentia sese habet: nempe in hac aliud est essentia simul atque esse quae consistunt in multitudine quam unitas quae, prout est unitas, multitudinem non admittit; atque esse ibi sequitur unionem quam unitas antecedit.

17   Quorsum haec? Ut intelligas ipsam animae formam cuius esse idem est quod et essentialis unitas eius esse prorsus indissolubilem quemadmodum est indissolubilis unitas, praesertim quia, si esse ubique in rebus est per formam, sequitur ut forma simplex in se ipsa subsistens esse suum semper in se ipsa continuet. Praeterea si forma simplex non mixta materiae perdenda sit, in nihilum redigetur;[15] si generanda, ex nihilo generabitur — id autem physica per se ratio non concedit. Est igitur anima sempiterna praesertim quia, si

this Idea is all things from one viewpoint and that Idea all things from another viewpoint, so similarly this soul is all things differently than is that soul and exploits its universe in a different way.

Furthermore, it is in agreement with reason that things composed of four elements can be resolved into pure elements. And if lower elements are unable to exist in total independence from the higher ones, although elsewhere the higher elements at least can subsist in their purity as separated from the lower; similarly, that which is composed from matter and form as though from a pair of elements can somehow be resolved into pure matter and altogether reduced to some form that is in itself pure and existing through itself and in itself without matter, although matter cannot subsist remote from all form. Just as a formal element (as I have said) exists in isolation from a material one, although the opposite situation does not occur, intellectual souls are numbered in the genus of forms of this kind. Indeed, a form of this kind is a simple essential being, possessing in itself its own being through itself, and thereby having this being and its essential unity as one and the same. The essential being of composites has a status opposite to that. Certainly, in this case the simultaneous essence and being established in multiplicity is different from the unity which, according to its unity, does not admit multiplicity: here, the being follows the union which the unity precedes. 16

Why are we arguing in this way? In order that you may understand that the form itself of soul, whose being is identical with its essential unity, is an indissoluble being by the same token that it is an indissoluble unity. This is especially the case given that, if its being is omnipresent in things through form, it follows that this form which subsists as simple in itself always maintains its being in itself. Moreover, if a simple form that is not blended with matter is to be destroyed, it will be reduced to nothing; if it is to be produced, it will be produced from nothing—something that physical reasoning in itself does not permit. Therefore, the soul is 17

de aliquo sit fingenda neque tamen ex ullo queat materiali, cogetur
Deus eam eius auctor de sua substantia procreare—unde cogetur
esse mutabilis—praesertim si quando faciat quod ante non fecerat.
Haec ergo Plotinus significat ut animam asserat sempiternam:
quae quantum affirmanda sint in *Theologia* nostra satis est dictum.

18   Inter haec animadverte formas eiusmodi unamquamque esse in
se[16] unum quiddam numero ab aliis non per accidens sed per se
distinctum: per se inquam quoniam animae non accipiunt numerum ex numero corporum vel corporalium qualitatum—quasi
una mundi anima per diversas affectiones corporum propagetur in
multas. Iam vero quaelibet anima ita per se subsistit semper unum
numero sicut in sua essentia suum habet esse atque esse suum
idem est quod et unitas eius. Sicut ergo essentia simpliciter animae tamquam simplex et in se ipsa consistens sempiterna est, sic
et quodlibet singulare illius esse, siquidem esse suum est solum in
ipsius essentia. Item sicut esse est sempiternum, sic et unitas quaelibet numeralis, siquidem illic idem est esse quod et unum aliquid
esse. Non enim per externa sed per interna distinguitur essentia
simplex permanens in se ipsa—ut nemini liceat somniare nostras
animas personalibus quandoque dimissis proprietatibus in generalem quandam animam confundendas. Res quidem corporeae ex
materia formaque compositae[17] unitatem speciei perpetuam successione conservant, unitatem vero numeralem propriamque nequaquam. Atqui neque specialem conservarent in se unitatem nisi
ab anima generationis fonte perpetuo hanc haurirent. Anima igitur tamquam longe praestantior unitatem in se ipsa quaelibet

everlasting especially since, if it were to be fashioned from something but could not be fashioned from anything material, God as its author will be forced to procreate it from his own substance — whence he will be forced to be mutable — especially in a case where he makes something that he had not previously made. Therefore, these are the points that Plotinus makes in order to assert that the soul is everlasting, and how much these should be affirmed has been stated sufficiently in our *Theology*.[19]

In the course of this discussion, you should note that each single form of this kind is in itself a certain unity distinguished from others in number not accidentally but through itself, and indeed distinguished "through itself" because souls do not acquire their number from the number in bodies or in corporeal qualities — as if the single world-soul were propagated into many souls through different conditions of bodies. Moreover, each and every soul always subsists in itself as a unity in number, just as it has its being in its essence and its being is the same as its unity. Therefore, just as the essential being *simpliciter* of soul which is as though simple and self-subsistent is everlasting, so is each and every instantiation of that soul's being everlasting —, given that its being is only in the essential being *simpliciter*. Again, just as being is everlasting, so also is each and every numerable unity, since in that realm being is identical with being some one being. For simple essential being remaining in itself is distinguished not through external but through internal characteristics, and consequently it is not legitimate for anybody to have the delusion that our souls can at some point be blended into a certain generic soul with our personal properties discarded. Corporeal things composed of matter and form preserve a perpetual unity of the specific form in succession but by no means a numerical and proper unity. However, they could not even preserve the specific unity in themselves if they did not derive this from the soul that is the perpetual source of generation. Therefore, as though far superior, each and every soul

numeralem propriamque retinet semper, non solummodo specialem. Immo sicut per ipsam composita quae dissolvuntur, similibus temporibus redeuntibus, similia prorsus et eadem specie revertuntur, sic anima mutans quodammodo in se ipsa formam, velut praestantior corpore, ad eandem numero quandoque redit et ad idem corpus eandemque personam.

19   Posthac, ubi quaeritur quomodo forma simplex intellectualisque anima sive mundi sive nostra dicatur aliquando infinita, respondetur non quia in infinitum dividi queat sed quia sine fine vigeat et ubique semper agere possit. Sic igitur nec anima mundi vel in animas dividitur infinitas vel qualitatis corporeae more distenditur — quatenus moles[18] mundi protenditur — sed unica permanet et, quantumcumque corporis ex ea quicquam potest accipere, ipse ubique integra vegetat. Animae quoque nostrae, sicut non fiunt numero totidem ex tot corporeis portionibus atque qualitatibus, sic neque protenduntur in molem et more albedinis extenduntur extensa materia, sed et totidem sunt quot proprietates intimae et, quantum molis ad earum praeparatur influxum, tantum formant in dividuo quodam et ubique toto perpetuoque vigore. Neque secatur anima nostra in plures animas sive propter diversa membra sive membro quolibet amputato, sicut nec anima mundi ipsa in se vel dividitur vel fit plures animae partibus inter se mundi divisis. Haec enim una permanens, quantumcumque disiungatur pars mundi vivens haec ab alia, tamen tota simul est in utraque. Est et in medio propter continuitatem materiae primae,

always retains in itself a numerical and proper unity and not just a specific one. Indeed, just as composite things that are dissolved undergo reversion as precisely similar and in the same specific form on the return of similar times through this soul; in the same manner the soul somehow changing its form in itself, being as though superior to body, reverts at some point to a form numerically the same, to the same body, and to the same person.

After this, when it is asked how a simple form and an intellectual soul, whether it be that of the world or that of ours is at some point said to be infinite, the reply is that this is not because the soul is able to be divided to infinity but because it is vigorous without limitation and can act everywhere and always. Therefore, even the world-soul cannot be divided into infinite souls or distended in the manner of corporeal quality as far as the mass of the world is stretched out but remains simple while, however large a portion of body is able to receive something from it, this soul itself in its entirety animates this portion. Our souls also, just as they do not as a result of the many corporeal portions and qualities become as many in number, similarly are not stretched out through the mass and extended together with the extension of matter in the manner of whiteness. Rather, they are as many as are their internal properties and, whatever portion of the mass is prepared for their influx, so much do they confer form in a given divisible thing with a force that is everywhere entire and perpetual. Moreover, our soul is not cut into a plurality of souls either on account of different limbs or the amputation of any limb, just as the world-soul itself is neither divided in itself nor becomes a plurality of souls when the parts of the world are divided among themselves. However much this living part of the world might be separated from this other part, the world-soul remains one, albeit being as a whole simultaneously in both parts. The world-soul is also in the middle on account of the continuity of primal matter, or rather of

19

immo et essentiae quintae quae est proprium animae susceptaculum.

20   Inter haec si cui Plotinus videtur in plantis et animalibus ex
putrefactione genitis non aliam ponere animam quam mundanam,
tu cave ne facile id concesseris: id enim ipse videtur in libro *De
animae immortalite* refellere. Dices ergo ipsam mundi animam omnibus quidem talibus esse praesentem neque cogi hanc ipsam
plures fieri animas propter sectiones plures atque animantes, sed
interea non hanc solam his esse vitam quamvis ipsa vitas in his
generet atque animas. Quae quidem animae si a Platonicis aliqui-
bus et ab ipso Plotino alicubi dicantur esse secundum proprias
substantias sempiternae, non tunc primum ab anima mundi gene-
rabuntur sed universali illius instinctu genitis infundentur. Poterit
et aliquis dicere omnem quidem vitam esse perpetuam, sed animas — si quae sunt tales — proprio motu carentes non tam in se
quam in communi post obitum vita subsistere; quae vero proprios
edunt motus, praesertim si liberos, propriam quoque formam per
se ipsas perpetuo conservare. Semper vero memento praeter vitas
animantium proprias subesse cunctos communem vim ex mundi
anima vegetalem in arbore mundana ubique vigentem quae et
praeparet materias propriis animabus et tempore certo conservet
et in unum viventia cuncta conciliet. Hunc Pythagorici, referente
Sexto Pyrrhonio, esse dicunt spiritum in modum animae rebus
cunctis infusum qui homines conciliet ceteris animantibus conci-
liatos aliunde numinibus. Hoc iam vigente communiter, accedit in
nobis ad foetum rationalis anima, atque sub hoc communi lumine

primal matter and also of the quintessence which is the proper receptacle of the soul.

Among these matters, if it seems to anybody that Plotinus posits as soul in plants and animals generated from putrefaction only the world-soul, you should have caution in readily conceding this point, for he himself seems to refute this position in his book *On the Immortality of the Soul.*[20] You will therefore say that the world-soul itself is present in all such things, but that this soul itself is not compelled to become many souls because of many dissections of living things. Meanwhile, you will say that this soul is not the only life in such things, although it itself generates lives and souls in the latter. And if these souls are said by certain Platonists and by Plotinus himself[21] elsewhere to be everlasting according to their proper substances, they will not be generated primarily by the world-soul but infused into things generated by the universal inspiration of that soul. One will be able to say that all life is perpetual, but that souls lacking a proper motion—if there are such—subsist after death not so much in themselves as in the general life, whereas souls that produce their own motions, especially if they are free motions, also preserve their own form through themselves in perpetuity. Indeed, you should always remember that, besides the proper lives of living beings, there is underlying all things in the tree of the world a general vegetative power coming from the world-soul, and that this power, which is vigorous as a whole everywhere, prepares the matters proper to souls, preserves them at a specific time, and also brings together all living things into a unity. According to Sextus the Pyrrhonian, the Pythagoreans say that this unity is a spirit infused into all things in the manner of soul, a spirit which brings humans—brought into accord with the divinities of the other realm—into accord with other living beings.[22] With this spirit now flourishing in the common domain, the rational soul is added to the embryo in the human sphere, the soul itself thereupon diffusing into the body—

ipsa deinceps lumen propriae peculiarisque vitae diffundit in corpus. Quod et in obitu ipsa secum contrahat proprium, quemadmodum et mundi anima suum atque commune conservat.

: VIII :

Quot modis insinuetur anima corpori; et qualis sit anima mundi, et quomodo faciat mundum et dimensionem eius, et quomodo sit ubique.

21 In capite libri nono ubi secunda incipit quaestio: quomodo insinuatur anima corpore, animadvertes duobus imprimis id fieri modis, nam aut ab incorporeo statu aut a corpore venit in corpus. Et hoc quidem secundum divisionis membrum in quattuor iterum membra dividitur: nempe aut a liquido corpore transit in liquidum aut a liquido in solidum aut a solido in aliud solidum vel a solido rursus in liquidum, ubi notabis, si quando ex Plotini sententia omne corpus exuere possit, excogitari posse semper extra corpus esse victuram — quod et Plato in *Phaedone* significat et Porphyrius atque Iamblichus suspicantur —, sin autem, ut ait Proculus, semper est in aliquo corpore, poterunt consequenter fingi vicissitudines corporum sempiternae.

22 Ut autem cognoscas quomodo anima tua, immo prius, quomodo mundi anima suo insinuetur corpore, cogita in anima mundi vim intellectualem eius in summo ceu lumen, rationalem in medio ut splendorem, vegetalem in infimo ut calorem. Praeterea circa eius essentiam considera duo: primum prout ipsa aliud quiddam

in subordination to the general light—the light of its proper and peculiar life. At death, the soul draws the light[23] back into itself as proper to it, just as the world-soul preserves the light that is its own and communal.

In how many ways the soul is inserted into the body; and of what kind is the world-soul; and how it makes the world and its dimensions; and how it is everywhere.

In the ninth chapter[24] of the book, where the second investigation: how the soul is introduced into the body, begins, you will note that this occurs primarily in two ways, for it comes into the body from an incorporeal status or from a body. This second member of the division is subdivided into four parts, for clearly the soul passes either from a liquid to a liquid body, or from a liquid to a solid body, or from a solid to another solid body, or from a solid back to a liquid body. Here, you will note that, if ever the soul is able—in accordance with Plotinus' opinion—to free itself entirely from body, it can be thought as destined to live always outside body. Plato indicates this conclusion in the *Phaedo*,[25] Porphyry[26] and Iamblichus[27] also surmising that this is the case. But if, as Proclus says,[28] the soul is always in some body, then everlasting exchanges of bodies can be imagined. 21

But in order that you may understand how your soul or rather, prior to that, how the world-soul is introduced into its body, you should think that—in the case of the world-soul—its intellectual power is at the highest level like light, its rational power is in the middle as radiance, and its vegetative power is on the lowest level as heat. Moreover, you should consider two things in connection 22

est quam illa tria, secundum prout tribus iam illis est insignita. Iam vero quo momento est aliud, quodammodo obscura est et deformis et frigida: obscura quidem nondum habens intelligentiae lucem, deformis item nondum rationis splendorem possidens, frigida denique non adhuc adepta vegetalis naturae fomentum. Ex hac ergo essentia sic egena cogita prodire primam mundi materiam prorsus egenam et omnino tenebrosam deformemque et frigidam. Sed interim ab essentia quatenus tribus iam illis est insignita contemplare mundi materiam prodeuntem protinus exornari per intelligentiam quidem formis penitus permanentibus, per rationem vero formis quae moveantur stabiliter, per vegetalem ⟨naturam⟩ denique formis quae mobiliter moveantur—ita tamen ut quae intelligentia rationeque procedunt tam naturaliter inde profluant quam naturaliter quae vegetali natura nascuntur.

23   Atqui sic anima mundi praedita in mundo formando exemplar praecipuum (ut Timaeus innuit) non mobilem et quasi generabilem spectat naturam vel rationem—si modo sit ratio mobilis—sed intellectualem potius formam omnis generationis expertem sive sit animalis intelligentia sive prima. Cogita rursum animam, quatenus mobilis est intrinsecus, naturaliter anniti ut eatenus moveatur extrinsecus; ex hoc ergo nixu materiam iam natam statim longe lateque protendi[19] adeo ut ex animae motu micante foras dimensio materiae sit exorta simul et mundi motus. Sic ergo locus inde

with its essential being: first, according to its being itself something other than those three and second, according to its being now distinguished into the three. Now, in the moment when it is other, it is somehow dark, and ill-formed, and cold. It is dark in not yet having the light of intelligence, ill-formed in not yet possessing the radiance of reason, and finally cold in having not yet received the fomentation of the vegetative nature. Therefore, you should think how from this essential being that is destitute in this way there comes forth the primal matter of the world that is entirely destitute and altogether dark, ill-formed, and cold. Meanwhile, you should contemplate how from this essential being, to the extent that it is now distinguished into those three, the matter of the world coming forth is immediately adorned through that being's intelligence with absolutely stable forms, through its reason with forms that are moved in a stable way, and finally through its vegetative nature with forms that are moved in a mobile way, these things being however so arranged that the forms proceeding through intelligence and reason flow forth from there as naturally as do the forms given birth naturally through the vegetative nature.

Now the world-soul thus endowed, in forming the world, primarily looks not toward an exemplar (as Timaeus intimates) which is mobile and as though a generative nature or reason-principle — assuming that a reason-principle can be mobile — but rather toward an intellectual and immobile form free of all generatedness, this being either the intelligence of the soul or the primal intelligence. Again you should think of the soul to the extent that it is moved internally as striving naturally to be moved to the same extent externally, and therefore of the matter that is now born from this striving as immediately stretched out in length and breadth to such a degree that from the motion of soul flashing toward the exterior the extendedness of matter and the motion of the world simultaneously arise. Accordingly, place and time are

23

simul nascitur atque tempus: locus quem habitet anima vegetando, tempus quo locum—id est, corpus—moveat vegetando. In exemplari primum intellectuali destinata est idealiter certa tum mundi tum mundanarum dimensio rerum: ad quam sane destinationem tanta suborta est ad motum formalis efficacia in vegetali natura quae pro mensura tali tantam mundo quantitatem exhibet tantasque mundanis quanta simul et quantae praesignantur in ipsa mentis idea.

24   Potest autem anima per essentiam suam tota simul adesse parti cuilibet mundi tam grandis, quoniam et tantus hic est factus quantum ipsa processit quae procedendo fecit. Et ipsa quidem anima neque dimensio est neque qualitas extensa dimensione sed individuum quiddam, non tamquam aliquis dimensionis terminus alicubi in dimensione signatus sed inde solutum in se consistens extra totum quantitatis genus in quodam plus quam substantiae genere molem totam longissimo naturae virtutisque supereminens intervallo. Unde hoc ipso individuo sui totam undique molem possidet neque totum possidetur ab ipsa.

born from there simultaneously: place in order that the soul might inhabit it by enlivening it, and time in order that the soul might move place: that is, body, by enlivening it. In the intellectual exemplar first, a certain extendedness both of the world and of worldly things is appointed in an ideal manner, and indeed at this appointing there springs up in the vegetative nature a formative power toward motion that is so immense that, in proportion to a measure of such a kind, it presents to the world and to worldly things a quantity and quantities that are as great as the quantity or quantities simultaneously prefigured in the Idea itself within the mind.

However, the soul can through its essential being be present simultaneously and as a whole to each and every part of such a great world, given that the world is made as great here as that which made it by procession was great when it itself proceeded. Moreover, this soul is neither dimension nor a quality extended by dimension, but rather a certain indivisibility albeit not as though a certain limit of dimension marked out somewhere else in the dimension but rather as something freed from that and self-subsistent, outside the whole genus of quantity, in a certain genus that is more than the genus of substance, and transcending the entire bulk by the largest interval of nature and power. Hence, in its own indivisibility itself it possesses the entire bulk on all sides but is not totally possessed by the latter.

24

: IX :

Quomodo anima mundi agit in se ipsa
atque ita naturaliter gignit mundum sic omniformem
sicut omniformis est ipsa.

25 Caput decimum docet, quemadmodum summus aer subest lumini, lumen vero soli—semper tamen simul sunt ab aevo—, sic
mundi animam intellectui divino semper, intellectum denique
bono; item mundum semper naturaliterque pullulare ex seminaria
suae animae potestate, sicut vivens quodlibet ex semine suo: haec
enim inde vim eiusmodi nanciscuntur; cum vero natura particularis in quolibet vivente non egeat ad motum generationemque consilio vel machinis ullis, multo minus his universalem egere naturam; hanc insuper facere movereque omnia facilitate mirabili; cum
enim ex ea pendeat tota mundi moles eiusque forma, nihil usquam
ei posse resistere, praesertim quia inde omnia subsequenti serie ita
dependent ut agentia vel levissimo primum nutu pulsata mox omnia moveantur atque ad actionem primi moventis finemque condu-
cant. Proinde quae non vivunt foras et in alienam tantum materiam agunt, in se ipsis vero torpent; quae vero vivunt, agunt etiam
in se ipsis aguntque perpetuo.

26 Anima ergo vivendi principium, mundana praecipue, agit semper atque potissimum in se ipsa prout intelligentia eius: hinc quidem suam rationem format, inde suam quoque naturam. Atqui et

: IX :

*How the world-soul acts in itself;
and how it naturally produces a world as omniform in the
manner in which it itself is omniform.*

The tenth chapter teaches that, just as the highest air is always   25
subjacent to light and light subjacent to the sun, although these
things exist simultaneously in derivation from eternity, so is the
world-soul always subjacent to the divine intellect, and finally the
intellect to the Good. It also teaches that the world always and
naturally springs forth from the seminal power of its soul, just as
each and every living thing springs forth from its seed, for it is
thence that the world and living things obtain such a force. It further teaches that, since the particular nature in each and every
living thing does not need deliberation or any contrivances for the
purposes of motion and generation, much less so will universal
nature need these things. Moreover, it teaches that the universal
nature also makes and moves all things with wondrous facility. It
also teaches that, given that the entire bulk of the world and its
form depends upon universal nature, nothing can ever resist it,
especially since all things in the subsequent series so depend on it
that all active things, even if at first impelled by the most gentle
stimulus, are soon moved and contribute to the action and end of
the first mover. Accordingly, the things that are not alive act toward the exterior and only on an alien matter, being sluggish in
themselves, whereas the things that are alive act also in themselves
and act perpetually.

Therefore, soul as causal principle of life — and especially the   26
world-soul — acts always and primarily in itself, in accordance with
its intelligence which on one side forms its reason-principle and on
the other also its nature. However, its reason-principle in itself

ratio naturaliter secum ipsa discurrit et omnia turget gestitque seminibus rerum omnium, etiam corporum divinorum. Ex quo quidem intimo rationalique per rationes rerum seminales motu nascitur forma rationalis[20] mundi similiter omniformis: forma inquam
animae quam simillima. Si enim generantia quae sequuntur sibi
similia generare contendunt, nimirum universalis et proximus hic
mundi genitor mundum sibi generat quam simillimum.[21]

: X :

De descensu animae, Dionysio, Iove, curriculis vitarum,
ordine mundi, consonantia universi.

27　Hic naturam ipsam: id est, vegetalem animae mundanae potentiam appellat Dionysium cuius membra sunt rationes rerum seminales in ipsa natura. Quae quidem membra quando per generati-
onem quasi procedunt in materiam, hic magis inter se divisa iam a
Titanibus: id est, daemonibus geniturae praefectis, discerpta videntur quasi membra Osiridis: id est, vivificae providentiae, dilaniata
a Typhone: id est, daemonum[22] geneficorum duce. Animae igitur in
divino quodam mundo viventes aliquando per imaginationem quae
in eis erat ultimum prospexerunt formas in materia mundi iacentes
quae sunt imagines Dionysii eiusque membrorum. In materia
quasi speculo prospexerunt vero eas forsan intuendo recto quodam
aspectu in naturam atque inde aspectum in materiam deflectendo.
Quorsum vero se ita convertit imaginatio, illuc statim ratio se

naturally runs to and fro, makes all things swell and exults in the seeds of all things, even those of divine bodies. From this innermost and rational motion through the seminal reason-principles of things, the rational form of the world is born as similarly omniform, a form indeed as similar to soul as possible. For if subsequent things that are generative strive to generate things that are similar to themselves, then certainly this universal and proximate generator of the world generates a world that is as similar as can be to itself.[29]

: X :

On the descent of soul, Dionysus, Jupiter, the cycles of life, the order of the world, and the consonance of the universe.

Here, Plotinus calls nature itself—that is, the vegetative power of the world-soul—Dionysus, his various limbs being the seminal reason-principles of things in that nature. When these limbs proceed, so to speak, through generation into matter, here now divided more in themselves by the Titans—that is, the daemons presiding over geniture—, they seem to be scattered as though being the limbs of Osiris—that is, life-giving providence—dismembered by Typhon—that is, the leader of the daemons who facilitate generation. Therefore, the souls living in a certain divine world at some point, through the imagination that was in them their lowest phase, surveyed those forms lying in the matter of the world that are the images of Dionysus and of his limbs. They surveyed them in matter as though in a mirror perhaps by looking at them with a certain direct gaze into nature and thence by deflecting that gaze into matter. Indeed, imagination turns itself thus toward that place, and reason immediately turns itself thither and

divertit ab intellectu et utraque non aspiciendo solum sed amando. Amor eiusmodi exstitit descendendi principium atque post casum etiam permanendi, quoniam provincia haec indiget assidua nostrae rationis attentione. Sed intellectus interea quem non tangit affectus eiusmodi se in mundo superiore servavit immotum.

28   Benignitas vero Iovis instituit curricula temporum in hac quidem laboriosa vita fore brevia, in vita vero apud superos longa, longissima tandem apud supremos. Revertuntur autem animae nostrae quandoque ad animae mundanae gradum ubi[23] providentiam eius publicam contemplentur et facilitate gubernationis propriae circa corpus tunc suum et circa suam provinciam imitentur. Praeterea mundi anima quasi mundanus Apollo canit quidem in natura, pulsat autem in caelo lyram. In natura rationum omnium evolutio statutis temporibus atque revolutio universalis est concentus ex multis cantibus modulisque compositus; in caelo similiter perpetua quaedam dispositio stellarum atque motionum sonus est Apollineus ad perpetuam cantus illius concordiam institutus. Si quis igitur dispositionem continuam illius cantus inspiceret, in ea statim caelestes sonos contueretur et quasi iam (ut proprie loquar) audiret. Animae quin etiam nostrae progressiones suas tum in descensu tum in hac habitatione tum in ascensu quasi tripudio concordi saltantes cantui mundano sonoque coaptant. Cum enim ab eodem patre proficiscantur a quo et anima mundi eiusque germanae sint et provinciam eius inhabitent, nimirum ad cantum sonumque illius ipsae saltant—non impulsae quidem inde sed volentes—et naturaliter simul atque libenter ipsae mundanae mundanum ordinem aemulantur. Hinc efficitur ut per caelestia progressiones humanas—etsi non ubique quasi per causas, saltem

away from intellect, both of these not only gazing but loving. A love of this kind is the initiating cause of descent, and — after the fall — also that of remaining below, given that this region is lacking in the assiduous attention of our reason. However, intellect in the meantime, which is not touched by such affectivity, has preserved itself as unmoved in the higher world.

The benevolence of Jupiter has established that there will be brief cycles of times in this burdensome life, long ones in the life among the higher beings, and the longest ones among the highest beings. Our souls return at some point to the level of the world-soul, where they may contemplate its communal providence and then imitate it with the ease of proper governance both with respect to their body and their domain. Moreover, the world-soul as though a worldly Apollo sings in nature and plucks his lyre in the heaven. In nature, the unfolding and enfolding of all the reason-principles at established times is a universal harmony composed of many melodies and rhythms. Similarly in the heaven, a certain perpetual arrangement of stars and motions is the Apollonian sound established in perpetual harmony with that song. Therefore, if anyone examines the continuity and arrangement of that song, he will immediately perceive the heavenly sounds in that continuity, and will be as though now hearing them (if I may speak for myself). And indeed, our souls attune their progressions in descent, in this present dwelling, and in ascent with the world's song and sound, as though dancing with a concordant step. For since they proceed from the same father from whom both the world-soul and its sibling souls have their existence, also inhabiting his domain, then surely they themselves dance to his song and sound — not impelled from there but going voluntarily —, and they themselves as worldly beings emulate naturally and at the same time freely the order of the world. Hence, it comes about that one can make conjectures through heavenly things — albeit not ubiquitously as though through causes but at least through certain

28

quasi per signa quaedam—coniectare quis valeat, praesertim quia universalis naturae caelique forma exemplari quadam ratione continet quaecumque geruntur[24] intra mundum sive ab ea ipsa sive a se ipsis sive quomodolibet aliunde ducantur.[25]

29   Habitant vero animae aliquando extra caeleste corpus, aliquando in caelesti puro, aliquando sub caelesti. Et quatenus anima diversum intra se habitum induit, diversam foris induit et figuram. Itaque aliquando in hominem caelestem venit, aliquando in aerium, alias in terrenum; atque hic rursum quatenus minus magisve degenerat, in hominem venit vel divinum, vel humanum, vel quasi ferinum. Nempe ita nos Plotini verba emendare solemus, nam rationalem animam bovini corporis vel suilli formam aliquando fieri a Platonicis non est receptum neque etiam ab ipso Plotino concedendum erat cum proposuisset mutationem in anima ab imaginatione principium habuisse quae in essentia speciem mutare non potest. Tot quidem intellectus in humana specie esse quot sunt et animae receptum est. Intellectum vero nostrum in divinis restare felicem dum rationalis potentia quasi ad terram praecipitata sit miserrima ab Iamblicho quidem non videtur penitus dissidere: a Porphyrio tamen Plotini discipulo spretum est, a Proculo reprobatum dicente tantam fore potentiam beatissimae apud Deum mentis ut vim sibi contiguum et simillimam rationem sit interim retentura quatenus ipsa minime declinaverit et in hac vita nos minime peccaturos—neque consentire videtur stomachum infirmissum fore quamdiu firmissimum iecur exstiterit.

signs — regarding the progress of human affairs. This is especially so given that the form of universal nature and of the heaven contains, in a certain exemplary reason-principle, whatever is done within the world, whether these things are guided by the form, by themselves, or by any other originary cause whatsoever.

The souls sometimes live outside the body of the heaven, sometimes in the pure body of the heaven, and sometimes below the body of the heaven. And to the extent that the soul takes on a different condition in itself, so also it takes on a different shape externally. Therefore, at one point it enters into a celestial man, sometimes into an airy one, and sometimes into an earthy one, and again, to the extent that it degenerates here less or more from that status, it enters into a divine man, or a human one, or a bestial one, so to speak. To be sure, we are wont to correct Plotinus' words, for it was not acceptable to the Platonists[30] that a rational soul could at some point become the form of a cow's or a pig's body. Moreover, it was not acceptable even on the authority of Plotinus himself since he proposed that a change in the soul took its origin from the imagination, given that the soul is not able, in its essential being, to change a specific form. It was the received view that there are as many intellects in the specific form of humanity as there are souls. The view that our intellect can remain blessed in the divine sphere while the rational power as though cast down to earth becomes most wretched does not seem totally at odds with Iamblichus,[31] although it was rejected by Porphyry[32] the student of Plotinus and criticized by Proclus.[33] He said that there will be so much power of the most blessed mind that is with God that it will in the meantime retain the power contiguous with it and the reason most similar to it to the extent that it will itself have not lapsed at all and we will sin very little during that life — although he does not seem to agree that the stomach will be the weakest organ as long as the liver exists as the strongest one.

29

30   Subdit Porphyrius casum animae non ab imaginatione vel natura sed ab intellectu coepisse: non enim trahi ab inferioribus superiora sed vim illam superiorem agere pro mensura quadam virtutis suae; itaque intentionem agendi quandoque in ea remitti atque eatenus intendi virtutis inferioris actum: id est, imaginationis atque naturae, cum anima undique otiari non possit; contra vero remitti rursum inferiorum actus quando superiorum actus intenditur. Ubi vero dicit intellectum agere pro mensura virtutis suae, sic emendandus est ut quando intellectus apud Deum est beatus, agat non tam virtute sua quam divina sub cuius forma iam agit. Itaque animam semel ita beatam putandum est numquam inde discessuram. Cetera illi viderint: nobis vero sat fuerit narravisse id potius probaturis quod theologi nostri potissimum comprobaverint.

: XI :

Lex iudicium iustitia universi ducit intrinsecus
animos tum sponte, tum necessitate
ad suum quemque terminum.

31   Sicut aliquis lactucam porrigens allicit anserem per exteriorem sensum, ita magus sensum interiorem allicit per nonnulla sensus interioris amica. Atque ita libens hic[26] movetur sicut et anser ita rursus divina providentia voluntatem omnemque affectum animi

Porphyry adds that the fall of the soul began not from the 30
imagination or nature but from the intellect, and that the higher
things are not drawn by the lower but exercise that superior force
in proportion to a certain measure of their power.[34] Therefore, the
intensity of acting in that power is sometimes remitted, and to
that extent the intensity of a lower power's acting—the lower
power being imagination and nature—is increased, since the soul
cannot be inactive in all its faculties. In a contrary fashion, the action of lower things is remitted when the intensity of the higher
powers' actions is increased.[35] However, where Porphyry says that
intellect acts according to the measure of its power, he should be
corrected in that, when intellect with God is blessed, it acts not so
much by its own as by the divine power, acting now in dependence
on the divine Form. Therefore, one should hold that, when it has
once become blessed in this way, the soul will never depart from
this condition. On the other questions, let these writers think
whatever they like. It will be sufficient for us to have described
these things, being rather prepared to accept that teaching which
our theologians have primarily sanctioned.

: XI :

The law, judgment, and justice of the universe leads our
souls from within both voluntarily and necessarily
each to its own term.

Just as someone can by stretching out a lettuce entice a goose 31
through its exterior sense, so can the magician entice the interior
sense through some things friendly to the inner sense. Thus, the
sense is here moved freely, just as the goose in its turn by divine
providence draws its will and the entire affectivity of its soul to an

ad terminum trahit sibi convenientem: videlicet per affectionem
certam in animo secundum actiones suas et electiones iam con-
ceptam qua et ita volens et tam vehementer ad terminum iustum
fertur sortemque competentem quemadmodum aliquis clam magia
raptus. Movet enim Deus animam non solum interius quam ars
sed etiam quam natura atque certis temporibus sicut natura solet.
Animae igitur ab initio sponte sua agentes et sic agendo factae
tales demum statutis a Deo temporibus non solum sponte sed
etiam necessitate legis intimae ad sortem decretam iuste perveniunt. Est autem in universo lex iudicium iustitia. Lex quidem in
mente divina ipsa scilicet rerum omnium dispositio, iudicium in
mente animae mundi ad divinae legis normam singula decernente,
iustitia in voluntate eiusdem ita volente et ita singula exsequente
sicut iam est iudicatum. Animas ergo transfert impuras quidem
deorsum per impuritatem suam illuc inclinantem quemadmodum
natura universalis movet ad centrum gravia per propriam gravita-
tem; puras autem sursum vicissim per puritatem suam eodem
quoque vergentem sicut et natura levia sursum per propriam levi-
tatem. Hac interim summula licet interpretari quae Orpheus in
tribus hymnis canit de lege iudicio iustitia Dei et quae Plato in
quarto *Legum* imitatus Orpheum de lege divina iudicioque definit.

end suitable to it: that is to say, draws through a certain affectivity now conceived in the soul with respect to its actions and choices by which it is borne so willingly and so earnestly toward a just end and a suitable destiny, like somebody secretly seized by magic. For God moves the soul not only more internally than does art but even more internally than does nature, doing this at certain times as nature is wont to do. Therefore, souls acting initially through their own choice and being rendered of such a kind through acting in this way, finally at times established by God arrive not only through their own choice but through the necessity of an inner law at a destiny justly decreed. There is in the universe law, judgment, and justice: the law being the arrangement itself in the divine mind: namely, that of all things, the judgment being in the world-soul's mind which determines individual things according to the pattern of the divine law, and the justice being in the same world-soul's will which wills and accomplishes individual things in accordance with the judgment already made. This justice transfers downward the impure souls inclining in that direction through their own impurity, just as universal nature moves heavy things through their own heaviness to the center. In a reciprocal manner, it transfers upward the pure souls also tending toward the same place through their own purity, just as nature also transfers light things upward through their own lightness. In the meantime, it is legitimate to interpret according to this little summary that of which Orpheus sings in the three hymns concerning the law, judgment, and justice of God,[36] and also that which Plato, imitating Orpheus in the fourth book of the *Laws*,[37] has explained regarding the divine law and judgment.

: XII :

De connexione huius mundi ad superiorem
et Prometheo statuisque loquentibus.

32 Mundanae sphaerae intimas habent animas et propria hinc imprimis vitalia dona per quas quidem animas perque animales dotes
velut per media quaedam sortiuntur intellectualia quaedam dona
consequenter ab intellectibus individuis suarum ducibus animarum per quos insuper nonnulla etiam divina munera nanciscuntur
ab ipsis divinae mentis ideis quibus (ut Plotinus putat et Iamblichus) inseparabiliter coniuncti sunt intellectus: ut non mirum sit
divinum mundum illum mundo huic undique esse prorsus infusum. Post haec animadvertes naturalem quandam providentiam in
vitali animae mundi parte regnantem sub Promethei cognomento
ex luto: id est, materia prima statuas: id est, res naturales effingere;
atque esse huic opificio partim quidem alligatam, partim quoque
solubilem, nec esse hic Epimetheo: id est, temeritati locum; item
rebus naturalibus non solum vires animales inesse sed dotes etiam
quasdam intellectuales atque divinas et omnia numina huic opificio aliquid ex se conferre: opificio inquam non universo tantum
sed etiam unicuique.

33 Alludit inter haec Plotinus, statuae fictilis vocem nactae men-
tione, ad magos praecipue illos qui loquentes statuas construebant
in quibus nec propriae quidem ullae statuarum animae nec sidera
loquebantur sed daemones ab eodem sidere ducti sub cuius imperio statuae fingebantur. Arbitror etiam in puero illo regis filio quo
die natus est locuto, ut testatur Aly qui et interfuisse[27] se dicit,

: XII :

On the connection of this world to the higher one;
and concerning Prometheus and talking statues.

The spheres of the world have inner souls and their own vital gifts 32
derived primarily from there. Through these souls and through
the psychic gifts, as though through certain mediate terms, they in
due sequence have certain intellectual gifts allocated to them by
the individual intellects that are the leaders of their souls. Through
these intellectual gifts they additionally obtain certain divine gifts
from the Ideas themselves in the divine mind to which (as Plotinus and Iamblichus[38] think) their intellects are inseparably joined,
there being accordingly no surprise that that divine world is everywhere totally infused into this world. After this, you will observe that a certain natural providence ruling in the vital part of
the world-soul to which the name of Prometheus is given fashions,
from "mud": that is, from primal matter, "statues": that is, natural
things, this natural providence being partly bound to this work of
creation and partly also detached from it, there being no place for
Epimetheus: that is rashness, here. You will further observe that
there are in natural things not only psychic powers but also certain
intellectual and divine gifts, all these numinous things contributing something from themselves to this created work: that is, not
just the universal created work but also each individual one.

During these remarks Plotinus, in mentioning the manufac- 33
tured statue that has obtained a voice, sports particularly with
those magicians who were constructing talking statues,[39] for neither did any souls proper to the statues nor did the stars speak but
only daemons led by the same star under whose rule the statues
were fashioned. I also think that in that boy who was the son of a
king and spoke on the day when he was born, according to the

non coniunctionem planetarum quattuor in eius horoscopo concurrentium formavisse verba nec etiam infantis animam verba vaticiniumque fecisse de paterni regni calamitate paulo post secuta sed daemonem potius illic fuisse locutum. Daemonem inquam Mercurialem, nam in octavo Librae gradu horoscopo qui et terminus est Mercurii Mercurius ipse cum Venere Ioveque et Marte fertur fuisse coniunctus. Sed non licet ulterius in praesentia digredi. Immo neque licet tenorem ab initio librorum exponendorum hactenus continuatum ultra servare. Si enim longa similiter argumenta immo et commentaria seorsumque ab ipsis Plotini capitibus disposita prosequamur, et confusa continget interpretatio et opus excrescet in immensum. Satis evagati sumus; satis multa iam diximus. Sat igitur erit deinceps breves quasdam annotationes, ut in Theophrasto fecimus, Plotini capitibus interserere.

: XIII :

34 De animarum descensu transmigratione differentiis fato arbitrio providentia; et quomodo providentiae ordo tamquam latissimus connectit sibi fatum pariter et arbitrium.

testimony of Haly[40] — who also says that he was present at the event —, it was not a conjunction of four planets coming together in his horoscope that formed the words, and it was not the soul of the infant that made the words and the prophecy concerning the disaster that befell his father's kingdom shortly thereafter, but rather a daemon who spoke there. Indeed, it was a Mercurial daemon, for in the horoscope of the eighth degree of Libra which is also the boundary of Mercury, Mercury itself is said to have been in conjunction with Venus, Jupiter, and Mars. But we ought not to digress too far at present, and indeed we should not any longer maintain the course of expounding the books set at the beginning and continued thus far. For if we pursue similarly lengthy analyses and indeed commentaries arranged separately from Plotinus' chapters themselves, a confused interpretation will arise and the project will expand to immense proportions. We have been sufficiently discursive and have already said sufficiently many things. Henceforth, it will be enough to insert certain brief notices between the chapters of Plotinus, as we have done in the case of Theophrastus.

: XIII :

On the descent, transmigration, differences, fate, free will, and providence of souls; and how the order of providence, as though most extensive, joins fate and free will alike to itself.

34

: XIV :

35 Cum mundus supercaelestis atque etiam caelestis sit ordinatissi-
mus, necessario ordinatus est etiam sublunaris in quo, cum inferiora homine sint ordinata, ergo multo magis humana. Singula igitur hominibus contingentia iuste divinitus dispensantur.

: XV :

36 Sicut summum aeris primum omnium ignitur ab infimo ignis, sic
caelum summum corpus primo animatur ab anima quae est ultimum divinorum. Item ipsum bonum est quasi centrum, mens lumen inde micans atque permanens, anima lumen de lumine se
movens. Corpus per se opacum illuminatur ab anima, sed animae
in caelo securae illuminant, sub caelo non absque cura.

: XVI :

37 Animae secundum Plotinum atque Iamblichum sunt extra omne
corpus et tunc potentia rationalis est adeo efficax et expedita ut
quae sibi porriguntur ab intellectu comprehendat cuncta sine tempore vel saltem quam brevissimo. Item animae inter se conversantes
in caelis sine sermone quasi per nutus mutuo se intelligunt, sed in
corporibus aeriis animae atque daemones voces formant.

: XIV :

Since the supercelestial and also celestial world is the most or-   35
dered, the sublunary world is also necessarily ordered. In the latter, since things below man are ordered, therefore human things
are so to a much greater extent. Therefore, individual things befall-
ing man are dispensed justly from the divine sphere.

: XV :

Just as the highest part of air — the first of all things — is rendered   36
fiery by the lowest part of fire, so is the heaven — the highest
body — enlivened by soul which is the lowest of divine things.
Also, the Good itself is as though a center, mind a light flashing
forth from there and being stable, and soul a light from light moving itself. Body in itself dark is illuminated by soul, although souls
in heaven illuminate being free of concern while those below the
heaven do so not without concern.

: XVI :

According to Plotinus and Iamblichus,[41] souls are sometimes out-   37
side all body. Then, the rational power is so efficacious and unen-
cumbered that it grasps all the things stretched out to them from
intellect without time or at least in the shortest time. Also, souls
interacting among themselves in the heavens without speech, understand one another as though through nodding, whereas souls
and daemons in airy bodies form sounds.

: XVII :

38   Vita sensualis est conflata ex proprietate individua et dividua. Dicitur enim dividua circa corpus, quia singulis partibus eius se accommodat; dicitur etiam individua quia singulis adest tota. Ratio vero ac mens dicitur simpliciter impartibilis quia corporeo instrumento non utitur et propterea separata.

: XVIII :

39   Anima non est in corpore sicut in loco vel vase, nec ut pars in toto vel totum in partibus nec ut qualitas in subiecto nec ut species in materia, sed corpus est in anima ut in vivificante comprehendente moventeque stabili.

: XIX :

40   Anima non proprie inest sed adest corpori, non tamem ut gubernator navi sed virtus gubernatoria infusa gubernaculo.

: XVII :

The sensory life results from a combination of the properties of 38
indivisibility and divisibility. It is said to be "divisible around bodies" because it accommodates itself to the individual parts of the
body, and it is said to be "indivisible" because it is present as a
whole to individual parts. Reason or mind is, however, said to be
indivisible *simpliciter* because it does not use a corporeal instrument
and is therefore separate.

: XVIII :

The soul is not in the body as though in a place or in a vessel. And 39
it is not there as a part in a whole or as a whole in parts, or as a
quality in a substratum, or as a specific form in matter. Rather, the
body is in the soul as in something that enlivens, contains, and
moves it in a stable manner.

: XIX :

The soul, properly speaking, is not in the body but present to the 40
body. However, it is present to the body not as a pilot is present to
a ship but as the power of piloting is infused into the helm.

: XX :

41   Anima adest corpori separabiliter sicut lumen aeri; corpus est in anima sicut aer in lumine; mens et ratio non adsunt corpori quia cum eo non communicant[28] in agendo; sensus et vegetalis potentia adsunt quia et haec per corpus agunt et corpus indiget eis neque tamen a corpore sustinentur.

: XXI :

42   Quaelibet vis animae est in qualibet parte corporis tota—sicut anima—, sed dicitur ibi agere ubi sibi servit instrumentum et ibi principaliter ubi instrumentum habet principium. Sic ergo sentiendi movendique actus attribuitur capiti, unde videlicet derivantur nervi instrumenta sensus et motus; sic iracundiae actus circa cor ubi instrumentum eius, scilicet sanguis igneus; sic nutritio circa iecur ubi sanguis aerius est instrumentum eius. Actus vero rationis, etsi non habet communionem cum corpori, attribuitur quodammodo capiti quoniam imaginationis actus est ratione propinquus eiusque fit particeps.

: XX :

The soul is present to the body inseparably, as light is present to   41
air. The body is in the soul as air is in light. The mind and the
reason are not present to the body because they do not enter into
communion with it in acting. The sense and the vegetal power are
present to the body because they act through the body and because the body needs them, although they are not sustained by the
body.

: XXI :

Each and every power of the soul is as a whole in each and every   42
part of the body—as the soul is—but is said to act where there is
an instrument serving its purpose and primarily where the instrument contains the causal principle of the act. In this manner,
therefore, the act of sensing and moving is assigned to the head—
the nerves, instruments, senses, and motions obviously being derived from there—; the act of being angry is associated with the
heart, where its instrument—that is, the fiery blood—is located;
nutrition is thus associated with the liver, where its instrument is
the airy blood. However, the act of reason, even if it does not enter into communion with the body, is somehow assigned to the
head, given that the act of imagination is close to reason and becomes participant in it.

: XXII :

43 Anima quia est substantia incorporea in se exsistens non determinatur ad aliquem locum nisi per inclinationem et actionem circa illum. Soluta igitur e corpore terreno, si nullam retinet inclinationem eiusmodi, nusquam terrarum est et ubique, nisi forte sit in sphaera superiore per inclinationem ad illam; sin autem inclinationem adhuc retinet ad terrena, circa haec revolvitur cum corpore spiritali in quo et corporea patitur. Praeterea sicut apud astrologos nonnulli fatum suum etiam nolentes implent dum ignari aliquid eligunt per quod incidunt clam in fatum, sic omnes animae divinam implent in se legem eligendo aliquid ex quo in[29] latentem incidunt legis divinae sententiam.

: XXIII :

44 In intellectu non est reminiscentia quia nihil novi illic accidit vel extrinsecus vel intrinsecus quod conservandum sit atque recolendum; nec ulla de potentia in actum ibi sit commutatio. Sed recordationis officium ad animam pertinet.

: XXII :

The soul, because it is an incorporeal substance subsisting in itself,   43
is not limited to any place except through an inclination and action around it. Therefore, when it is freed from an earthy body,
and if it retains no inclination of this kind, it is nowhere and everywhere on earth, the exception being perhaps when it is in a
higher sphere through inclination to that sphere. However, if the
soul still retains an inclination to earthly things, it goes around
these with its spiritual body and in this body also suffers corporeal
things. Moreover, just as according to the astrologers, some people
fulfill their fate even unwillingly, when out of ignorance they
choose something through which they secretly light upon their
fate, similarly all souls fulfill the divine law, choosing something as
a consequence of which they light upon the hidden judgment of
the divine law.

: XXIII :

There is no recollection in intellect, because nothing new can oc-   44
cur there either externally or internally that should be preserved
and revisited. Moreover, there is no change from potency to act
there, the function of recollection pertaining to soul.

: XXIV :

45 Animal est unum quiddam: non unum dico factum ex transmutatione ambarum partium in aliquid tertium sed ex transmutatione corporis in formam actumque animalem. Ad hoc unum commune pertinet effectus sentiendi ferme sicut et vegetandi. Sed effectus memoriae: id est, conservandi et recolendi, ad animam proprie pertinet stabilem non ad corpus instabile quod est oblivionis occasio, nam et multa per memoriam servantur et suggeruntur quae numquam cum corpore sunt percepta.

: XXV :

46 Opinio quasi poetica esse geminas in homine animas per substantiam inter se differentes: rationalem quidem ab ipso mundi opifice, irrationalem vero a mundi vita; utramque[30] sempiternam esse ac post obitum posse rationalem esse apud deos et interim irrationalem quae est eius idolum apud homines; et hanc reminisci rerum in hac vita gestarum—plurimum quidem passionum suarum minus autem rerum ad rationalem animam pertinentium—item in homine, non dico temperato sed continente vel incontinente, ambas simul animas commigrare rerumque humanarum memores esse—facilius quidem quatenus vivunt in aerio corpore, difficilius autem si terrenum corpus quandoque recipiant. Probabilius forte foret dicere unam nobis inesse animam atque ex hac vitalem vim

: XXIV :

The animate being is a certain unity. However, this unity is pro-   45
duced not from the transmutation of its two parts into a *tertium
quid*, but from the transmutation of the body into the psychic act
and form. It is to this common unity that the effect of sensing
pertains, more or less as the effect of enlivening also pertains. But
the effect of memory: that is, of preserving and revisiting, pertains
properly to the stable soul and not to the unstable body which is
the starting point for forgetfulness. For many things are preserved
through memory and suggested which were never perceived together with the body.

: XXV :

His somewhat poetic view is that there are two souls in man dif-   46
fering from one another in substance, and that the rational soul
comes from the craftsman of the world but the irrational soul
from the world's life. He says that both souls are everlasting and
that, after death, the rational soul is with the gods while the irrational soul which is its *idolum* is among men; he says that the irrational soul remembers the things done in this life—to the greatest extent, indeed, its passions but to a lesser degree the things
pertaining to the rational soul; he further says that in a man—not
indeed in the man who has a balanced temperament but in the one
who restrains or does not restrain his passions—the two souls
migrate together and recall human affairs more easily to the extent
that they live in airy body and with more difficulty if they at some
point receive an earthy one. It might perhaps have been more
probable to say that there is one soul in us and that the vital power

vel actum vivificum corpori huic influentem appellari quasi alteram animam. Quae ideo dicitur ab universi vita fieri quia ex nostra profluit sub universae vitae virtute.

: XXVI :

47 Potentia sensitiva aliud quiddam est quam potentia concupiscendi vel irascendi atque haec utraque excitatur a sensu et ex frequenti incitamento acquirit inclinationem propensiorem. Quae tamen non est memoria: memoria enim ad sensum pertinet atque rationem.

: XXVII :

48 Quando in sensu memoriam ponimus, hanc in sensu interiore: id est, imaginatione, locamus. Haec enim absentia repetit et conservat; et ubi haec potentior est, memoria est etiam validior, praesertim si corporis qualitas et meditatio conducat ad idem.

: XXVIII :

49 Sunt in nobis imaginationes geminae: una in vita irrationali, altera in anima rationali, atque illa est summum sensuum, haec infimum cogitationum. Suntque contiguae et ad utramque[31] pertinet

and the vital act flowing thence into this body is called the 'other soul' so to speak. This other soul is said to come into being from the life of the universe because it flows forth from our soul in subordination to the power of the universal life.

: XXVI :

The sensitive power is something other than the concupiscent or irascible power. Both the latter are aroused by sense and acquire a greater inclination from frequent stimulus which, however, is not memory. For memory pertains to sense and to reason. 47

: XXVII :

When we place memory in sense, we situate it in the inner sense: that is, the imagination, for the latter revisits and preserves absent things. Where imagination is more powerful, memory is stronger, especially if quality of body and meditation contribute to the same effect. 48

: XXVIII :

There are two imaginations in us: one in the irrational life and the other in the rational soul, the former being the highest of the sensitive and the latter the lowest of the cogitative functions. They are contiguous with one another, and noticing pertains to both of 49

animadversio. Sicut ergo saepe nonnulla videmus nec tamen animadvertimus nos videre nisi huc imaginatio sensualis intendat et nisi in hanc visio ipsa resultet, ita nec intelligere neque cogitare nos animadvertimus nisi actiones eiusmodi quoquo modo attingant imaginationem sibi continuam et in ea quasi resultent. Ad hanc quoque imaginationem perveniunt et sensuum et imaginationis inferioris actus atque in hac ipsa rationalis memoria collocatur.

⁚ XXIX ⁚

50   Si animae nostrae duae locis inter se separentur, duas habebunt imaginationes manifestas atque memorias. Quatenus vero sunt simul, inferior praestantiori cedit in corpore formando sicut lumini maiori minus lumen. Et ideo non sunt hic animalia duo quia superior anima est quasi inferioris forma atque haec sub illius forma actuque naturaliter agit in corpore. Praeterea quamvis imaginatio memor naturaliter sit in utraque, tamen quando una frequentius imaginatur atque validius, altera vel vacat vel ita remisse agit; sicut saepius visus quasi non videt, imaginatione interim circa aliud attentius laborante. Decet autem—ut naturale est et fit communiter—imaginationem inferiorem superiori cedere. Quae quidem superior, quia comprehendit intelligibilium notas simul et sensibilium formas, declarat in nobis animal esse unum; et quando egreditur corpore, si alteram sibi educatione subegerit, vilia quidem mandat oblivioni, honestiora resumit.

them. Therefore, just as we often see certain things, albeit without noticing that we see unless the sensitive imagination leads in that direction and unless vision itself rebounds in it, similarly we do not notice that we think unless actions of this kind in some way reach the imagination that is continuous with them and rebound in it, so to speak. The acts of the senses and of the lower imagination also reach this imagination, and in the latter the rational memory itself is established.

: XXIX :

If our two souls were separated from one another by place, they will obviously have two imaginations and two memories. But to the extent that the souls are together, the lower yields to the higher in the forming of body just as lower light yields to higher light. And there are not in this case two animate beings, because the higher soul is as though the form of the lower soul and the lower soul acts in the body naturally in subordination to the form and act of the higher one. Moreover, although imagination is naturally recollective in both cases, nevertheless when one of them imagines more often and more forcefully, the other is either inactive or acts weakly. It acts as weakly as sight often does when it is as though not seeing, the imagination meanwhile struggling in its greater attention to something else. It is fitting — as it is natural and comes about generally — that the inferior imagination should yield to the superior. This superior imagination, indeed, because it simultaneously grasps the signs of intelligible things and the forms of sensible things, makes clear that the animate being in us is single. When it leaves the body, if it subjects the lower to itself in education, it consigns base things to forgetfulness and revisits the more worthy.

: XXX :

51 In utraque anima post obitum humanorum memoria remanet, sed
in inferiore cum perturbatione—praesertim quando superiori non
prorsus obtemperaverit—in superiore vero sine perturbatione—
praesertim quando talia parvi penderit. Item in corpore aerio remi-
niscimur mortalium quamplurimum, in caelesti pauciorum, extra
caelum paucissimorum. Recordari vero illic pauciorum non provenit ex debilitate memoriae sed ex attentione circa meliora ne-
gligente deteriora, nisi quatenus haec per illa conspiciuntur.

: XXX :

The memory of human affairs remains in both souls after death. 51
However, in the case of the lower soul, the memory is together
with perturbation, especially when it has not completely obeyed
the higher, whereas in the higher soul it is without perturbation,
especially when it has treated such human affairs as having little
value. Moreover, in the airy body we have extensive remembrance
of many mortal things, in the heavenly body of fewer things, and
outside the heavenly body of even fewer. The recollection of fewer
things arises there not from the weakness of the memory but from
the attention to better things that neglects worse things, except to
the extent that the worse things are observed through the better.

[LIBER IV]

DE DUBIIS ANIMAE

: I :

1 Anima corpus omne vel caeleste quandoque exuta et mente divina tunc formata attentissime divina conspicit simul cuncta sine discursu: ideo dicitur non recordari rerum humanarum non quia ignoret inferiora, dum omnes inferiorum causas contuetur ac se perfectissime possidet, sed quia negligentissime repetit minima quando est in maximis attentissima, ac etiam quia non repetit per modum discurrentem atque mutabilem quemadmodum solet humana recordatio fieri. Contuetur autem et per intellectum et per rationem quaecumque cognoscit uno quodam intuitu sine motu quoniam conspicit per unam Dei formam. Veruntamen per ipsam seriem idearum habentem gradus non tempore sed ordine inter se distinctos discernit alia aliis ordine ibi esse priora. Quod autem aliquis apud nos attentissime cogitans aliquid nequeat interim aliud perspicue cogitare accidit cum ex debilitate potentiae tum etiam ex eo quod non cogitat principium aliorum. Ibi vero potentia et validissima est et omnium principia contuetur: ergo et in illis omnia simul, praesertim quia a motu ac tempore iam est penitus separata. Anima denique, postquam mente divina ideisque for-

[BOOK IV]

ON DIFFICULTIES CONCERNING
THE SOUL [SECOND BOOK]

: I :

The soul which has at some point put aside its body — even the 1
celestial one — and is then formed by the divine mind most attentively perceives all divine things at once and without discursive
motion. Accordingly, it is said not to recall human affairs, not because it does not know lower things while beholding all the causes
of the lower and being most perfectly self-possessed, but because it
pays little attention to dealing with the most insignificant things
when it is most attentive with respect to the most important, and
also because it does not revisit things in a discursive and mutable
way as human recollection is wont to do. However, it beholds
through both intellect and reason whatever it knows in a certain
single intuition without motion, given that it beholds its object
through the single Form of God. Nevertheless, it does distinguish,
within the series itself of the Ideas having degrees marked off from
one another not in time but in order, certain terms as there being
prior in the order to other terms. The fact that someone in our
world thinking of something in a most attentive way is meanwhile
unable to think clearly of something else comes about both from
the weakness of his power and also from his not thinking of the
causal principle of other things. But there in the higher world his
power is exceedingly great and perceives the causal principles of all
things: therefore, it perceives all things together in those causal
principles especially because it is now absolutely separated from
motion and time. Finally, after it has been formed by the divine

mata fuit, attingit ipsum unum mente ideisque superius. Et tamen adhuc inde conspicit omnia—potestas enim ipsius unius, cum primum in alio: id est, mente vel anima percipitur, in plurima derivatur.

: II :

2 Anima in hoc quidem corpore, dum attentior est ad aliud, se ipsam interim non cognoscit quia et potentia hic eius debilis est et quod cogitatur ab ea non est principium animae. Sed quando divinum mundum contemplatur, utpote quae et corroborata est et principia sui conspicit, se ipsam habitumque suum et gesta prorsus agnoscit. Anima in hoc corpore ad imaginationem et per hanc ad sensibilia plurimum est conversa, sed post obitum si in corpore vivat aerio, ad rationem postremo tota convertitur perque hanc ad intellectum suum semper omnia contuentem et in discursu interim temporali versatur. In corpore vero caelesti ratio quasi effecta est intellectus et suus atque communis praeteritumque discursum ad intuitum ferme redegit. Hic ergo et quatenus ingenitas sibi repetit formas, agnoscit se ipsam et quatenus se, formas quoque vicissim: ipsa enim est ipsae formae. Anima denique extra caelum sic formata est divina mente eiusque ideis sicut corpus anima viribusque animae et sicut ignitum ferrum igne. Videt igitur agitque per ideas divinae mentis quasi per vires quasdam suae[1] formae, igitur et actu stabili et cognoscens ibi principia sui agnoscit profecto se ipsam.

mind and the Ideas, the soul attains to the One itself that is superior to the mind and the Ideas, although from this vantage point it still beholds all things. For the power of the One itself, although it is first perceived in another thing: that is to say, mind or soul, is distributed to all things.

: II :

The soul in this body, while being more attentive toward something else, does not in the meantime know itself, both because its power is weak here and because that which is thought by it is not the causal principle of soul. But when it contemplates the divine world, inasmuch as it is both strengthened and beholds its own causal principles, it precisely recognizes itself, its status, and its deeds. The soul in this body is for the most part turned toward the imagination and through the latter to sensible things. But after death, if it lives in an airy body, it is finally turned completely toward reason and through the latter to its intellect that beholds all things everlastingly, being in the meantime engaged in temporal and discursive activity. In the celestial body, indeed, reason is as though made into an intellect that is both its own and general, and has virtually reduced its erstwhile discursiveness to intuitive gaze. Here therefore, to the extent that it revisits forms inborn in itself, the soul recognizes itself, and to the extent that it recognizes itself, it also recognizes the Forms in turn, for it is itself those Forms. Finally, the soul outside the heaven is formed by the divine mind and by its Ideas in a manner similar to that in which the body is formed by the soul and the powers of the soul and the glowing iron is formed by the fire. It therefore sees and acts through the Ideas of the divine mind, as though through certain powers of its own form. Therefore, in a stable act and in knowledge of its own causal principles in that act, it certainly recognizes itself.

2

: III :

3   Anima extra caelum in mundo divino constituta dicitur esse unum quoniam agit dumtaxat per intellectum. Descendit tandem in corpus caeleste quando suam ipsam in se explicat multitudinem, agens iam videlicet per intellectum rationem imaginationem. Tunc et sui rerumque suarum ita ferme iam reminiscitur quemadmodum apud[2] homines consueverat, scilicet cum per rationis agitationem — quamvis ibi celerrimam — tum per imaginationis formationes atque simulacra. Plurimum vero interest qualia cum affectu cogitat animus, nam cum formas ipse suas in se latentes producendo in actum cogitet, nimirum evadit illa ipsa quae cogitat locumque et condicionem eis convenientem subinde sortitur.

: IV :

4   Anima in mundo supercaelesti contemplans divinae mentis ideas per ipsam mentem velut per diaphanum luminosum cernit ipsum bonum velut solem atque, dum per principia sui videt se ipsam, nimirum et se cognoscit intelligentem esse et se ipsam prorsus agnoscit, sed per eundem penitus actum eiusdemque potentiae divina[3] suam naturam actionem⟨que⟩ propriam contuetur. Ideo non proprie dicitur se ipsam suumque actum et vitam priorem animadvertere quia non utitur rationis discursu atque imaginatione in quibus recordatio et animadversio consueta versatur.

: III :

The soul outside the heaven and established in the divine world is   3
said to be one, since it acts only through intellect. At length, it
descends into a celestial body when it unfolds its own multiplicity
within itself: that is, acting now through intellect, reason, and
imagination. Then it remembers itself and its affairs almost in the
way it usually did when it was among men: that is to say, both
through the activation of the reason — albeit there the swiftest activation — and through the formativity and representations of the
imagination. It is of the utmost importance to know what kind of
things the soul thinks with its affectivity, for when it itself thinks
its own forms hidden in itself by bringing them forth into actuality, surely it emerges as itself what it thinks, getting hold subsequently of the place and condition befitting the latter.

: IV :

The soul in the supercelestial world, contemplating the Ideas in   4
the divine mind through the mind itself as though through an illuminated transparent medium, perceives the Good itself as though
it were the sun and, while it sees itself through the causal principles of itself, it certainly both understands itself to be exercising
intelligence and also completely recognizes itself. But through absolutely the same act and that of the same power, the soul being
divine beholds its own nature and its proper action. Therefore it is
not properly said to observe itself and its act and the previous life,
because it does not use the discursiveness if reason and imagination in which recollection and habitual observation are engaged.
However, when it comes from there first into the heaven and after-

Sed cum primum inde venit in caelum et post in aerem duo haec exercet. Omnino vero formae rerum in potentia animae cognitrice non sunt accidentia quaedam sic animae adiacentia, ut in tabella sunt litterae, sed rationes proprietates vires quaedam essentiales, sicut rationes seminales membrorum qualitatumque corporalium in potentia vegetali et sicut proprietates plantae totius in semine. Anima igitur semper est haec omnia sed alias quidem potius in potentia quadam alias vero magis in actu. Est autem anima magis res ipsae divinae si per solum intellectum agit in ipsis quam si interim per rationis quoque discursum vel imaginationis figmenta id ipsum animadvertat: haec enim distrahunt.

: V :

5 Anima in hac vita potest cognoscere divina non per imaginationem nec etiam per rationem sumentem ab imaginatione principia sed per intellectum et rationem principia sumentem ab intellectu. Quando anima per rationem surgit in mentem velut in speculam, quamvis autem memoria communiter dicta omni imaginatione versetur, tamen memoria quaedam in ratione etiam et intellectu consistit. In anima supra caelum actus intelligentiae consuetum rationis et imaginationis occupat usum, sed in caelo resurgit usus eiusmodi per quem reminiscitur humano quasi modo humanae quondam vitae rerumque humanarum, nam haec supra caelum modo quodam eminentiore prospexit. Agnoscunt igitur in caelo se invicem animi, amici praesertim atque quondam noti, cum per

ward into the air, it does exercise these two faculties. Indeed, the forms of things in the cognitive power of the soul are not annexed to the soul as certain accidents, in the way that letters are in a tablet, but are present there as certain reason-principles, properties, and essential powers, in the way that the seminal reason-principles of corporeal members and qualities are in the vegetative power and the properties of an entire plant in its seed. Therefore, the soul always is these things, albeit in some cases more in a certain potency and in others more in act. However, the soul is the divine things themselves, more if it acts among them through its intellect alone than if it observes the same thing in the meantime also through the discursiveness of reason or the figments of the imagination. For the latter distract it.

: V :

The soul in this life is able to know divine things neither through 5 the imagination nor even through the reason taking its originative stimulus from the imagination, but through the intellect and the reason taking its causal principles from the intellect. When the soul through reason rises up to the mind as though to a watchtower, although memory as generally described is exercised in the imagination as a whole, a certain memory takes its stand in the reason and also the intellect. In the soul above the heaven, the act of intelligence takes over the normal function of reason and imagination, but in the heaven a function of this kind rises up again through which there is recollection somewhat in the human manner of the erstwhile human life and human affairs, given that the soul in heaven has looked upon things in a certain more elevated way. Therefore, souls recognize one another in the heaven, especially those of friends and of those formerly known to one another,

ipsos motus affectusque vividos animorum tum per corpora quae ibi habere possunt figuram huiusmodi similem in materia liquida cedente multo magis animo quomodocumque formatori quam terrena materia nunc affectibus animae. Tum vero si corpora illic orbicularia sint, differentia tamen erunt indifferentibus signa indiciaque differentium animorum sive in figura (ut diximus) sive magnitudine qualitate motu gestu nutu luce — quemadmodum fit in oculis ex affectibus animorum et in variis nubibus figurae differentes atque colores. Sunt qui velint caelicolas inter se voces edere, nam et caelos posse sonare. Saltem vero mutuis inter se nutibus colloquentur: recordantur vero in caelis divinorum magis quam humanorum. Lapsae vero in aerem e converso possunt autem — et quando in caelo et quando in aere sunt — propter motum naturaliter liberum et ibi per multa saecula gradum sistere et altius inde regredi. Denique quidnam prohibet optima quadam electione in superioribus semper esse? Nihil, apud Porphyrium et Iamblichum atque Iulianum.

: VI :

6 Conservatricis memoriae ministerium necessarium est ubi praeterire aliquid rursumque accedere potest vicissim praeteriturum. Animis ergo caelestibus non videtur memoria necessaria: neque enim discurrunt ut novum aliquid vel inveniant vel acquirant.

both through the motions themselves and the lively affections of the souls and also through the bodies which are there able to possess a shape similar to that of bodies of this world, this shape residing in a flowing matter which yields much more to the soul forming it in every possible way than does earthy matter now to the affections of the soul. Moreover, if the bodies there are spherical, there will nevertheless be different signs and indications of different souls for things that are not differentiated, these signs and indications residing in shape, as we have said, or in quantity, quality, motion, gesture, nodding, or light—just as in the eyes there arise such things from the affections of the soul, and in various clouds there arise different shapes and colors. Some believe that the inhabitants of heaven emit sounds, for the heavens are able to sound. But at least, they converse among themselves with noddings to one another, for in heaven they recollect divine things more than human things. On the other hand, those souls which have fallen into the air—both when they are in the heaven and when they are in the air—are able because of their naturally free motion also to stop their course there after many ages and return thence to the higher. Finally, what is to prevent souls from being forever in the higher realm through a certain best choice? Nothing—according to Porphyry,[1] Iamblichus,[2] and Julian.

: VI :

The agency of a memory that retains is necessary when something   6
is able to pass away and come back which will pass away in turn. Therefore, memory does not seem necessary to celestial souls, for they do not have discursive motion in order to find or acquire something new.

: VII :

7 Animis caelestium corporum rectoribus non est necessarium recordationis obsequium vel in cognitione vel vita vel motu: suspiciunt quidem divina intuitu numquam interrupto. Ubi animadvertere quidem possunt se videre, non tamen est opus repetere se vidisse cum ibi non sit ipsum vidisse sed videre numquam intermissum numquam igitur resumendum. Similis est et eorum vita semper eadem, similis et motus perpetuus in eorum corporibus atque continuus ideoque uniuscuisque illorum semper unus quamvis nobis multiplex vel accidat vel videatur. Prospiciunt res quoque mutabiles intuitu quopiam non mutato, sicut et quispiam eadem inspectione ad aliquam horae partem continuata cernit[4] deambulantem in rectum aliter[5] aliterque mutatum, prospectu videlicet non mutato. Quo quidem si iudicaverit illum hic esse, ibi fuisse, illic fore, mutationes eiusmodi non propterea in visione contingent quod in spectaculo contingere iudicentur.

: VIII :

8 Anima cuiuslibet stellae contemplans ideas principiaque rerum omnium habet semper in se certam universi notitiam — sive intellectualem hanc sive rationalem appellare volueris —, atque interea per corpus caeleste suum corporalia sentit. Sed quod minima quaeque sentiat interea nec per imaginationem animadvertit,

: VII :

The service of recollection either in their thinking, their life, or 7
their motion is not necessary to the souls that rule the celestial
bodies, for they look up at divine things with an intuitive gaze that
is never interrupted. When they are able to observe their seeing of
themselves, there is however no need for them to revisit their having seen, since there is no "having seen" but only a seeing never
intermitted and therefore never to be resumed. Similar to this is
their life that is always the same. Also similar is the perpetual motion in their bodies which is continuous and therefore always unified in each of their cases, although it comes about as multiple for
us or seems to be so. They also look over mutable things without
change of any kind in their intuitive gaze, just as any person with
the same gaze maintained until a certain part of an hour discerns
someone walking away in a straight line and changed from one
position to the next: that is to say, discerns him with a surveillance
that is not changed. If he judges in this surveillance that this man
is here, has been there, and will be there, changes of this kind do
not occur in his act of vision as a consequence of their been judged
to occur in the public view.

: VIII :

The soul of each and every star contemplating the Ideas and causal 8
principles of all things always has in itself a certain knowledge of
the universe—whether you wish to call that knowledge intellectual
or rational—and in the meantime senses corporeal things through
its celestial body. But because it might sense every least significant
thing but does not meanwhile observe them through imagination,

ideoque nec in memoria collocat cum quia haec omnia altius iam comprehendit tum quia apud ipsum nullius sunt momenti tum etiam quoniam tamdiu iam omnia sentit ut nihil ultra sensum moveat tamquam novum. Veruntamen per imaginationem animadvertit ea particularia se sentire quae universo sunt apprime necessaria: ut stellae caelestia elementa. Profecto cum propositum sit caelestibus animis non per hanc quidem solum partem vel hucusque tantum vel tamdiu dumtaxat moveri sed contemplari et simpliciter semperque moveri, et cum quolibet in momento earum motio sit perfecta, sintque animae illae certae praescriptum in se ipsis ordinem universi ita procul dubio evasurum, nulla nimirum eas cura tangit de parte quapiam loci vel temporis aut motus vel de re vel de quavis re mutabili. Itaque neque dum talia sentiunt imaginationem attentionemque talibus adhibere coguntur. Nota circularem caeli motum nec esse alterationem—quia non mutat formam—nec esse localem—quia non mutat locum—sed esse vitalem: id est, proprium vitae interioris actum pariter et indicium, nam agere in se moverique ex intimis proprium est viventium. Caelestium vero motus est eiusmodi quemadmodum in animalibus pulsuum cordisque motus nutritioque in plantis.

: IX :

9   Rector mundi Iuppiter per unam simplicemque sui formam omniformem virtute infinitam infinitorum effectricem videt et efficit infinita: non duobus quidem actibus sed quo actu videt eodem

it therefore does not place them in the memory given that it already comprehends these things from a higher vantage point, and that they are of no importance considered on its level, and also that it now senses all things through such an extent of time that nothing beyond that sensing can move it as a novelty. Nevertheless, it observes through imagination that it senses those particulars which are primarily necessary to the universe: that is, the stars, celestial things, and elements. Certainly, since the plan of the celestial souls is not to move through only this part, or only thus far, or only for so long, but rather to contemplate and move simply and always, and since their motion is complete in each and every moment, and that these souls are certain that the predetermined order of the universe will without doubt be realized in them, surely no concern touches them with respect to any part of space, of time, of motion, or of a thing, or of any mutable thing. Therefore, even when they sense such things, they are not compelled to apply imagination and attention to them. You should note that the circular motion of the heaven is neither alteration — since it does not change its form — nor locomotion — since it does not change its place. It is rather a vital motion — that is, the proper act of the inner life — and equally its indicator — since acting and moving in itself from within is the proper characteristic of living things. Indeed, the motion of celestial things is of the same kind as is the motion of the pulses and the heart in animals and nutrition in plants.

: IX :

Jupiter, the ruler of the world, through his single, simple, and om- 9
niform Form that is infinite in power and efficacious of an infinite number of things, sees and effects an infinite number of things albeit not in two acts: rather, he effects by the same act by which

efficit atque vicissim. Absurdum vero foret dictu eum notitiam rerum ex rebus ipsis colligere, nam per notitiam res antecedentem res efficit. Neque posset infinita comprehendere si notitiam ex infinitis aucuparetur. Nunc vero, non aliter per unam sui formam conspicit infinita quam si sol per unam sui lucem radios innumerabiles micantes inde conspiciat.

: X :

10 Ordo universi qui paulatim evolvitur in materia simul totus est immutabilisque in utroque Iove tum in primo qui est intellectus purus mundi artifex segregatus tum in Iove secundo qui est intellectualis anima dux mundi coniunctus. Neuter itaque Iuppiter cogitatione discurrit ambiguo more de rebus agendo, praesertim quia anima aeterno quodam intuitu suspicit universi ordinem in primo Iove tenetque firmum totamque mundi materiam subiectam habet et intrinsecus eam agitat ex una sui vita quasi ex uno cardine cuncta facillime versans: ut merito nihil eius actioni resistat, nulla incidat ambiguitas.

he sees and *vice versa*. It would be absurd to say that he gathers his knowledge of things from things themselves, for he effects things through a knowledge that precedes things. Moreover, he would not be able to grasp an infinite number of things if he went in pursuit of knowledge derived from the infinity of things. This being the case, he does not perceive the infinite number of things through his single Form in a manner different from that in which the sun through its single light perceives the innumerable rays shining forth from itself.

: X :

The order of the universe that gradually unfolds in matter is as a   10
whole, all at once, and immutable in both Jupiters: both in the first Jupiter which is the pure intellect and the separate craftsman of the world, and in the second Jupiter which is the intellectual soul and the leader joined to the world. Therefore, neither Jupiter runs discursively through thinking in an uncertain manner regarding things to be done, especially since the soul looks up with a certain eternal gaze at the order of the universe in the first Jupiter. Moreover, it holds that order stably, has the entire matter of the world subject to it, and activates it internally through its unitary life as though turning all things easily from a single hinge. Therefore, it is right that nothing should resist its action and no uncertainty befall it.

: XI :

11 Qua proportione singulae naturae partium singularum in quolibet
vivente dependent ab una quadam viventis totius natura communi,
eadem omnes mundanorum naturae ab una communi totius
mundi natura. Sicut ergo viventis cuiusque natura in se continens
naturaliter seminales partium effectuumque naturalium rationes
nec laborat neque consultat in agendo neque transmutatur dum
diversa producit—praesertim quoniam agit ex intimis nec ex multis velut partibus inchoat opus sed ex uno velut omnium cardine
cuncta derivat—, ita neque natura mundi consultat in opere vel
laborat vel permutatur, quippe cum sic ad opus se suum habeat
sicut naturam particularem ad suum se modo dicebamus habere
atque etiam multo praestantius, praesertim quia instrumentum est
aeternae infinitaeque sapientiae ductum semper ad eadem vicissim
eodemque tenore totique materiae praesidet. Ars quin etiam
quando per habitum naturae similem denique agit, sine consul-
tatione vel electione vel attentione iam agit. Immo vero, si tunc ad
attentionem eiusmodi redeat, impeditur saepius et aberrat, quasi
attentio talis non pertineat ad naturam.

: XI :

It is according to the same proportion in which the individual na- II
tures of individual parts, in the case of each and every living being,
depend on a certain general nature of the entire living being, that
all the natures of worldly things depend on the one general nature
of the entire world. Therefore, just as the nature of each living
thing naturally containing in itself the seminal reasons of natural
parts and effects neither expends effort nor deliberates in acting
nor undergoes change while producing different things — especially
since it acts from within and does not begin a work from many
parts, as it were, but distributes all things from a single hinge of all
things, so to speak —, so similarly the nature of the world does not
deliberate in its work, neither expending effort nor undergoing
change, given that it relates to its own work as we have just said
that the particular nature relates to its own. Indeed, the nature of
the world relates to its work in this manner to a much greater degree, especially because it is an instrument of the eternal and infinite wisdom always led around to the same things and in the same
course, and because it presides over the whole of matter. Moreover, when an art finally acts through a condition similar to that
of nature, it now acts without deliberation, choice, or attentiveness; indeed, if it then returns to attentiveness of this kind, it is
more often impeded and goes astray, as though such attentiveness
did not pertain to nature.

: XII :

12 Cogitatio per plura deinceps ordine currens est motus aliquis absoluta notitia carens atque ob indigentiam veritatem sapientiamque appetens consummatam. Ideo discursio eiusmodi vel consultatio vel electio non pertinet ad mentem vel animam mundi rectricem possidentem ab aevo habitum sapientiae plenum et integram cum idearum tum rationum seminalium plenitudinem. Qua quidem plenitudine res futuras anticipat in praesentibus et quibus modis sint futurae discernit quarum ipsamet est opifex sola toti suae materiae dominans nec impedimentis obnoxia ideoque nec sollicita vel ambigua vel inquirens, sed natura sua omniformi universum sibi conformans. Cum vero haec ipsa natura sit intelligentia et voluntas, merito non consilio tractat mundi materias sed sapientia firma tum[6] naturaliter tum etiam voluntarie fabricante.

: XIII :

13 Mens divina idearum suarum sigillo imprimit formas animae mundi adeo vehementur ut non solum figuret supremum animae: id est, intelligentiam, sed etiam medium eius: id est, imaginationem, et usque ad infimum eius: id est, naturam, formarum notas inurat. Formae sive rationes rerum seminales in natura sunt ultima quaedam vestigia divinorum. Ideo cognitione carent, quamvis vita non careant, aguntque in materiam sicut ignis atque

: XII :

Thinking that runs successively through many things is a certain   12
motion that lacks absolute knowledge and, because of its indi-
gence, strives after complete truth and wisdom. Accordingly, discursiveness of this kind, or deliberation, or choice pertains neither
to the mind nor to the soul that governs the world and possesses
from eternity the full disposition of wisdom and an integral plenitude both of Ideas and of seminal reason-principles. By means of
this plenitude the soul anticipates future things in the present and
discerns in what ways there exist the future things of which it itself is the maker, being the only maker which masters the whole of
its matter and is not subject to impediments. Accordingly, this
soul is neither troubled, nor uncertain, nor questioning, but brings
the universe into conformity with itself by means of its omniform
nature. Indeed, since its very nature is intelligence and will, it
rightly handles the materials of the world not with deliberation
but with a stable wisdom, fashioning naturally and also voluntarily.

: XIII :

The divine mind impresses forms in the world-soul with the seal   13
of its Ideas so strongly that it not only shapes the highest part of
the soul: that is, the intelligence, but imprints marks of the forms
into its middle part: that is, the imagination, and right through to
its lowest part: that is nature. The forms or seminal reasons of
things of things in nature are certain last vestiges of divine things.
Therefore, they lack thought although they do not lack life. They
act upon matter in the manner of fire and similar things. Indeed,

similia: et artificiose quidem, quoniam sunt vivae quaedam expressiones divinae cuiusdam intelligentiae atque huius verba loquentis. Natura dum agit in materiam pati dicitur non a materia sed ab anima; anima vero non tam patitur a mente quam se agit ad ipsam.

: XIV :

14 Natura universalis: id est, vivifica quaedam virtus animae mundanae omnium plena seminum adest corporibus omnibus ex se genitis non tamquam qualitas quaedam his permixta factaque horum propria — sicut calor aeri —, sed tamquam actus animae quodammodo separatus separabiliterque praesens — sicut aeri lumen. Natura quidem se habet ad animam sicut lumen ad solem, forma vero materialis ad naturam sicut calor ad lumen ex lumine genitus in materia.

: XV :

15 Actio animae mundi intima non tempore transfigitur paulatim sed momento tota simul impletur. Extima vero: id est, processio quaedam virtutis illinc in mundum et ipse mundi actus temporis successione peragitur. Ipsa igitur propria huius animae actio non est in tempore sed tempus generat in materia.

they act in a craftsmanlike manner, since they are certain living expressions of a certain divine intelligence and the words of this intelligence giving utterance. While nature acts upon matter, it is said to be passive not to matter but to soul. However, soul is not as much passive to matter as it is active toward it.

: XIV :

Universal nature: that is, a certain enlivening power of the world-soul that is filled with all the seeds is present to all the bodies generated by it not in the manner of a certain quality blended with them and made a property of them — as heat is blended with air — but in that of an activity of the soul which is somehow separate and present in a separable way — as light is present to air. Nature is with respect to soul as light is to the sun, and material form with respect to nature as heat is to the light, the heat being generated in matter from the light. 14

: XV :

The innermost action of the world-soul is not accomplished gradually in time but is fulfilled all at once in a moment. However, its most external action: that is, a certain procession of power from there into the world, and the action itself of the world is carried out in the successivity of time. Therefore, the proper action itself of this soul is not in time but generates time in matter. 15

: XVI :

16 Formae rerum quae in materia distant inter se loco in anima mundi distant differentia tantum inter se formali. Item quae in materia priora sunt inter se tempore atque posteriora in anima solo quodam ordine discrepant quo aliis alia cedunt potius quam succedant. Est enim anima per essentiam omniformem ordo quidam specialis et firmus futuri ordinis universi exemplar pariter et effector. Et quantum in se est efficere potest simul omnia si materia posset simul omnia capere. Moveri quidem dicitur anima haec ad bonum qua ratione per mediam mentem ad illud appetendo convertitur; mens vero in bono quiescere quoniam nullo ad id medio utitur; mundus vero circa animam, immo intra animam, tempore volvitur. Plotinus in libro *De Tempore*, etsi non ponit tempus motumque in anima mundi superiore, ponit tamen in anima eiusdem inferiore: id est, in vestigio superioris atque natura, non quia formas acquirat ullas[7] vel amittat sed quia formae in ea quaedam quasi e somno statutis temporibus prodeunt in vigiliam.

: XVII :

17 In anima mundi non est ambigua consultatio temporalisque discursio quia quod optimum est in ea ab aevo semper ceteris suis viribus dominatur. Est tamen in nostra quoniam e multis partibus

: XVI :

The forms of things, which are in matter spatially distinguished   16
among themselves, differ among themselves in the world-soul with
a purely formal distinction. Likewise, things which are in matter
temporally prior and posterior among themselves are differentiated
in the soul only in a certain order where one yields to another
rather than takes its place. For the soul is through its omniform
essential being a certain specific and stable order which is the exemplar and likewise effector of the entire future order of the universe: to the extent that it is in itself it could accomplish everything simultaneously, if matter were able to receive everything in
simultaneity. This soul is said to move toward the Good in so far
as it reverts in striving toward it through a mind which mediates,
whereas the mind is said to rest in the Good on the grounds that
it does not put any mediator to use for this purpose. However, the
world revolves around the soul or rather revolves within the soul
in time. Plotinus in his book *On Time*,[3] although not placing time
and motion in the higher world-soul, does nevertheless place it in
the lower phase of the same soul: that is, in the trace of the higher
soul and in nature. He does this not because it gains or loses any
forms but because certain forms in it are awakened as though from
a dream at specific times.

: XVII :

In the world-soul there is neither changeable deliberation nor tem-   17
poral discursiveness because that which from eternity is best in it
always dominates its other powers. However, deliberation and
discursiveness are in our soul because, among our many parts and

viribusque nostris nunc una, nunc alia dominatur; item quia et
ignorantes sumus tum etiam quoniam plurimis indigemus, tum
denique quia plurimae nobis ab externis incidunt passiones. Vis in
nobis rationalis, etsi non est ipsa natura debilis ac etiam si non sit
caeca, tamen ab irrationali aliquando superatur et quia haec quieta
est, illa vero turbulenta, et quia haec est unica, illa vero multiplex.
Homo pessimus similis est populari gubernationi pessimae, minus
vero malus populari minus malae. Bonus optimatum gubernationi
optimus regno: pessimum forsan diceret aliquis similem esse ty-
ranno.

⁖ XVIII ⁖

18 Sicut ex sole micat lumen ab eo inseparabile quod non fit aeris
propria qualitas — sed a lumine generatur calor propria iam qualitas aeris —, sic ab anima nostra emicat vivificus actus qui non fit
quidem propria corpori qualitas sed generat vitale aliquid in corpore factum iam corpori proprium. Anima quidem substantia est
et vita, actus ille suus inseparabilis substantiale aliquid est et vivificum. Qualitas hinc tributa corpori accidentale quiddam est et
quasi vitale. Actum illum appellamus idolum animae in quo sensus
est vegetalisque natura; 'qualitatem' vero illam imaginem animae
nominamus et 'umbram.' Ex hac et corpore fit compositum in quo
voluptates doloresque sunt corporales quarum passionum sensus
ad idolum animamque perveniunt, passiones vero nequaquam.
Superior comparatio magis propria fuerit, si idolum animae ab

powers, now one and now another is dominant, and also because we are ignorant both because we lack very many things and also finally because many passions befall us from external things. The rational power in us, even if it is not weak in its very nature and also even if it is not blind, is nevertheless overcome at times by the irrational power, this occurring both because the rational power is tranquil and the irrational power disturbed and because the former is single and the latter multiple. The worst man is similar to the worst democratic government, a less bad man to a less bad democratic government. A good man is similar to the rule of the aristocrats, the best man to a kingdom. One might perhaps say that the worst man is similar to a tyrant.

꞉ XVIII ꞉

Just as a light shines forth from the sun that is inseparable from it, 18 because it does not become a proper quality of the air — heat rather being generated from light now as the proper quality of air —, so from our soul there shines forth a life-giving act which does not indeed become a quality proper to the body but generates something vital in the body which is now made the proper characteristic of the body. The soul indeed is a substance and a life, and its inseparable act is something substantial and life-giving, whereas the quality assigned from that source to the body is something accidental and *quasi*-vital. We call this act the *idolum* of the soul in which its sense and vegetative nature reside, whereas we name that image of the soul "quality" and "shadow." It is from this image and from the body that the composite being arises in which are the corporeal pleasures and sorrows, the sensing of these passions reaching the *idolum* and the soul, although the passions in no way do. The above comparison will be more proper if we compare the

anima non seiunctum comparaverimus radio visuali ab oculo non disiuncto. Qui si quando ab oculo rubente processerit, ruborem aspicienti procreabit in oculo cui similem esse dixeris umbram animae in corpore resultantem.

: XIX :

19 Passio dissolutiva vel voluptas instaurativa non fit in sensu et anima sed in corpore per animae praesentiam quasi vitaliter iam affecto; in sensu autem et anima fit perceptio passionis illius minime patiens. Duobus quasi nodis anima cum corpore devincitur: unus quidem vergit ad animam: id est, vivificus eius actus emicans erga corpus, alter vero declinat ad corpus: id est qualitas ipsa quasi vitalis per hunc actum infusa corpori. Itaque corpus sic affectum atque sic alligatum animae ad animam pertinet fitque nostrum. Id ergo curamus et, quando motio huic incidit dissolutoria vel instauratoria, passionem hanc sensu percipientes ad ipsam vel vitandam inclinamur[8] vel prosequendam. Si in anima sentiente fieret peremptoria passio, et impediretur sensus atque iudicium et in quo membro praecipue sit passio non discerneret. Anima enim individua simul est in quolibet tota: si igitur patiatur ipsa, passio ubique totam animam occuparet.

idolum of the soul that as not separated to a visual ray not separated from the eye. If this at some point has proceeded from a reddened eye, it will for the one looking generate a redness in the eye, to which you will say that the shadow of the soul rebounding in the body is similar.

: XIX :

The passion that destroys and the pleasure that restores do not 19 arise in the sense or the soul but through the presence of soul in the body which is now as though vitally affected. However, the perception — which itself is not passive — of that passion arises in the sense and the soul. The soul is bound to the body as though with two ligatures, one of these being a tendency toward soul: that is, its life-giving act springing forth toward the body, the other being an inclination toward body: namely, the *quasi*-vital quality itself that is infused into the body by means of the life-giving act. Therefore, the body thus affected and thus bound to the soul belongs to the soul and becomes ours. We look after this and when a destructive or restorative motion falls upon it, perceiving this passion with sense, we either incline toward avoiding it or pursuing it. If a destructive passion were to arise in the soul *as it senses*, then the sense and judgment would be impeded and would not discern in what bodily part the passion is primarily. For the undivided soul is simultaneously present in each and every bodily part as a whole, so that if it were passive, the passion would everywhere take over the entire soul.

: XX :

20 Sicut in corpore levi est stimulus ad ascensum, in radice ad humorem, in folio ad calorem, sic in corpore per animam quasi vitaliter iam affecto insurgunt naturalia quaedam incitamenta: pro indigentia quidem ad impletionem, pro repletione ad evacuationem, pro alteratione nimia ad oppositam. Natura interim vegetalis quae vitalem in corpore affectionem genuit et conservat, patiente tali corpore, laborat dum conatur et agit intentius circa conservandam vel instaurandam affectionem in corpore naturalem. Quo quidem conatu dicitur concupiscentia illa quae exordiebatur in corpore tali adolescere in naturam. Dum vero natura haec agit obnixius, pervenit perceptio passionis in sensum atque hinc ad imaginationem atque iudicium.

: XXI :

21 Incitamentum ad concupiscenda oblectamenta corporea non oritur in ipsa animae virtute concupiscente sed in corpore tali: id est, per animam affecto vitaliter. Id sane coniicimus primo, quia, cum in corpore tali sit indigentia simul atque passio, merito appetitus hinc incitantur; secundo, quoniam, quatenus aliter se habet corpus tale pro differentia aetatum valetudinis habitus loci temporis, eatenus diversi surrepunt appetitus — virtus autem concupiscendi in anima permanens non permutatur — ; tertio, quia nonnunquam in tali corpore stimulus aliquis est ad aliquid ad quod non statim vis ipsa concupiscendi se dirigit; quarto, si etiam mox ad hoc intenderit,

: XX :

Just as there is a stimulus in a light body toward ascent, in a root   20
toward moisture, and in a leaf toward heat, so in a body now affected as though vitally through a soul certain natural incitements
rise up — toward replenishment in the case of lack, toward evacua-
tion in the case of surfeit, and toward its opposite in the case of
excessive alteration. Meanwhile, the vegetative nature which has
generated and preserves a vital affection in the body, with the com-
pliance of such a body, toils as it strives and acts more intently
toward the conserving or restoring of the natural affection in the
body. In this endeavor, that desire which began in such a body is
said to come to maturity in the nature. Moreover, while this nature acts strenuously, the perception of the passion arrives at sensation, and after that at imagination and judgment.

: XXI :

The incitement to desire for corporeal pleasures does not arise in   21
the desiring power itself of the soul but in a body of such a kind:
that is, one affected vitally by the soul. We certainly surmise that
this is the case first, because when there is both a lack and passion
in a body of this kind, rightly are the appetites aroused from that
source; second, because to the extent that such a body has different conditions according to difference of age, health, lifestyle,
place, and time, to the same extent different appetites steal upon
us — however, the power of desiring that remains in the soul is not
changed —; third, because sometimes in such a body there is a
certain stimulus toward something to which the power itself of
desiring does not immediately direct itself; fourth, if one also

non tamen animus semper hoc admittit; quinto, surgit saepe in corpore depravato stimulus ad aliquid naturae minime consentaneum: ut ad cinerem comedendum, quod natura corporeae habitudinis moderatrix non asciscit neque coaptat corpori neque sibi; denique, nec impletur nec evacuetur nec quomodolibet alteratur vis ipsa concupiscendi animae insita eiusve idolo, sed corpus tale. Hinc igitur non inde appetitus ad talia suscitantur.

: XXII :

22 Terra cum animalia generet sitque animalis mundani membrum, et necessarium et minime contemnendam. Est animal intellectuale atque divinum. Habetque sensum, nam in anima vis iudicaria viget quae coniuncta corpori suo percipit et iudicat sui corporis passiones: id autem est sentire. Quamquam Plotinus et multi unicuique elementorum suam tribuunt animam, poterit tamen aliquis forsan non absurde dicere sphaeras quidem caelestes, quia et immutabiles sunt et permanent in se ipsis invicem non confuse, animas inter se distinctas habere; elementa vero, quoniam compositi gratia instituta sunt et in se ipsis permutantur et invicem confundentur suntque in globum unum redacta numerisque competentibus in formam unam concorditer colligata, unicam cunctorum animam possidere, uni eorum materiae complexionique humorum quasi quattuor prorsus accommodatam, vigentem in aere et igne quamplurimum—per haec in aqua simul atque terra cuius

strives toward this something immediately, the soul however does not always allow it; fifth, there often rises up in a corrupted body a stimulus toward something not at all in agreement with nature: for example, the eating of ash which nature the governor of the corporeal condition neither takes up nor fits to the body or to itself. Finally, the power itself of desiring implanted in the soul or its *idolum*, is neither replenished nor evacuated nor altered in any way whatsoever. Only a body of a certain kind undergoes these processes. For these reasons, therefore, the appetite toward such things is not aroused from that source.

: XXII :

Since the earth generates living beings and is a constituent part of the world-animal, it is something necessary and not to be despised. It is an intellectual and divine animate being. It also has sensation, for there thrives within it a power of judgment which perceives things connected with its body and judges the passions of its body. This indeed amounts to sensing. Although Plotinus and many others attribute to each of the elements its own soul, someone will perhaps be able to say without absurdity that the heavenly spheres, because they are immutable and also remain in themselves without confusion with one another, also have souls that are mutually distinct; but that the elements — since they have been established for the sake of the composite, undergo change in themselves, are blended with one another, and are brought back to a single sphere in being bound concordantly into a single form with suitable numbers —, possess a soul that is single in all things. As though fully accommodated to the single matter and complexion of the humors in its quadriplicity, this soul flourishes to the highest degree in air and fire, and through these simultaneously in

22

virtute vitalem vim composita etiam illa reportent. In quibus elementorum portiones simili quadam ad totum proportione ligantur: in terra quidem et aqua animalia manifesta, in aere vero daemones habentes corpora connexa similiter, quamvis tenuia nobisque occulta.

: XXIII :

23 Sentire non est simpliciter cognoscere sensibilia sed per passiones sive impressiones quasdam factas vel a rebus sentiendis prope animam vel ab anima circa eas. Anima ab omni corpore separata, sicut in se vivit, sic ad se conversa per formas sibi insitas a divinis divina cognoscit perque illa velut principia comprehendit et sensibilia. Neque tamen hoc est sentire: nequit enim sentire tunc corporalia quia nullam habet cum eis proportionem per quam impressio ulla vel expressio inter hanc et illa fiat. Sed quando corpori coniuncta est, spiritu utitur ut instrumento quodam medio inter eam atque externa proportionem inter utraque faciente[9] in quo qualitates vel passiones extrinsecus venientes in speciem spiritalem puramque evadunt animaeque propinquam adeo ut per hanc anima formas excitet sensibilium in se latentes: quae quidem excitatio est sentire. Id vero totum diligentius in libro Theophrasti *De Anima* una cum Prisciano et Iamblicho declaramus.

water and earth, those things that are composite also gaining vital strength from its power. In composite things, the portions of the elements are bound to the totality by a certain similar proportion, there being in earth and water animate beings that are manifest, and in the air daemons having bodies similarly connected albeit more subtle and hidden from us.

: XXIII :

To sense is not to know *simpliciter* sensible things but to know   23
them through passions or certain impressions that have been made either by things that are sensed in proximity to the soul or by the soul in response to them. Just as it lives in itself, so does the soul separated from all body—having been turned toward itself through the forms inborn in it—know divine things through the divine. Through these divine things, as though causal principles, it also knows sensible things. However, this is not sensation, for it is not able at that point to know corporeal things, since it has no proportion to them through which any impression or expression between it and them could come about. But when it is joined to the body, it uses spirit as a kind of instrument that is mediate between itself and external things and makes a proportion between the two in which qualities or passions coming from outside turn into a spiritual and pure form that is close to soul to such an extent that the soul through this form stirs up the forms of sensible things that are hidden within it. This excitation is indeed sensation. We state the whole of this matter more carefully together with Priscian and Iamblichus in our book concerning Theophrastus' *On the Soul*.[4]

: XXIV :

24 Cum animam corpori coniunctam necessario consequatur sensus, animae sphaerarum stellarum mundi sentiunt. Mundus sentit per aliam sui partem vicissim partem aliam, item per totum partes. Praeterea totius habitudinem quasi quodam sui consensu sentit per⟨que⟩ amplissimam sphaeram praecipue quasi per oculum intus omnia contuetur. Si enim tu per oculum tuum, quoniam animatus est et diaphanus atque lucidus, quamplurima vides ac per radium eius ad caelestia procedentem caelestia suspicis, cur non et mundus per caelestem oculum suum vivum perspicuum lucidum radiosque suos ad omnia diffundentem omnia cernat?

: XXV :

25 Animae sphaerarum stellarumque et anima mundi humana vident atque audiunt sed interim talia se sentire minime sentiunt quoniam imaginatio ad quam talis animadversio pertinet intentissima semper est ad intelligentiarum notas in se fingendas. Etsi sentire se nostra forsan non animadvertunt, tamen precantibus benefaciunt qualicumque sensu et occulto quodam naturae consensu. Haec Plotini sententia est inter obiectiones ex textu mendoso. Dicet fortasse quispiam imaginationes caelestium animarum adeo efficaces esse ut vel intelligibilium notas derivent in sensibus atque ita

: XXIV :

Since sensation is a necessary consequence of soul's joining with 24
body, the souls of the spheres of the world's stars exercise sense.
The world senses one part of itself reciprocally through another
part and likewise the parts through the totality. Moreover, it
senses the condition of the totality as though with a certain cosensation of itself, and it beholds all things within it especially
through the most extensive sphere as though through an eye. For
if you through your eye, given that it is enlivened and transparent
and light-filled, see very many things, and if you look up at celestial things through its ray going forth to the celestials, then why
should not the world perceive all things through its celestial eye
which is living, transparent, light-filled, and diffusing its rays to
them all?

: XXV :

The souls of the spheres and stars and of the world-soul see and 25
hear human affairs. But in the meantime, they in no way sense
that they sense such things, since the imagination to which such
an observation pertains is always most intent on fashioning within
itself the traces of the intelligences. But even if perchance they do
not observe that they sense our affairs, they impart benefits to
those who pray with a sensation such as it is and a certain cosensation of nature. This opinion of Plotinus is presented as something to which he objects because of a faulty text. There will be
someone who will perhaps say that the imaginations of the heavenly souls are so efficacious that they either distribute the traces of
intelligibles into sensible things and thus sense internally in a cer-

intrinsecus quodammodo sentiant vel simul valeant tam sensibilia quam intelligibilia miris quibusdam modis imaginari.

: XXVI :

26 Sphaerae mundi stellaeque sensus habent et preces nostras exaudiunt. Caelestia visum quidem habent etsi specie differentem a nostro visu generali tamen natura convenientem: natura scilicet viva perspicua lucida. Dicuntur et auditum habere sed genere quodam ab auditu nostro longe diversum, quia videlicet audientium exaudientiumque more saepe voventium preces impleant. Inter omnes mundi partes quasi unius animalis membra dicitur esse communio quaedam vel contiguitas vel continuitas aut unio cuius quidem quinque fundamenta videntur. Primum est una omnium ubique materia; secundum concordia qualitatum nam, sicut elementa quamvis discordia quibusdam tamen proximis inter se qualitatibus concordia sunt, sic et rerum omnium gradus sive componantur ex elementis sive non componantur, quamvis inter se differentes, tamen concordibus vicissim terminis se contingunt; tertium spiritus ubique unus nam, sicut caelum unus est spiritus in excelsis, sic intra caelum unus inde spiritus vel caelestis omnino vel caelo simillimus omnibus est infusus quo et caelitus regantur omnia et anima mundi inferioribus quoque corporibus per spiritum coniungatur et omnia per hunc viventia coalescant: spiritum intellige spiritui nostro consimilem; quartum est una natura genitalis omnia fovens per spiritum sequentibus colligata; quintum

tain manner, or else that they are able to imagine both intelligible and sensible things in certain marvelous ways.[5]

: XXVI :

The spheres of the world and the stars have senses and they hearken to our prayers. Celestial things have sight even if this differs in its specific form from our sight albeit agreeing with it in its general nature: that is, as a living, transparent, and light-filled nature. They are also said to have hearing, albeit in a certain genus far different from our hearing, given that in the manner of hearers and listeners they often fulfill the requests of those praying. Among all the parts of the world being as though constituents of a single animate being, there is said to be a certain communion or contiguity — or continuity or union — of which there seem to be five foundations. The first foundation is the single matter of all things that is everywhere. The second foundation is the concord of qualities for, just as the elements although being discordant are however concordant among themselves in the proximity of their qualities, so the levels of all things whether composed or not from elements, although different among themselves, nevertheless touch one another with concordant boundaries The third foundation is the spirit that is everywhere single for, just as the heaven is a single spirit on high,[6] so within the heaven there is subsequently infused into all things a single spirit which is either wholly celestial or most similar to the heaven in order that all things might be governed from on high, that the world-soul might also be joined to lower bodies through spirit, and that all things might coalesce into vitality through it — you should understand this spirit as similar to our own. The fourth foundation is the single generative nature that fosters all things having been bound through spirit to the

447

anima mundi ubique una per naturam spiritui ceterisque connexa. Per hanc igitur unionem fundamentis quinque constantem vehementissimus quisque motus sive voventium pervenit ad caelestia sive caelestium pervenit ad voventes, praesertim si non solum anima mundi sed etiam divinae omnes sunt ubique praesentes, quamvis alicubi potius actiones suas quandoque declarent — quod velle videntur Plotinus Porphyriusque et Iamblichus. Praesentissimus autem singulis adest primus Deus omnium potentissimus imperioque latissimus. Anima terrae sensus omnes exercet per spiritum ibi quasi caelestem et caelestium radiis illustratum suaeque naturae subiectum et terrena regentem. Praeterea preces exaudit.

: XXVII :

27 Terram habere animam apparet ex plantis lapidibusque crescentibus quidem quamdiu terrae radicitus inhaerent, contra vero nequaquam. Sicut in animali dentes ungues pili, in plantis terrae inhaerentibus apparet virtutis genitalis effectus. Ipsa vero virtus[10] in eis propria nulla videtur esse, alioquin etiam avulsae per virtutem propriam pariter coalescerent. Vegetalis igitur ipsa virtus non tam est propria quam communis: scilicet in anima terrae. Item masculina virtus et feminina: id est, generandi et concipiendi quae in animalibus sunt discretae, coniunctae sunt in plantis — in eodem plantae corpore ob hoc dumtaxat quia natura plantae ita est inserta

things that follow it. The fifth foundation is the world-soul which, being everywhere single, is connected through nature to spirit and the other things. Therefore, through this union established in five foundations, every very powerful motion either reaches the celestial beings—when it is a motion of those praying—or reaches those praying—when it is a motion of the celestial beings. This is especially the case if not only the world-soul but also all the divine souls are everywhere present although they display there actions at some point more in a certain place—as Plotinus, Porphyry,[7] and Iamblichus[8] seem to hold. However, the first God himself who is most powerful of all and most broad in his authority is most present to individual things. The soul of the earth exercises all its senses through the spirit there which is as though celestial, illuminated by celestial rays, subject to its nature, and ruling earthly things. Moreover, it hearkens to prayers.

⁚ XXVII ⁚

That the earth has a soul is apparent from the fact that plants and stones grow as long as they inhere root-like in the earth but in no way grow in the opposite situation. Just as teeth, nails, and hair appear in an animal, so in plants fixed to the earth there appears the effect of the generative power. However, the power in them seems not to be anything proper to them, for if it were, they would become vigorous through their own proper power equally when torn from the earth. Therefore, the vegetative life itself is not as much proper as it is general: that is to say, in the soul of the earth. Likewise, the masculine and feminine power—the power of generating and conceiving—which are distinct in animals—are conjoined in plants, and in the same body of a plant, for this reason alone: namely, that the nature of the plant is thus implanted in

27

communi naturae sicut plantae corpus communi corpori. Vis autem masculina et feminina ad naturam pertinentes coniunctae sunt in universali natura, quamvis in aliis separatae: sicut visus ubi perfectus est vim perspicacem habet cum illuminante coniunctam, similiter intellectus. Sic Orpheus naturam mundanumque Iovem marem appellat et feminam, similiterque Mercurius. Hac ratione aeris animam Iovem Iunonemque appellant, animam terrae non solum Cererem atque Vestam sed etiam Plutonem cum Proserpina coeuntem. Coniunxit vero natura utrumque sexum in arbore quia nequit haec ad aliam coeundi gratia progredi quamvis alibi praevaleat alter: tunc oportet plantas appropinquare.

: XXVIII :

28 Vegetalis genitalisque natura animae in complexione humorum imprimit quoddam vitale vestigium ex quo corpus vitaliter evadit affectum in quo quidem sic affecto sunt passiones animalis corporeae perturbationumque principia. In toto quidem voluptas corporalis et dolor: in iecore potissimum concupiscendi principium, in praecordiis maxime principium irascendi: ibi enim nutritio viget et generatio, hic autem vigor igneus. Motus autem iracundiae aut quasi extrinsecus exordiuntur aut intrinsecus: extrinsecus ira quando, illata foris corpori passione, ad primum sensus motum fervet vigor igneus imaginationemque movet et per hanc provocat rationem; intrinsecus ira quando ratio vel imaginatio iniuriam excogitans humorem ferventem incitat. Libido quin etiam proclivitatem habet in corpore et quandoque ex ipso corpore seminibus

the general nature as the body of the plant is in the general body. The masculine and feminine powers pertaining to nature are conjoined in the universal nature although they are separated in other things—just as vision, when it is perfect, has a transparent power joined to the illuminator, there being a similar situation in the case of intellect. Thus, Orpheus[9] calls nature and the worldly Jupiter male and female, and so does Mercury.[10] By the same criteria, they call the soul of air both Jupiter and Juno, the soul of earth not only Ceres and Vesta but also Pluto in coition with Proserpine. Nature indeed joins the two sexes in a tree because this tree cannot proceed toward that one for purposes of coition, although elsewhere one of the sexes is more powerful—in which case, it is necessary for plants to be in proximity.

⁝ XXVIII ⁝

The vegetative and generative nature of the soul impresses a certain vital trace in the complexion of the humors as a result of which the body turns out to be affected in a vital manner. In the body thus affected are the passions of the corporeal animal and the beginnings of the emotions. In the body as a whole is corporeal pleasure and grief, the beginning of desire being primarily in the liver but the beginning of anger primarily in the spleen, for in the former flourish nutrition and generation but in the latter the fiery power. The motions of anger commence either *quasi*-externally or internally. The external anger commences when, a passion having been inflicted externally on the body, the fiery power seethes with respect to a primal motion of sense, moves the imagination, and through that provokes the reason. The internal anger commences when the reason or imagination in thinking up some unjust deed arouses the seething humor. Sensual desire indeed has its proclivity in the body and is sometimes supported by the body itself as

28

quasi turgido suscitatur, quandoque ex primo aspectu corpore in-
citato imaginationemque movente vel etiam rationem, aliquando
vero ex imaginatione vel etiam ratione oblectamentum excogitante
corpusque movente. Sunt autem concupiscendi et irascendi vires
quasi geminae, nam proclives ad libidinem sunt etiam propen-
siores ad iram atque vicissim: ut non immerito Martem cum Venere poetae coniunxerint.

: XXIX :

29　In corpore animato non solum est anima et actus vivificus animae
continuus—sicut luminoso lumen in corpus suum emicans—, sed
etiam est quoddam vitale vestigium, quasi sub lumine calor. Calorem dico naturalem spiritumque motibus aptum qui ad breve
restare potest in corpore post discessum animae et motum quendam edere. Nulla vita, nullum vivificum perit. Sed numquid hoc
vitale vestigium? Profecto ibi naturalis calor brevi esse desinit,
spiritus quoque naturalis cito resolvitur. Vitalis autem et animalis
⟨spiritus⟩ potest diutius superesse et sequi animam contentus ab
anima velut coagulo futurum quasi fermentum aerio corpori post
obitum congregando afficiendoque vitaliter. Sin autem in vestigio
hoc vitali cogites esse aliquid praeter calorem atque spiritum quod
ad animam lumenque eius se habeat non ut calor sed ut splendor
resultans ex lumine animae, id quidem non perit sed lumen abeun-
tis animae comitatur. Opinatur lumen nullo modo ab illuminato
sed tantum a luminoso pendere idque semper sequi una cum
splendore quomodolibet resultante. Tangit opinionem dicentem

though swollen with seeds, and at other times by the body aroused by a first glance and moving the imagination or also the reason, and at other times by the imagination or even the reason thinking up some pleasure and moving the body. Desire and anger are twin powers, so to speak, for in having proclivity to sensual desire these powers also have greater propensity to rage and *vice versa*. Therefore, not without justification have the poets made Mars cohabit with Venus.

∶ XXIX ∶

In an animated body there is not only a soul and a continuously life-giving act of soul—just as in a luminous body there is light shining forth into its body—but also a certain vital trace, as though heat underneath the light. I refer here to a natural heat and a spirit suited to motions, which for a short time is able to remain in a body after the departure of the soul and give rise to a certain motion. No life and nothing life-giving perishes. But does this vital trace perish? To be sure, the natural heat ceases to be there in a short time, and the natural spirit is quickly released. The vital and the animate spirit is able to survive longer and follows the soul, being sustained by the soul which is as though a coagulative principle gathering and vitally affecting something that will be after death as though a leaven for an aerial body. But if you think that there is in this vital trace something besides heat and spirit which relates to the soul and its light not as heat but as a brightness rebounding from the light of the soul, this indeed does not perish but accompanies the light of the departing soul. Plotinus thinks that light depends in no way on the thing illuminated but only on the luminous thing, and that it follows the latter together with a brightness rebounding in all directions. He touches on the

29

omnium colorum vires et quasi flosculos esse in lumine; neque
perire sed latere potius et iterum apparere; item lumina quae videntur extingui non disperdi sed in perspicuum aeris lucidumque
eius occultum nobis obire; denique quicquid in nobis vitae inferioris est nostram sequi superiorem neque perire vestigiumque vitale
in corpore servari ab anima — vel propria vel communi — saltem ad
tempus postquam propria deseruerit.

: XXX :

30 Stellae visum auditumque habent, memoria vero non indigent.
Praeterea preces exaudiunt. Sicut qui corpus suum opportune lumini solis exponit naturaliter inde fovetur, ita qui animum spiritumque suum per votum superiorum influxibus applicat ubique
praesentibus beneficia[11] inde reportat naturaliter influentia. Antiqui aliqui praeter solem stellas etiam adorabant; plurimi vero —
praesertim Platonici atque id genus philosophi — solum adorabant
inter caelestia solem. Orationem ad solem composuit Iulianus[12] et
Iamblichus. Solem Plato filium et imaginem summi Dei visibilem
appellavit; solem Socrates orientem salutans ecstasim saepe patie-
batur; orienti soli Pythagorici hymnos lyra canebant. De cultu
quidem solis illi viderint. Deus certe in sole posuit tabernaculum
suum.

opinion stating that the powers of all colors and as though their blossoms are in light, and that these do not perish but rather lie hidden and then reappear; that the lights which are seen to be extinguished are not destroyed but go down into the transparency of air and into its lucidity which is hidden from us; and finally, that whatever there is of our lower life follows our superior life and does not perish, and that the vital trace in the body is preserved by the soul — either the individual or the general soul — at least for a time after the individual soul has deserted the body.

: XXX :

The stars have sight and hearing, albeit having no need of memory. Moreover, they hearken to our prayers. Just as a person who exposes his body to the sun at an opportune moment is naturally warmed by it, so a person who connects his mind and spirit through prayer to the emanations that are everywhere present of higher beings naturally obtains benefits flowing down. Some of the ancients worshipped also the stars in addition to the sun. However, most of them — and especially the Platonists and philosophers of that kind — only worshipped the sun among the celestial beings. Julian and Iamblichus[11] composed orations to the sun. Plato called the sun the son and visible image of the supreme God. Socrates often experienced ecstasy when greeting the rising sun. The Pythagoreans chanted hymns with the lyre to the rising sun. Regarding the worship of the sun let them think what they like. But God has certainly placed his tabernacle in the sun.

: XXXI :

31 Actiones aliae quidam naturales sunt, aliae autem artificiosae. Naturales aut sunt universi mundi erga partes suas aut partium ad universum aut partium vicissim erga partes. Artificiosae actiones vel desinunt in opus arte constructum, ut statuaria in statuam, vel ad opus naturae ministrant, ut medicina agricultura magia cum qua similitudinem quandam habet oratoria persuasio et poetica musicaque lenocinia. Actiones caelestium ad inferiora non solum fiunt per calorem et aliam elementis similem qualitatem sed per vires quasdam a notis qualitatibus longe diversas. Quod enim differentiae in nobis morum ingeniorum professionum fortunarum per caelestia vel fiant vel portendantur non potest referri ad differentias qualitatum caelestium similes elementis. Neque etiam consilio et electione caelestia in nos agunt singula, alioquin et illorum animi solliciti semper erunt et cottidie ministri malorum.

: XXXII :

32 Caelum in omnia haec inferiora agit non consilio quodam eligente talia vel taliter agere neque tantum corporeis qualitatibus: scilicet calefaciendo, rarefaciendo, vel contra. Sed naturalibus quibusdam vegetalis animae viribus, similibus quibusdam viribus inter consilium et corporeas qualitates quasi mediis, anima nostra corporis humores et membra eorumque figuras et qualitates cottidie reficit.

: XXXI :

Some actions are natural and some artificial. Natural actions are 31
either those of the entire world toward its parts, or of the parts to
the entire world, or conversely of the parts to one another. Artificial actions are either completed in a work constructed by art: for
example, the act of statue making in a statue, or else attend to a
work of nature: for instance, medicine, agriculture, and magic to
which rhetorical persuasion and poetical and musical panderings
bear a certain similarity. The actions of the celestial bodies on the
lower come about not only through heat and another quality similar to the elements but through certain powers very different from
qualities that are known. The fact that differences of customs,
abilities, professions, and fortunes among us either come about or
are portended through the heavenly bodies cannot be referred to
differences of qualities of the heavenly bodies similar to elements.
Moreover, the heavenly bodies do not produce individual effects in
us through deliberation and choice. If that is the case, their souls
will always be troubled and also the agents of evil every day.

: XXXII :

The heaven acts on all these lower things neither by means of a 32
certain deliberation choosing to act on such things and in such a
manner nor by means of corporeal qualities alone: that is, by heating, moistening, rarefying, or the opposite. But by means of certain natural powers of the vegetative soul, certain similar powers
being as though mediate terms between deliberation and corporeal
qualities, our soul renews the humors and members of the body
together with their configurations and qualities on a daily basis.

Cum mundus sit unum animal, omnia corporea duobus modis sunt partes mundi: primo, quia singula corpora sunt quaedam universi portiones; secundo, quia in quolibet corpore est et ipsa mundi anima et propria quaedam huius animae virtus efficax[13] dos huic corpori distributa. Quatenus ergo corporea singula sunt animalis mundani membra, facile tum a toto tum invicem patiuntur, quippe cum etiam quae loco inter se distare videntur sint propinqua ob mirabilem naturae unius communionem.

⁘ XXXIII ⁘

33 Totus mundus est animal unum ratione musica saltans et saltando consequenter una secum omnia varians. Anima mundi habet in sua intelligentia cogitatione imaginatione natura descriptas quasi praesentes futuras omnes revolutiones mundi secundum musicas earum proportiones, item designatos habet omnes eventus qui vel revolutiones necessario comitantur in caelis vel quomodocumque sub caelo consequuntur easdem. Ad eiusmodi musicam designationem, quasi ad cantilenam sonorumque concentus, per affectum sequuntur revolutiones in mundo quasi gestus quidam arte tripudiantis. Ipse quidem saltator intentione spectat primo insitam sibi musicam, deinde per hanc membrorum mundanorum revolutiones, tertio per eas prospicit quodammodo quae inde sequuntur vel saltem significantur. Potest et sapiens aliquis quasi musicus praevidere qualia ubique quales sequuntur revolutiones mundi, sicut quales gestus membrorum ad quales sequantur soni partes —

Since the world is a single animate being, all corporeal things are parts of the world in two ways: first, because individual bodies are certain portions of the universal body; second, because in each and every part of the body both the soul itself of the world and a certain efficacious power of this soul is distributed as a gift to this body. To the extent that individual corporeal things are members of the animate being that is the world, they have a ready passivity both to the totality and to one another. This is also because things that seem to be separate from one another in place are close on account of the wonderful mutual participation in a single nature.

: XXXIII :

The entire world is a single animate being dancing according to a 33 musical reason-principle, and by means of the dancing consequently changing all things together with itself. The world-soul has delineated in its intelligence, thinking, imagination, and nature — according to their musical proportions — all the future cycles of the world as though these are present. Likewise, it has all the events marked out which either the cycles in the heavens necessarily accompany or which below the heaven somehow follow those cycles. In order to represent a music of this kind — as though a melody and harmonies of sounds —, certain gestures of a man dancing according to art follow the cycles in the world in a sympathetic way. The dancer himself directs his gaze first, at the music implanted in him and then, through that music at the cycles of the members of the world. Third, through those members he somehow foresees the things that follow from these cycles or are at least indicated by them. A certain wise man, as though a musician, can foretell what kind of things everywhere follow what kind of cycle of the world, just as he can foretell what kinds of gestures of the

praeterquam ubi vel inepta superis materia non omnino cedit vel nimis debilis patitur supra modum, sicut et arbitrium hominis potest non sequi caeli tenorem et vicissim humana debilitas ultra modum inde pati. Denique sicut in chorea passiones quasdam membrorum vel aliorum contingunt ultra gestus artificiosos, sic et similia quaedam ex tripudio mundi contingunt.

: XXXIV :

34 Corpus nostrum tamquam mundi pars sequitur fatalem mundi circuitum, anima quoque, quatenus obsequitur corpori: potest tamen et magnanimitate passiones corporis parvi pendere et eas arte declinare vel levare. In variis mundi sphaeris partibusque earum et stellis naturaliter variae sunt virtutes. Sunt et virtutes variae in differentibus ibi figuris ex stellis invicem firmiter constitutis: virtutes inquam firmae. Oriuntur et differentes deinceps virtutes in differentibus figuris quae inter stellas perpetua motus diversitate contingunt. Ad has utique virtutes tam naturarum quam figurarum consequuntur quae sub luna fiunt: partim quidem velut inde necessario facta—ceu qui saltantis manu capti corripiuntur—, partim vero tamquam liberius consonantia—velut qui ad sonum choreamque gestiunt et canunt saltantque libenter. Figurae quidem caelestes haec inferiora significant, naturae vero una cum figuris

members follow what kinds of parts of sound. This occurs except where a matter as unsuitable does not wholly yield to the higher things or where as too weak it is affected beyond due measure — just as the choice of a man is able not to follow the course of the heaven and conversely human weakness suffers beyond due measure the effects of that course. Finally, just as in dancing certain passions of the members or of other things happen beyond the artificial gestures, thus certain similar things arise from the dancing of the world.

⦂ XXXIV ⦂

Our body, as though a part of the world, follows the fatal circuit 34 of the world, and our soul, likewise, to the extent that it obeys the body. However, it can also through its greatness of soul also treat the passions of the body as having little worth, avoiding or alleviating them through art. In the various spheres of the world and their parts and in the stars there are naturally various powers. There are also various powers in the different figures there constituted by the stars' stable interrelations, these powers being indeed stable. After these, different powers arise in the different figures which occur among the stars in the perpetual diversity of their motion. Indeed, following upon these powers — which are as much those of natures as those of figures — are the things that come to be below the moon. These are partly as though made necessarily from there — being like those people who are captivated by the ecstatic dancer's hand —, but also partly as though more freely in consonance — being like those who posture, sing, and dance freely in relation to his song and dance. These celestial figures signify lower things, and natures produce effects together with the figures

efficiunt pro dispositione materiae. Multa vero figurae significant quae non caelitus sed aliunde fiunt.

: XXXV :

35 Anima mundi in ipsa idearum serie universum hoc ab aevo contemplata una semel communi elegit electione totum mundi cursum, ita fore comprobans. Interea natura vegetalis eius imago sibi subdita absque electione sic totum transfigit mundi cursum. Singulae quoque sphaerarum stellarumque animae se similiter habent ad Deum atque mundum, et usque adeo cum anima mundi tum voluntate tum natura consentiunt ut omnes in mundo actiones earum recte possint animae mundanae actio nominari. Omnes ergo res corporeae sunt animalis mundani partes; omnes rerum naturalium actiones sunt animalis huius motus; omnes revolutiones mundanae sunt gestus et quasi sermones eiusdem. Nihil vel in eo vel ex eo est aut fit fortuitum: ad rationes enim omnia referuntur huic insitas seminales vel altius exemplares. Singula igitur vel ordine proficiscuntur vel statim rediguntur in ordinem. Sol mundi cor plus admodum vitae naturalis habet atque affert quam ceterae mundi partes: in hoc igitur nonnulli ipsam mundi animam posuerunt per radios eius usquequaque diffusam. Virtutes rerum naturalium omnes primo sunt in seminalibus rationibus naturae communis. Hinc mox traducuntur in mundi sphaeras earumque figuras tam volubiles quam firmas; hinc in rerum

in accordance with the disposition of matter. Moreover, the figures signify many things which arise not from the heaven but from somewhere else.

: XXXV :

The world-soul, having contemplated this universe from eternity   35
in the series itself of the Ideas, has once chosen the entire course of the world in a single general act of selection, thus assenting to what will come to be. Meanwhile, the vegetative nature which is the image of soul and subordinate to it thus transfixes the entire course of the world without any act of selection. Also, the individual souls of the spheres and stars have the same relation toward God and the world, being so concordant with it both in will and in nature that all their actions in the world can rightly be called the action of the world-soul. Therefore, all corporeal things are parts of the animate being that is the world. All the actions of natural things are the motions of this animate being. All the world's revolutions are its gestures and as though the utterances of the same animate being. Nothing either in it or from it is or becomes fortuitous, for all things are referred back to reason-principles implanted in it as seminal or higher up as exemplary. Therefore, individual things come forth from it in order or are immediately brought back to order. The sun that is the heart of this world has and imparts much more natural life than do the other parts of the world. Consequently, some placed the world-soul itself in the solar body, having been diffused everywhere through its rays. All the powers of natural things are primarily in the seminal reason-principles of the general nature. From here they are immediately transmitted to the spheres of the world and to their figures: both the revolving and the stable ones. From here

naturalium species in quibus inde latent vires super elementa mirabiles atque ex ipsis caeli figuris in figuras inferiores vires quoque mirifice. Habent et vultuum[14] nostrorum figurae proprias quasdam alliciendi vel deterrendi virtutes: unde appareat vim propriam figuris non minus quam coloribus inesse posse.

: XXXVI :

36   Sicut vegetalis vita nostra singulis membris — quamvis aliis aliter se impertit viresque articulis alias aliis mirabiles inserit —, sic multoque excellentius una mundi anima omnes — licet aliter alias — vegetat mundi partes; atque ipsa innumerabilium mirabiliumque plena virtutum, quasi gravida tumensque, exundat in totum: singula quidem sed praecipue superiora mundi membra viribus ubique mirificis implens quas nec elementares vires aemulari ullo modo valent neque nos effari facile possumus. Sunt autem eiusmodi vires quasi propriae propagines quaedam animae mundanae per corporis universi membra diffusae. Quas quidem vota supplicium operaque magorum conciliare sibi et quasi per insitionem quandam inserere quandoque possunt.

they are transmitted to the specific forms of natural things in which are thereupon concealed amazing powers over the elements and also—as derived from the figures of heaven themselves—powers over lower figures in a wonderful way. Moreover, the figures of our facial expressions have certain powers proper to them of attracting or repelling: from which it appears that a proper power can be present as much in figures as in colors.

: XXXVI :

Just as our vegetative life enlivens our individual members, albeit imparting itself in various ways to various parts and implanting different amazing powers in different limbs, so much more and so much more excellently does the single world-soul enliven all the parts of the world, albeit in different ways in different places. The world-soul itself which is full of innumerable and wonderful powers, as though being pregnant and tumescent, overflows into the totality, filling individual members of the world but primarily the higher ones everywhere with wonderful powers. Elemental powers cannot in any way equal them, and we cannot easily express them. The powers of this kind are as though certain proper offshoots of the world-soul diffused through the members of the universal body. The prayer, entreaty, and operation of magicians can adapt these powers for their use, implanting them—as though through a certain grafting—at various times.

: XXXVII :

37 Sicut membra nostra tam interna quam externa vires ad actionem atque motum habent ab anima nostra, sic omnia mundi membra ab ipsa mundi anima. Mirabiles supra naturam elementarem actiones in lapillis metallis herbis animam esse testantur in mundo a qua minima quaeque vires ubique maximas habeant. Item quod exiguus ignis tam procul agat, tam facile cuncta in se assumat, quod luceat, habet ab anima—immo, singula quod aliquid generent. Et ipse ordo motuum atque formarum ab anima regitur contrariorumque connexio et motus caelestis machinae tam ingentis in quam velut animae proximam genitalis anima potissimum propagatur: per hanc in ignem per hunc in aerem per hunc in cetera. Atqui genitalis haec mundi vita non electione quasi practica nec actionis suae animadversione in haec, sed ita naturaliter agit ut sol et ignis—immo ut in nobis anima vegetalis. Naturalis autem actio est antiquior quam electio practica, quamvis contemplativa et universalis ipsa excelsae mentis electio antiquior sit quam actio naturalis.

: XXVIII :

38 Intellectualis anima mundi et sphaerae cuiuslibet atque stellae subiunctam habet vegetalem vitam suo infusam corpori per quam non electione sed naturaliter generantur moventurque sequentia et be-

: XXXVII :

Just as our members, both internal and external, have powers to- 37
ward action and motion through our soul, so do all the members
off the world have them through the world-soul. The marvelous
actions above their elemental nature in gems, metals, and herbs
prove that there is a soul in the world through which each smallest
thing everywhere has the greatest powers. Again, that a small fire
acts from such a distance, so easily consumes all things in itself,
and shines: these things it has through soul. Indeed, the ability of
individual things to generate something is similarly derived. The
very order of motions and forms is governed by soul, and likewise
the connection of opposites and the motion of such a great celestial mechanism. The generative soul is propagated primarily into
this mechanism which is as though in proximity to soul, and
through this mechanism into fire, through fire into air, and through
air into the rest. However, this generative life of the world acts on
such things neither in choosing, as though in a practical sense, nor
in consciousness of its action. Rather, it acts as naturally as do the
sun and fire, and indeed as naturally as does the vegetative soul in
us. Natural action is more primordial than is practical choice, although the contemplative and universal choice itself of the superior mind is more primordial than is natural action.

: XXXVIII :

The intellectual soul of the world and of each and every sphere 38
and star has a subjoined vegetative life infused into its body, and
through this life subsequent things are generated and moved not
by choice but naturally, and benefits are conferred on things capa-

neficia capacibus conferuntur. Quicquid usquam ex eiusmodi vita profluit vitale hinc affluit et beneficum, sed evadit alicubi noxium vel quia materia non est capax—sicut infirmus ad solis lumen se habet atque calorem—vel quia ex diversorum mixtione aliud quiddam inde resultat—ut aureum solis lumen in nube rubrum evadit et viride atque fuscum. Vegetalis vita nostra vitae superius dictae admodum est conformis; similiter spiritus noster radiis illius tam occultis quam manifestis omnia penetrantibus. Evadit etiam longe cognatior quando erga vitam illam vehementer afficimur consentaneum illi beneficium exoptantes atque ita spiritum nostrum in illius radios transferentes amore, praesertim si cantum et lumen adhibemus odoremque numini consentaneum—quales Orpheus hymnos mundanis numinibus consecravit—; item caelo incensi turis odorem aetheri ferventem crocum stellis aromata soli tus et manna lunae et naturae aromata Saturno et Iovi styracem Neptuno myrrham Mercurio tus. Spiritus enim per affectum cantum odorem lumen cognatior effectus numini uberiorem haurit illinc influxum.

: XXXIX :

39 Super vegetalem mundi vitam quae et natura et rerum naturalium seminarium appellatur est intelligentia omnia latius ordinans quam natura. Ex intentione seminarii est quaecumque ex ipso nascuntur formosa nasci efficaciaque ad motum, praeterea solito quodam et dumtaxat naturali ad suum profectum tenore proce-

ble of receiving them. Whatever flows forth at any time from a life of this kind flows from there as vital and beneficial, although elsewhere it comes to be harmful, either because matter is not capable of receiving it—just as a sick person reacts to the sun's light and heat—or else because something else rebounds from there through the blending of different things—just as the golden light of the sun comes to be reddish, green, and tawny in a cloud. Our vegetative life is very much in conformity with the one mentioned above, and likewise our spirit with the latter's rays penetrating all things in both a hidden and a manifest way. Our spirit can become even more akin to these rays when we are strongly disposed toward that life, pray for a benefit in agreement with it, and thus transfer our spirit into its rays through love. This is especially so if we apply chant, light, and fragrance harmonious with its divinity—it was hymns of this kind that Orpheus consecrated to the worldly spirits—; and also if we apply to the heaven the odor of burned frankincense, to the aether boiling saffron, to the stars spices, to the sun frankincense, to the moon manna, to nature spices, to Saturn and Jupiter storax, to Neptune myrrh, and to Mercury frankincense. For the spirit, affected through disposition, chant, fragrance, and light becomes more akin to the divinity and imbibes a more abundant emanation from that source.

: XXXIX :

Above the vegetative life of the world that is called both nature   39 and the seedbed of natural things is the intelligence that orders all things more broadly than does nature. It is according to the intentionality of the seedbed that whatever is born from it is born well-formed and efficacious toward motion. and furthermore that it should progress in a certain habitual and purely natural course to

dere. Quod ergo deformia debiliaque contingant ob materialem quandam necessitatem et alia interimantur ab aliis impedianturque solitum peragere ordinem et crescere suumque tempus implere ac suo vicissim semine alia propagare: id inquam totum ex nulla est intentione naturae. Neque igitur id contingens ordinari potest intentione naturae cum sit eius ordini inimicum. Ordinandum tamen est: omnia enim sub uno rediguntur in unum. Per intelligentiam igitur natura superiorem accidentia eiusmodi in ordinem revocantur, per eandem arbitrii quoque liberi motus et effectus pro meritis ordine disponuntur. Anticipantur nostrae preces, ut ait Iamblichus, et implentur vobis interim libere obscrantibus, nec divina voluntate mutata nec rerum ordine perturbato. Dispositio itaque rerum latior est in mente quam in ipsa natura: in mente inquam non[15] solum prima sed etiam mundanae caelestisque animae.

40   Dispositionem vero rerum in mente prima 'legem Saturni' Plato nominat in *Politico.* eandem in intellectu animali 'legem' appellat 'Iovis' in *Politico* atque *Legibus,* eandem in natura 'legem fatalem' vocat in *Politico* et *Timaeo.* Quoniam vero ubique firma est inevitabiliterque procedit in *Phaedro* nominat 'Adrastiae legem.' Tum vero, quoniam simul cum lege liberam conservat efficaciam animorum, in *Legibus* ait in animis quidem exsistere principium actionum in lege vero terminum; atque in *Phaedro Timaeoque* legis edictum introducit semper cum condicione quadam hunc in modum: si anima perpetraverit talia quaedam, reportet et talia. Quod autem inquit in *Timaeo* animas non prius fatales audivisse leges quam

its proper outcome. Therefore, it is because of a certain material necessity that things arise as ill-formed and feeble, that some things are killed by others, and that they are prevented from accomplishing their habitual course, from growing, from completing their own time span, and from procreating with their own seed other individuals in due succession, all this indeed resulting from no intentionality of nature. Therefore, such a contingent thing cannot be ordered according to the intentionality of nature since it is incompatible with nature's ordering. However, it *is* ordered in the sense that all things are reduced to unity beneath the one. Therefore, through intelligence superior to nature accidents of this kind are called back to order, and through the same intelligence the motions of free choice and consequences in accordance with deserts are arranged in an orderly way. As Iamblichus says, our prayers are anticipated and fulfilled, although we pray freely in the meantime, there being neither change in the divine will nor disturbance of the order of things.[12] Therefore, the arrangement of things is broader in the mind than it is in nature—meaning by this not only the primal mind but also that of the world and of the heaven.[13]

Plato in the *Statesman*[14] names the arrangement of things in the primal mind the "law of Saturn," calling the same arrangement in the intellect of soul the "law of Jupiter" in the *Statesman*[15] and the *Laws*,[16] and the same arrangement in nature the "fatal law" in the *Statesman*[17] and the *Timaeus*.[18] Since it is everywhere stable and comes forth inevitably, he names it the "law of Adrastia" in the *Phaedrus*.[19] Then indeed, since Plato maintains a free ability of souls in simultaneity with the law, he says in the *Laws*[20] that the beginning of actions is in souls but the end of actions in the law; and in the *Phaedrus*[21] and *Timaeus*[22] introduces a decree of the law that is always together with a certain condition in this manner: namely, that if the soul has committed deeds of such and such a kind, then it will obtain such and such recompenses. However, when he says in the *Timaeus*[23] that souls have not heard the laws of

40

vehiculis iungerentur, declarat animas ex se liberas esse, fatum vero ad corpora pertinere. Pertinet vero fatalis necessitas non solum ad corpus sed ad vitam quoque corpoream. Qualis utique vita in mundano caelestique corpore latens non electione libera sed necessitate fatali vim suam ad inferiora diffundit; quae quidem vis emicat inde benefica etiam a Marte vel Saturno stellisque similibus.

41 Potest tamen magus maleficam reddere non aliter atque ille qui e concavo speculo collectos solis radios coniicit in oppositum atque comburit. Si quis enim decem Saturni vires mundo nobisque necessarias atque sparsas in materiis decem una coniunctis cogat in unum, perdet eum—videlicet non toleraturum—in cuius perniciem congregaverit; innocens interim est Saturnus. Venus varias fecunditatis conciliationisque proprietates variis passim rebus inseruit: magus igitur materias eligens omnes virium eiusmodi quomodocumque capaces adhibensque regnante Venere collectas in unum homini huic et illi immoderatos inter eos conflat amores, Venere non peccante. Dotes quoque Iovis similiter accumulat aliis, Iovio interim animali non advertente. Ioviale vero animal et Saturnium et Venereum appellamus stellae corpus vegetali virtute vivium: qualia quidem corpora excogitavit Pythagoras ubi ait invocatos deos influere nobis quadam necessitate compulsos.

fate until they are joined to vehicles, he shows that souls are free in themselves and that it is to bodies that fate pertains. Indeed, fatal necessity pertains not only to the body but also to the corporeal life. This kind of life concealed in the world's body and the body of the heaven diffuses its power to lower things not by a free choice but by a fatal necessity, this power indeed springing forth as a beneficial one thereupon also from Mars or Saturn and similar stars.

However, a magician can render this power maleficent in a 41 manner not dissimilar to that in which a man directs the rays of the sun collected in a concave mirror in the opposite direction and causes a fire. For if anyone were to direct the ten powers of Saturn that are necessary with respect to the world and to us and in a dispersed state, having collected them in ten matters, toward one man, he would kill that man for the purpose of whose destruction he had collected them — the latter being unable that is, to bear the powers gathered — although Saturn is harmless in the meantime. Venus has everywhere implanted various properties of fecundity and conciliation in various things. Therefore, a magician who selects all the matters that are in whatsoever manner receptive of such powers and, when Venus is in the ascendant, applies them after collection into a unity to this and that person, will stir up immoderate loves between them, Venus not being the sinner. The magician similarly amasses the gifts of Jupiter for other men, the Jovian animate being meanwhile not paying any attention. We call the "Jovian animate being," the "Saturnian animate being," and the "Venereal animate being" the body of a star enlivened by the vegetative power. Pythagoras formed a conception of such bodies with his utterance to the effect that the gods, when invoked, flow down upon us compelled by a certain necessity.

: XL :

42 Quodlibet animalis membrum vim habet ad portionem nutrimenti propriam attrahendam et cor ad aromata, iecur ad dulcia,
venae ad sanguinem, ad spiritum arteriae, ad semen vero testiculi.
Sunt et medicinae quae certos asciscant humores et membra quaedam petere videantur. Eadem est animalis mundani condicio in
quo passim dispersa sunt quae rem hanc aut illam ad se rapere
possint, si congregata in unum admoveantur. Per sua enim retia vel
illicia homines, per sua equi et per propria similiter homines, Hi
vel illi clam illaqueari possunt, quemadmodum oblectamentis
formarum atque musicae palam inescantur. Denique sicut ferro
paleisque compertum est quod trahat magnes—scilicet atque suci-
num—, sic diligens et fortunatus perscrutator inveniet escam
omnibus attrahendis. Singulis enim animalis mundani membris
coaguli vis est insita connectens in unum cuncta vivum: temperate
quidem suapte natura intemperate vero quotiens undique congregata in aliquid transferatur, mundo nec patiente interim neque
peccante. Sunt et differentes in hoc animali vires inter se a natura
disiunctae quae frequenter a mago coniunctae et in membrum hoc
coniectae vel illud violentius agant atque perdant, in his (ut dixi)
non peccante mundo.

43 Nominat Plotinus quattuor quibus mirabilis insit virtus: scilicet
qualitates specierum occultas et figuras concentusque et vota,

: XL :

Each and every bodily part of an animal has a power for attracting   42
its proper portion of nutriment: the heart having a power with
respect to spices, the liver with respect to sweet things, the veins
with respect to blood, the arteries with respect to spirit, the testi-
cles with respect to semen. There are also medicines which appropriate certain humors and seem to seek certain bodily parts. There
is an identical condition in the world-animal in which things are
everywhere distributed able to attract strongly to themselves this
and that, if the latter are brought together into a unity and moved
toward them. For men are attracted through their own nets and
snares. Horses are attracted through things associated with them,
and men similarly by things belonging to them. And both men
and horses can be secretly ensnared, just as they are enticed openly
by the amusements of forms and music. Finally, just as it has been
discovered in the case of iron and filings that the magnet attracts — amber having the same property, indeed —, so a careful
and lucky investigator will find the bait for attracting all things.
For in the individual bodily parts of the world-animal there is implanted a power of coagulation joining all things into one living
being — in a tempered manner according to its own nature but in
an untempered manner whenever, as collected from all sides, it is
transferred into something, the world in the meantime not suffering or erring. There are also different powers in this animal
which, disconnected from one another by nature, are often connected by the magician. Put together with respect to this or that
bodily part they act upon it more violently and destroy it, the
world not erring (as I have said) in these activities.

Plotinus names four things in which the wonderful power is   43
present: namely, the hidden qualities of specific forms, figures,
chants, and prayers, for those qualities are certain offshoots of the

quippe cum qualitates illae propagines quaedam sint virium in vita mundi latentium et figurae concentusque inferiores caelestium figuras saepe referant et concentus; votum vero motus quidam est animae nostrae[16] vehemens erga numen quod obsecramus. Si contrito sulfure subtilissimum eius pulverem proiicias versus ignem, ignis in longum producta flamma se pulveri huic protinus applicabit. Similiter qui stellam obsecrat opportune paratus ad stellam spiritum suum proiicit in radios stellae—manifestos pariter et occultos—ubique diffusos atque vivificos per quos vitalia sibi stellae munera vindicat. Denique, sicut omnes stellae fixae connexae sunt firmamento, sic omnium stellarum numinumque mundanorum connexae sunt vitae mundanae cui et connexa est vita nostra: ut non mirum sit vehementes animae nostrae motus effusos per communem vitam ubique vigentem usque ad numina mundana produci[17] vicissimque motus horum numinum per eandem vitam ad nos usque deduci.

: XLI :

44   Qualis est in quolibet animali perfecto textura nervorum atque venarum talis in mundano est animali naturarum contextus atque vitarum. Sicut ergo motio passioque pedis in nobis pertinet ad cervicem et cervicis ad pedem, sic et in mundano hoc animali motus inferiorum ad superiora proveniunt atque vicissim et quasi aequalium similiter ad aequalia. Motus autem omnis venit quidem salutaris ex alto dummodo qualis venit taliter capiatur et capi

powers in the life of the world, while the inferior figures and chants often announce the figures and harmonies of celestial things, prayer indeed being a certain strong motion of our soul toward the divinity that we implore. If you crumble sulfur and throw its most subtle dust toward a fire, a flame of the fire drawn out in length will forthwith connect itself with this dust. Similarly, the man who implores a star having been made ready for this star in an opportune manner sends forth his spirit into the rays of the star—manifest and hidden alike—that are everywhere diffused and life-giving and through which he obtains the enlivening gifts of the star. Finally, just as all the fixed stars are connected to the firmament, so the worldly lives of all the stars and worldly spirits are connected to the life of the world to which our life is also connected. It is therefore not surprising that powerful motions of our soul when poured out are extended right through the general life that flourishes everywhere to the worldly spirits, and that the motion of these spirits is in return conducted down through the same life as far as ourselves.

: XLI :

The weaving together of nerves and veins in each and every complete animate being is of the same kind as the connection of natures and lives in the animate being that is the world. Just as the motion and passivity of our foot reaches back to the neck and those of our neck to the foot, so in this world-animal the motions of lower things go forth to the higher and *vice versa*, and those of things that are as though equal go forth similarly to their equals. However, every motion which comes from above is healthful provided that it is received—and is able to be received—in the way

44

possit. Neque distantia loci prohibet quin motus vicissim utrimque proveniant, ubi ultra communem texturam res inferior cognatam habet cum superiore proprietatem tam acquisitam quam naturalem—sicut nervi motus in lyra ad nervum alterum pervenit distantem quidem sed similiter temperatum.

: XLII :

45 Magi quondam multi vitae praesentis amatores bonorumque corporeorum cupidi excogitaverunt corporea sacrificia votaque vivis stellarum corporibus et vivo mundi corpori consentanea ut inde quod optabant consequerentur. Ad eadem corporea sacrificia dedicata stellis populum assuefecisse videntur. Dubitabant ergo nonnulli utrum stellis ad hoc ipsum opus sit sensu imaginatione memoria electione ut vota eiusmodi impleant. Respondet Plotinus non oportere, nam ex vivis mundi corporibus vitalis vigor suapte natura derivatur in alia qui et in corpora spiritus animas, quando per votum et cetera competentia ad hauriendum aptius exponuntur, uberius affluit—naturali scilicet proprioque influxu—etiamsi non adsit electio.

46 Sed Plotinus vivis stellarum sphaerarumque corporibus intellectuales earundem animas anteponit a corpore quodammodo segregatas ad quas non perveniat passio motioque ulla per corporeas continuata naturas ideoque nec hauriantur inde bona eiusmodi attractu quasi magico. Idemque Porphyrius atque Iamblichus asserunt qui una cum Plotino in illis voluntatem electionemque collocant: electionem inquam non ab inferioribus persuasam sed ex se

that it comes. No separation in place prevents motions from coming forth in both directions, when a lower thing has a property shared with a higher over and above the general weaving together, this property being either acquired or natural. It is just as the motion of a string on a lyre reaches another string that is indeed separated from it but similarly tuned.

: XLII :

Many magicians of former days who were lovers of the present life 45 and desirous of corporeal things contrived corporeal sacrifices and prayers in harmony with the living bodies of the stars and the living body of the world, in order that they might gain from there the thing desired. They seem to have habituated the people to the same corporeal sacrifices dedicated to the stars. Therefore, some of them questioned whether the stars had any need of sense, imagination, memory, and choice in order to further this project: namely, of answering prayers of such a kind. Plotinus replies that there is no such need, for the vital force is dispersed to other things from the living bodies of the world through its own very nature. This vital force, when things are laid out — using prayers and other actions — that are more suitable for drawing it in, flows forth into bodies, spirits, and souls more abundantly, that is, by its own natural and proper emanation, even if no choice is present.

But Plotinus places before the living bodies of the stars and 46 spheres their intellectual souls that are somehow separate: no passion and motion connected through corporeal natures can reach these, and therefore goods cannot be drawn off by any *quasi*-magical attraction of this kind. Porphyry and Iamblichus[24] say the same thing. They agree with Plotinus in placing will and choice together in those intellectual souls — choice here being not some-

ipsa ab aevo constituentem imitari quidem summum Deum et sequentibus omnibus providere ⟨atque⟩ exaudire supplicum preces
intellectuali vita imitantium intellectuales mundi rectores. In sacri-
ficiis quidem votisque corporeis ad corpora mundi directa repor-
tant et eiusmodi bona homines etiam corpore mancipati: bona
vero diviniora per segregatum cultum viri tantum divini a divinis
mundi rectoribus.

47   Addit Porphyrius ac Iamblichus hos etiam ultra intellectualia
etiam corporalia quaedam et externa[18] bona referre officio numinum mediorum superioribus numinibus obsequentium et eorun-
dem tutela saepe mala imminentia devitare. Adiungit astrologus
Abraham religiosas animas ex applicatione ad Deum caelo superiorem acquirere potestatem per quam fatalia bona quidem augeant
mala vero minuant. Proponunt Platonici intellectualibus animis
mundi rectoribus intellectus puros, his intellectum divinum, huic
patrem eius ipsum bonum. Mundanis diis sacrificia corporea con-
stituunt, superioribus segregatam dedicant sanctimoniam, primo
segregatissimam — idque confirmat Apollonius Theaneus — ; adorationem prae ceteris eligunt superioribus et supremo denique
consecratam; illinc enim bona ampliora referri ⟨dicunt⟩. De his
apud Iamblichum et Porphyrium quos nuper interpretati sumus
legere latissime poteris.

thing persuaded by lower things but from itself eternally determining to imitate the supreme God and provide for all subsequent things, and to hear the prayers of those who humbly imitate with an intellectual life the intellectual rulers of the world. With corporeal sacrifices and prayers, men given over to the body obtain only goods directed toward the bodies of the world and of the same kind; only divine men obtain more divine gifts from the divine rulers of the world through a detached worship.

Porphyry and Iamblichus[25] add that those men who even sur-   47
pass intellectual things also refer certain corporeal and external goods to the favor of intermediate spirits that obey the higher ones and often avoid evils threatening them through the protection of these spirits. The astrologer Abraham[26] adds that religious souls through submission to the God superior to the heaven acquire a power through which they increase the goods and diminish the evils accruing through fate. The Platonists place pure intellects before the intellectual souls ruling the world, the divine intellect before the pure intellects, and the Good its father before the divine intellect.[27] They establish corporeal sacrifices for the worldly gods and dedicate a detached chastity to the superior ones and a most detached one to the primal God: something that Apollonius of Tyana confirms.[28] For the higher gods they choose a worship more select than any other and ultimately consecrated to the supreme God, saying that the greater goods are to be referred to that worship. You will be able to read more extensively about these topics in the works of Iamblichus and Porphyry which we have recently translated.

: XLIII :

Magica fascinatio nititur viribus naturalibus tam
caelestium quam inferiorum rerum, scilicet
atque verborum. Attingit igitur proxime spiritum nostrum
et per hunc non solum humores
sed etiam vitam irrationalem dependentem etiam ab
ipso mundo. Animam vero
rationalem natura vitaque corporea mundi[19] *superiorem et*
solum a mente divina pendentem nequit
attingere, nisi quatenus
cum vita inferiore consentit.

48 Si quis hunc quidem sucinea induat veste, illum vero paleari, ad
hunc attrahet illum. Ita perscrutati magi multa passim recondita —
non naturalia solum sed etiam verba — quae vim suam eminus
effundentia trahere valeant, multa etiam quae ab his trahi possint — et illa quidem viro, haec autem feminae — clam adhibentes,
feminam ad virum rapiunt. Admovent etiam quae seiungere possint, sicut et nautae suspendentes ferrum ita cum magnete librant
ut rapiatur ad Ursam atque vicissim inficientes allio raptum eiusmodi solvunt.

49 Qua vero siderum positione quidam opportunius ad haec utan-
tur et quas fingant imagines quasve materias conflent narrare non
expedit,[20] nec etiam quibus incantamentis clam alliciant. Verbis
quidem praeest Mercurius, cantibus vero Phoebus, incantamentis

: XLIII :

*Magical enchantment strives for its effects with the natural
powers both of celestial and lower things: obviously
including those of words. This enchantment, therefore, affects
our spirit directly, and then by means of the latter not only our
humors but also our irrational life which also is causally
dependent on the world itself. However, the enchantment is
unable to affect our rational soul which is superior to the
corporeal nature and life of the world and is dependent
causally on the divine mind alone, except to the extent
that the soul enters into a compact with the lower life.*

If anyone dresses one person in an amber-colored garment and 48
another person in a chaff-colored one, he will attract the latter toward the former. Magicians expert in such matters, who secretly
apply many objects hidden all around that are able to attract in
emitting their power from a distance — not only natural objects
but also words —, and who also apply many objects that are attracted by such things — the former being applied to a man and
the latter to a woman — : these magicians forcefully bring a woman
to a man. They also introduce things that are able to bring about
separation: just as sailors suspend a piece of iron and so balance it
with a magnet in order to move the iron forcibly to the Great Bear
and conversely by smearing the piece of iron with garlic disengage
a forced motion of this kind.

It is not advantageous to report what position of the stars cer- 49
tain people opportunely exploit for such purposes, what images
they fashion, what matters they bring into combination, and also
by what incantations they secretly entice. Mercury presides over
words, Phoebus over songs, and Mercury in conjunction with

autem Mercurius cum Phoebo coniunctus.[21] Sed ubi et qua rationne iunctus soli et quali stellarum aspectu fretus vim praebeat cantionibus, item quo aspectu malefica quove benefica praestet incantamenta docere iustitia vetat. Forte vero sicut ceterae materiarum qualitatumque mixtiones vim novam adipiscuntur, ita certae quaedam iuncturae verborum et intra animam conceptae et extra animam prolatae adhuc quasi vivae vim quandoque mirabilem consequuntur vel ex praesenti siderum positura vel etiam ex ipsius hominis genitura aut ex singulari quadam animae potestate adeo ut in effectu verborum haec ipsa eorum iunctura processioque in obiectum intenta sit quasi directio et applicatio virtutis intimae ad externum,[22] quemadmodum praegnantis cupidae digitus genam signans rei nimium affectatae nota.

50   Procedit vero in rem distantem incantamenti vigor motu quodam non solum per aerem sibi similem propagatus — sicut in aqua semel percussa circuli — sed etiam per radios spiritus excantantis quos quidem procul imaginatio vehemens affectusque iaculatur. Radialis namque natura subito procedit in longum secumque producit vires eiaculantis: immo vero res omnes infra lunam imitatae stellas naturae suae vires et quasi vapores quosdam radiorum instar emittunt foras quibus obiecta etiam distantia pro natura sua bene aut male frequenter afficiant; idque facilius quoniam singula eiusdem sunt animalis membra mundani — quod odores ipsi declarant longius et diutius a canibus apibusque percepti.

51   Mitto quantam daemones veneficiis magicisque operibus adhibeant potestatem, quod sane in *Symposio* Plato confirmat. Hos etiam magus cultorque diligens demulcendo sibi conciliare potest,

Phoebus over incantations. But at what time, joined by what ratio to the sun, and relying on what aspect to the stars Mercury furnishes power to incantations; and again, in what aspect he provides maleficent and in what aspect beneficent incantations: these things, justice forbids me to teach. Perhaps, just as other blends of matters and qualities obtain a novel power, so similarly do certain couplings of words both conceived within the soul and expressed externally but still living, so to speak, sometimes obtain a wonderful power either from the present disposition of the stars, or also from the geniture of a man himself, or from a certain singular power of the soul. This is to such an extent that in the effect of the words, the joining of these things as such and their procession is stretched toward the object and is as though a directing and application of the inner power to the exterior, in the way that the finger marking the thigh of a pregnant woman who is lustful is the sign of a thing desired to excess.

The power of an incantation proceeds into a distant thing having been propagated in a certain motion not only through the air which is similar to it — as do circles in water that is struck once — but also through the rays of the enchanter's spirit which a powerful imagination and affection throws from afar. For the nature of rays suddenly proceeds into length, and in itself extends the powers of the one casting. One could even say that all things below the moon emit powers of their nature which imitates the stars, and that they give out certain vaporous emissions akin to rays. Such rays frequently affect objects at a distance in accordance with their own nature for better or worse. This happens the more easily given that individual things of this kind are the bodily parts of the world-animal: something that the very smells perceived from a greater distance and for a longer time by dogs and bees reveal. 50

I pass over how much power daemons apply to potions and magical operations — something Plato establishes in the *Symposium.*[29] A diligent magician or worshipper can procure the favor of 51

quemadmodum et abiectus[23] mimus[24] musicusque puer regem il-
laqueat generosum et bestiae quaedam hominem quandoque fasci-
nant: sicut enim se habet ad hominem bestia, ad virum puer, ita
vir magus ad inferiores daemones nobisque propinquos. Huc forsan tendit illud Albumasar aliorumque astrologorum: scilicet,
preces vim habere quamplurimum quando Caput Draconis medium tenet caelum et Iuppiter vel in eo sit vel id aspiciat, lunaque
vel coniuncta sit cum Iove vel ab ipso procedens coitum cum
Ascendentis Domino prosequatur aut Ascendentis Dominus con-
gressum cum Iove petat Capitisque Draconis aspectum. Putant
etiam sidus eiusmodi vel efficaciam prosperitatemque spiritui nostro votisque praebere ad daemonas Iovi Capitique subditos allec-
tandos; si modo caelestibus his influxibus subiungantur, ex omni
genere sensibilium multa tam huic daemoni quam suo illi sideri
competentia — quae et perscrutari laboriosum est et observare
periculosum.

52   Tutius vero de hoc Ioviali sidere physicus aliquis opinabitur
spiritum hominis tunc bona caelestia vehementius affectantis beneficio Iovis caelestibus bonis largius hauriendis exponi; ad ma-
lignos autem spiritus loco movendos divinationemque per mortuos
explendam Ptolemaeus in *Quadripartito* conferre putat harmoniam
caelestem quando luna fuerit Magisterii Domina colatque Iovis
Aedes: Sagittarium scilicet, aut Pisces.

53   Haec ad Plotinicum illud dicta sint ubi ait: magum quodammodo daemonas irretire ac per universum in partes agere atque per
superiora facile inferiora movere. Ego vero suspicor ne forte

these daemons for himself by flattering them, in the same manner in which a lowly actor or boy musician ensnares a noble monarch and certain animals sometimes bewitch a man. For just as an animal relates to a human being and a boy to a man, so does the magician relate to the daemons that are lower and proximate to us. These facts are perhaps suggested by the doctrine of Albumasar[30] and other astrologers: namely, that prayers have their greatest power when the Dragon's Head occupies the midpoint of the heaven and Jupiter is either in this constellation or in aspect to it, when the moon is either in conjunction with Jupiter or, in proceeding from him, seeks union with the Lord of the Ascendant, or when the Lord of the Ascendant seeks combination with Jupiter and the aspect of the Dragon's Head. The astrologers think that a star of this kind even grants efficacy and success to our spirit and our prayers in enticing the daemons subject to Jupiter and the Head, and that there are many things among every kind of sensible object due as much to this daemon as to that star of his, provided that things are made subject to these celestial emanations. But such questions are laborious to investigate and dangerous to be concerned with.

With greater safety any natural philosopher will hold, with regard to this star of Jupiter, that the spirit of a man striving more forcefully for celestial goods is at this time exposed more broadly to the imbibing of celestial goods through the beneficence of Jupiter. In the *Tetrabiblos*, Ptolemy[31] thinks that the heavenly harmony makes a contribution to the removal of malignant spirits from a place and to the performance of divination through the dead when the moon is the Mistress of the Instruction and abides in the Temple of Jupiter: that is Sagittarius or Pisces. 52

Let these things be said in relation to Plotinus' comment when he says that the magician somehow ensnares daemons and acts through the totality upon its parts and moves lower things easily through the higher. As for myself, I am wary of this, lest perchance 53

daemones subdoli simulent magicis quibusdam machinis allici vel expelli. Nam Porphyrius et Iamblichus aiunt per Deum proprie perque bonos angelos adversus infimos spiritus imperium nos habere qui alioquin nos fallere frequenter soleant atque laedere. Et quoniam perturbatione tanguntur—quod et Plotinus affirmat—, merito Plotinus una cum Porphyrio atque Iamblicho damnat eam superstitionem quae exquisitis illecebris studeat fallacibus perturbatisque daemonibus adulari. Qua[25] vero ratione ex corpore mundi ubique vivo vivisque tum stellis tum ceteris mundi partibus naturali quodam quasi agricolarum medicorumque more vitales carpere auras valeamus satis in libro *De Vita* tertio disputamus. Platonici denique adorationem intentissimam sacrificiorum omnium efficacissimam esse putant, praesertim si ad intellectus mundo superiores—scilicet, angelos—dirigatur, maximeque si ad Deum quoque superiorem; sed ab his similiter atque ab hoc nihil impetrari naturali quodam caelestique favore cuius motus illuc usque non transit, sed elevatione quadam coniunctioneque mentis ad illos. Quae vero in superioribus de virtute imaginationis fascinationibusque et de magia praetermisimus in *Theologia* nostra et libro *De Amore* et libro *De Vita* tertio latius pertractamus.

cunning daemons might pretend that they are being attracted or expelled by certain magical contrivances, for Porphyry and Iamblichus[32] say that we have through God properly and also through the good angels a position of authority in opposition to these lower spirits which, otherwise, are wont to deceive us frequently or bring us harm. Given that they are touched by perturbation—as Plotinus also asserts—, rightly Plotinus together with Porphyry and Iamblichus condemns that superstition which strives to flatter deceitful and troubled daemons with choice enticements. We discuss sufficiently in the third book On Life[33] how we are able to take living drafts from the body of the world that is everywhere vital, and from both the living stars and the other parts of the world in a certain natural manner as though that of farmers and physicians. Finally, the Platonists think that worship is the most intense and most effective of all sacrifices, especially if it is directed to the intellects superior to the world: that is, the angels, and most of all if it is directed also to the God superior to them. They also think that from the former and likewise the latter nothing can be obtained by means of a certain natural and celestial approbation whose motion does not pervade as far as their level; something can only be obtained by means of a certain elevation and conjunction of the mind with them. We examine at greater length in our Theology,[34] the book On Love,[35] and the third book On Life[36] the matters concerning the power of imagination, enchantments, and magic which we have passed over in the above discussion.

: XLIV :

Vita contemplativa libera est, activa ministra actionum et rerum atque fortunae, voluptuosa serva corporis.

54 Cum mens rerum contemplandarum formas ingenitas habet ipsaquemet sit ipsae formae, merito, quatenus in his contemplandis nativa voluptate se versat, eatenus libera secum habitat. Qui vero corpus et externa curiose colit, corpori hominibus fortunae servit. Actio atque passio inter se opponuntur. Omnis igitur motus noster qui incitamentum ex corporea humanaque passione habuit passio quaedam est et servitus. Denique natura ipsa vitaque mundi quasi maga imagines ipsius boni veri pulchri ubique fingit velut escas quibus animas huic mundo per voluptatem avaritiam inanem gloriam deditas fallit et quasi mancipia detinet atque trahit.

: XLIV :

The contemplative life is free; the active life is the attendant of actions, things, and fortune; the voluptuous life is the servant of the body.

Since the mind has inborn in it the forms of things to be contem- 54
plated and is itself these forms, rightly, to the extent that it occupies itself in the contemplation of these things with a natural
pleasure, to the same extent it lives in freedom with itself. But a
man who devotes himself inquisitively to the body and external
things is a servant to the body, to men, and to fortune. Action and
passion are opposed to one another. Therefore, every motion of
ours which has taken its stimulus from corporeal and human passivity is a certain passivity and servitude. Finally, the nature itself
and life of the world, like a magician, everywhere fashions of the
Good itself, the True, and the Beautiful images that are as though
baits with which it deceives souls that are dedicated to this world
through pleasure, greed, and vainglory. It detains them and drags
them along as its hirelings.

: XLV :

Homo non solum tamquam mundi pars quaedam
fataliter agit patiturque multa, sed etiam
substantiam habet propriam naturaliter quidem partim
superioribus, partim inferioribus cognatam. Ac libero motu
potest insuper affectionem et habitum induere tam
cum superioribus quam cum inferioribus congruentem.

55   Eiusmodi habitus fit anima tandem: quasi natura cuius[26] instinctu
sub divino iudicio fertur in sortem atque locum aut superis aut
inferis competentem.

: XLV :

Man not only, as though a certain part of the world, acts in a fatal manner and suffers many things, but also has a proper substance that is related in a natural sense partly to higher things and partly to lower things. With a free motion, he is also able to take on an affection and a condition that is as much in agreement with the higher as with the lower.

The condition of the soul becomes ultimately as though a nature 55 under whose impulse and subject to divine judgment the soul is borne toward an allotment and a place associated either with higher or lower things.

[LIBER V]

DE DUBIIS ANIMAE
VEL DE VISIONE

: I :

1 Sentire est percipere corporea singulatim per instrumenta corporea. In perceptione sensuali deprehendimus externorum corporum qualitates aut actus usque ad animam vel circa animam quodammodo pervenire necnon quandoque vim actumque animae ad corporea se porrigere. Quod quidem fieri nullo modo posset nisi anima proportionem quandam ad haec haberet: hanc vero non habet nisi ipsa per vim vegetalem suo quodam pacto formet manifestum corpus et praecipue spiritum; atque ita sibi conformet ut vis eius actusque per hoc suum corpus quasi instrumentum ad externa quandoque se porrigat et externorum motus ad hoc veniendo quodammodo videantur ad animam pervenisse. Denique ut visus percipiat rem videndam, non opus est foris corpore medio quasi ad videndum necessario[1] adiuvante: satis enim per se visus oculusque natura paratus est ut versetur[2] circa luminosum atque hoc vicissim circa visum. Corpus vero medium, siquidem opacum est, impedit; sin diaphanum, hoc tantum habet ut visioni non obstet sicut solet opacum. Absque hoc ergo forte videbitur.

[BOOK V]

ON DIFFICULTIES CONCERNING
THE SOUL OR ON VISION

: I :

To sense is to perceive corporeal things one by one by means of corporeal instruments. In sensitive perception we discern that qualities or acts of external bodies reach as far as the soul or somehow the vicinity of the soul, and also that the power and act of the soul sometimes stretches itself out to bodily things. But this could in no way happen if the soul did not have a certain proportion to those things, and it does not have this proportion if it does not itself through its vegetative power in a certain manner of its own form a palpable body and especially a spirit. Moreover, the soul conforms this body and spirit to itself in order that the latter's power and act may, through the instrumentality of the soul's own body, stretch itself out sometimes to external things, and that the motions of external things may seem to have somehow reached the soul in coming to this spirit or body. Finally, in order that sight might perceive the thing to be seen, there is no need of a body on the exterior as a medium as though assisting necessarily in the process of seeing. For the sight through itself and the eye is sufficiently prepared by nature for the purpose of dealing with the luminous object and similarly the luminous object sufficiently prepared for its dealings with sight. A mediate body impedes if it is opaque. But if it is transparent, its only salient feature is that it does not obstruct the vision as an opaque one is wont to do. Therefore, it will perhaps be seen in the absence of an opaque object.

495

: II :

2 Inter visum atque visibile medium per se necessarium est lumen
vel commune externumque vel proprium sive oculi seu obiecti natura valde lucentis; corpus autem non adeo necessarium inter haec
medium est. Visio fit potissimum quia vel radius ab oculo visualis
proficiscitur ad visibile vel a visibili iam luminoso nonnihil procedit ad visum vel utroque simul pacto; et omnino quoniam tam
oculus quam visibile ita in natura mundi vivente[3] sunt disposita ut
proprietatem habeant invicem valde conformem per quam a se invicem facile moveantur agantque mutuo vel patiantur. Corpus igitur nec est per se necessarium ad emicantem ex oculo radium
sustinendum atque perferendum qui sine sustentaculo in rectum
profluit naturaliter; nec ad lumen ita vehendum sive sit lumen
obiecti sive sit alienum; nec etiam ad compassionem inter visibile
visumque complendam—satis enim per se mutuae sunt exposita
passioni[4]—; denique nec necessarium est aerem medium ab obiecto colorari figurarique, modo cerae, per quam passionem visus
subinde similiter patiatur: alioquin ad[5] cernendum non oporteret
oculum ad obiectum ipsum convertere procul positum—satis
enim foret oculum attingi a contigua nobis parte aeris iam[6] formata. Omnino vero spiritales sub lumine visibilium species perve-
nientes ad oculum absque aeris passione perveniunt.

: II :

Between vision and the visible, the medium necessary in itself is 2
light—either a communal and external light or a light proper to
the eye or the object that is naturally shedding much light. However, a body is not such a necessary medium between these things.
Vision arises primarily because either a visual ray comes forth
from the eye toward the visible object, or something proceeds toward the sight from the visible object that is already luminous, or
because both these things occur simultaneously. Vision in general
also arises because both the eye and the visible object are so arranged in the living nature of the world that they have a property
very much in conformity with both of them through which they
are easily moved in a reciprocal manner and are active or passive
with respect to one another. Therefore, a body is not in itself necessary for the maintenance and conveyance of a ray springing forth
from the eye, this ray flowing forth naturally in a straight line
without a support. A body is also not necessary for the conveyance
of the light—either the light of the object or some other light—
nor even for the achievement of a copassivity between the visible
and the vision, the fact of their exposure to a mutual passivity being sufficient. Finally, it is not necessary for color or shape to be
given from the object to the medium of air—as wax is colored and
shaped—, with sight itself thence becoming similarly passive
through the air's passivity. If this were the case, the eye would not
have to turn toward the object itself that was placed at a distance
in order to perceive it, for it would be sufficient for the eye to be
touched by the part of the air already formed that is contiguous
with us. Indeed, spiritual forms below the light of visible things in
general that reach the eye do so without the passivity of air.

: III :

3   Inter visum atque visibile non est necessarius aer medius ad hoc
ipsum proprie ut forma obiecti imprimatur deinceps per partes
aeris succedendo, unde tandem imprimatur et oculo. Ratio ad hoc
prima paulo superius assignata est. Sequuntur duae quarum una
est eiusmodi: quando nocte profunda igniculum longissime distans[7] cernimus, non est putandum ex igniculo formam continuatis
aeris partibus gradatim imprimi. Non enim potest hunc ita pin-
gere, nisi et easdem partes illuminet; nec tamen illuminat eas:
alioquin alia quoque multa in recto hoc spatio cerneremus. Ratio
altera talis est: si aer modo quodam suo: id est, corporeo, a persona videnda pingatur, sequetur ut exigua illa pars aeris pupillae
proxima et aequalis id dumtaxat minimum de persona tota quod
praefert ostendat oculo; nunc autem in qualibet aeris portiuncula
totum videmus obiectum. Denique, aer nihil patitur ab illa specie
si qua mittitur ab obiecto, sicut neque patitur ab ipso lumine per
quod mittitur: ab ipso inquam qua ratione lumen. Sic enim momento adest et abest, neque remanet illuminante subtracto, et est
ubique totum. Ex quo apparet lumen neque fieri propriam aeris
qualitatem nec esse re vera corporeum. Proinde incorporeum hoc
non tam provenit ex corpore quam vita mundi. Nam et quando ad
longissimum spatium scintillam vides, exiguum locustae sonum
audis; et animalia quaedam audiunt minima quaeque; item apes et

: III :

It is not necessary that air should be a medium between vision and   3
the visible in the proper sense in order that the form of the object
might be imprinted by coming in sequence through parts of the
air and as a result of this be finally imprinted also in the eye. The
first reason for this was given a little earlier. There are two further
reasons of which one is as follows. When we perceive at the dead
of night a little fire burning at a very great distance, we should not
think that a form derived from the fire is impressed by stages on
parts of the air continuous with one another, for the form is not
able thus to color the air unless it also illuminates the parts of the
said air. However, it does not illuminate them, for if it did, we
would perceive many other objects in the linear trajectory of the
space. The second reason is as follows. If the air in a certain way of
its own: that is, in a corporeal way, is colored by a person to be
seen, it will follow that that smallest part of the air closest to the
pupil and equal to it will show to the eye only that smallest part of
the whole person that it presents. However, we do see the entire
object in each and every smallest portion of the air. Finally, the air
has no passivity with respect to that form if the latter is somehow
sent from the object, just as it also has no passivity with respect to
the light itself through which it is sent: with respect to the light,
that is, to the extent that it is light. For the light is present and
absent in a moment and does not remain if the illuminating substance is removed. Moreover, it is everywhere as a whole, and from
this fact it appears that light can neither become a proper quality
of the air nor be truly corporeal. Therefore, this incorporeal does
not come forth so much from the body as from the life of the
world. For at the same time when you see a spark at the greatest
distance you also hear the faintest sound of a locust. And certain
animals hear every slightest sound. Similarly, bees and ants smell

formicae mellita olfaciunt remotissima; conchae quin etiam distantia gustant;[8] et torpedo piscis per longam saepe virgam stupefacit te quasi tangens.

4   Non est existimandum, praesertim in superioribus, a minimo quoque obiecto longissimum spatium frangi et materialiter affici, sed intervenire nescio quid quodammodo spiritale quod per tam longum spatium agat in sensum: id est, actum quendam specialem ab ipsa speciei rei sentiendae provenientem. 'A specie' inquam non tam quia in materia sit quam quia a spirituali vivaque dependet idea; actum quoque 'specialem' inquam et 'spiritalem' sive hic[9] intra nos fiat in instrumento sensus — ut in tactu atque gustu — sive etiam extra nos in aere — ut circa visum auditum olfactum — sive etiam a visu proveniat in obiectum: qui sane actus in omnibus sentiendis fit ubique inter passionem[10] etiam materialem ab obiecto in aere factam circa sensus inferiores. Fit igitur opportune tunc virtute quadam vitae communis cuius beneficio cuncta ligante tam facile a rebus distantibus et movetur sensus et corpus conforme procul patitur a conformi — quod etiam apparet in magia. Et caelestia aliaque multa vires suas impartiunt remotissimis. Denique, vita mundi communis ita sensum hunc cum hoc sensibili temperat ut agente sensibili moveatur sensus et agat, sicut in lyra dum movetur haec chorda statim et contemperata movetur et te clamante paries conclamat sic expositus. De superioribus diligentius in *Commentariis Theophrasti* tractamus.

things sweetened by honey at the farthest remove. Indeed conches taste distant things and the electric ray will often numb you through its long tentacle as though by touching.

You should not think, especially with respect to the things 4 above, that the greatest extension of space is broken up and materially affected by every smallest object. Rather, you should think that a spiritual entity of some kind or other intervenes in a certain manner, and that this acts over a great distance on the sense, this spiritual entity being a certain formal act coming forth from the form of the thing being sensed. I use the phrase "from the form" not so much because it[1] comes to be in matter but because it depends on a spiritual and living Idea. I speak of the act as "formal" and "spiritual" whether this arises within us in the instrument of sense — as in the cases of touch and taste —, or also outside us in the air — being around the sight, hearing, and smell —, or also comes forth from the sight into the object. Indeed, this act in the case of all things sensed arises everywhere amid the passion which, as made by the object in the air around the lower senses, is also material. It therefore arises at that point opportunely by means of a certain power of the general life according to whose favor binding all things the sense is so easily moved by distant things and a conformed body is passive to a conformed body at a distance — this also appears in magic. Moreover, celestial beings and many other things impart their powers to distant things. Finally, the communal life of the world so attunes this sense with this sensible thing that the sense is moved by the agency of the sensible and also acts: just as in the case of a lyre, when this string is moved, immediately another string attuned to it is moved, and when you shout, a wall thus exposed echoes the shout. We discuss the points mentioned above in more detail in our *Commentaries on Theophrastus*.[2]

: IV :

5 Si quod medium necessarium est inter visum atque visibile, id quidem non corpus est sed lumen vel nativum oculo sive visibili vel alienum. Confert autem ad videndum non passio medii oculique sed actio quaedam atque lumen. Tres hic de visu tangit opiniones. Una putat animam ita per radios visuales sicut per capillos sese propagare vel manus, atque ita sensibilem tangere, et id quidem absque reflexione; secunda, animam non propagari per radios sed eos quasi virgas extendere ad obiectum eosque ad animam inde reverberari; tertia[11] lumen figurari ab obiecto atque ita figuratum ad oculos pervenire. Circa primam ludit, secundum deridet, tertium reprobat. Et ubique tandem id molitur: tantam esse compatiendi conformitantem inter visum atque visibile ut satis circa se vicissim moveantur et agant, etiamsi nulla passio contingat in medio, sicut neque patitur medium, vel saltem non tale quiddam patitur quando tremente hac chorda altera contremescit, oscitante hoc oscitat ille, et imaginante aliquid amicissimo imaginatur interdum idem et alter amicus.

: IV :

If any medium is necessary between the sight and the visible. this   5
is indeed not a body but a light either natural to the eye or to the
visible or else alien to them. However, it is not a passion of the
medium and of the light that contributes to seeing but a certain
action and light. Plotinus here touches upon three views regarding
light. The first view holds that the soul extends itself through visual rays just as it does through hairs or hands, and that it thus
touches the sensible and does so without reflection. The second
view is that the soul does not extend itself through rays but extends the rays as though wands to the object, and that they
bounce back to the soul. The third view holds that light is shaped
by the object and that so shaped it thus reaches to the eyes. Plotinus plays around with the first view, mocks the second, and criticizes the third. Ultimately, he labors everywhere in order to establish that there is so great a conformity of passivity between the
visible and sight that they are sufficiently moved and act around
themselves reciprocally, even if no passion occurs in an intermediary. It is just as there is no passive intermediary or at least no intermediary passive to a certain particular thing when, together
with the vibration of this string, another string also vibrates, or
when one man yawns and so does another, or when a man bound
by great friendship imagines something and another man who is
his friend imagines the same thing in the meantime.

: V :

6 Si qua materialis passio a rebus sentiendis affertur in medium,
quia nimium diversa est ab incorporea natura sensus, ideo et saepe
sua vehementia confundit sensum et numquam est accommodata
causa sentiendi, nisi praeter illam suboriatur spiritale aliquid vel in
medio vel saltem in instrumento sensus. Id quidem spiritale
accommodatum sensui etiam apparet in voce. Quod enim ubique
totum circa vocem a multis eodem momento percipitur significaturque spiritale quiddam esse videtur. Tale vero aliquid circa
quemlibet sensum non corporea causa generat, sed procreat ipsa
mundi vita in subiecto tunc opportune disposito. Est autem hoc
adeo cognatum sensui ut, cum primum id circa sensum viget actu,
ipse quoque sensus ipsius actus circa id simul expergiscatur —
quemadmodum aliis hominibus alius praecipue concentus est amicus et alius alios ad cantum excitat atque tripudium. Quod autem
ad actum huius obiecti sensibilis statim hic sensus agat conficit
eadem ubique vita mundi, hoc potissimum cum illo contemporans
simulque movens, sicut ad talis humoris motum movetur et imaginatio talis atque vicissim, item ad varios lunae motus habitusque
varie moventur et afficiuntur humores, ad motum sulfuris movetur
et flamma. Quorsum intendis dextrum oculum, intenditur et si-
nister.

: V :

If in some way a material passion is borne into the intermediary 6
from things sensed, because the passion is very much distinct from
the incorporeal nature of the sense, it therefore often confounds
the sense with its strength, the cause of the sensing being never
adapted to the sense unless in addition to the cause a certain
spiritual entity rises up either in the intermediary or at least in the
instrument of sense. Indeed, this spiritual entity adapted to sense
is even apparent in the case of voice. For that which is everywhere
as a whole perceived and signified with respect to voice at the same
moment by many people seems to be something spiritual. Indeed,
it is not a corporeal cause that produces such a thing around each
and every sense but rather the life itself of the world that generates
it, being in a subject that is at this point opportunely arranged.
This thing[3] is so akin to sense that, when it first grows strong in
act in relation to the sense, the very act of the sense itself is simultaneously awakened in relation to it — in the way that different
harmonies are especially amicable toward different men, the different harmonies arousing some men to song and others to dance.
The same ubiquitous life of the world brings it about that this
sense immediately acts in relation to the act of this sensible object,
this life especially attuning this object with that sense and simultaneously moving it. It is just as when such an imagination is moved
in relation to the motion of such a humor and *vice versa*. Likewise,
the humors are moved and affected in different ways in relation to
the motions and conditions of the moon, and a flame is moved in
relation to the motion of sulfur. To whichever point you direct
your right eye the left eye is also directed.

: VI :

7 Lumen non ab illuminato sed ab illuminante dependet; similiter vita omnis non ab animato sed ab anima pendet tamquam proprius actus et regitur, etiamsi omne foris defuerit sustentaculum. Primum corpus est caelestis ignis; prima huius qualitas est lumen. Ideo usque adeo perfecta est ut per modum actus potius quam otiosae qualitatis exsistat. Actus quidem tam efficax ut per omnia sese porrigat a fonte proprio non disiunctus. Appellatur et ignis eiusmodi color qui usquequaque diffusus colores omnium otiosos suscitat atque circumfundit. Praeterea in quocumque sub caelo corpore praevalet igneus quidam vigor caelesti similis; emicat et inde lumen quasi familiaris color.

8 Sub praesentia solis lumen calefacit aerem. Calefactio quidem utroque indiget: scilicet, et praesentia solis et aere. Haec vero calefactio competens medium est inter lumen atque calorem. Calor sane potest etiam sine praesentia luminis in aere superesse. Ergo lumen sine aere penes solem exsistere potest, sed calor quidem a lumine relictus in aere non multo tempore superest, quoniam est alienus, lumen vero circa solem semper, quia proprium; proprium enim inseparabile est. Alicuius certe proprium est lumen non diaphani per se quidem obscuri; ergo solis ipsius corporisque solaris. Et merito, sicut est forma quaedam in ordine rerum in seipsa consistens, quaedam alio sustentata, sic et actus[12] est duplex: alter quidem formae dumtaxat agentis. alter insuper iacens in patiente.

9 Lumen vero non fieri propriam diaphani qualitatem alibi diximus, quia neque suscipitur paulatim neque etiam retinetur; neque

: VI :

Light depends not on the illuminated but on the illuminating 7
thing. Similarly. all life depends not on the ensouled thing but on
the soul, being as though its proper act and also governed by it,
even if every external support is lacking. The first body is the celestial fire, and its first quality is light. For that reason it is so
perfect that it exists more in the manner of an act than in that of
an inactive quality. Indeed, the act is so efficacious that it extends
itself while being not disconnected from its proper source. A fire
of this kind is also called color which, being diffused so far on all
sides, arouses and pours around the inactive colors of all things.
Moreover, in whatever body below the heaven a certain fiery force
similar to the celestial one predominates, light springs forth from
there being as though a color in attendance.

In dependence on the sun's presence, light heats air, the heating 8
indeed needing both things: that is to say, the presence of the sun
and the air. Indeed, this heating is a sufficient medium between
light and heat. Of course, heat is able to endure in air even without the presence of light. Therefore, light is able to exist in the sun
without air, whereas heat left in the air by light does not endure
for very long, since this heat is other than the sun whereas light is
always around the sun as its property. For the property is an inseparable one. Certainly, the light is not a property of a certain
transparency which is in itself dark. Therefore, it is a property of
the sun itself and of the solar body. And rightly, just as there is in
the order of things a certain form subsisting in itself and a certain
form supported by something else, so is act twofold. One is the act
of a form that is only active, and the other an act also immanent in
something passive.

We have said elsewhere that light does not come to be as a 9
proper quality of the transparent, because it is neither taken up

simul cum hoc inficitur vel movetur. Neque confunduntur inter se lumina neque igitur cum ceteris qualitatibus commiscentur: non confundi apparet ex eo quod, si tribus luminibus corpus unicum opponatur, tres in oppositum umbrae resultant, quoniam tria ibidem lumina sunt distincta. Praeterea si tribus candelis opponatur ingens tabula in cuius medio sit foramen, tria lumina in oppositum inde resiliunt: aliud quidem in rectum, alia duo e transverso se invicem intersecantia non confusa. Similiter mentes et animae coniunctae invicem minime confunduntur.

10   Lumen merito neque subiecto capitur neque commiscetur alicubi, quoniam omne lumen caelestis luminis est imago. Illud vero animae caelestis est actus. Sicut enim verbum emittitur ab anima velut actus imaginationis extra porrectus in quo tria sunt: aer, motus, significatio; sic a luce intellectuali caelestis animae per omnia efficacissimus actus effunditur in quo tria sunt: lumen, calor, vis occulta; et aliquo pervenit lumen quo non calor et e converso. Vis autem in hoc actu occulta quae in eo potissimum est per omnia transit facitque mirabilia non formaliter calefaciendo vel palam illuminando sed speciales inferendo virtutes.

: VII :

11   Sicut reliqua corpora proiiciunt semper foras[13] ex se nonnihil: scilicet, vaporem vel virtutem vel imaginem, ita sidereum corpus

gradually nor even retained, and because it is neither blended nor moved simultaneously together with it. Moreover, lights are not confused with one another and therefore are also not commingled with the other qualities. That they are not confused is apparent from the fact that, if a single body is placed opposite three lights, three shadows leap forth into the opposite space, since there are three distinct lights in the same place. Moreover, if a large tablet having a hole in its middle is placed opposite three candles, three lights leap forth thence into the opposite space: one in a straight line and the other two intersecting one another diagonally, these lights being not confused. Similarly, minds and souls are conjoined to one another but are not at all confused.

Rightly is light neither seized by a subject nor commingled with   10 anything else, since every light is an image of the celestial light, the latter being indeed the act of the celestial soul. For just as a word is sent forth from the soul—like an act of the imagination put forth externally in which there are three components: the air, the motion, and the meaning—, so from the intellectual light of the celestial soul is poured forth through all things a most efficacious act in which there are three components: light, heat, and a hidden power. Light reaches to a point where heat does not and *vice versa*. The hidden power in this act, which is its most powerful component, passes through all things and accomplishes wonderful effects, not heating formally or illuminating openly but implanting the powers of specific formality.

∶ VII ∶

Just as other bodies always send forth something from themselves   11 to the exterior: that is to say, a vapor or a power or an image, so does the sidereal and a similar body externally give forth its own

atque simile actum suum emittit foras; et quia efficaciter, ideo procul eiusmodi actus est lumen attingens quidem externa et interim fontem proprium non relinquens. Inter lucem prorsus intimam lucido corpori atque calorem iam aeri factum intimum est lumen partim quidem lucenti intimum, partim etiam extra procedens — ferme sicut sermo inter cogitationem atque fabricam. Lumen quo momento penetrat molle diaphanum, eodem diaphanum transverberat vel durissimum: incorporeum est igitur cui duritia corporis non resistit. Verumtamen quoniam est caeleste, ideo obstaculum natura terreum, etiamsi minus durum sit, non capit lumen. Quoniam igitur incorporeum est, non debemus huic passiones corporis attribuere: id est, accedere recedere refluere transfluere contrahi dilatari. Sed potius ubi coram diaphanum exponitur lucido, statim lumen illic exsistere, illic agere; sin minus, non exsistere ibi, non agere: neque tamen simpliciter esse desinere quamdiu corpus est lucidum. Lumini simile est radialis actus spectaculi directus in speculum; item vitalis actus animae directus in corpus. Actus vitalis omnis est immortalis. Et qui ab anima nostra in corpus intenditur eam perpetuo comitatur; et qui in corpus idem manat ab anima mundi: hanc quoque animam assidue sequitur.

: VIII :

12 Cum mundus sit universum corpus atque sensibile, poni re vera non potest sensibile aliquid extra mundum. Quod si fingas corpus

act. Because it does so efficaciously, the light of such an act is spread afar, reaching to external things but in the meantime not departing from its proper source. Between the light that is absolutely internal to the lucent body and the heat which is now made internal to the air there is a light that is indeed partly internal to the lucent body and partly also going forth to the exterior, almost in the manner that there is a speaking between thinking and making. At the moment when light penetrates the soft transparency, it simultaneously pierces through the transparency however hard it may be. It is therefore an incorporeal which no hardness of body can resist. Nevertheless, since it is a celestial light, an obstacle that is earthy in nature, even if it is less hard, does not capture light. Therefore, since the light is incorporeal, we should not attribute the passions of body to it: namely, approaching, receding, flowing back, flowing through, being contracted, and being dispersed. Rather, when a transparency is placed in front of a lucent body, immediately light subsists and acts in the transparency. But if this occurs less, the light neither subsists nor acts in the transparency, although it does not cease to be *simpliciter* as long as the body is lucent. Similar to light is the radiating activity of something seen when directed toward a mirror, and likewise the vital act of the soul directed toward the body. Every vital act is immortal. The vital act stretched forth to the body by our soul accompanies the soul perpetually, the vital act flowing from the world-soul into the same body also following that soul assiduously.

: VIII :

Since the world is a universal and sensible body, it is certainly not possible for something sensible to be posited outside the world. That certain body which you might imagine to exist outside the

12

aliquod extra nulla in re cum mundo communicans, non sentietur sensu mundano; sin vero quoquomodo communicans, iam non erit extra sed intra. Quod patiente digito pedis statim compatiantur inguina—et haec quidem potius quam genua quamvis remotiora—inde contingit quia in eodem animali sunt et praecipue inter se conformia. Similiter ad passionem cerebri patitur stomachus atque vicissim. Simili ratione quod sensus etiam longe distantes ad levissimos sensibilium suorum motus, etiam non patiente medio annuant, efficit una mundi inter haec continuata natura. Sicut continuitas longissimi intentique nervi facit ut, vibrata parte vel infima, statim vibretur et summa. Hinc quoque contingit ut rerum series caelitus imminentes et adhuc futuras imaginemur vel occultiore quodam instinctu saepius imitemur, et amicum ad nos proficiscentem antequam perveniat occulto quodam sensu nonnumquam praeveniamus.

world and not communicating with it in any way will not be sensed by any worldly sense. On the other hand, if that body does somehow communicate with the world, it will not be outside the world but inside it. That the groin immediately joins in suffering the ill effects of that which the toe suffers, doing so more than do the knees, although the groin is further away — this occurs because these things are in the same animate being and primarily because they share formal properties among themselves. In a similar manner, the stomach suffers in relation to the ill effects suffered by the brain and *vice versa*. According to a similar reasoning, the fact that the senses even when located at a distance give acknowledgment to the most nimble motions of their objects of sense, even when there is no intermediary passive to the effect — this is something that the single nature of the world accomplishes between things related by continuity. It is in this same manner that the continuity of the longest string in a state of tension brings it about that, when even the lowest part of the string is set in vibration, the highest part immediately also vibrates. From this it also comes about that we may imagine the sequence of things threatening us from on high and still in the future or may more often imitate them with a certain more hidden impulse; also that we may sometimes with a certain hidden sense anticipate the coming of a friend before he arrives.

[LIBER VI]

DE SENSU ET MEMORIA[14]

: I :

1 Non imprimuntur sensibilium formae in anima. Non imprimi a sensibilibus formas in anima tamquam a sigillo in cera[15] Boetius noster in *Consolatione* probat, nos in *Theologia* et *Commentariis Theophrasti*. Plotinus existimat formam animae sic impressam sortiri iam obiecti sensibilis rationem. Itaque si in visu impressa fuerit forma caeli, quinque absurda sequi; primum non oportebit oculum ad caelum ultra dirigere; secundum non metiemur quantum distet caelum ab oculo, immo neque distare putabimus; tertium non apparebit caelum oculo latius; quartum non caelum videbimus sed hanc forsan in nobis caeli formam; quintum non discernemus rem sensui sic impositam.

: II :

Sentire non est pati a rebus sentiendis
sed agere circa illas.

2 Anima, quoniam rebus sentiendis absque proportione excellentior est neque cum eis in materia vel natura communicat, formas ab eis numquam suscipit; et quoniam in sentiendo recte iudicatura est—

[BOOK VI]

ON SENSE AND MEMORY

: I :

The forms of sensible things are not imprinted in the soul. Our 1
Boethius in the *Consolation*[1] demonstrates that forms are not impressed by sensible things in the soul as though by a seal in wax,
and we demonstrate this in the *Theology*[2] and in the *Commentary on
Theophrastus*.[3] Plotinus thinks that a form thus impressed in the
soul is now selecting the reason-principle of the sensible object.
Therefore, if the form of the heaven has been impressed in the vision, five absurd things follow. First, it will not be necessary also to
direct the eye toward the heaven; second, we will not measure how
far distant the heaven is from the eye, and indeed we will not
think that it is distant; third, the heaven will not appear to be
broader than the eye; fourth, we will not see the heaven but rather
the form of the heaven in us; fifth, we will not discern the thing
thus imposed on the sense.

: II :

*To have sensation is not to be passive with respect to things to
be sensed but to be active in relation to them.*

Since the soul is more excellent than the things to be sensed with- 2
out having proportionality to them, and since it does not communicate with them in matter or nature, it never takes on forms from
them. Moreover, since it will exercise judgment correctly in the act

passio vero confundit iudicium—nihil patitur ab obiectis. Si qua vero passio contingit ab eis, in corpus pervenit atque spiritum: quo[16] quidem spiritu sic ab externis aut [sic] pulsato vel affecto statim anima praesens affectiones eiusmodi percipit. Id vero percipere non est pati, sed potius agere: id est, aliter tunc spiritum atque aliter vegetare et innatas (ut Iamblichus ait) sensibilium formas edere. Intelligentia multo magis quam sensus est a passione remota, nam et interiores habet formas nec extra convertitur.

∶ III ∶

Meminisse et reminisci non est conservare atque repetere rerum formas aliquando impressas animo.

3 Quando dicunt animam tamquam rerum incorporearum[17] atque corporearum mediam utrarumque in se formas habere, non intelligimus has formas tamquam accidentia quaedam iacere in anima—sicut litteras in tabella—sive aliquando inscriptae sint sive ingenitae. Nam animae divinae natura neque novas subit impressiones, neque rationes rerum quas habet ab initio tam diversas habet ab ipsa sui natura ut[18] accidentia referant sed, ut alibi diximus, sicut sunt in anima naturales substantiae vires: intellectus ratio imaginatio sensus et potentiae vegetales, ita rerum quoque cognoscendarum rationes habet quasi vires essentiales, quemadmodum et membrorum seminales possidet rationes. Quando igitur anima

of sensing—whereas passivity confuses judgment—it has no passivity with respect to objects. If passivity arises in any way from these things, it reaches the body and the spirit: indeed, it is when the spirit is thus either struck or affected by external things that the soul being present immediately perceives affections of this kind. In truth, this perception is not passivity but rather activity: that is, under these circumstances in one way or another enlivening the spirit and putting forth (as Iamblichus says)[4] the inborn forms of sensible things. Intelligence is much more removed from passivity than is sense, for it has internal forms and does not turn toward the exterior.

: III :

To remember and recall is not to preserve and revisit forms of things at some point impressed on the soul.

When they say that the soul, as though an intermediary between incorporeal and corporeal things, has the forms of both these within itself, we do not understand these forms as lying in the soul as though they were certain accidents—like letters in a tablet—whether these forms were at some point inscribed or inborn there. For the nature of a divine soul does not take on fresh impressions and does not have the reason-principles of things which have been its possession from the beginning as so diverse from its own nature that they might represent accidents. But as we have said elsewhere, just as there are in the soul natural powers of substance: intellect, reason, imagination, sense, and the vegetative potencies, so the soul also has reason-principles of things to be known which are as though essential powers in the same way that it also has the seminal reason-principles of its bodily parts. Therefore, when the

3

aliquid meditatur, seipsam ex naturali virtute in actum naturalem circa id ipsum educit. Quod si attentius diutiusque meditatur idem, in hoc ipsum valentius se conformat; idque est meminisse — hinc et facilius reminiscitur.

soul thinks about something, it brings itself out from its natural power into a natural act with respect to that thing. But if it thinks about this same thing with greater attentiveness and for a longer time, it conforms itself more forcefully to that thing, and this amounts to remembering it. And from this, recollection is easily accomplished.

[LIBER VII]

DE ANIMI IMMORTALITE

: I :

Unusquisque nostrum totus est immortalis,
siquidem est ipse animus immortalis.

1 Anima dupliciter se habet ad corpus: partim quidem ut substantialis quaedam species ad materiam, quoniam per eius praesentiam certa quaedam humorum temperatura spiritusque vitalis in corpore nascitur; partim vero tamquam utens ad instrumentum quantum pro arbitrio movet corpus. Atque est a corpore separabilis et iam quodammodo separata.

: II :

Nullum corpus qua ratione corpus propriam et insitam habet
vitam; anima vero habet. Igitur anima non est
corpus; ergo neque fit ex
corpore vel corporibus cum sit natura praestantior.

2 Corpus sua proprietate dissolubile est; anima proprietate sua connectit corpus conciliatque contraria dum certa quadam ratione commiscet; neque igitur dissolubilis est neque corpus neque ex certa corporum mixtura concipitur; immo vero vicissim ordinata

[BOOK VII]

ON THE IMMORTALITY OF THE SOUL

: I :

Each one of us is immortal as a whole,
given that the soul itself is immortal.

The soul has a twofold relation to the body: partly in relation to 1
matter in so far as it is a certain substantial form — since through
its presence a certain definite temperament of humors and a vital
spirit[1] is born in the body —, and partly as though using the body
as an instrument to the extent that it moves the body in conformity with choice. Moreover, the soul is separable from body and is
separate in a sense now.

: II :

No body, to the extent that it is body, has its own inborn life.
However, the soul does have this. Therefore, the soul is not a
body. Therefore also, it does not come to be from body or
bodies, since it is superior in nature.

Body in its own proper quality is dissoluble. Soul in its own 2
proper quality binds the body together and harmonizes contraries
while blending them according to a certain definite proportionality. Therefore, soul is not dissoluble, is not a body, and is not
brought into being through a definite blending of bodies. On the

ratio mixtionis in corporibus procedit ab anima. Erimus in hoc libro brevissimi, nam circa eadem in *Theologia* latissimi sumus.

: III :

Omne corpus efficit distantia partium ut
parte alia patiente non
statim compatiantur et aliae. Per ipsam vero animam
corpus vivum habet ut ad[19] *partis unius*
motionem passionemque cunctae statim
commoveantur. Anima igitur nec est corpus
neque forma distenta per corpus.

3 Non est corpus crassum, alioquin non facile penetrabit totum; non est corpus labile, alioquin labilissimum corpus non continebit; non est impressa corpori forma, alioquin nec expedite corpori dominabitur ad vivificandum et movendum et continendum, et a forma praestantiore pendebit in seipsa manente vitamque effundente per corpus. Atque haec ipsa forma praestantior potius erit anima; quae cum individua sit ubique tota et extra contrariarum qualitatum genus, facile contraria inter se conciliat et distenta dissipabiliaque connectit in unum.

contrary, indeed, an ordered proportion of blending in bodies comes forth from the soul. In this book, we will be very brief, for we range more widely around the same issues in the *Theology*.[2]

: III :

Every body brings it about, through separation of parts,
that when one part suffers an affect the other parts do not
immediately suffer together with it. It is through the soul that a
living body has the wherewithal to bring it about that all parts
are immediately moved in response to the motion and passion
of a single part. Therefore, the soul is neither a body
nor a form extended through body.

The soul is not a solid body: otherwise, it will not readily pene- 3 trate a totality. It is not a volatile body: otherwise, it will not sustain the most volatile body. It is not a form impressed in a body: otherwise, it will not expeditiously take command of a body in order to enliven, move, and sustain it, and it will depend on a higher form which remains in itself and effuses life through the body. Moreover, it is this very higher form that will rather be the soul. Since the soul is indivisible everywhere as a whole and outside the genus of contrary qualities, it easily harmonizes contraries with one another and binds together separate and disparate things into a unity.

: IV :

Stoici et Epicurei animam esse spiritum suspicabantur:
id est, subtilissimum corpus. Illi quidem potius
igneum, hi vero magis aerium; et utrique
non quemlibet spiritum sed certa quadam
proprietate affectum[20] *animam nominabant.*

4 Haec ipsa certa proprietas et quodammodo incorporea corporeque
excellentior non a corpore generatur sed a substantia penitus incorporea quae potius anima iudicabitur. Quae quidem cum ad
oppositas in corpore qualitates et motiones tam edendas quam re-
gendas aeque se habeat, merito neque certum aliquod corpus vel
corporeum est, neque ex corpore quodam corporibusve dependet.

: V :

Anima motus effectusque omniformes tam
vegetali virtute per rationes seminales quam
electione profert; et corpus
certo quodam ordine ad certum auget terminum,
permanetque ipsa interea eadem. Item tota anima est in
qualibet — vel ficta portione animae
vel vera corporis portione —; totaque virtus animae
in qualibet seminis gutta servatur.

5 Haec autem munera ad molem vel qualitatem corpoream pertinere
non possunt. Anima igitur est incorporea.

: IV :

The Stoics and the Epicureans surmised that the soul was a
spirit: that is to say, a most subtle body. The Stoics thought of
the spirit more as fiery, the Epicureans more as airy. Both
groups named as soul not any kind of spirit but the one
bestowed with a certain definite property.

This definite property itself which is somehow incorporeal and   4
superior to body is not generated by a body but by a substance
that is completely incorporeal and will be judged rather to be a
soul. Indeed, since this property has an equal relation to opposite
qualities and motions in the body that are as much to be brought
forth as governed, it is rightly neither some definite body or corporeal thing nor dependent on a certain body or bodies.

: V :

The soul puts forth its omniform motions and effects as much
using the vegetative power operating through seminal rational-
principles as using choice. It increases the body according to a
certain definite order toward a definite limit, while in the
meantime remaining the same. Moreover, the soul is entire in
each and every thing—either an imagined "part" of the soul
or a true part of the body. The entire power of the soul is
preserved in each and every drop of semen.

These functions cannot pertain to bulk or corporeal quality.   5
Therefore the soul is incorporeal.

: VI :

Necesse est diversa per sensus varios
influentia ad intimum et unum
individuumque sensum redigi omnia inter se comparantem.

6   Nisi ad individuum denique colligantur, non poterunt comparari
per iudicium prorsus eundem: colligi vero ibi sic apparet, quoniam
colliguntur ferme similiter in pupilla. Sensus hic intimus neque
dividi ad sensibilium divisionem potest neque quantitate illis aequari; neque esse humidus, alioquin cessaret memoria; neque du-
rus: periret namque docilitas. Et omnino si sit corporeus, formae
ibi rerum se invicem impedient atque confundent.

: VII :

Principalis sensus passionum iudex passiones
cuiuslibet membri subito percipit;
in qua particula membri sint distincte discernit;
huc oculos manusque statim admovet.

7   Id autem efficere non valeret nisi esset ubique totus: non est ergo
corporeus.

: VI :

It is necessary for different things flowing in through various senses to be taken back to an innermost, unitary, and indivisible sense that compares all things among themselves.

If they are not gathered ultimately into something indivisible, they 6
will not be able to be compared by means of a judgment that is absolutely self-identical. It appears that they are gathered there because they are gathered in the pupil of the eye in a broadly similar manner. This innermost sense can neither be divided in relation to the division of sensible things nor equated with them in quantity. It cannot be moist, for otherwise, memory would cease, and it cannot be hard. for otherwise, docility would be destroyed. Altogether, if it were corporeal, the forms of things will impede and be confused with one another there.

: VII :

The primal sense which is the judge of passions suddenly perceives the passions of each and every bodily member. It clearly discerns in what part of the member these passions are and immediately moves the eyes and the hands to that part.

The primal sense could not do this if it were not present every- 7
where as a whole. Therefore, it is not corporeal.

: VIII :

Intelligentia frequenter attingit et penetrat incorporea,
formasque separat a corporibus. Fit igitur absque corpore;
intellectus ergo non est corporeus.[21]

8   Cum indivisibile non aliter quam per indivisibile possit attingi, intellectus attingens individua est individuus; et ubi separatis se coniungit, est a corpore separatus; et quando coniuncta separat, maxime separatum se esse declarat.

: IX :

Essentia corporea tamquam imperfecta dependet
ab incorporea perfecta; quae quidem cum ex
seipsa primoque sit et vivat, semper est et vivit:
in cuius genere anima continetur.

9   Anima quoniam in genere divinorum est ultima, ideo cum caducis videtur inire commercium ex quo optimus eius habitus intermittitur. At quoniam in divinorum genere comprehenditur, naturam assidue servat seque potest in dignitatem pristinam revocare.

: VIII :

Understanding frequently reaches and penetrates incorporeal things, and it separates forms from bodies. It therefore comes about without body. Therefore, intellect is not corporeal.

Since the indivisible cannot be reached except through the indivis- 8
ible, the intellect that reaches the indivisible is indivisible. When it
joins itself to separate things, it is separate from the body, and
when it separates conjoined things, it declares itself to be separate
to the highest degree.

: IX :

An essential being that is corporeal, as though being imperfect, depends upon something incorporeal and perfect. Since the latter exists and lives through itself and primally, it exists and lives everlastingly. The soul is contained in this genus.

Since the soul is the last in the genus of divine things, it therefore 9
seems to enter into dealings with mortal things, as a result of
which its optimal condition is neglected. But since it is included
within the genus of divine things, it continuously maintains its
nature and is able to call itself back to its original status.

: X :

Duae sunt mentium divinarum dotes: una quidem claritas
intellectus omnia cernens, altera vero optimus vitae habitus.
Eiusmodi dotes maxime consequitur animus quando seipsum
ab omni labe corporea segregans revertitur in seipsum. Ex quo
apparet eum esse divinis mentibus natura cognatum.

10 Duo sunt apud nos argumenta divinitatis: alterum prophetia, alterum prodigiosorum operum demonstratio. Quicumque vero divina haec munera reportarunt, ex hoc uno dumtaxat officio haec
sibi vindicavisse videntur: quod animam a corpore revocaverint ad
seipsam. Unde constat ipsam naturam per se esse cum divinitate
coniunctam.

: XI :

Corpus animatum ipsius animae beneficio habet ut ex se
quodammodo moveatur. Igitur anima
potissimum habet idem; igitur et vitam ex
se habet; igitur et in se a corpore non
dependentem: semper ergo vivit etiam
a corpore separata.

11 Animam ex se et in se moveri vivereque etiam sine corporis sustentaculo apparet, praeterea maxime quando contra inclinationes corporis sese movet et quando se ad incorporea transfert. Si quod

: X :

There are two gifts of divine minds: one the clearness of intellect perceiving all things, the other the optimal condition of life. The soul most fully obtains such gifts when it separates itself from all corporeal blemishes and returns to itself. From this it appears that it is by nature akin to divine things.

There are two proofs of the divinity among us: one being proph- 10 ecy, the other the evidence of miraculous works. All those who have successfully performed these divine functions seem to have gained this privilege through their discharge of one obligation: that of having recalled the soul from the body to itself. From this it is established that the nature of soul is through itself conjoined with divinity.

: XI :

The enlivened body has through the favor of the soul itself the ability to be self-moved in some way. Therefore the soul has the same ability most of all. Therefore it also has life through itself. Therefore it also has life in itself not depending on the body. Therefore, it always lives even when separated from the body.

It appears that the soul moves from itself and in itself and that it 11 lives even without the support of the body. Moreover, this is especially so when the soul moves itself contrary to the inclinations of the body, and when it transfers itself toward incorporeal things. If

vero accidentale vitae vestigium corpori est impressum, redigen-
dum est ad substantialem animae vitam in se exsistentem, sicut
calor vel pallor nubis ad lumen; atqui ut lumen ad solem, sic
anima refertur ad mentem.

: XII :

Anima nostra mundi animam motu rerumque[22]
intelligentia imitans sempiterna est,
sicut et illa, praesertim quoniam, dum
revocando se ad intima sui res intelligit, declarat
absolutas rerum formas sibi ingenitas se habere.

12 Denique cum anima sit forma simplex individua non alligata
materiae, neque dissolvi potest neque dividi neque disperdi.

: XIII :

Anima nostra, etsi est in genere divinorum, tamen quia
in eo genere ultimum tenet gradum, merito
descendit in corpus — et id quidem caducum —
ad divinum gradum iterum reversura.

13 Natura intellectus longe diversa est a corpore: agit enim in seipsa
fugiens interim a corporeis. Igitur inter puros intellectus et corpora sunt naturae habentes partem quidem intellectualem, partem

any accidental trace of life is impressed on the body, it must be traced back to the substantial life of the soul subsisting in itself, just as the heat or paleness of a cloud must be traced back to light. But as light is traced back to the sun, so is the soul referred back to the mind.

: XII :

Our soul, imitating the world-soul in motion and the under-standing of things, is everlasting, just as the world-soul also is. This is especially so because, when it understands things by recalling itself to the innermost part of itself, our soul shows that it has inborn in it the transcendent forms of things.

Finally, since it is a form that is simple, indivisible, not bound to body, the soul can neither be dissolved, nor divided, nor dispersed. 12

: XIII :

Our soul, even if it is in the genus of divine things, because it nevertheless holds the lowest rank in that genus, rightly descends into a body — and indeed, a mortal body. However, the soul will return once more to the divine rank.

The nature of intellect is distinct by far from the body, for it acts 13 in itself, in the meantime fleeing from corporeal things. Therefore, between pure intellects and bodies there are natures having a part that is intellectual and a part that is psychic: that is to say, a part

etiam animalem: id est, ad corpora sibi conformanda vergentem. Sunt in his tres[23] gradus, nam in animis quidem caelestibus intellectuale superat animale, in nostris vero vicissim, in daemonicis aeque se habent. Nihil ergo mirum est animam nostram, quamvis divinam, in corpus mortale descendere quando in seipsa descendit ad tertia: id est, sub intellectu per rationem et imaginationem ad potentiam vegetalem.

: XIV :

Omnes animae proprias immortalesque vitas habent.

14 Quicquid vitae ab anima nostra in nostrum corpus emicat abeuntem hinc[24] animam comitatur. Quod vero in foetu vitale caelitus impressum fuerat caelitus conservatur. Circa quod et noster animus hinc impurus emigrans amore se versat purus vero relinquit.

: XV :

Animae defunctorum nostra haec
memoriter tenent sentiunt curant
malefaciunt benefaciunt.

15 Quamdiu[25] corpus habent qualecumque vel aerium vel aetherium, proprios habent et sensus; sin omne corpus exuant, eminentia

that tends toward the conforming of their bodies to themselves. There are three ranks among these, for in celestial souls the intellectual prevails over the psychic, in our souls however the reverse is the case, while in daemonic souls the intellectual and the psychic are in equilibrium with one another. Therefore, there is no surprise that our soul, although being divine, descends into a mortal body when it descends to a third level *in itself*: that is to say, descending below intellect through reason and imagination to the vegetative power.

: XIV :

All souls have lives that are their own and immortal.

Whatever vitality shines forth from our soul into our body accompanies the soul as it departs from here. That which from the heaven was impressed in the embryo as vital is preserved in the heaven as vital. As to that around which our soul turns itself with love when departing from here as impure: this it leaves behind when it is pure.

14

: XV :

The souls of the dead hold the things of our world in their memory. They exercise sensation and care, and they do good and ill.

As long as they have a body of whatever kind — either airy or aetherial — they have their own proper senses. But if they shed all body, they are judged to employ in place of the senses a certain

15

quadam intelligentiae ad singula discernenda uti pro sensibus iudi-cantur. Nam et imaginatio, praesertim perfecta, sensus praefert, et ratio imaginationem agit atque sensus, et intellectus rationem atque sequentia modo quodam praestantiore.

Marsilii epilogus.

16 Desideras, magnanime Laurenti, brevem tandem longae disputationis summam: disputationis inquam de immortalite et in *Theologia* et in praesentia in longum iam productae. Desiderabat et idem noster ille Bernardus cum Veneti senatus hic orator nos hac[26] de re latissime disputantes audiret: Bernardus inquam Bembus, vir apprime doctus doctorumque patronus atque meus in sidere genioque frater. Tibi igitur atque illi pariter haec erit summa quattuor distincta capitibus: primo quidem, quod anima rebus caducis dominari potest incitamentisque corporeis repugnare; secundo, quod multa a corporibus separata frequenter excogitat sive res ipsas attingat per se separatas sive separet ipsa; tertio, quod naturaliter aeterna desiderat ac saepe aeternorum fiducia negligit temporalia; quarto, quod aeternum colit Deum vitae sempiternae gratia. Tota denique religio naturalis homini firmissimum immortalitatis est fundamentum.

greatness of intelligence for the distinguishing of individual things. For imagination also, especially when it is perfect, exhibits sensation, reason acts upon the imagination and the senses, and intelligence in a certain more excellent manner activates the reason and the faculties that follow it.

Marsilio's epilogue.

You desire, O magnanimous Lorenzo, at long last a brief summary 16 of the protracted discussion: indeed, the discussion of the immortality of the soul both in the *Theology*[3] and in the present instance has already been extended to a great length. Our friend Bernardo also desired the same thing when, being here as ambassador of the Venetian senate, he heard us very lengthily discussing this topic: we are referring to Bernardo Bembo, a man preeminently learned, a patron of learned men, and brother to me with respect to star and genius.[4] Therefore, to you and to him alike, this will be the summary distinguished into four points: first, that the soul is able to prevail over mortal things and to combat corporeal urgings; second, that it frequently thinks about many things separate from bodies, whether it reaches the very things that are separate in themselves or else separates them; third, that it naturally desires eternal things and often spurns temporal things in its reliance upon the eternal; fourth, that it worships the eternal God for the sake of everlasting life. Finally, natural religion in its totality is the firmest foundation of immortality for man.

[LIBER VIII]

DE ANIMAE DESCENSU IN CORPORA

: I :

Animae nostrae intellectuales in corpus descendunt per
naturam vivificam intelligentiae suae subiunctam et
corpus naturaliter asciscentem sicut flamma sulfur; similiter
et caelestium intellectuales animae corporibus suis
per eiusmodi medium copulantur.

1 Voluit Deus ad sui intellectus exemplar in qualibet mundi sphaera et in caelo et infra caelum animalia quaedam intellectualia fore; ac ne intellectus quasi per violentiam forent ad corpora protrahendi per naturam animalem: id est, vegetalem eis agnatam quasi plantam, corporibus libenter asciscendis conciliavisse videtur.

[BOOK VIII]

ON THE SOUL'S DESCENT INTO BODIES

: I :

*Our intellectual souls descend into bodies through the life-giving
nature that is subjoined to their intelligence and naturally
adopts a body in the way that a flame adopts sulfur. Similarly
the intellectual souls of the celestial bodies are joined to their
bodies through a medium of this kind.*

God willed that in each and every sphere of the world, both in the   1
heaven and below the heaven, there should be certain intellectual
animate beings after the paradigm of his own intellect. In order
that the intellects should not be things to be dragged forth, as
though by force, in the direction of bodies through the psychic —
that is to say: vegetative — nature born as though a scion of their
family, God seems to have harmonized them with bodies freely
adopted.

: II :

Coniunctio animae cum corpore, etsi est
secundum quandam animae naturam atque etiam ad
universi perfectionem, tamen duplici ratione animis nostris
obest, quia et intelligentiam quodammodo
impedit et animum perturbationibus implet; animis vero
caelestibus haec impedimenta non accidunt.

2 Quoniam per naturam genitalem coniunctio cum corpore naturalis est animae, ideo caelestes animae quae hac sola potentia utuntur ad corpus in habitu naturali felicique consistunt. Cum enim
earum corpora nec dissolvenda nec externis passionibus subdita
nec ullius egena sint, facile per solam animae suae vim genitalem
reguntur atque moventur nec earum contemplationem tranquilli-
tatemque impediunt; animis vero nostris contraria ratione accidit
et contrarium: datur tamen reditus ad superna siquidem quandoque fit ad superna conversio.

3 Ad inferiora vero labi Porphyrius ait, quando animus quasi ager
iam depravatur ut qui multis annis produxerit triticum, reddat
denique pro tritico lolium: id est, solitus notiones intellectuales
edere iam ferat imaginales. Tunc e radicibus animae pullulat, inquit, vegetalis actus quasi germen per quod in corpus iam por-
rectum anima corpori se conglutinat. Porphyrius hic animarum
lapsum casui daemonum ab Hebraeis introducto facit similem, vi-
tio videlicet intelligentiae vel voluntatis effectum, unde secuta sit
concupiscentia demens. Quod etiam de daemonibus disputans[27]

⁘ II ⁘

Although the conjunction of the soul with the body is in accordance with a certain nature of the soul and also with the perfection of the universe, it obstructs our souls in a twofold manner inasmuch as it somehow impedes the intelligence and fills the soul with disturbances. However, these impediments do not arise for the celestial souls.

Since conjunction with the body through the generative nature is 2 natural to the soul, the celestial souls which use this power alone with respect to bodies subsist in a natural and felicitous condition. For since their bodies are not to be dissolved nor subjected to external passions nor lacking with respect to anything, these bodies are governed and moved easily by the generative power alone of their soul, and do not impede the contemplation and tranquility of the celestial souls. The opposite of this situation occurs with respect to our souls and in accordance with a contrary reason-principle, although a return to the higher realm is given to them if and when a turning toward the higher things comes about.

However, Porphyry says that the soul falls toward the lower 3 realm when it is now barren in the manner of a field which has produced wheat for many years but eventually yields darnel in place of the wheat: that is to say, the soul having been accustomed to bring out intellectual concepts now bears imaginary ones. At this point, he says, a vegetative act comes forth from the roots of the soul, being as though a sprout through which when now extended through the body the soul cements itself to that body. Porphyry here makes the fall of souls similar to the fall of daemons of which the Hebrews make mention: that is to say, produced by a defect of intelligence or will from which a mindless

Dionysius ait qui ibi videtur daemonas animalia ponere, sicut et Basilius plurimique Graeci theologi putaverunt. Tum vero si verum sit illud Damasceni ultimos tantum angelos cecidisse atque evaserint animalia, valde similis erit Platonicus animarum lapsus daemonibus apud Hebraeos Christianosque cadentibus.

4 Proinde ubi apud Plotinum atque Proculum legis particulares animas agere particulares vicissitudines tum ad superiora tum ad inferiora, ne intelligas animam tuam infinita corpora mutaturam: finitae namque sunt et paucae unius animae mutationes in anno mundi magno, atque in anno sequenti, ut aiunt, eadem penitus retexuntur. Praeterea nec oportet[28] omnem animam omnes induere species nec quamlibet animam pariter ascendere vel descendere. Sunt enim (ut Platonice loquar) inter animas hominum differentiae quaedam quodammodo speciales — sicut in stellis quae videntur aspectu consimiles — differuntque inter se animae nostrae non sicut pyrum a pomo persico sed sicut a pyro pyrum. Sunt ergo determinati singulis pro natura progressus: excellentiores igitur animae ascendunt quidem altius minusve descendunt, deteriores vero vicissim. Humanas dico animas et ad corpora tantum humana descendere: sic enim opinionem Platonicam moderamur quae erit insuper moderatior si ab Hebraeis accipiatur existimantibus ter solum animam in hominem devenire, postremo semper fore vel miseram vel beatam.

concupiscence will follow. Dionysius[1] in discussing daemons also says this, for there he seems to postulate daemons as ensouled beings, just as Basil and most of the Greek theologians thought them to be. Moreover, if the Damascene's statement that only the lowest angels fell is true and that the fallen daemons did turn into ensouled beings,[2] then the Platonic fall of souls will be very similar to the falling daemons mentioned by the Hebrews and the Christians.

Therefore, when you read in Plotinus and Proclus[3] that particular souls have particular alternations of movement sometimes to the higher and sometimes to the lower sphere, you should not understand that your soul will take on an infinite number of bodies. For the changes of a single soul are finite and few in number within the great year of the world while in the following year, as they say, absolutely the same things are woven anew.[4] Moreover, it is neither necessary for every soul to take on all the specific forms nor for each and every soul to ascend or descend in a similar manner, for there are among human souls (speaking Platonically) certain somewhat specific differentiae—just as in the case of stars those that are seen are similar in appearance—, our souls differing among themselves not as a pear differs from a pomegranate but as a pear differs from a pear. Therefore, there are courses of life that are determined for individual souls in accordance with their nature: the more worthy souls ascend higher or descend to a lesser extent while the less worthy have a comparable situation but in reverse. I refer here to human souls and to descent only toward human bodies, thus tempering the Platonic doctrine which will be even more moderate if it is received in the form adopted by the Hebrews. They think that the soul enters only three times into human form and in the end will be permanently either wretched or blessed.

4

: III :

Quoniam omnis natura praeter primam[29] simplicissimam
infinitam multiplicabilis est, ideo in genere intellectuali multi
sunt intellectus, in genere animali multae sunt animae.
In ordine animarum multae sunt intellectuales quales sunt
caelestes, daemonicae, nostrae.

5   Animae nostrae praeter intellectum in mundo intelligibili semper
agentem habent rationem imaginationem sensum vim vegetalem.
Quas sane vires officiis propriis quandoque oportet uti. His autem
utuntur in corpore: itaque consentaneum est eas in corpora quandoque descendere.

: IV :

Intellectus divinus impressit intellectui nostro omniformem
universi formam quae facile in rationem vacantem inde
surrutilat. Quando igitur
ratio ad eam penitus se convertit secumque
rapit imaginationem, in eodem statu quo
et mundi anima permanet.

6   Id est: simili divinorum contemplatione fruitur et interim caelum
habitans ad universalem mundi gubernationem intuitum convertit
similiter et affectum. At quando ratio una cum imaginatione, universali mundi forma neglecta, particularem quandam diligentius

: III :

*Since every nature except the first, most simple, and infinite
nature is capable of multiplication, there are many intellects in
the intellectual genus and many souls in the psychic genus.
Within the order of souls there are many intellectual souls
such as the celestial, daemonic, and our own.*

Our souls have, besides an intellect always active in the intelligible 5
world, reason, imagination, sense, and the vegetative power. It is
indeed necessary to employ these powers in their proper functions
at one time or another. Our souls use these powers in the body,
and so it is proper for them to descend into bodies from time to
time.

: IV :

*The divine intellect has imprinted the omniform Form of
the universe in our intellect. From there, this Form readily
casts its glimmer into the reason which is free to receive it.
Therefore, when the reason completely turns itself toward
the Form and snatches away the imagination, it
remains in the same status as that of the world-soul.*

That is to say: it enjoys a similar contemplation of divine things 6
and, dwelling in the meantime in heaven, it turns its intuitive gaze
and similarly its affectivity to the universal governance of the
world. But when the reason together with the imagination gazes
more intently on something particular and loves it more ardently,

intuetur et amat ardentius, iamque et vegetalis ipsa natura eandem prorsus affectat, tunc anima facta iam angustior corpus asciscit angustum passionibusque subiectum; hinc igitur curis innumerabilibus sollicitata vexatur.

: V :

De animae descensu Empedoclis Heracliti Platonis dicta consentiunt.

7 Anima quoniam divina est in hac regione caduca saepe convertitur ad divina, et quoniam est ultimum divinorum per instinctum affectumque naturalem venit in corpus: ideo voluntate venit, scilicet naturali, insuper electione quadam: venit et necessitate, quoniam divina lege necessarium est animas quae sic affectae sunt, sic eligunt, e vestigio devenire—sponte veniunt velut ad bonum, non sponte interim incidunt et in malum. Venire huc animas ad ordinem pertinet universi—ad exercitationem ⟨videlicet⟩ inferiorum animae virium ad mali peritiam. Peccantes animae levius commutatione puniuntur ex feliciore homine in hominem felicem minus vel infelicem; peccantes vero gravius vexantur etiam a daemonibus—quod Mercurius et Orpheus Iamblichusque confirmant. Vir puerum atrocitate vultus personatisque terriculamentis facile terret. Saturni Martisque influxus atrae bilis vel croceae motibus imaginationes vexant. Saturnii quidam Martisque daemones horrendis imaginationibus suis quasi vultibus personatis imaginationes peccantium miserabiliter agitant: possunt quin etiam eas humorum motibus afflictare

the universal Form of the world having been neglected, and when the vegetative nature itself strives after the same thing, then the soul which has now become more contracted adopts a body[5] that is contracted and subject to passions. So hereupon, the soul is beset by the disturbance of innumerable cares.

: V :

The statements of Empedocles, Heraclitus, and Plato are in agreement concerning the descent of the soul.[6]

Since the soul is divine, it often turns, in this region of mortality, toward divine things. Since the soul is the last divine thing, it comes into body through its impulses and natural affectivity. Therefore, it comes by an inclination of a natural kind and in addition by a certain choice. It also comes by necessity, since it is necessary according to divine law that souls so affected and making such choices instantly reach a point where they come willingly as though to a good while in the meantime falling unwillingly into an evil. That souls should come to this point: that is, to the exercise of the lower powers of the soul with respect to the experience of evil, pertains to the order of the universe. Souls that sin more moderately are punished by change from being a happy man to being one less happy or unhappy. Those that sin more grievously are harassed also by daemons: something that Mercury,[7] Orpheus,[8] and Iamblichus[9] confirm. A man easily frightens a boy with a frowning facial expression and feigned menaces. The emanations of Saturn and Mars disturb our imaginations with the motions of black or yellow bile. Certain daemons of Saturn and Mars pitiably assail the imaginations of sinners with their fearsome apparitions which are as though feigned expressions. Indeed, they can also afflict them with the motions of the humors.

: VI :

Anima venit in corpus non solum infirmitate
quadam in divinis ultra consistere non valente,
sed etiam potestate naturae fecundae
pullulantis in germen; forma namque corporea est
animae fecundae propago.

8 Simili quadam fecunditate primum bonum in mentem exuberat omniformem, haec in similem mundi animam, haec in mundum similiter omniformem; item causae omnes in effectus ubique suos. Denique superiorum providentiam imitatus animus ad inferiora se transfert quodam studio providendi.

: VII :

Sicut aer inter ignem aquamve medius,
illinc quidem igneus, hinc vero fit aquaeus,
ac vicissim ad utraque fertur; sic animus
ad divina se habet atque caduca.

9 Omnia corpora sui aliquid inferioribus largiuntur, sed caelestia quidem nihil interim accipiunt a sequentibus, elementaria vero dando vicissim quoque recipiunt. Similiter caelestes animae inferioribus providentes inde nequaquam inficiuntur. Daemonicae vero quaedam atque nostrae, dum perficiunt corpora, quodammodo

: VI :

The soul comes into the body not only through inability to
remain any longer in the divine realm because of a certain
weakness but also through the power of the fertile nature
sprouting into a shoot. For indeed, the corporeal form
is an offshoot of the fertile soul.

Through a certain similar fertility, the First Good overflows into   8
the omniform mind, the mind into the world-soul that is similar,
and the world-soul similarly into the omniform world. Next, all
causes overflow everywhere into their effects. Finally, having imitated the providence of the higher causes, the soul directs itself
toward lower things with a certain desire to be provident.

: VII :

Just as air is the intermediate between fire and water,
becoming fiery in one part of itself but watery in the other,
and being borne by turns in either direction, so is the soul
disposed toward the divine and the mortal.

All bodies impart something of themselves to lower things. How-   9
ever, celestial bodies in the meantime receive nothing from the
things that follow them, whereas elemental bodies in the process
of giving also receive something in turn. Similarly, celestial souls
provide for lower things while being in no way corrupted by them.
However, certain daemonic souls and our souls, while bringing

inficiuntur inde propter curiosiorem providentiam circa provinciam duriorem. Sed loci malignitas et mundi superioris felicitatem
commemorat et admonet illum vehementius affectare.

: VIII :

*Cum animus noster vires et actus caelestibus
animis consimiles habeat, probabile est saltem intellectum
nostrum, sicut et illorum, circa divina semper agere, sicut
natura vegetalis in nobis circa corporea versatur assidue.*

10 Verum sicut actiones vegetales nostrae nos latent, sic et intellectuales nostrae nobis plurimum sunt occultae, nec motus ullus in
parte vegetali sensuve[30] concupiscentia factus patet nobis, nisi ad
imaginationem et per hanc ad rationem usque perveniat; similiter
nec actus intelligentiae se patefacit nisi in rationem vacantem
quandoque surrutilet perque hanc ad[31] imaginationem similiter
vacuam transferatur ubi fieri solet animadversio. Caelestes animae
oboedientia sibi corpora solo tum naturae instinctu tum mentis
nutu facillime regunt; nostrae vero imaginationem quoque et rationem circa corpus id occupant eiusmodi providentiam exigens.
Ideo constitutum est divinitus ut quandoque hinc abeuntes ad
caelestia revertantur.

bodies to completion, are somehow corrupted by the latter on account of a providence which is more meddlesome as orientated to a harsher domain. However, the meanness of the place does recall to mind the blessedness of the higher realm and admonishes us to strive more earnestly after the latter.

: VIII :

Since our soul has powers and activities similar to celestial souls, it is at least probable that our intellect acts always around divine things just as does their intellect, and just as the vegetative nature in us is engaged continuously around bodies.

It is true that, just as our vegetative actions are hidden from us, so are our intellectual actions mostly concealed from us. Any motion in the vegetative part or the sense made by concupiscence sensation is not apparent to us unless it reaches the imagination and ultimately the reason by means of the latter. Similarly, an act of intelligence does not reveal itself unless at some point it casts its glimmer into a reason that is free to receive it, and is similarly passed through this reason to an imagination similarly free to receive it, awareness being wont to occur only here. The celestial souls govern with ease the bodies that obey them only with the instinctiveness of nature and at the same time with the assent of mind. However, our souls also employ imagination and reason with respect to that body fulfilling this kind of providence. Therefore, it has been established by divine dispensation that souls can sometimes depart from here and return to the celestial realm.

[LIBER IX]

UTRUM OMNES ANIMAE
UNA SINT ANIMA

: I :

*Plotini sententia est mundum unam habere
propriam sibi animam et animalia omnia
suas propriasque habere.*

1 Nisi mundus haberet unam, non esset compositum perfectum ve-
reque unum, nec reliquae in mundo animae ordine inter se facile
convenirent; item nisi nos proprias <animas> haberemus, affectio
passioque et actio animalis in uno mox ad omnes universumque
pertineret. Plotinus exercitaturus ingenium circa opinionem po-
nentem unicam in cunctis animam ludit utro citroque, aliud interea moliens.

[BOOK IX]

WHETHER ALL SOULS
ARE ONE SOUL

: I :

*The opinion of Plotinus is that the world has
a single soul proper to it, and that all animate beings
have their own proper souls.*

If the world did not have one soul, it would not be a composite 1
that is perfect and truly one, and the other souls in the world
would not readily come together with one another in an order.
Moreover, if we did not have our own proper souls, the affection,
passion, and action of the animate being in the case of one individual would immediately lead to all souls and to the universe.
Plotinus, intending to perform an intellectual exercise with respect
to the opinion that posits a single soul in all things, shifts playfully
in one direction and another, in the meantime working out a different position.

: II :

*Concessurus revera Plotinus animas esse distinctas,
non facile cedit rationi iam dictae: scilicet,
passionem animalis unius mox in aliud
universumque transituras.*

2 Dici mallet animalium corpora neque sibi invicem neque toti continua distinctas animas postulare; item ubi tota prorsus animalis
virtus congregatur in uno, hanc ipsam animam summum in animali genere possidentem merito passiones defectusque in animalibus[1] apparentes ipsam in se minime perpessuram.

: III :

Ludit adhuc Plotinus noster.

3 Verum sicut mutuus hominum amor unionem significat animarum, sic et perpetua diraque inter se odia diversitatem: non enim
minus dissidet homo ab homine et animal quodvis ab animali
quam ignis ab aqua, neque minus ergo distinguitur. Magicus vero
raptus magna ex parte confictus est et quas habeat causas in superioribus declaravimus. Alibi diximus formalem rei cuiusdam rationem esse in essentias plures multiplicabilem, excepta causa
prima. Igitur sicut ratio formalis corporis qualitatis naturae in
plura corpora naturas qualitates distincta est, sic et animae

: II :

*Being in reality ready to admit that souls are distinct, he does
not readily yield to the argument now stated: namely, that
passivity in the case of one animate being will immediately
cross over to another individual and to the universe.*

He would prefer it to be said that the bodies of animate beings   2
that are continuous neither with themselves nor with the totality
require souls that are distinct, and further that, when the entire
animating power is absolutely concentrated in one animate being,
that soul itself which possesses the highest rank within the genus
of animate beings will rightly not at all suffer in itself the passions
and defects that appear in animate beings.

: III :

Our Plotinus continues his playful exploration.

It is true that, just as the mutual love of men signifies the union of   3
souls, so do perpetual and dire hatreds signify their diversity, for a
man is no less separated from another man and whatsoever animate being from another animate being than fire is separated from
water, and therefore men and animate beings are no less distinct
than are those things. Magical seizure is to a large degree produced by assemblage, and we have stated above what the causes of
this are. Elsewhere, we have said that the formal reason-principle
of a certain thing can be multiplied into many essential beings, the
first cause being excluded from this rule of multiplication. Therefore, just as the formal reason-principle of a body, a quality, and a
nature is distinct in passing into many bodies, natures, and quali-

intellectusque in[2] animas intellectusque plures: tum vero si anima excellentior formaliorque est quam qualitas. Certe providentia divina constitutum est esse multos animarum gradus, sicut et qualitatum formaliter inter se distinctos: non sicut hic calor ab illo subiecti causa, sed sicut calor a frigore siccitas ab humore. Quod et Plotinus in fine capituli iam innuit ubi ait intellectus esse multos atque sensus ipsos iudiciales simul esse cum intellectibus: id est, cum intellectualibus animis. Significat vero disputationem hanc annuere: unam esse in cunctis corporibus animam non rationalem quidem sed vegetalem sensus cuiusdam confusi participem; verumtamen rationalem quamlibet animam posse corpus suum vita irrationali formare si non sit ab anima mundi formatum.

: IV :

Opinionem dicentem cunctis inesse animam numero unam iam respuit; tangit vero dicentem esse unam specie distinctam numero, atque singulas esse derivatas ex una divisa.

4 Hanc quoque refutat, nam anima est substantia incorporea individua in se consistens. Non potest igitur una communis anima in[3] plures derivari sicut vel continuum in partes vel albedo in plures albedines divisione continui vel sicut ex uno sigillo plures in multis ceris fiunt impressiones.

ties, so are souls and intellects distinct in passing into many souls and intellects, this being especially the case if soul is more excellent and more formal than is a quality. Certainly, it has been established by divine providence that there are many levels of souls, just as there are many levels of qualities formally distinct among themselves, this occurring not in the way that this heat is distinct from that heat as a consequence of their substrata but in the way that heat differs from cold and dryness from wetness. This is what Plotinus now suggests at the end of the chapter where he says that there are many intellects, and that the judging senses themselves are simultaneous with the intellects: that is to say, with the intellectual souls. However, he indicates his approval of the argument that there is one soul in all bodies—not the rational soul but the vegetative soul that partakes of a certain confused sensation—, although each and every rational soul would nevertheless be able to form its own body with irrational life were that body not formed by the world-soul.

: IV :

He now rejects the opinion stating that soul is numerically one
in all things. However, he touches upon the one stating that
it is one in species but distinguished in number and that
individual souls are distributed from a single divided soul.

He also refutes this view, for the soul is an incorporeal substance,   4
indivisible, and subsisting in itself. Therefore, it is not possible for
a single universal soul to be distributed into a multiplicity of souls
as a continuous thing is distributed into parts, or whiteness into a
multiplicity of whitenesses by division of a continuous thing, or
else as a multiplicity of impressions can arise in many pieces of
wax from a single seal.

: V :

Animae, quamvis per essentias inter se distinctae sint,
omnes tamen quodammodo una sunt anima
tribus videlicet modis.

5 Primo quia omnibus praeest una animarum generalis idea et tota
singulis inest; secundo quia quaelibet anima est forma penitus
omniformis, ideo quaelibet anima ceteras complectitur animas—
differt tamen haec ab illa quoniam sub differenti actu proprietate-
que haec et illa sunt omniformes, sicut conveniunt et differunt
propositiones inter se geometricae; tertio quia omnes in eodem
puncto esse possunt sicut lumina imaginesque colorum absque
confusione. Non esse unicam in singulis animam aut mentem satis
in *Theologia* probavimus. Haec ergo tibi sit summa. Cave suspiceris
suspicari Plotinum non distingui inter se essentias animarum: id
enim omnibus eius libris et huius etiam fini adversaretur; quin
etiam disputationem propriam fecit in hac *Enneade* contra eos qui
animam esse unicam opinantur.

6   Sed memento Plotinum ubique conari omnia quantum fieri
potest ad unum quiddam redigere, servata interim proprietate naturae. At 'unum quiddam' dico: id est, ad communionem affectionis actionisque et passionis, ut concors in universo harmonia ser-
vetur et traductio virtutis et actionis mutuo facileque per singula
fiat: quod quidem fieri non posset nisi singulae animae, quamvis
servata essentiae distinctione, contineantur et regantur ab una,

: V :

*Although the souls are distinct among themselves through their
essential being, they are all nonetheless a single soul in a
certain sense: namely, in three ways.*

First, because there presides over all things a single universal Idea   5
of soul, and this is present as a whole in individual things; second,
because each and every soul is an absolutely omniform form, and
therefore each and every soul embraces the other souls — however,
this soul differs from that soul because this soul and that soul are
omniform on the basis of a different act and proper character, just
as geometrical propositions agree and differ among themselves;
third, because all souls are able to be in the same point without
confusion, just as are lights and the images of colors. We have
demonstrated sufficiently in the *Theology*[1] that there is not a single
soul or mind in individual things: therefore, let this be your summary of the matter. You should take care not to surmise that Plotinus believes that the essential beings of souls are not distinguished from one another, for this surmise would be in opposition
to all his books and also to the conclusion of the present one. Indeed, he has in this *Ennead* made his own argument against those
who think that the soul is single.

You should remember that Plotinus everywhere strives, as much   6
as possible, to trace all things back to a certain unity, while in the
meantime preserving the proper characteristic of their nature:
tracing them back indeed to a "certain unity" in the sense of a universality of affectivity, action, and passion in order that a concordant harmony in the universe might be maintained and that a
transfer of power and action might occur with reciprocity and facility through individual things. This indeed could not come about
if individual souls were not sustained and governed by one soul,

ferme sicut virtutes omnes membrorum a virtute cordis et a cervice nervi. Adducit igitur multa ad unionem eiusmodi signa quae, ut tamquam validissima confirmet, concedere videtur etiam tanti vigoris videri posse ut valeant adduci non solum ad talem unionem sed ad maiorem etiam suspicandam. Quasi dicat: si posset quispiam per haec signa suspicari unionem essentiae — quod tamen ego non probo — multo magis nos[4] possumus per eadem signa unionem inter animas affectionis et actionis consensionisque et compassionis asseverare.

albeit having preserved the distinction of their essential being, more or less in the way that all the powers of the bodily members are sustained and governed by the power of the heart and all the tendons by the neck. Therefore, Plotinus introduces a multiplicity of evidences with respect to such a union and, in order to establish them as being the most compelling, he also seems to admit that they can be seen as having so much force that they can be adduced not only toward the surmise of such a union but even toward that of a greater one. It is as though he were to say: if anyone were able through these evidences to surmise that there was a union of essential being—something which I do not approve—, much more can we assert through the same evidences the union between souls of affectivity, action, concord, and sympathy . . .

Note on the Text

ॐ

In establishing the Latin text in the present volume, I have for the most part followed the principles set out in my edition of the *Commentary on the Third Ennead* in volume 4 (ITRL 80). As in the earlier volume, the *editio princeps* of 1492 [*E*] has been employed as the foundational text, although in the present instance the edition of Basel 1580 [*Ba*]—which also prints the Greek text of Plotinus—has been used as the control rather than that of Basel 1559 [*B*]. Both these latter versions are excellent and follow the *editio princeps* very closely.

In connection with the *Fourth Ennead*, the *editio princeps* has confused the chapter numbering in several places, this numbering being only partially rectified in the *corrigenda* of the *editio princeps* [*E^c*] and by a later scribe *in Plut* [*Plut^c*]. The chapter numbering of Book 4 is particularly chaotic (a situation that may well go back to the author's archetype), and contains further variations between *E* and *Ba*. For the convenience of the reader, the chapters in this book have been completely renumbered by the editor.

SIGLA

B *Plotini divini illius è Platonica familia philosophi De rebus philosophicis libri LIIII in Enneades sex distributi, à Marsilio Ficino Florentino è Graeca Lingua in Latinam versi et ab eodem doctissimis commentariis illustrati, omnibus cum Graeco exemplari collatis et diligenter castigatis* (Basel: Pietro Perna, 1559). Copy used: University of Notre Dame.

Ba *Plotini Platonicorum facile coryphaei operum philosophicorum omnium libri LIV [. . .] cum latina Marsilii Ficini interpretatione et commentatione* (Basel, 1580); facsimile edition with an introduction by Stéphane Toussaint (Lucca: Société Marsile Ficin, 2010).

E   [Plotinus. *Opera*, translated with a commentary by Marsilio
           Ficino] (Florence: Antonio di Bartolommeo Miscomini, May
           7, 1492). See [British Library], *Incunabula Short Title Catalogue*,
           no. ip00815000. Electronic facsimile in the Digitale Biblio-
           thek of the Munich Staatsbibliothek. Copy used: Trinity
           College, Cambridge.

E^c *corrigenda* in E.

O   *Marsilii Ficini Florentini [. . .] opera et quae hactenus extitere et quae*
           in lucem nunc primum prodiere omnia, 2 vols. (Basel, 1576);
           photographic reprint (Torino, 1959, 1962, 1983; Lucca, 2011).

Plut   Florence, Biblioteca Medicea Laurenziana, Plut. 82.10 and 82.11.
           The dedication copy for Ficino's patron Lorenzo de' Medici,
           in 2 volumes. Copied by Ficino's amanuensis, Luca Fabiani,
           in 1490. For a full description, see *Marsilio Ficino e il ritorno di*
           Platone, pp. 147–50, item 115. An electronic facsimile may be
           viewed online via the website of the Biblioteca Laurenziana
           ("Plutei online").

$Plut^c$ hand of corrector in *Plut*.

⟨ ⟩   word or words supplied by the editor.

[ ]   editorial deletions.

Notes to the Text

❧❧❧

Book V

1. porrigit *Plut EB*: corrigit *O*
2. dii *Plut E^c BO*
3. multa *BO*: muta *E*
4. temperatae *conjectured*: temperata *EBO*
5. *This paragraph (3.5.9) is omitted in Plut.*
6. *The entire capitulum is lacking in O.*

Book VI

1. rursus *Plut E*: rursum *BO*
2. subterfugiunt *Plut O*: subterfugium *EB*
3. protrahitur *Plut E*: praetrahitur *B*: pertrahitur *O*
4. protractioni *Plut E*: pertractioni *BO*

Book VII

1. an *Plut EB*: ad *O*

Book VIII

1. in *omitted in O*
2. vita *omitted in O*
3. substantia *Plut EB*: substantiali *O*
4. essentia *Plut EB*: essentiali *O*
5. instrumento *Plut E^c BO*
6. eaedemque *Plut EB*: eaedem quae *O*
7. ad *omitted in O*

8. esse *omitted in Plut E*: esse BO

9. rationes *Plut E*: rationis BO

10. quod *omitted in O*

11. cessat *Plut EB*: cesset O

12. ad *omitted in O*

13. sit *omitted in O*

14. vero *omitted in Plut*

15. ad *omitted in O*

16. est *omitted in O*

17. contueri *Plut EB*: converti O

Book IX

1. quot *Plut EB*: quod O

2. essentiali *Plut E*: essentialis BO

3. se cum *corrected*: secum *Plut EBO*

4. super essentiam *Plut O*: superessentiam EB

5. immobilis EB: mobilis *Plut O*

6. ea enim *Plut EB*: eam O

7. nona *Plut EB*: non O

ENNEAD IV

Books I and II

1. individua *Plut EBa*: dividua O

2. etiam *Plut EO*: etiam et *Ba*

3. *corrected to* entelechiam: endelechiam *Plut EBaO*

Book III

1. Platonis *Plut EBa*: Platonicis O

2. calor *Plut EBa*: color O

3. cuilibet *Plut EBa*: cuiuslibet O

4. in quo *Plut EBa*: in duo *O*

5. multae *Plut EBa*: multi *O*

6. internis *Plut EBa*: aeternis *O*

7. summum *Plut EBa*: summam *O*

8. inesse *Plut EBa*: esse *O*

9. sint *Plut EBa*: sunt *O*

10. et *omitted O*

11. partes *omitted O*

12. omniformis *Plut EBa*: uniformis *O*

13. conferente *Plut EBa*: confitente *O*

14. se *omitted O*

15. redigetur *Plut EBa*: redigitur *O*

16. se *omitted O*

17. compositae *Plut BaO*: composita *E*

18. moles *Plut EBa*: molis *O*

19. protendi *Plut EBa*: protendit *O*

20. rationalis *Plut EBa*: rationales *O*

21. *In the dedication copy, Plut (f. 13r), Ficino added, after* simillimum, *a "chapter" which he numbered (incorrectly) as Cap. XI, with the title* In quo consistat secundum Plotinum virtus favorem caelitus attrahens: scilicet in eo quod anima mundi et stellarum daemonumque animae facile alliciuntur corporum formis accommodatis *(In what, according to Plotinus, the power of attracting favor from the heavens consists: namely, that the world-soul and the souls of the stars and daemons are easily enticed by forms of bodies that are well adapted). There follows the full text of Book 3 of Ficino's* De vita *(i.e., chapters 1–26) in the earlier recension (see J. R. Clark in* Manuscripta *27 [1983]: 160–61). A critical edition of this text by John R. Clark with an English translation by Carol V. Kaske is available (see Bibliography to Ennead 3, part 1). The translation of Plotinus carries a further heading or annotation:* Magica trahit vim proprie ab anima mundi diisque mundanis — per haec a superioribus *(Magic draws its strength properly from the world-soul and the mundane gods,*

and also from the higher powers through the mediation of these things). At the end of this passage in Plut, Ficino adds (f. 59r): Revertimur tandem ad interpretationem Plotini continuam et caput aggredimur duodecimum in quo naturam ipsam, etc. *(We return finally to the running commentary on Plotinus and begin with the twelfth chapter in which nature itself, etc.).*

22. daemonum *Plut EBa:* daemon *O*

23. ubi *Plut EBa:* unde *O*

24. geruntur *Plut EBa:* generantur *O*

25. ducantur *Plut EBa:* dicantur *O*

26. hic *Plut EBa:* hoc *O*

27. interfuisse *Plut EBa:* interesse *O*

28. communicant *Plut EBa:* communicent *O*

29. in *omitted O*

30. utramque . . . virtute *after* opinio . . . vita *Plut:* utramque . . . virtute *printed as if the words of Plotinus in E:* opinio . . . vita *after* utramque virtute *Ba:* utramque . . . virtute *omitted O*

31. utramque *Plut EBa:* utraque *O*

Book IV

1. suae *omitted O*

2. apud *Plut EBa:* ad *O*

3. divina *Plut EBa:* divinam *O*

4. cernit *Plut EBa:* cerni *O*

5. aliter *omitted O*

6. firma tum *Plut EO:* firmatum *Ba*

7. ullas *Plut EO:* ullus *Ba*

8. inclinamur *Plut E^c BaO:* inclinamus *E*

9. faciente *Plut E^c BaO:* facientia *E*

10. virtus *Plut EBa:* virtutis *O*

11. beneficia *Plut EBa*: benefica O

12. Iulianus *corrected*: Iunianus *Plut EBaO*

13. efficax *conjecture*: efficacia *Plut EBaO*

14. vultuum *Plut E*: vultum *BaO*

15. non *omitted O*

16. nostrae *omitted O*

17. produci *Plut E*: producit *BaO*

18. externa *Plut EBa*: aeterna O

19. vitaque corporea mundi *Plut EᶜBaO*: vitaque corpore amundi E

20. expedit *Plut EBa*: expedis O

21. coniunctus *Plut EBa*: coniunctis O

22. externum *Plut EBa*: extremum O

23. abiectus *Plut EBa*: abiectis O

24. mimus *Plut EBa*: minimus O

25. qua *Plut EBa*: quia O

26. cuius *Plut EBa*: cuique O

Book V

1. necessario *Plut EBa*: necessaria O

2. versetur *Plut BaO*: versertur E

3. vivente *Plut EBa*: vidente O

4. passioni *Plut BaO*: possioni E

5. ad *omitted O*

6. iam *Plut EBa*: tam O

7. distans *conjectured*: distantem *Plut EBaO*

8. gustant *Plut EBa*: gestant O

9. hic *Plut EBa*: hinc O

10. passionem *Plut EBa*: passiones O

11. tertia *Plut BaO*: tartia *E*

12. actus *EBa*: tactus *Plut*: affectus *O*

13. foras *Plut Eba*: foris *O*

Book VI

1. vel septimus *deleted by Plut^c*

2. cera *Plut EBa*: certa *O*

3. quo *omitted O*

4. incorporearum *Plut EBa*: in incorporearum *O*

5. ut *omitted O*

Book VII

1. ad *omitted O*

2. affectum *Plut EBa*: effectum *O*

3. corporeus *Plut EBa*: incorporeus *O*

4. motu rerumque *Plut E^c BaO*: motur erumque *E*

5. tres *BaO*: tris *Plut E*

6. hinc *Plut EBa*: hic *O*

7. quamdiu *Plut EBa*: quando *O*

8. hac *Plut EO*: ac *Ba*

Book VIII

1. disputans *Plut EBa*: disputant *O*

2. oportet *Plut EBa*: oporteret *O*

3. primam *omitted O*

4. sensuve *conjectured*: sensu *Plut EBaO*

5. ad *omitted O*

Book IX

1. animalibus *Plut EBa*: animabus *O*
2. in *Plut E*: et *BaO*
3. in *omitted O*
4. nos *EBa*: non *Plut O*

Notes to the Translation

ENNEAD III, part 2

BOOK V

1. Ficino is presumably referring here to Lorenzo's *Comento de' miei sonetti*, finished around 1490/91, just as he was finishing his commentary on Plotinus.

2. On this doctrine, see Analytical Study §2.32 and Excursus 2.

3. That is, it takes place in the *intellectual* world-soul, as argued above.

4. Ficino, *Platonic Theology* 4.1.13, 16.6.4.

5. Apuleius, *De Deo Socratis* 8.137–38.

6. *Orphei Hymni* 38.30.1–25.

7. *loc. cit.*

8. Porphyry, *De Abstinentia* 2.42.3, 2.46.2.

9. Iamblichus, *De Mysteriis* 5.10.212.3–7.

10. Porphyry, *De Abstinentia* 2.40.2–3.

11. Cf. Diels-Kranz: *Die Fragmente der Vorsokratiker* 2, "Democritus," A78 and B171.

12. Iamblichus, *De Mysteriis* 2.10.91.12–15.

13. Plotinus, *Ennead* 3.5.6.35–45.

14. Iamblichus, *De Mysteriis* 1.20.63.5–12.

15. Plotinus, *Ennead* 3.5.6.30–35.

16. Porphyry, *De Abstinentia* 2.38.1.

17. Plato, *Timaeus* 41d.

18. Proclus, *In Alcibiadem* 68.4–11. The goddess is Rhea or Hecate. Cf. Proclus, *Theologia Platonica* 5.11.35.22–39.24, 5.30.109.1–110.17, 5.30.112.1–113.12, 5.31.113.14–5.32.120.25; *Commentarius in Timaeum* 3.249.30–255.10.

19. Plotinus, *Ennead* 3.5.6.28–35.

20. Plotinus, *Ennead* 3.5.7.9ff.

21. On this passage, see Analytical Study §4.1.

22. For more details of Ficino's epistemological doctrine, see *Commentarius in Parmenidem* 23.1–24.2.

Book VI

1. That is, Plotinus, *Ennead* 3.6.1–5 and 3.6.6–19, respectively.

2. Porphyry, *Sententiae ad intelligibilia ducentes* 18.8.9–10 = Ficino, *De occasionibus sive causis ad intelligibilia nos ducentibus* 67.7–9.

3. Porphyry, *Sententiae* 21.12.8–11 = Ficino, *De occasionibus* 69.20–22; Porphyry, *Sententiae* 21.13.4–6 = Ficino, *De occasionibus* 69.29–30.

4. Cf. *Sententiae* 15.7.1–2 = *De Occasionibus* 66.11–12.

5. See Plotinus, *Ennead* 3.6.5.3, "the image, so to speak, which enters into [the soul] at the point said to be passive" (τὸ εἰς αὐτὴν ἐπὶ τοῦ λεγομένου παθητικοῦ οἷον φάντασμα).

6. Plotinus, *Ennead* 3.6.7.2–3 and 9–11; Porphyry *Sententiae* 20.11.3–4 = Ficino, *De Occasionibus* 68.19–20.

7. Plato, *Parmenides* 137c ff.

8. Plato, *Sophist* 237b ff.

9. See Proclus, *Commentarius in Parmenidem* 6.1039.1–1040.17; Ficino, *Commentarius in Parmenidem* 50.3–4, 54.1–2, 55.1–2, 102.1–2 (ed. Van Haelen).

10. On this point, see Analytical Study §4, p. lxxiii ff., and Excursus 1.

11. Plotinus, *Ennead* 3.6.6.33ff.

12. Plotinus, *Ennead* 3.6.7.23–27.

13. Ecclesiastes 1:2.

14. 1 Corinthians 13:12.

15. The reference to "Perspectivists" in the plural suggests that Ficino is referring loosely to a well-known group of thinkers who wrote treatises entitled *Perspectiva*. this group includes Roger Bacon, Witelo, and especially John Pecham.

16. Cf. Plotinus, *Ennead* 3.6.7.24–26 and 41; Porphyry, *Sententiae* 20.11.12–16 = Ficino, *De Occasionibus* 69.4–8.

17. On this point, see Analytical Study §4, p. lxxiii ff. and Excursus 1.

Book VII

1. For the full definition, see Plotinus: *Ennead* 3.7.3.36–38, ἡ περὶ τὸ ὂν ἐν τῷ εἶναι ζωὴ ὁμοῦ πᾶσα καὶ πλήρης ἀδιάστατος πανταχῇ τοῦτο = Ficino, *Versio Plotini* (Basel 1580, p. 327E, *circa ens in ipso esse vita simul tota et plena et ubique prorsus indistans*).

2. Ficino uses two Latin terms, *aeternitas* and *aevum*, to translate the single term αἰών in Plotinus' text. Cf. *Versio Plotini* (Basel 1580, 325A and 328E–29C). We have rendered the Latin terms "eternity" and "the always."

3. Plotinus contrasts the status of the things that come to be at *Ennead* 3.7.4.24–28. The term ἀϊδιότης (= Ficino's *sempiternitas*) occurs at *Ennead* 3.7.3.2 and 3.7.5.15.

4. See Proclus, *Elementatio Theologica*, prop. 54.52.8–10.

5. See the definition quoted in note 1.

6. The notion of circularity is suggested to Ficino by the application of the phrase "around the one" (περὶ τὸ ἕν) at Plotinus, *Ennead* 3.7.6.7.

7. See Plotinus, *Ennead* 3.7.4.19ff.

8. Plotinus, *Ennead* 3.7.2.17–19, 3.7.4.8–15.

9. For this systematic distinction between types of whole, see Proclus, *Elementatio Theologica*, props. 67.64.1–69.66.10.

10. See Plato, *Timaeus* 37d–e.

11. Plotinus, *Ennead* 3.7.6.1–9.

12. Plotinus, *Ennead* 3.7.7 Henry-Schwyzer [= 3.7.6 Ficino].

13. For this distinction see Proclus, *Elementatio Theologica*, prop. 191.166.26–168.10.

14. Paragraphs **6–8** summarize Plotinus, *Ennead* 3.7.7–10.

15. For this doctrine see Proclus, *Commentarius in Timaeum* 3.17.22–30.

Book VIII

1. See Ficino, *Theologia Platonica* 4.1.5–6. Cf. 1.3.13, 2.7.6.

2. This would represent the life that—together with being and intellect—constitutes an aspect of the second (Plotinian) hypostasis. Ficino is therefore stressing the continuity between this higher life and the life corresponding to the reason-principle as life or nature.

3. For the metaphysical principle involved see Proclus, *Elementatio Theologica*, props. 56.54.4–57.56.16, 70.66.11–30.

4. The reference is presumably to Aristotle's "unmoved mover" that is here identified with Plato's artificer as understood by Ficino via Plotinus.

5. See Plotinus, *Ennead* 3.8.2.19–22.

6. Plotinus, *Ennead* 3.8.4.15–16.

7. Plotinus, *Ennead* 3.8.2.22–34.

8. *Orphei Hymni* 10.10.7.

9. That is, its personal traits.

10. Ficino is loosely summarizing Plotinus' argument from *Ennead* 3.8.5–8.

11. This seems to develop into a full analogy, something merely suggested by Plotinus at *Ennead* 3.8.4.28–29.

12. Plotinus, *Ennead* 3.8.6–7 Henry-Schwyzer.

13. Plotinus, *Ennead* 3.8.8.1–12.

14. On this doctrine, see Analytical Study §2.2.2.3 and Excursus 3.

15. For the metaphysical doctrine of levels of wholeness, see Proclus, *Elementatio Theologica*, props. 67–69.64.1–32.

16. Plotinus, *Ennead* 3.8.9.1ff.

17. That is, the reason-principle equivalent to the *secundum rem* distinction mentioned above.

18. The argument concerning the first principle that follows has some affinities with that which begins Damascius' *De Principiis*: a work defi-

nitely utilized by Bessarion and Patrizi but which Ficino may also have seen. See *De Principiis* 1.1.4–2.20. However, Ficino does not follow Damascius in embracing the more radical *aporia* that the First both *is* and *is not* a "principle."

19. This explanation of the distinction between the nomenclatures of "Good" and "One" seems especially to recall Proclus, *Theologia Platonica* 2.6.40.1–43.10.

20. Or, alternatively, the distinction *secundum rem* mentioned above.

21. Cf. Plotinus, *Ennead* 3.8.7.19, ὠδίς.

22. Cf. Damascius, *De Principiis* 1.27.7–10, αὐτό; 1.84.13–21, ἐκεινή. However, this kind of language is also typical of Plotinus, by whom Damascius was also influenced.

23. Cf. Plotinus, *Ennead* 3.8.10.32, θαῦμα, and 3.8.11.32, θάμβος.

24. In his coupling of the Good and the True, Ficino recalls the Scholastic Aristotelian doctrine of the "transcendentals."

25. Ficino is recalling the passage at *Ennead* 3.8.11.33–45, where Plotinus is alluding to the derivation of intellect from the One as the generation of Kronos from Ouranos. The description of Kronos as "full" (κόρος) in Plotinus is reflected in Ficino's reference to *plenitudo*. On this passage, see Analytical Study §2.3.

Book IX

1. In actual fact, *nine* considerations follow.

2. Proclus, *Commentarius in Timaeum* 3.98.27–100.1.

3. The reference is a very general one. However, Proclus, *Commentarius in Timaeum* 3.98.27–100.1 provides a close parallel to Ficino's argument here. In this passage the relation between the artificer and the living creature is explained in terms of the relation between three intellects: those of Zeus, his divine father, and his divine grandfather. Ficino was obviously familiar with other passages in Proclus' *Commentarius in Timaeum* that combine Plato's teaching about the artificer and the living creature with the "Orphic" system worked out by his teacher Syrianus. See especially Proclus,

Commentarius in Timaeum 1.314.22–315.4, 1.449.25–451.17, 3.167.32–171.4.
In these passages the divine hierarchy is more complicated—consisting of
Phanes, Night, and the three *kronides* (sometimes together with their fe-
male partners and Dionysos)—and the living creature is identified with
Phanes rather than Ouranos.

4. Plato, *Timaeus* 39e.

5. On this passage, see Analytical Study §3.2.3.

6. See Plotinus, *Ennead* 3.9.1.21, τὸ διανοηθέν = *quod excogitat* in Ficino's
translation.

7. See the next note.

8. Ficino contrasts two possible views of how the intellective world-soul
produces the multiplicity of intellects: (1) it produces this multiplicity
directly as a series of *unparticipated* intellects; (2) it produces this multiplicity indirectly—through the mediation of the multiplicity of souls
participating in intellects—as a series of *participated* intellects; and attributes the latter to Plotinus. In fact, this distinction seems rather to result
from the study of the order of reality in post-Plotinian thought (especially that of Proclus) that is also revealed in the first paragraph of this
commentary. For multiplicities of unparticipated and participated terms,
see Ficino's summary of Proclus' *Platonic Theology* discussed in Excursus 3.

9. This position seems close to that favored by Ficino himself, who defi-
nitely identifies the divine artificer of Plato's *Timaeus* with the pure intellect and the intellect of the world-soul acting in collaboration. See *In
Enneadem* 3.2.42–43.

10. According to Proclus, by whom Ficino seems to be influenced here,
souls have eternal substance and temporal activity. See Proclus, *Elementatio Theologica*, prop. 191.166.26–168.10.

11. That is, even the *secundum rem* distinction characteristic of intellect.
Cf. Plotinus, *Ennead* 3.8.8.9–10.

12. On this passage see Analytical Study, §3.3.

ENNEAD IV

Books I and II

1. In the course of his commentary on the *Fourth Ennead*, Ficino occasionally refers to numbers of chapters, seemingly referring to sections of the Plotinus translation rather than to those of the Plotinus commentary. For reasons stated in our Note on the Text, these references will not correspond exactly with the chapters as numbered in the present separate edition of the commentary. See further our Concordance to the commentary on the *First Ennead*.

2. Ficino's references seem to be rather vague here, since there is a huge amount of "Plotinian" material (mostly not acknowledged as such) in the early books of the *Platonic Theology*. The doctrine of five levels of being, which he extracts from Plotinus, *Enneads* 4.1–2 and is prominent in the commentary on those treatises, is utilized most overtly at Ficino, *Platonic Theology* 1.1, 1.4, 3.1–2.

3. Plato, *Timaeus* 35a.

4. Aristotle, *De Anima* 2.1.412a.27–28.

Book III

1. Plato, *Philebus* 30a–b.

2. Plato, *Phaedrus* 246a–c.

3. Plato, *Timaeus* 41d–e.

4. Ficino, *Platonic Theology* 15.

5. That is, it is the presence of *order* that confers the unity rather than that of totality.

6. Ficino, *Platonic Theology* 9.4.

7. Plato, *Republic* 10.617d–19b.

8. Plato, *Phaedrus* 249a.

9. Plato, *Timaeus* 42b–c, 44b–c.

10. This doctrine was held by Alexander of Aphrodisias. See Simplicius, *In De Caelo* 380.5ff., and *In Physica* 1262.1ff., 1354.29ff.

11. These correspond to the unnamed thinkers mentioned by Plotinus, *Ennead* 4.3.1.17–18, and criticized during the next four chapters.

12. See the previous note.

13. See especially Ficino, *Platonic Theology* 3.2.1–9.

14. Averroes, *Commentum Magnum in De Animam* 3.4.703–28.

15. Plato, *Philebus* 30a.

16. Plato, *Phaedrus* 249b–d.

17. See note 1 above.

18. That is, the unnamed thinkers mentioned at Plotinus, *Ennead* 4.3.2.1ff.

19. See especially Ficino, *Platonic Theology* 5.5–9.

20. See Plotinus, *Ennead* 4.7.14.1–8.

21. Ibid.

22. Sextus Empiricus, *Adversus Physicos* 1.127.

23. Or "the body," the *quod* beginning the last clause in Latin being ambiguous.

24. See note 1 above.

25. Plato, *Phaedo* 114b–c.

26. Porphyry, *De Regressu Animae* at Augustine, *De Civitate Dei* 12.21.61–70, 13.19.39–44, 22.12.56–64.

27. Iamblichus, *De Mysteriis* 5.15.219.1–5.

28. Proclus, *Commentarius in Timaeum* 3.236.31–237.9, 3.298.2–299.9, 3.309.20–310.2.

29. The manuscript of the dedication copy (*Plut*), but not the printed editions, inserts at this point the entirety of Book 3 of Ficino's book on magic, the *De vita* (*On Life*). See Notes to the Text, note 21.

30. See Timaeus of Locri, *De Natura Mundi et Animae* 99d–e, 104b–105; Proclus, *Commemtarius in Timaeum* 3.294.22–295.32.

31. Iamblichus at Proclus, *Commentarius in Timaeum* 3.334.4–8.

32. Porphyry, *De Abstnentia* 1.39.1–3.

33. Proclus, *Commentarius in Timaeum* 3.334.8–15.

34. Porphyry, *Sententiae ad intelligibilia ducentes* 29.19.6–13.

35. Porphyry, *De Abstinentia* 1.30.6–7.

36. *Orphei Hymni* 62–64.

37. Plato, *Laws* 4.713c–14b.

38. Iamblichus, *De Mysteriis* 1.19.57.6–13, 1.19.59.1–4.

39. See *Corpus Hermeticum*: 'Asclepius' 13.37.347.3–13.38.349.8.

40. This is probably a reference to Haly Abenrudian ('Alī ibn Ridwān), possibly as reported by Pietro d'Abano.

41. Iamblichus, *De Mysteriis* 5.15.219.1–5.

Book IV

1. Porphyry, *De Regressu Animae*. See note 26 on Book 3.

2. Iamblichus, *De Mysteriis* 5.18.223.15–224.1.

3. Plotinus, *Ennead* 3.7.11.38–57, 3.7.12.3–8.

4. See especially Ficino, *Super Theophrastum de sensu*, chs. 4–5, 9, 13, 27–32 (*Opera* 2:1803, 1805–7, 1814–16).

5. This being the view to which Plotinus is really objecting.

6. The passage is complicated because Ficino seems to envisage numerous modalities of a universal spirit including (1) the spirit on high, (2) the spirit infused into things, and (3) our spirit, (4) the spirit that joins the world-soul to body, and (5) the spirit that connects nature to body.

7. Porphyry, *Sententiae ad intelligibilia ducentes* 29.18.16–19.13.

8. Iamblichus, *De Mysteriis* 1.8.29.4–8, 1.9.31.11–12, 6.3.243.4–5.

9. *Orphei Hymni* 10.18, 32.10.

10. *Corpus Hermeticum* 1.9.9.16–20.

11. See Julian, *Oratio* 4: *Ad Solem Regem* 157d–58a. Cf. 146a, 150d.

12. Iamblichus, *De Mysteriis* 5.26.237.8–238.6.

13. Or, possibly, "that of the world and that of the heaven."

14. Plato, *Statesman* 272a–b.

15. Ibid.

16. Plato, *Laws* 1.624a.

17. Plato, *Statesman* 272e.

18. Plato, *Timaeus* 41e.

19. Plato, *Phaedrus* 248c.

20. Plato, *Laws* 10.904c.

21. Plato, *Phaedrus* 248c–e.

22. Plato, *Timaeus* 42b–d.

23. Plato, *Timaeus* 41e.

24. Iamblichus, *De Mysteriis* 5.17.222.3–5.19.226.19.

25. Iamblichus, *De Mysteriis* 5.17.222.8–12, 5.18.223.15–224.1.

26. Abraham ibn Ezra, *Liber electionum*, fol. 67 r–v. Cf. Ficino, *De Vita* 3.22.95–97 (ed. Kaske-Clark, p. 368).

27. The doctrine is, of course, typical of Plotinus and most subsequent Platonists.

28. Philostratus, *Vita Apollonii* 4.40.1–2. Cf. 1.31.1–2.

29. Plato, *Symposium* 202e–3a.

30. Albumasar at Pietro d'Abano, *Conciliator*, differentia 156. Cf. Ficino, *Contra Iudicium Astrologorum* (Kristeller, *SF*, 2:39).

31. Ptolemy, *Tetrabiblos* 1.17.

32. See Iamblichus, *De Mysteriis* 4.1.181.2–4.3.186.5.

33. Ficino, *De Vita* 3.1.75–90, 3.4.1–3, 3.11.1–3 (ed. Kaske-Clark, pp. 246, 258, 288), etc.

34. Ficino, *Platonic Theology* 13.4.8–9.

35. Ficino, *De Amore* 7.4 (ed. Laurens, pp. 217–23), 7.10 (ed. Laurens, pp. 233–35).

36. Ficino, *De Vita* 3.12.1–3.21.155 (ed. Kaske-Clark, pp. 298–356).

Book V

1. That is, the act.

2. Ficino, *Super Theophrastum*, chs. 15, 26–27 (*Opera* 2:1808, 1814).

3. That is, the spiritual entity mentioned above.

Book VI

1. Boethius, *De Consolatione Philosophiae* 5.m.4.

2. Ficino, *Platonic Theology* 7.1.2. Cf. 7.6.1–3.

3. Ficino, *Super Theophrastum*, chs. 13, 30 (*Opera* 2:1806–7, 1815).

4. The attribution here seems to be indirect. Ficino refers to this doctrine in connection with Priscianus at *Super Theophrastum*, chs. 4–5, 10 (*Opera* 2:1803, 1805). However, at ch. 13 (*Opera* 2:1807) he describes Priscianus as being "an assiduous follower of Iamblichus" (*sedulus Iamblichi sectator*) with respect to all the matters under discussion.

Book VII

1. A possible albeit less probable meaning could be "a certain definite temperament of humors and of vital spirit."

2. The subtitle of Ficino's *Platonic Theology* is, of course, "On the Immortality of Souls" (*De immortalitate animorum*).

3. See note 2 above.

4. Bernardo Bembo (1433–1519), father of the better-known Pietro Bembo. Bembo was a Venetian aristocrat and humanist who served as an ambassador in Florence and became friendly with Ficino and other members of his circle.

Book VIII

1. Ps.-Dionysius, *De Divinis Nominibus* 4.23.

2. Cf. Thomas Aquinas, *Summa Theologiae* Ia, q, 63, a. 4; Ia, q, 63, a. 7 (citing Porphyry and John Damascene).

3. For example, see Proclus, *Commentarius in Timaeum* 3.274.14–275.23.

4. Ficino is also giving the classical doctrine of *apokatastasis* a Christian nuance by contrasting the present age with the resurrection.

5. Or, perhaps, *the* body.

6. See Plotinus, *Ennead* 4.8.1.12–50.

7. *Corpus Hermeticum* 10.19.122.13–21.124.2.

8. *Orphei Hymni* 38.14.

9. Iamblichus, *De Mysteriis* 3.13.129.15–130.5, 31.176.13–177.6.

Book IX

1. See Ficino, *Platonic Theology* 15.

Bibliography

For information regarding other works by Ficino and Ficino's classical and medieval intertexts, see the Bibliography in the preceding volume of the *Commentary on Plotinus* (ITRL 80). The following items supplement that material with special reference to the *Fourth Ennead*.

TEXT EDITIONS

OTHER EDITIONS OF WORKS BY FICINO

Commentary on Dionysius the Areopagite. *Dionysii Areopagitae De mystica theologia, De divinis nominibus, interprete Marsilio Ficino*. Edited by Pietro Podolak. Napoli: M. d'Auria, 2011.

———. *On Dionysius the Areopagite*. Edited by Michael J. B. Allen. 2 vols. The I Tatti Renaissance Library 66–67. Cambridge, MA: Harvard University Press, 2015.

Translation of the *Corpus Hermeticum*. *Mercurii Trismegisti Pimander sive De Potestate et Sapientia Dei*. Edited by Maurizio Campanelli. Torino: Nino Aragno, 2011.

Opuscula. *Marsile Ficin, Métaphysique de la lumière: opuscules 1476–1492*. Edited with a French translation by Julie Reynaud and Sébastien Galland. Chambéry: L'Act mem, 2008.

EDITIONS OF OTHER AUTHORS CITED

Abano, Pietro d'. *Expositio praeclarissimi atque eximii artium ac medicine doctoris Petri de Ebano Patavini in librum Problematum Aristotelis . . .* Venice: Ioannes Herbert Alemanus, 1482.

———. *Conciliator differentiarum philosophorum et medicorum . . .* Venice: Bonetus Locatellus, 1496.

Abraham ibn Ezra. *Abrahe Avenaris Judei astrologi peritissimi in re iudiciali opera ab excellentissimo philosopho Petro de Abano post accuratam castigationem in Latinum traducta . . .* Venice: Petrus Liechtenstein, 1507.

Abū Ma'shar. *Introductorium in astronomiam Albumasaris abalachi octo continens libros partiales*. Augsburg: Erhard Ratdolt, 1489.

Aquinas, Thomas. *S. Thomae Aquinatis Summa Theologiae: Pars Prima et Prima Secundae*. Edited by Pietro Caramello. Torino: Marietti, 1952.

Ps.-Aristotle. *Problemata*. In *Aristotelis Opera*. Edited by Immanuel Bekker. Revised by O. Gigon. 2 vols. Berlin: De Gruyter, 1960. In volume 2.

Firmicus Maternus. *Iulii Firmici Materni Matheseos Libri VIII*. Edited by Wilhelm Kroll, Franz Skutsch, and Konrat Ziegler. Stuttgart, Teubner, 1913. Reprint, Stuttgart: Teubner, 1968.

Iamblichus. *De Vita Pythagorica Liber*. Edited by Ludwig Deubner. Revised by Ulrich Klein. Stuttgart: Teubner, 1975.

Orphic Hymns. *Orphei Hymni*. Edited by Wilhelm Quandt. 4th ed. Dublin: Weidmann, 1973.

Philostratus. *Apollonius of Tyana*. Edited by Christopher P. Jones. 3 vols. Cambridge, MA: Harvard University Press, 2005. In volumes 1–2.

Picatrix. Das Ziel des Weisen von pseudo-Magriti. Translated into German from the Arabic by Helmut Ritter and Martin Plessner. London: Warburg Institute, 1962.

———. *The Latin Version of the Ghāyat al-ḥakīm*. Edited by David E. Pingree. London: Warburg Institute, 1986.

Plotinus. *Ennead IV. 4. 30–45 and IV. 5: Problems Concerning the Soul*. Edited and translated by Gary Gurtler. Las Vegas: Parmenides Publishing, 2015.

Priscianus Lydus. *Prisciani Lydi quae extant: Metaphrasis in Theophrastum et Solutionum ad Chosroem Liber (Supplementum Aristotelicum I. 2)*. Edited by Ingram Bywater. Berlin: Reimer, 1886.

———. *Priscian, On Theophrastus On Sense-Perception*. Translated by Pamela Huby. London: Duckworth, 1997.

Sextus Empiricus. *Against the Physicists, Against the Ethicists*. In *Sextus Empiricus*. Edited and translated by Robert G. Bury. 4 vols. Cambridge, MA: Harvard University Press, 1933–1949. Volume 3.

Simplicius. *In Aristotelis libros Physicorum Commentaria*. Edited by Hermann Diels. 2 vols. Berlin: Reimer, 1882–1895.

———. *In Aristotelis De Caelo Commentaria*. Edited by Johan L. Heiberg. Berlin: Reimer, 1894.

SECONDARY LITERATURE

Allen, Michael J. B. "Ficino's Theory of the Five Substances and the Neoplatonists' *Parmenides*." *The Journal of Medieval and Renaissance Studies* 12 (1982): 19–44. Reprinted in Allen, *Plato's Third Eye*, item VIII.

——. *The Platonism of Marsilio Ficino. A Study of His Phaedrus Commentary, Its Sources and Genesis*. Berkeley and Los Angeles: University of California Press, 1984.

——. "To Gaze upon the Face of God Again: Philosophic Statuary, Pygmalion, and Marsilio Ficino." *Rinascimento*, ser. 2, 48 (2008): 123–36.

——. "Sending Archedemus: Ficino, Plato's Second Letter, and its Four Epistolary Mysteries." In *Sol et Homo. Mensch und Natur in der Renaissance: Festschrift zum 70. Geburtstag für Eckhard Kessler*, edited by Sabrina Ebbersmeyer, Helga Pirner-Pareschi, and Thomas Ricklin, 405–20. München: Fink, 2008.

——. "Marsilio Ficino on Saturn, the Plotinian Mind, and the Monster of Averroes." *Bruniana et Campanelliana* 16 (2010): 11–29. Reprinted in *Renaissance Averroism and its Aftermath: Arabic Philosophy in Early Modern Europe*, edited by Anna Akasoy and Guido Giglioni, 81–97. Dordrecht: Springer, 2013.

——. "Prometheus among the Florentines: Marsilio Ficino on the Myth of Triadic Power." *Rinascimento*, ser. 2, 51 (2011): 27–44.

——. "Eurydice in Hades: Florentine Platonism and an Orphic Mystery." In *Nuovi maestri e antichi testi: Umanesimo e Rinascimento alle origini del pensero moderno: Atti del convegno internazionale di studi in onore di Cesare Vasoli (Mantova 1–3 dicembre 2010)*, edited by Stephano Caroti and Vittoria Perrone Compagni, 19–40. Florence: Olschki, 2012.

——. "*Ratio omnium divinissima*: Plato's *Epinomis*, Prophecy and Marsilio Ficino." In *Epinomide: Studi sull'opera e la sua ricezione*, edited by Francesca Alesse and Franco Ferrari with Maria Cristina Dalfino, 469–90. Napoli: Bibliopolis, 2012.

Armstrong, A. Hilary. "Was Plotinus a Magician?" *Phronesis* 1 (1955): 73–9. Reprinted in Armstrong, *Plotinian and Christian Studies*, item III.

——— . *Plotinian and Christian Studies.* London: Variorum, 1979.

Barbanti, Maria di Pasquale. "L'anima mediana e lo statu epistemologico della phantasia in Plotino." In Barbanti and Iozzia, *Anima e libertà in Plotino,* 247–70.

Barbanti, Maria di Pasquale, and Daniele Iozzia, eds. *Anima e libertà in Plotino: Atti del convegno nazionale, Catania 29–30 gennaio 2009.* Catania: CUCEM, 2009.

Blumenthal, Henry J. "Plotinus *Ennead* IV. 3. 20–21 and Its Sources: Alexander, Aristotle and Others." *Archiv für Geschichte der Philosophie* 50 (1968): 254–61.

——— . *Plotinus' Psychology. His Doctrines of the Embodied Soul.* The Hague: Nijhoff, 1971.

——— . "Soul, World-Soul, and Individual Soul in Plotinus." In Schuhl and Hadot, *Le Néoplatonisme,* 55–63. Reprinted in Blumenthal, *Soul and Intellect,* item III.

——— . "Plotinus' Psychology. Aristotle in the Service of Platonism." *International Philosophical Quarterly* 12 (1972): 340–64. Reprinted in Blumenthal, *Soul and Intellect,* item V.

——— . "Nous and Soul in Plotinus. Some Problems of Demarcation." In *Plotino e il Neoplatonismo in Oriente e in Occidente: Atti del convegno internazionale dell'Accademia Nazionale dei Lincei, Roma 5–9 ottobre 1970,* 203–19. Rome, 1974. Reprinted in Blumenthal, *Soul and Intellect,* item II.

——— . "Neoplatonic Elements in the *De Anima Commentaries.*" *Phronesis* 21 (1976): 64–87.

——— . "Plotinus' Adaptation of Aristotle's Psychology: Sensation, Imagination, and Memory." In *The Significance of Neoplatonism,* edited by R. Baine Harris, 41–58. New York: International Society for Neoplatonic Studies, 1976. Reprinted in Blumenthal, *Soul and Intellect,* item VII.

——— . "The Psychology of (?) Simplicius' Commentary on the *De Anima.*" In Blumenthal and Lloyd, *Soul and the Structure of Being in Late Neoplatonism,* 73–93.

——— . *Soul and Intellect. Studies in Plotinus and Later Neoplatonism.* Aldershot: Variorum, 1993.

——— . "On Soul and Intellect." In Gerson, *The Cambridge Companion to Plotinus,* 82–104.

——. *Aristotle and Neoplatonism in Late Antiquity: Interpretations of the 'De Anima.'* Ithaca, NY: Cornell University Press, 1996.

Blumenthal, Henry J., and Elizabeth G. Clark, eds. *The Divine Iamblichus. Philosopher and Man of Gods.* London: Bristol Classical Press, 1993.

Blumenthal, Henry J., and John F. Finamore, eds. *Iamblichus the Philosopher* = *Syllecta Classica* 8 (1997).

Blumenthal, Henry J., and Anthony C. Lloyd, eds. *Soul and the Structure of Being in Late Neoplatonism: Syrianus, Proclus and Simplicius.* Liverpool: Liverpool University Press, 1982.

Burkert, Walter. "Plotin, Plutarch und die Platonisierende Interpretation von Heraklit und Empedokles." In *Kephalaion. Studies in Greek Philosophy and Its Continuation Offered to Professor C. J. de Vogel,* edited by Jaap Mansfeld and Lambertus M. de Rijk, 137–46. Assen: Van Gorcum, 1975.

Caluori, Damien. "Plotin: Was fühlt der Leib? Was empfindet die Seele?" In *Klassische Emotionstheorien. Von Platon bis Wittgenstein,* edited by H. Landweer and U. Renz, 121–40. Berlin, 2008.

Celenza, Christopher. "Pythagoras in the Renaissance. The Case of Marsilio Ficino." *Renaissance Quarterly* 52 (1999): 667–711.

Chiaradonna, Riccardo, ed. *Studi sull'anima in Plotino.* Napoli: Bibliopolis, 2005.

——. "La conoscenza dell'anima discorsiva. Enn. V. 3 (49) 2–3." In Barbanti and Iozzia, *Anima e libertà in Plotino,* 41–69.

Copenhaver, Brian P. "Scholastic Philosophy and Renaissance Magic in the *De Vita* of Marsilio Ficino." *Renaissance Quarterly* 37 (1984): 523–54.

——. "Iamblichus, Synesius, and the *Chaldaean Oracles* in Marsilio Ficino's *De vita libri tres*: Hermetic Magic or Neoplatonic Magic?" In *Supplementum Festivum: Studies in Honor of Paul Oskar Kristeller,* edited by James Hankins, John Monfasani, and Frederick Purnell, 441–55. Binghamton, NY: Mediaeval and Renaissance Texts and Studies, 1987.

——. "Hermes Trismegistus, Proclus, and the Question of a Philosophy of Magic in the Renaissance." In *Hermeticism and the Renaissance: Intellectual History and the Occult in Early Modern Europe,* edited by Ingrid

Merkel and Allen G. Debus, 79–110. Washington, DC, London and Toronto: Folger Shakespeare Library, 1988.

——. "Hermes Theologus: The Sienese Mercury and Ficino's Hermetic Demons." In *Humanity and Divinity in Renaissance and Reformation: Essays in Honor of Charles Trinkaus*, edited by John O'Malley, Thomas Izbicki, and Gerald Christianson, 149–82. Leiden: Brill, 1993.

——. "Ten Arguments in Search of a Philosopher: Averroes and Aquinas in Ficino's *Platonic Theology.*" *Vivarium* 47 (2009): 444–79.

——. *Magic in Western Culture from Antiquity to the Enlightenment.* Cambridge: Cambridge University Press, 2015.

Corcilius, Klaus and Perler, Dominik, eds. *Partitioning the Soul. Debates from Plato to Leibniz.* Berlin: De Gruyter, 2014.

Dodds, Eric R. *Pagan and Christian in the Age of Anxiety. Some Aspects of Religious Experience from Marcus Aurelius to Constantine.* Cambridge: Cambridge University Press, 1965.

Emilsson, Eyólfur K. *Plotinus on Sense-Perception. A Philosophical Study.* Cambridge: Cambidge University Press, 1988.

Finamore, John F. *Iamblichus and the Theory of the Vehicle of the Soul.* Chico, CA: Scholars Press, 1985.

——. "The Rational Soul in Iamblichus' Philosophy." In Blumenthal and Finamore, *Iamblichus the Philosopher*, 163–76.

——. "Iamblichus on Light and the Transparent." In Blumenthal and Clark, *The Divine Iamblichus*, 55–64.

Gannon, Mary A. I. "The Active Theory of Sensation in St. Augustine." *New Scholasticism* 30 (1956): 154–80.

García Bazán, Francisco. "Jámblicho y el descenso del alma. Sintesis de doctrinas y relectura neoplatónica." In Blumenthal and Finamore, *Iamblichus the Philosopher*, 129–47.

Garin, Eugenio. *Astrology in the Renaissance: The Zodiac of Life.* Translated by Carolyn Jackson and June Allen. London: Routledge, 1983.

Gentile, Sebastiano. "Sulle prime traduzioni dal greco di Marsilio Ficino." *Rinascimento* 30 (1990): 57–104.

Gersh, Stephen. *Middle Platonism and Neoplatonism. The Latin Tradition.* 2 vols. Notre Dame, IN: University of Notre Dame Press, 1986.

Gerson, Lloyd P. ed. *The Cambridge Companion to Plotinus*. Cambridge: Cambridge University Press, 1996.

Giardina, Giovanna R. "Se l'anima sia entelechia del corpo alla maniera di un nocchiero rispetto alla nave. Plotino IV. 3. 21 su Aristotele *De anima* II. 1, 413a8–9." In Barbanti and Iozzia, *Anima e libertà in Plotino*, 71–112.

Giglioni, Guido. "Theurgy and Philosophy in Marsilio Ficino's Paraphrase of Iamblichus's *De Mysteriis Aegyptiorum*." *Rinascimento* 52 (2012): 3–36.

Hankins, James. "Ficino, Avicenna and the Occult Powers of the Rational Soul." In *La magia nell'Europa moderna: tra antica sapienza e filosofia naturale. Atti del Convegno (Firenze 2–4 ottobre 2003)*, edited by Fabrizio Meroi and Elisabetta Scapparone, 35–52. Florence: Olschki, 2007.

Helleman-Elgersma, Wypkje. *Soul-Sisters. A Commentary on Enneads IV. 3 (27), 1–8 of Plotinus*. Hildesheim and Amsterdam: Gerstenberg and Rodopi, 1980.

Helmig, Christoph. "Iamblichus, Proclus and Philoponus on Parts, Capacities, and *ousiai* of the Soul and the Notion of Life." In Corcilius and Perler, *Partitioning the Soul*, 149–77.

Huby, Pamela M. "Priscian of Lydia as Evidence for Iamblichus." In Blumenthal and Clark, *The Divine Iamblichus, Philosopher and Man of Gods*, 5–12.

Karfik, Filip. "Parts of the Soul in Plotinus." In Corcilius and Perler, *Partitioning the Soul*, 107–48.

Kristeller, Paul O. *The Philosophy of Marsilio Ficino*. Translated by V. Conant. Gloucester, MA: Peter Smith, 1964.

Lavaud, Laurent. "La dianoia médiatrice entre le sensible et l'intelligible." *Études platoniciennes* 3 (2006): 29–55.

Merlan, Philip, "Plotinus and Magic." *Isis* 44 (1953): 341–48.

Monfasani, John. "The Averroism of John Argyropoulos." *I Tatti Studies: Essays on the Renaissance* 5 (1993): 157–208.

O'Brien, Denis. "Le volontaire et la nécessité. Réflexions sur la descente de l'âme dans la philosophie de Plotin." *Revue philosophique de la France et de l'Étranger* 167 (1977): 401–22.

O'Meara, Dominic J. "Plotinus on how Soul acts on Body." In *Platonic Investigations*, edited by Dominic J. O'Meara, 247–61. Washington, DC: Catholic University of America Press, 1985.

———. *Pythagoras Revived. Mathematics and Philosophy in Late Antiquity.* Oxford: Clarendon Press, 1989.

Palisca, Claude V. *Music and Ideas in the Sixteenth and Seventeenth Centuries.* Urbana and Chicago: University of Illinois Press, 2006.

Pépin, Jean. "Plotin et le miroir de Dionysos (*Enn.* IV. 3 [27] 12. 1–2." *Revue internationale de philosophie* 24 (1970): 304–20.

———. "Héraclès et son reflet dans le Néoplatonisme." In Schuhl and Hadot, *Le Néoplatonisme*, 167–92.

Prins, Jacomien. *Echoes of an Invisible World. Marsilio Ficino and Francesco Patrizi on Cosmic Order and Music Theory.* Leiden and Boston: Brill, 2015.

Schuhl, Pierre-Maxime "Descente métaphysique et ascension de l'âme dans la philosophie de Plotin." *Studi internazionali di filosofia* 5 (1973): 71–84.

Schuhl, Pierre-Maxime, and Pierre Hadot, eds. *Le Néoplatonisme, Colloque international du Centre National de la Recherche Scientifique, Royaumont 9–13 juin 1969.* Paris: Centre National de la Recherche Scientifique, 1971.

Schwyzer, Hans-Rudolf. "Zu Plotins Interpretation von Platons Timaeus 35A." *Rheinisches Museum* N.F. 84 (1935): 360–68.

Shaw, Gregory. *Theurgy and the Soul: The Neoplatonism of Iamblichus.* University Park, PA: Pennsylvania State University Press, 1995.

Sicherl, Martin. *Die Handschriften, Ausgaben und Übersetzungen von Iamblichos de mysteriis: Eine kritisch-historische Studie.* Berlin: Akademie Verlag, 1957.

Steel, Carlos. *The Changing Self. A Study on the Soul in Later Neoplatonism: Iamblichus, Damascius, and Priscianus.* Brussels: Paleis der Akademiën, 1978.

Steel, Carlos, and F. Bossier. "Priscianus Lydus en de *In De Anima* van Pseudo (?) Simplicius." *Tijdschrift voor Filosofie* 34 (1972): 761–822.

Tomlinson, Gary. *Music in Renaissance Magic: Toward a Historiography of Others.* Chicago and London: University of Chicago Press, 1993.

Vasiliu, Anca. "Les limites du Diaphane chez Marsile Ficin." In *Marsile Ficin: Les Platonismes à la Renaissance*, edited by Pierre Magnard, 108–12. Paris: Vrin, 2001.

Védrine, Hélène. *Philosophie et magie à la Renaissance*. Paris: Librairie générale française, 1996.

Walker, Daniel P. "Medical Spirits and God and the Soul." In *Spiritus: Lessico Intelletuale Europeo: IVo Colloquio Internazionale, Roma, 7–9 gennaio 1983*, edited by Maria Fattori and Massimo Bianchi. Rome: Ateneo, 1984.

Warren, Edward W. "Memory in Plotinus." *Classical Quarterly* N.S. 15 (1965): 252–60.

——. "Imagination in Plotinus." *Classical Quarterly* N.S. 16 (1966): 277–85.

Zambelli, Paola. "Platone, Ficino e la magia." In *Studia Humanitatis: Ernesto Grassi zum 70. Geburtstag*, edited by Eginhard Hora and Eckhard Kessler, 121–43. München: Fink, 1973.

Zintzen, Clemens. "Bemerkungen zum Aufstiegsweg der Seele in Jamblichs 'de mysteriis.'" In *Platonismus und Christentum: Festschrift für Heinrich Dörrie*, edited by Dieter Blume and Friedhelm Mann, 312–28. Münster: Ascendorff, 1983.

Index

Abamon (Egyptian priest), 178, 258n137, 262n189

Abano, Pietro d', 189, 245n23, 265n231, 265n233, 581n40; *Conciliator*, 582n30

Abraham ibn Ezra, 189, 481; *Liber electionum*, 582n26

Adrastia, law of, 471

Albert the Great, 167

Albumasar, 158, 487, 582n30; *Introductorium Maius*, 189

Alexander of Aphrodisias, 166, 579n10

Amelius, 179

Anebo (Egyptian priest), 186

Aphrodite, 240

Apollo, 151, 245n24, 289n428, 383; Phoebus, 483–85

Apollonian sound, 152, 383

Apollonius of Tyana, 188, 481

Apuleius, 25; *De Deo Socratis*, 573n5

Aquinas, Thomas, Saint, 167, 266n235, 290n433; *Summa contra gentiles*, 251n73; *Summa theologiae*, 583n2

Arab/Arabic, 189, 282n355, 283n365

Arian, 255n101

Aristotelian/Aristotelianism, 163, 167, 189, 196, 197, 242n5, 244n14, 251n72, 269n249, 275n305, 282n353, 292n447, 327, 577n24

Aristotle, 25, 203, 278n324, 282n353, 327, 335, 576n4; *On the Soul*, 281n353; *On the Soul 2.1.412a.27–28*, 579n4; *On the Soul 2.7.418a–19b*, 281n353; *On the Soul, 3.5.430a*, 281n353

Aristotle (pseudo-), *Problems*, 245n23

Asclepius. See Corpus Hermeticum

Augustine, Saint, 167, 186, 225; *City of God 8*, 264n207; *City of God 10*, 216, 264n208, 286n385; *City of God 12*, 580n26; *City of God 13*, 580n26; *City of God 22*, 580n26; *On Music*, 264n209, 292n447; *On the Immortality of the Soul*, 167, 251n76; *On the Quantity of the Soul*, 167, 251n76; *On the Trinity*, 256n107

Augustinian, 172, 264n209

Averroes, 160, 165, 166, 189, 251n73, 333, 345; *Long Commentary on On the Soul*, 580n14

Averroism/Averroistic, 167, 195, 251n73, 251n77; anti-Averroistic, 195

Averroists, 251n73, 251n77

Avicenna, 283n367, 289n431

Publication of this volume has been made possible by

The Myron and Sheila Gilmore Publication Fund at I Tatti
The Robert Lehman Endowment Fund
The Jean-François Malle Scholarly Programs and Publications Fund
The Andrew W. Mellon Scholarly Publications Fund
The Craig and Barbara Smyth Fund
for Scholarly Programs and Publications
The Lila Wallace–Reader's Digest Endowment Fund
The Malcolm Wiener Fund for Scholarly Programs and Publications